The Complete Friday Q&A: Volume I
by Mike Ash

The Complete Friday Q&A: Volume I

Copyright © 2011 by Mike Ash. All rights reserved.

ISBN-13: 978-1-4583-7049-5

Table of Contents

About The Complete Friday Q&A: Volume 1 8

Introduction 9

Acknowledgements 10

Multithreaded Programming and Parallelism Overview 11

Blocks in Objective-C 14

Pros and Cons of Private APIs 21

Thread Safety in OS X System Frameworks 24

Interprocess Communication 29

How Key-Value Observing Works 33

Code Injection 40

Profiling With Shark 45

Operations-Based Parallelization 53

The Good and Bad of Distributed Objects 56

Holistic Optimization 60

Using the Clang Static Analyzer 63

Intro to the Objective-C Runtime 67

Objective-C Messaging 73

Objective-C Message Forwarding 77

Multithreaded Optimization in ChemicalBurn 82

Code Generation with LLVM, Part 1: Basics 88

Code Generation with LLVM, Part 2: Fast Objective-C Forwarding 96

Objective-C Class Loading and Initialization 115

4

- Introduction to Valgrind 118
- Mac OS X Process Memory Statistics 123
- Type Qualifiers in C, Part 1 127
- Type Qualifiers in C, Part 2 131
- Type Qualifiers in C, Part 3 135
- Format Strings Tips and Tricks 141
- Practical Blocks 146
- Writing Vararg Macros and Functions 158
- Intro to Grand Central Dispatch, Part I: Basics and Dispatch Queues 162
- Intro to Grand Central Dispatch, Part II: Multi-Core Performance 169
- Intro to Grand Central Dispatch, Part III: Dispatch Sources 174
- Intro to Grand Central Dispatch, Part IV: Odds and Ends 179
- GCD Practicum 183
- Care and Feeding of Singletons 194
- Defensive Programming 200
- Creating a Blocks-Based Object System 205
- A Preview of Coming Attractions 215
- Generators in Objective-C 216
- Linking and Install Names 233
- Dangerous Cocoa Calls 236
- Probing Cocoa With PyObjC 240
- Using Accessors in Init and Dealloc 246
- Building Standalone iPhone Web Apps 250

A GCD Case Study: Building an HTTP Server 256

Highlights From a Year of Friday Q&A 272

NSRunLoop Internals 273

NSNotificationQueue 284

Stack and Heap Objects in Objective-C 289

Toll Free Bridging Internals 293

Method Replacement for Fun and Profit 297

Error Returns with Continuation Passing Style 303

Trampolining Blocks with Mutable Code 311

Character Encodings 324

Futures 330

Compound Futures 342

Subclassing Class Clusters 356

OpenCL Basics 361

Comparison of Objective-C Enumeration Techniques 369

Implementing Fast Enumeration 373

Implementing a Custom Slider 382

Dealing with Retain Cycles 392

What Every Apple Programmer Should Know 401

Leopard Collection Classes 405

Implementing Equality and Hashing 412

Background Timers 419

Zeroing Weak References in Objective-C 428

Zeroing Weak References to CoreFoundation Objects 447

Implementing NSCoding 459

Defensive Programming in Cocoa 468

Index 480

About The Complete Friday Q&A: Volume I

Friday Q&A is a biweekly series on Mac programming. It can be found online at http://mikeash.com/pyblog/. Volume I is a full archive of all posts through August 2010.

The author gratefully acknowledges all of the topic and comment contributions to Friday Q&A from its readers.

The Complete Friday Q&A: Volume I Copyright © 2008-2010 by Michael Ash

Mike Ash
mike@mikeash.com
http://mikeash.com/

Introduction

I started NSBlog about five years ago with the intent of just having a place to occasionally write about code and technical matters. Attempting to limit myself to meaty posts ensured that content was sporadic, as meaty topics were hard to come by.

Eventually these posts drew in a relatively substantial amount of traffic. I wanted to satisfy this newfound readership, but thinking of interesting things to write about was tough. The solution to this dilemma was lurking in the cause: pull topics from the readership!

Thus I announced Friday Q&A. Each week I would take a reader-submitted topic and use that for a blog post. I didn't have high expectations but it seemed like it was worth a shot.

Response was tremendous! Each post gets a sizeable amount of readers who have posted many intelligent and interesting comments. And although there have been a couple of pauses in the schedule (and a shift to a biweekly schedule once the weekly schedule became too demanding), Friday Q&A has been more or less continuously published ever since. I have been honored to see a large number of unjustifiably kind comments and recommendations about the series.

The idea for a book version has been floating around for quite a while. After a disastrous encounter with the publishing industry, the thought of self-publishing began to look more attractive. With the introduction of the iPad and the success of iBooks, selling as an ePub through Apple's store seemed like the logical course of action.

This book is a compendium of all Friday Q&A articles from the first one on December 19, 2008 through the latest one as of this writing on August 27, 2010.

The content is mostly unedited from the original posts. This means that each chapter still talks about "last week", and encourages the reader to return "next week". There are two reasons for this. First, Friday Q&A is an inherently temporal series and this preserves that feel in the book. Second, fixing up all of the articles to appear as though part of a reference book would have been a lot of work, and like most programmers I am lazy.

Some articles link to code in my public Subversion repository. All of these links remain valid. However, you may wish to check my github page first, as I have moved several projects there and some of them are more up to date than the Subversion copy.

It's been a pleasure to write Friday Q&A over these past two years, and I hope to continue for many more. Although the "next week" is out of date, the reader-driven nature of the series is not. So as always, if you have an idea for a topic that you'd like to see covered in Friday Q&A, send it in!

Acknowledgements

I would like to thank my reviewers, whose valuable input dramatically improved this book. They are: Steven Vandeweghe, Vadim Shpakovski, Matthias Neeracher, Phil Holland, Landon Fuller, David Helms, Joshua Pokotilow, Mike Shields, Jeff Schilling, Jordan Breeding, Hamish Allan, Eimantas Vaiciunas, Ilya Kulakov, Cédric Luthi, Alex Blewitt, and Kevin Avila.

I would also like to thank everyone who contributed the topic ideas used throughout this book. Their names can be found at the beginning of each chapter.

Finally, I would like to thank everyone who has commented on one of my posts, e-mailed about Friday Q&A, or simply read it. No matter what your contribution, it is appreciated.

Friday Q&A 2008-12-19: Multithreaded Programming and Parallelism Overview

Related Articles

    Thread Safety in OS X System Frameworks 24

    Profiling With Shark 45

    Operations-Based Parallelization 53

    The Good and Bad of Distributed Objects 56

    Holistic Optimization 60

    Multithreaded Optimization in ChemicalBurn 82

    Mac OS X Process Memory Statistics 123

    Intro to Grand Central Dispatch, Part I: Basics and Dispatch Queues 162

    Intro to Grand Central Dispatch, Part II: Multi-Core Performance 169

    Intro to Grand Central Dispatch, Part III: Dispatch Sources 174

    Intro to Grand Central Dispatch, Part IV: Odds and Ends 179

    GCD Practicum 183

    Dangerous Cocoa Calls 236

Great response last week. This week I'm going to merge Sam McDonald's question about how I got into doing multithreaded programming and Phil Holland's idea of talking about the different sorts of parallelism available.

Like a lot of computer programmers, I was always interested in making code run fast. This led to better languages (I started in BASIC!), micro-optimization, and algorithms, but ultimate performance means multiprocessing. The distributed.net and SETI@Home projects showed the power of distributed computation.

Multithreading was also interesting in coming to OS X from the old Mac OS, where multithreading was a lot more limited and difficult. At the time it wasn't about performance, since most machines had only one CPU. But multithreading has lots of other benefits for organization, design, and interactive GUIs so it was still highly useful.

Then the ongoing multicore revolution kicked off and made it clear that multithreading was the way to go.

That's the why. The how is pretty boring. Just lots of work, reading, and experimentation on all sorts of multiprocessing, not just threading. They're very different, but many concepts are the same, and ideas from one can often help with the others. As with most things, practice and experience makes a big difference.

So then we have the different forms of parallel processing available. There are actually a lot of these, and I'm probably doomed to miss some, but:

1. **Distributed computing.** Probably the most visible example of this one for Mac developers is distributed builds in Xcode. This is generally the most difficult to build, the most expensive to take advantage of for the user, and therefore the least useful. Bandwidth and latency between computers are horrendous compared to what you get within a single machine, so it's hard to write something that goes fast. Xcode can get away with it because it (usually) does a lot of processing for each bit of data that it processes. Beyond the difficulty of achieving speed, you also have to deal with a much more error-prone environment. You want to recover gracefully if the user wanders out of wifi range, not lose a bunch of data. Most of the time this is not worth it, especially if you're going to be shipping consumer-level software.
2. **GPGPU.** Basically using the video card for computation. This is what GPULife does. It's capable of immense power. A top-of-the-line video card can easily outperform a top-of-the-line CPU by a factor of 50 with the right program. It's also really hard. GPUs are extremely parallelized and have a considerably different architecture from CPUs, so coding for them is hard and making them go fast is harder. (Although even slow GPU code can run really fast due to the amount of power available.) Technologies like CUDA and OpenCL promise to make this sort of thing a lot better, although you're always going to be dealing with the fact that it's a massively parallel system with really different performance characteristics. My recommendation here is to wait for Snow Leopard and then hope OpenCL delivers on its promise.
3. **Multiple processes.** Again Xcode is a prominent example of this approach, where you can see it spawn multiple instances of gcc when compiling. This is often talked about as being an easier, safer way to go than multithreading because the OS protects processes from each other and forces a better separation of concerns. I don't buy it, personally. For just about any non-trivial program, a dead subprocess is going to mean that the whole thing comes crashing down, and all you've done by splitting it into multiple processes is make it harder to debug. What's worse, OS limits on the number of processes tend to be frighteningly low, so your program would need to gracefully handle being unable to spawn as many subprocesses as it likes. (And all the other apps on the system would need to as well!)
4. **Multithreading.** The standard technique. Often very difficult to get right, and very difficult to debug, but potentially very rewarding in terms of performance. Threads can also help to better organize a program. It's often much cleaner to put long-running processing or blocking operations into a separate thread than to try to multiplex them together.

Multithreading is the one we're most familiar with and the one that's the most generally useful. It's useful because it's very generalized, so you have various ways to use multithreading to actually get things done:

1. **Locks.** "Standard" multithreading. You have shared data protected by locks. Acquire the locks before you fiddle with the data. Often used to build more sophisticated machinery. This level can be tricky to get right so I recommend avoiding it where you can, and using it sparingly to build better abstractions where you must.
2. **Message passing.** With message passing, you avoid shared data, and have threads communicate using message queues instead. (The message queues generally have shared data inside them, but that's an implementation detail.) Cocoa has some nice facilities for this with the `-performSelectorOnMainThread:...` and `performSelector:onThread:...` calls. The threading-heavy language Erlang uses this model extensively and is the main force behind its multithreading power.
3. **Operation units.** This is kind of like message passing, except the operations just fly off and get executed on a queue which uses threads outside your view. When set to only execute one operation at a time, a queue can act like a synchronization point, replacing locks in a way that's often easier to work with. NSOperationQueue provides this and Grand Central Dispatch in Snow Leopard is rumored to provide similar facilities.
4. **Atomic/transactional objects.** Rather than using mutual exclusion (locks, queues) to avoid destroying shared data, you can build objects that operate using transactions. Grab a snapshot, make changes, commit them. (Often this is implemented as a loop: snapshot, change, try to commit and start over with a new snapshot if something changed in the middle.) TransactionKit is a great example of this sort of thing in a Cocoa context.

As for what to use, here are my thoughts. Avoid distributed computing unless your code is going to be run by a single client with a lot of available hardware. Being able to snarf up CPU cycles from idle hardware sitting around in the user's house sounds cool but just doesn't pay off most of the time. Avoid GPGPU on the Mac until Snow Leopard ships unless you have a *really* good application for it. OpenCL will make GPGPU a lot more practical and flexible, so trying to shoehorn your computationally expensive code into GLSL or CoreImage today just doesn't seem worth it.

Using multiple processes is a good idea if the subprograms are already written. If you're invoking gcc as a subprocess, invoking it simultaneously on four files instead of one by one is pretty easy. If you're writing your code from scratch, I don't recommend it unless you have another good reason to write subprocesses, as it's difficult and the reward just isn't there.

For multithreading, concentrate on message passing and operations. Multithreading is never easy, but these help greatly to make it simpler and less error prone. Good OO design will also help a lot here. It's vastly easier to multithread an app which has already been decomposed into simple objects with well-defined interfaces and loose coupling between them.

Friday Q&A 2008-12-26: Blocks in Objective-C

Related Articles

    Practical Blocks 146

    Creating a Blocks-Based Object System 205

    Error Returns with Continuation Passing Style 303

    Trampolining Blocks with Mutable Code..311

    Futures...330

    Compound Futures..342

    Background Timers...419

Welcome to another Friday Q&A. This week I thought I would take fellow amoeboid Jeff Johnson's suggestion and talk about blocks in Objective-C.

The word "blocks" is kind of ambiguous, so to clarify, I'm not talking about the compound statement structure which has existed in C since the beginning of time. I'm talking about a new addition to the language being created by Apple which adds anonymous functions to the language. [Note: since this chapter was written, Apple's blocks implementation has been made public and is now completely mature and usable. While this chapter remains relevant, good up-to-date documentation on blocks can now be found on developer.apple.com.]

Since they're not available to the public in finished form yet, the discussion is going to be a bit imprecise in terms of syntax. But since I mainly want to talk about what they will do for us and not the absolute precise details of how to type them out, that's not a big problem. First let's see how they look:

```
x = ^{ printf("hello world\n"); }
```

That's a block. The funny caret before the braces is what distinguishes it from boring old compound statements. Now we can simply call this block like so:

```
x();
```

And the resulting code will print "hello world". Now let's introduce a couple of parameters:

```
x = ^(int a, char *b){ printf("a is %d and b is %s", a, b); }
```

And then we can call this just the way you'd think:

```
x(42, "fork!");
```

Now let's remove the parameters again:

```
int a = 42;
char *b = "fork!";
x = ^{ printf("a is %d and b is %s", a, b); }
x();
```

This illustrates one of the really interesting things about blocks: they can capture variables from their enclosing scope. This is not particularly interesting here (why didn't we just pass a and b when invoking it?) but it gets really interesting when we start passing the block around to other functions:

```
int a = 42;
char *b = "fork!";
callblock(^{ printf("a is %d and b is %s", a, b); });
```

When the `callblock()` function calls that block, the block will still get access to our local variables a and b even though we never passed them to the function explicitly.

We're just about done with the basics of what blocks are. One more quick example, a block that returns a value:

```
x = ^(int n){ return n + 1; };
printf("%d\n", x(2));
```

This code will print "3". Note that there is no need to declare the type of the return value as the compiler can simply infer it from the return statement.

So what's the big deal? A major advantage of blocks is that they essentially allow you to write your own control structures in the language without having to alter the compiler. As one example, take the `for(... in ...)` syntax that appeared in Leopard. This syntax is a wonderful addition to the language. Previously we had to write a bunch of code just to iterate over an array:

```
NSEnumerator *enumerator = [array objectEnumerator];
id obj;
while((obj = [enumerator nextObject]))
    // finally we can do something with obj
```

And the new syntax cuts this down to a single line:

```
for(id obj in array)
```

Which is great. The only trouble is that we went years and years without it. We had to wait for Apple to add it for us. With blocks, no more! You don't get quite the same syntax, but you can get the same convenience with a method you wrote entirely yourself:

```
my_for(array, ^(id obj){ /* loop body goes here */ });
```

Or in a perhaps slightly stranger but much more interesting object-oriented form:

```
[array do:^(id obj){ /* loop body goes here */ }];
```

The implementation of the `-do:` method is left up to the reader, but rest assured that it's relatively simple.

As another example, consider the `@synchronized` directive. This could be redone using blocks too:

```
[obj synchronized:^{ /* this is protected by the lock */ }];
```

OK, you say, I get it, but what's the big deal? After all, `for/in` and `@synchronized` are already part of the language, why would you rewrite them?

Of course you wouldn't. That would be silly. Those examples serve only to illustrate the idea: that you can build your own control structures. But of course it's only interesting to build control structures that are new! So here are some ideas.

- Open a file and ensure that it gets closed when you're done:

    ```
    [[NSFileHandle fileHandleForReadingAtPath:path]
       closeWhenDone:^(NSFileHandle *handle){
         /* use handle here */
    }];
    ```

- Build a new array by working with the objects of an existing one:

    ```
    newArray = [existingArray map:^(id obj){ return [obj stringByAppendingString:@"suffix"]; }];
    ```

- Filter the contents of an array:

    ```
    newArray = [existingArray filter:^(id obj){ return [obj hasPrefix:@"my"]; }];
    ```

- Main thread synchronization:

```
/* threaded code */
PerformOnMainThread(^{ /* synchronized code */ });
/* more threaded code */
```

- Delayed execution:

```
PerformWithDelay(5.0, ^{ /* will run 5 seconds later */ });
```

- Parallel enumeration:

```
[array doParallelized:^(id obj){
    /* will get executed on all of your CPU cores at once */
}];
```

And many other examples abound.

Another place where blocks will make things much nicer is when dealing with callbacks. If you've ever written much Cocoa code you've probably had to write a sheet callback, and it's a pain in the ass. If you need to pass variables through to the other side then it gets really frustrating with code like this:

```objc
- (void)method {
    int foo;
    NSString *bar;
    /* do some work with those variables */
    NSDictionary *ctx = [[NSDictionary alloc] initWithObjectsAndKeys:
        [NSNumber numberWithInt:foo], @"foo",
        bar, @"bar",
        nil];
    [NSApp beginSheet:sheet
        modalForWindow:window
        modalDelegate:self
        didEndSelector:@selector(methodSheetDidEnd:returnCode:contextInfo:)
        contextInfo:ctx];
}

- (void)methodSheetDidEnd:(NSWindow *)sheet returnCode:(int)code contextInfo:(void *)ctx {
    NSDictionary *ctxDict = ctx;
    [ctxDict autorelease];

    int foo = [[ctxDict objectforKey:@"foo"] intValue];
    NSString *bar = [ctxDict objectForKey:@"bar"];
    /* do some more stuff with those variables */
}
```

Wow! What a pain that is. Since I removed all the stuff that does work, nearly everything that remains is just boilerplate. Horrible boilerplate whose only purpose is to tell the sheet who to call, and to pack up local information in a way that the sheet can give it back to you later on. Now let's imagine we were redoing this API using blocks and see how it would look:

```objc
- (void)method {
    int foo;
    NSString *bar;
    /* do some work with those variables */
    [sheet beginSheetModalForWindow:window
        didEndBlock:^(int code){
            /* do stuff with foo */
            /* do stuff with bar */
            /* do stuff with code, or sheet, or window, or anything */
        }];
}
```

Isn't that great? All that horrible boilerplate just flies right out the window. Code flow suddenly becomes completely logical, you can read it top to bottom, and you can access any local variables you please.

Let's take another example, sorting an array with a custom comparison function using some variables that you pass in. NSArray has functionality for this, with the `-sortedArrayUsingFunction:context:` method. The old-style code is annoying, and I'm not going to write it. It's much like the sheet method above. You have to define a separate function, way outside of your code where it's not really visible. You have to set up the context to pass into it. If you're passing more than one thing then you have to pass a dictionary (and unpack it) or a pointer to a struct. Now here's the blocks version of a custom comparator:

```
sorted = [array sortedArrayUsingBlock:^(id a, id b){
    /* compare, use local variables to decide what to do, run wild */
}];
```

And that's all there is to it.

Callbacks are one of the most powerful things in C and Objective-C but in many situations their use can be extremely difficult and unnatural. Blocks promise to allow callbacks and custom control constructs to be created and used in a much more natural fashion.

So far I've only shown examples of using a blocks API, but how about creating one? Well, it's a little worse, but not much. The only problematic thing is that the syntax for declaring a block type is kind of ugly, as it's modeled after function pointer syntax. But it's not too bad, and the rest is nice and simple. For example, here's how you could write that `-map:` method from above:

```
- (NSArray *)map:(id (^)(id))block { // takes an id, returns an id
    NSMutableArray *ret = [NSMutableArray array];
    for(id obj in self)
        [ret addObject:block(obj)];
    return ret;
}
```

Pretty straightforward, especially considering the power it gives us.

Information on Apple's implementation of blocks is still a bit sparse. Some more details can be found in a mailing list post to the Clang development list. For more purely conceptual ideas on how blocks can be used, check out the Smalltalk language, where blocks are used for virtually every control structure right down to if/then and basic loops.

Here's hoping that blocks allow for some major changes in how we work on Snow Leopard!

Friday Q&A 2009-01-02: Pros and Cons of Private APIs

It's a new year, and that means a new Friday Q&A! This week I'm going to take Steven Degutis's suggestion and discuss the ups and downs of using private APIs.

Getting Started
I'm not going to discuss what private APIs are out there or how to figure them out, as that would cause me to badly miss my deadline and make this thing way too long. Instead I just want to address this question: *should* you use them at all, and if so, when?

There are two pretty obvious extremes to the answer, and a lot of people who believe each end. One extreme is that private APIs should never be used, period, full stop. They're bad, don't want to touch them, don't even acknowledge that they exist. The other extreme is that they're fine and dandy, use them like you'd use anything else.

As with most things, I believe the truth lies somewhere in the middle. But where, exactly, and how do you determine if something is worth using?

First let's review the disadvantages, which you're probably familiar with already. An API is essentially a contract between the creator of the API (generally Apple in the context of this blog) and the user of that API. When an API is public, the creator promises not to change that API in an incompatible fashion. With private APIs no such promise exists, and they can change at any time. This change can cause your application to malfunction, crash, or refuse to start.

And the advantages? Well that one's easy. Private APIs let you do stuff you couldn't otherwise do.

So like most of engineering, it's a tradeoff. You have benefits and disadvantages, and you have to decide which one is more significant.

Elements of the Tradeoff
Using a private API is, ultimately, a maintenance issue. (Except on the App Store, where it's a legal issue, but that's outside the scope of this post.) If you use nothing but public APIs, your app is basically guaranteed to work forever. (Where "forever" really means "until Apple decides not to maintain backwards compatibility anymore". But note that ancient PowerPC-only Carbon apps still run on the latest Mac OS X, and that Classic didn't disappear until 10.4; Apple still keeps old stuff working for a good long time.) If you use a private API, your app is likely to break at some point.

But when? That's one of the big questions you need to answer. There are basically four levels to consider:

1. **Never.** Sometimes a private API may be so fundamental and so widely used that it gets essentially fixed in stone despite not being public. A good example of this on Mac OS X is the `mach` APIs, which are technically private but which underly everything at a very fundamental level.
2. **Major releases.** Most private APIs fall into this category, where you can be reasonably (although never 100%) confident that they will continue to work throughout the lifetime of the current major OS release. In other words, it will keep working on 10.5 but is likely to break on 10.6. Typically private APIs end up forming part of a support structure for the public APIs and can't be changed without a major reworking of those public APIs, and that only happens with a new major release.
3. **Minor releases.** Occasionally something can't even be relied upon to keep working during the life of a major release. Early versions of LiveDictionary were like this. They relied on fiddly internal details of WebCore's implementation, like C++ method and ivar layout. These offsets were subject to change at pretty much any time, so LiveDictionary generally broke every single time Safari got updated. (Later on, public APIs became available that I was able to use instead, which solved the problem once and for all. For more details of what was going on under the hood in those dark days before the public APIs were available, see Hacking C++ From C.)
4. **Any time.** Generally this means that you aren't using the private API right. This is much more common than with public APIs since you don't have any documentation, you have no guarantee as to the API's requirements, constraints, preconditions, postconditions, etc.

Another big question you need to answer is how bad the break, when it comes, is likely to be. Again, there are different levels to consider:

1. **No effect.** It's unlikely that you'll get here. If there's no effect from having it break, why are you even using the thing?
2. **Lose a feature.** Often you can write your code in such a way that the breakage is *likely* to be detectable and so you can simply disable whatever feature uses it.
3. **Crash your app.** This is pretty common.
4. **Crash other apps.** For developers of stuff that loads into other programs this is very common, for self-contained processes not so much. LiveDictionary did this. When LiveDictionary broke, it didn't just crash, it crashed Safari too.

Which category you fall into depends not only on what you're using but how. For example, LiveDictionary would toss up a warning and offer to disable itself for the duration if the WebCore version was higher than what it knew about. A brave user could try to use it anyway (and there was at least one time when that version changed in unexpected ways and stopped this precaution from working) but this helped a lot. Obviously the higher up this list you are, the better off you are.

And lastly you need to figure out how long it will take you to fix the break. This depends greatly on your skill, your availability, what you're using, how critical it is, how it broke, and other such factors.

Coming to a Conclusion
Now you have enough information to run the cost/benefit analysis. The benefit side is pretty easy. The cost side can be determined by looking at how often you're likely to break, how bad it's likely to be, and how much time and effort it will take to fix. If it's a huge feature and will almost never break and will be trivial to fix when it does, then go for it. If it's a minor feature and will cause huge problems when it breaks every three months, pass. For LiveDictionary, the entire app was built around this feature, so it was worth it even though it required frequent difficult fixes.

Remember that the cost is not just to you, but to your users. If you're really unlucky, the break will be so bad that it's not even obvious that it's your fault, and they'll figure it out only after much head-scratching. Once they do figure it out, they will hate you if your fix doesn't come really fast. This means that for a really crucial and breakable feature, you need to stay available and ready to create and release a fix.

Private APIs can be invaluable, but their use must be weighed carefully. Sometimes it pays off very well, and sometimes it's a terrible choice. By carefully examining your app's vulnerability to breakage and your ability to fix it, you can decide whether it's the right move for you.

Friday Q&A 2009-01-09: Thread Safety in OS X System Frameworks

Related Articles

    Multithreaded Programming and Parallelism Overview 11

    The Good and Bad of Distributed Objects... 56

    Multithreaded Optimization in ChemicalBurn 82

    Care and Feeding of Singletons 194

    Dangerous Cocoa Calls... 236

    Probing Cocoa With PyObjC 240

    Using Accessors in Init and Dealloc... 246

    NSRunLoop Internals 273

    NSNotificationQueue.. 284

    Implementing a Custom Slider 382

    Dealing with Retain Cycles 392

    What Every Apple Programmer Should Know 401

    Leopard Collection Classes.. 405

    Implementing Equality and Hashing 412

    Implementing NSCoding 459

    Defensive Programming in Cocoa 468

Greetings one and all. I caught my mistaken writing of "2008" in this blog post title almost instantly instead of only noticing after I'd already posted it like I did last week, so the year must be coming along. Welcome to the second Friday Q&A of 2009 (and only the fourth in all human history!) where I'll be taking Ed Wynne's suggestion and talking about the various meanings and implications of thread safety as they apply to Mac OS X system frameworks.

Thread Safety? What's That?

Hopefully not too many readers are actually asking the above questions, but just as a quick refresher, thread safety is about whether it's safe to access a particular module, API, or data structure from multiple threads. These things are typically unsafe due to making assumptions of single-threadedness, such as updating multiple pieces of data in a non-atomic fashion, in such a way as to expose inconsistent data to the outside world. There's the classic example:

```
x++;
```

Which is not thread safe (assuming x is globally accessible) because down at the very bottom it breaks down into multiple operations:

```
get x
increment
store x
```

And if multiple threads are doing this at once, they interleave and you miss increments. Not too dire here, but apply it to pointers and objects and you can hopefully see why you'll crash at best, and silently corrupt data if you're unlucky.

So to start off with there are two kinds of thread safety in the world:

1. **Not thread safe.** The normal state. Code is not thread safe by default. Special effort needs to be taken to make it thread safe, and if you haven't done it, your code falls into this category.
2. **Thread safe.** Can be called from any thread without a care or worry. Nice to have, often painful to make.

Three Kinds

But what does this really *mean*? Well, **thread safe** is easy enough to understand. But **not thread safe** can't really mean it can't be called from any thread, because all code runs from *some* thread.

Of course what it really means is that this code can't be run from *more than one thread at the same time*.

But that doesn't really do it either. For example, `NSMutableArray` is not thread safe. But you can call NSMutableArray from multiple threads simultaneously, as long as each thread is working on a different array. So maybe we should say that thread unsafe means that the code can't be run *on the same data* from more than one thread at the same time.

Well, that's better, but still not there. Take the `atoi()` function. Not thread safe, says so in the man page. But you only ever feed it constant data, and it's unsafe even if you feed it completely different data on your different threads. What's the deal? Simple: behind the scenes, it has some shared data.

How can you tell one from the other? We'll need another classification:

1. **Never thread safe.** The normal state. Code is not thread safe by default. Special effort needs to be taken to make it thread safe, and if you haven't done it, your code falls into this category.
2. **Not thread safe with shared data.** Can safely be called from multiple threads simultaneously as long as each thread is dealing with a distinct set of data.
3. **Thread safe.** Can be called from any thread without a care or worry. Nice to have, often painful to make.

It's actually really easy to write code that falls into category #2. All you have to do is not have any global state, which is pretty common anyway. If you're writing an array class, your method for adding a new object to the array isn't going to deal with global state, it's going to deal with that one array. So while #1 may be the "normal state", #2 is actually really easy to come by, and most code falls into that category.

The System Screws It All Up
These categories are sufficient in a relatively simplistic program which controls every action taking place and for which all the code is known. It gets more complicated when you start pulling in a ton of big, complex external frameworks such as AppKit and Foundation. Take `NSView` as an example. It can fall into category #1 or #3 depending on what you're doing with it. (Drawing is safe, creation/resizing/etc. is unsafe.) But that #1 is complicated by the fact that the shared global data which makes NSView unsafe can be *accessed by code that isn't yours*.

NSView isn't just unsafe from multiple threads, it's **main thread only**. This is because your NSView doesn't just belong to you, it belongs to the framework. And this means that you can't synchronize all accesses to it, because some of those accesses come from code that does not belong to you! Let's put this in its own paragraph, because it's important:

If an API is never thread safe and you do not absolutely control every access to this API, then you can only call it from the main thread.

And since virtually every system API is going to be, at least potentially, called by other system APIs, we can rewrite our three types of thread safety:

1. **Main thread only.** The normal state. Code is not thread safe by default. Special effort needs to be taken to make it thread safe, and if you haven't done it, your code falls into this category.
2. **Not thread safe.** Can safely be called from multiple threads simultaneously as long as each thread is dealing with a distinct set of data.
3. **Thread safe.** Can be called from any thread without a care or worry. Nice to have, often painful to make.

Singletons
Keep in mind that singletons qualify as global shared data. This has an important impact on their thread safety. Practically speaking, it means that singletons provided by system frameworks only ever fall into category #1 or #3. Take NSFileManager as an example. It's listed as not being thread safe. What this really means is that `[NSFileManager defaultManager]` can only be safely used from the main thread, because you can't control what other code might access it. (On 10.5 and above you can `alloc/init` your own private instances which then fall into category #2.)

Terminology and the Apple Way
This is all fine and dandy except that Apple, in their infinite wisdom, does not always distinguish between **main thread only** and **not thread safe**. To make things worse, they even sometimes use the term **thread safe** to mean what we have defined here as **not thread safe**.

Let's take that second one first, because it's pretty weird. As a concrete example, look at the `CFNetDiagnostics` API. The documentation for this API is full of quotes like this:

> ```
> This function is thread safe as long as another
> thread does not alter the same CFNetDiagnosticRef at
> the same time.
> ```

Huh??

So why is it labeled "thread safe"? What they're trying to convey here, through the fog of inadequate terminology, is that this API falls into category #2 and not category #1. In other words, you can use it from any thread as long as only one thread at a time is using this API on any given piece of data. This as opposed to an API which requires you to call it only from the main thread.

Other APIs are less explicit about it. The `Search Kit` reference simply states "Search Kit is thread-safe". And yet I'm pretty sure it's not. Again, it's trying to convey that Search Kit is in category #2 rather than category #1.

Why do they do this? Well, back in the day, on the classic Mac OS, nearly all code ran in what might be considered the "main thread" today. As a consequence, nearly every API required only calling it from there. Being able to run from multiple threads was novel and unusual and was worth documenting. Alas, not only does this no longer make sense on Mac OS X, but this sort of terminology abuse is actively destructive because it ends up making guarantees which aren't actually true.

As an example of the first, look at `NSAppleScript`. In the big master guide it's marked as being not thread safe. This is true! However what they don't tell you is that `NSAppleScript` can only be safely used from the main thread, due to AppleScript itself being a main thread only API. And yet it's right next to other classes such as `NSMutableArray` which are clearly category #2.

Figuring It Out
So we've established the three basic categories of thread safety, and we've established that Apple doesn't consistently distinguish between them in its documentation. So what do we do?

Fortunately it's *usually* possible to figure out the real story.

1. Check the documentation. Not only the API documentation but also the big list. Is the API listed as being thread safe? Is it written in a relatively unambiguous way that makes it clear that this really is thread safe, and not the "thread safe" that means "not thread safe"? Fortunately for us, this abuse of the term "thread safe" is relatively rare and relatively obvious. It generally shows up in older APIs

27

which have no reason to be thread safe in the first place. If after all this you have determined that your API is **thread safe** then you're done! If not go to the next step.
2. When in doubt, assume it's unsafe. In the absence of an explicit guarantee of thread safety, consider the API to be unsafe. But what kind of unsafe? That's the tricky thing.
3. Does it access shared global data? Singletons fall into this category, as do things like user interface elements. If the answer is yes, then it's category #1: **main thread only**.
4. Does it potentially invoke other code which may not be thread safe? `NSAppleScript` falls into this category (scripting additions) as do things like user interface elements which may broadcast notifications when they're manipulated. Again, if the answer is yes, it's main thread only.
5. If you got this far then it's *probably* category #2, **thread unsafe**, and usable on any thread as long as you synchronize calls on shared data.
6. To verify, think about how simple or self-contained an API is. If it's pretty self-contained then it's very likely category #2. If it calls out to a zillion other things then it's very likely category #1. Therefore we can be pretty sure that NSMutableArray (self-contained) is merely not thread safe, whereas NSAppleScript (calls out to all sorts of other stuff, including arbitrary third-party components) needs to run on the main thread.

It would be good if Apple would properly distinguish between the different kinds of thread safety. However you can *usually* do a good job of figuring out any given API if you work it through.

Friday Q&A 2009-01-16: Interprocess Communication

Related Articles

The Good and Bad of Distributed Objects...56

Happy Friday to everyone, and welcome back to another Friday Q&A. This week I'll be taking Eren Halici's suggestion to discuss the various ways to do interprocess communication on OS X.

IPC is an interesting and sometimes complicated topic, especially on OS X, which has a veritable zoo of IPC techniques. It can be hard to decide which one to use, and sometimes hard to even know what's available.

OS X is a funny mixture of mach and UNIX so you end up with IPC mechanisms from both:

- **Mach ports:** The fundamental IPC mechanism in mach. Fast, light-weight, extremely capable, and difficult to use. Mach ports will not only let you talk to other processes, but do things as drastic as inject code into other people's programs. The poor state of the mach documentation makes it hard to get started and easy to make mistakes with it. On the other hand, the core `mach_msg` function is probably the most optimized syscall in the system, so they're really fast to use, and your machine will barely blink if you decide to allocate a million mach ports at once.
    - **CFMachPort:** A very thin wrapper around mach ports. `CFMachPort` essentially exists to allow a mach port to be used as a runloop source. It can also help with creating and destroying the ports. It helps a little with receiving messages and not at all with sending them.
    - **CFMessagePort:** This nice CoreFoundation wrapper around some mach functionality makes it easy to set up synchronous back-and-forth communication between two unrelated processes. You can start a server with just a few lines of code. Another program can then look up that server by name and message it. You get the speed advantages of mach without all the messy stuff going on underneath.
    - **NSPort/NSMachPort/NSMessagePort:** Cocoa has some mach port wrappers too. They're mainly geared toward use with Distributed Objects (more on that below) but can be used on their own as well, if you're brave.
- **POSIX file descriptors:** There are actually several kinds of these but they can all be used with the typical `read` and `write` calls once they're set up.
    - **Pipes:** The archetypal POSIX IPC mechanism. If you've ever used the | pipe operator in a UNIX shell, you've used a pipe. Pipes get created in

pairs within the same process, so they're good for communicating between parents and children (or between two children of a single, coordinating parent) but not so good for communicating between unrelated processes. Make them with the `pipe` call.
- **FIFOs:** It's like a file, but it's like a pipe! A FIFO gets an entry in your filesystem, just like a file, but writes don't go to the filesystem, instead they go to whatever process has opened the fifo for reading. You can make these with the `mkfifo` call. The end result is a pipe that has a filesystem entry, which can make it easy for two unrelated processes to hook up. The processes don't even have to know that they're talking to a fifo. Try it out in your shell:

```
$ mkfifo /tmp/fifo
$ cat /tmp/fifo

# in another shell
cat > /tmp/fifo
type some junk here
```

- **Sockets:** You probably know these from working with TCP/IP, but they can also be used to communicate locally, and not just by connecting to `localhost`. If you create a socket in the `AF_UNIX` family you get a socket that's only for local communication and uses more flexible addressing than TCP/IP allows. `AF_UNIX` sockets can be created using a filesystem path much like a FIFO by using the `socket` and `bind` calls, but allowing multiple clients and more options for how the communication works. They can also be created anonymously using the `socketpair` call, giving you something much like a pipe, except bidirectional.
- **Shared memory:** Shared memory is a magical piece of memory which appears in multiple processes at once. In other words, you write to it from process A, and read from it in process B, or vice versa. This tends to be very fast, as the data itself never touches the kernel and doesn't have to be copied around. The downside is that it's really difficult to coordinate changes to the shared memory area. You essentially get all of the disadvantages of threaded programming *and* most of the disadvantages of multi-process programming bundled together in one neat package. Shared memory can be created using either mach or POSIX APIs.
- **Miscellaneous, not really IPC:** There are some techniques which don't really count as "IPC" but can be used to communicate between programs if you want to.
  - **ptrace:** This system call exists mainly for writing debuggers, but could in theory be used to do non-debugger things too. Not recommended, included only for completeness.

- **Files:** Sometimes it can be useful to communicate using plain old files. This can be as simple as creating a lock file (a plain empty file that works simply by being there) for mutual exclusion, or you can transfer actual data around by writing it to a file, then having the other program read it. This tends to be inefficient since you're actually writing to the filesystem, but it's also easy and nearly universal; every application can read files!

Those are all what I would call system-level functionality, things which are either provided directly by the kernel/libSystem, or which are thin wrappers around them. OS X also provides a bunch of higher-level IPC mechanisms at the framework level:

- **Apple Events:** Scourge of the Skies, Champion of the Ugly Contest, King Slow, Emperor Horrible. Apple Events are all of these things, but they're also tremendously useful. They're the only IPC mechanism which is universally supported by GUI applications on Mac OS X for remote control. Want to tell another application to open a file? Time for Apple Events. Want to tell another application to quit gracefully? Apple Events time. Underneath it all, Apple Events are built on mach ports but this is mostly not exposed in the API.
    - **AppleScript:** Everything Apple Events is and worse, but still often useful, AppleScript is a scripting language built on top of Apple Events. Generally it's best to avoid AppleScript and simply send the corresponding raw Apple Events instead, either directly or through a mechanism like Scripting Bridge. AppleScript support is the standard way to allow users to script your application, although if you ever try to add AppleScript support to your application you'll find yourself wishing for a different standard.
- **Distributed Objects:** It's like Objective-C, but it happens over there! DO gives you proxy objects that can be used (mostly) just like local objects, with the exact same syntax and everything, except that your messages fly across to the other process and get executed there. DO normally runs over mach ports but can also be used with sockets, allowing it to work between computers as well. DO is really cool technology and it's the sort of thing that tends to blow people's minds when they come to Objective-C from lesser languages such as Java or C++. Unfortunately DO is also really old and crufty and tends to be strangely unreliable. This is especially true when using it with sockets to talk to remote machines, but is even true when using it locally. DO is also completely non-modular, making it essentially impossible to swap out the IPC mechanism it uses for something custom (like if you want to encrypt the stream). It is worthy of investigation if only to learn about how it works, and despite the shortcomings can still be very useful in certain situations.
- **Distributed Notifications:** These are simple one-way messages that essentially get broadcast out to any process in the session that's listening for them. Extremely easy to use, and available in both Cocoa and CoreFoundation flavors. (And they interoperate!) The downside is that they don't guarantee delivery and

they're very resource-intensive due to potentially messaging every application on your system. They would be completely unsuitable for something like transmitting a large picture to another process, but are great for simple one-off things like "I just changed my preferences, re-read them now". Internally this is implemented by using mach ports to talk to a centralized notification server which manages the task of getting notifications to where they want to go.
- **Pasteboard:** Probably the IPC mechanism that you've directly used the most. Every time you copy and paste something between applications, that's IPC happening! Inter-app drag and drop also uses the pasteboard, and it's possible to create custom pasteboards for passing data back and forth between applications. Like distributed notifications, pasteboards work by talking to a central pasteboard server using mach ports.

So which one is right for you? Well, it all depends on what you're doing. I've used nearly every one of these to accomplish different things over the years. You'll have to see which one fits your problem best, and I hope the above gives you a good place to get started.

Friday Q&A 2009-01-23: How Key-Value Observing Works

Welcome to the first Friday Q&A of the new Presidential administration. Unlike Mr. Obama, I'm afraid of change and so this week's edition will be just like all the other ones. This week I'll be taking Jonathan Mitchell's suggestion to talk about how Key-Value Observing (KVO) is actually implemented at the runtime level.

What Is It?
Most readers probably know this already, but just for a quick recap: KVO is the technology that underlies Cocoa Bindings, and it provides a way for objects to get notified when the properties of other objects are changed. One object *observes* a key of another object. When the observed object changes the value of that key, the observer gets notified. Pretty straightforward, right? The tricky part is that KVO operates with no code needed in the object being observed... usually.

Overview
So how does that work, not needing any code in the observed object? Well it all happens through the power of the Objective-C runtime. When you observe an object of a particular class for the first time, the KVO infrastructure creates a brand new class at runtime that subclasses your class. In that new class, it overrides the set methods for any observed keys. It then switches out the `isa` pointer of your object (the pointer that tells the Objective-C runtime what kind of object a particular blob of memory actually is) so that your object magically becomes an instance of this new class.

The overridden methods are how it does the real work of notifying observers. The logic goes that changes to a key have to go through that key's set method. It overrides that set method so that it can intercept it and post notifications to observers whenever it gets called. (Of course it's possible to make a modification without going through the set method if you modify the instance variable directly. KVO requires that compliant classes must either not do this, or must wrap direct ivar access in manual notification calls.)

It gets trickier though: Apple really doesn't want this machinery to be exposed. In addition to setters, the dynamic subclass also overrides the `-class` method to lie to you and return the original class! If you don't look too closely, the KVO-mutated objects look just like their non-observed counterparts.

Digging Deeper
Enough talk, let's actually see how all of this works. I wrote a program that illustrates the principles behind KVO. Because the dynamic KVO subclass tries to hide its own existence, I mainly use Objective-C runtime calls to get the information we're looking for.

Here's the program:

```
// gcc -o kvoexplorer -framework Foundation kvoexplorer.m
#import <Foundation/Foundation.h>
#import <objc/runtime.h>

@interface TestClass : NSObject
{
    int x;
    int y;
    int z;
}
@property int x;
@property int y;
@property int z;
@end
@implementation TestClass
@synthesize x, y, z;
@end

static NSArray *ClassMethodNames(Class c)
{
    NSMutableArray *array = [NSMutableArray array];

    unsigned int methodCount = 0;
    Method *methodList = class_copyMethodList(c, &methodCount);
    unsigned int i;
    for(i = 0; i < methodCount; i++)
        [array addObject: NSStringFromSelector(method_getName(methodList[i]))];
    free(methodList);

    return array;
}

static void PrintDescription(NSString *name, id obj)
{
    NSString *str = [NSString stringWithFormat:
        @"%@: %@\n\tNSObject class %s\n\tlibobjc class %s\n\timplements methods <%@>",
        name,
        obj,
        class_getName([obj class]),
        class_getName(obj->isa),
```

```objc
    [ClassMethodNames(obj->isa)
componentsJoinedByString:@", "]];
    printf("%s\n", [str UTF8String]);
}

int main(int argc, char **argv)
{
    [NSAutoreleasePool new];
    
    TestClass *x = [[TestClass alloc] init];
    TestClass *y = [[TestClass alloc] init];
    TestClass *xy = [[TestClass alloc] init];
    TestClass *control = [[TestClass alloc] init];
    
    [x addObserver:x forKeyPath:@"x" options:0
context:NULL];
    [xy addObserver:xy forKeyPath:@"x" options:0
context:NULL];
    [y addObserver:y forKeyPath:@"y" options:0
context:NULL];
    [xy addObserver:xy forKeyPath:@"y" options:0
context:NULL];
    
    PrintDescription(@"control", control);
    PrintDescription(@"x", x);
    PrintDescription(@"y", y);
    PrintDescription(@"xy", xy);
    
    printf("Using NSObject methods, normal setX: is %p, overridden setX: is %p\n",
            [control methodForSelector:@selector(setX:)],
            [x methodForSelector:@selector(setX:)]);
    printf("Using libobjc functions, normal setX: is %p, overridden setX: is %p\n",
method_getImplementation(class_getInstanceMethod(object_getClass(control)
                                    @selector(setX:))),

    method_getImplementation(class_getInstanceMethod(object_getClass(x),
                                    @selector(setX:))));
    
    return 0;
}
```

Let's walk through it, top to bottom.

First we define a class called TestClass which has three properties. (KVO works on non-`@property` keys too but this is the simplest way to define pairs of setters and getters.)

Next we define a pair of utility functions. `ClassMethodNames` uses Objective-C runtime functions to go through a class and get a list of all the methods it implements. Note that it only gets methods implemented directly in that class, *not* in superclasses. `PrintDescription` prints a full description of the object passed to it, showing the object's class as obtained through the `-class` method as well as through an Objective-C runtime function, and the methods implemented on that class.

Then we start experimenting using those facilities. We create four instances of TestClass, each of which will be observed in a different way. The `x` instance will have an observer on its `x` key, similar for `y`, and `xy` will get both. The `z` key is left unobserved for comparison purposes. And lastly the `control` instance serves as a control on the experiment and will not be observed at all.

Next we print out the description of all four objects.

After that we dig a little deeper into the overridden setter and print out the address of the implementation of the `-setX:` method on the control object and an observed object to compare. And we do this twice, because using `-methodForSelector:` fails to show the override. KVO's attempt to hide the dynamic subclass even hides the overridden method with this technique! But of course using Objective-C runtime functions instead provides the proper result.

Running the Code
So that's what it does, now let's look at a sample run:

```
control: <TestClass: 0x104b20>
    NSObject class TestClass
    libobjc class TestClass
    implements methods <setX:, x, setY:, y, setZ:, z>
x: <TestClass: 0x103280>
    NSObject class TestClass
    libobjc class NSKVONotifying_TestClass
    implements methods <setY:, setX:, class, dealloc,
_isKVOA>
y: <TestClass: 0x104b00>
    NSObject class TestClass
    libobjc class NSKVONotifying_TestClass
    implements methods <setY:, setX:, class, dealloc,
_isKVOA>
xy: <TestClass: 0x104b10>
    NSObject class TestClass
    libobjc class NSKVONotifying_TestClass
    implements methods <setY:, setX:, class, dealloc,
_isKVOA>
Using NSObject methods, normal setX: is 0x195e, overridden
setX: is 0x195e
Using libobjc functions, normal setX: is 0x195e,
overridden setX: is 0x96a1a550
```

First it prints our control object. As expected, its class is TestClass and it implements the six methods we synthesized from the class's properties.

Next it prints the three observed objects. Note that while -class is still showing TestClass, using object_getClass shows the true face of this object: it's an instance of NSKVONotifying_TestClass. There's your dynamic subclass!

Notice how it implements the two observed setters. This is interesting because you'll note that it's smart enough not to override -setZ: even though that's also a setter, because nobody has observed it. Presumably if we were to add an observer to z as well, then NSKVONotifying_TestClass would suddenly sprout a -setZ: override. But also note that it's the same class for all three instances, meaning they all have overrides for both setters, even though two of them only have one observed property. This costs some efficiency due to passing through the observed setter even for a non-observed property, but Apple apparently thought it was better not to have a proliferation of dynamic subclasses if each object had a different set of keys being observed, and I think that was the correct choice.

You'll also notice three other methods. There's the overridden -class method as mentioned before, the one that tries to hide the existence of this dynamic subclass.

There's a `-dealloc` method to handle cleanup. And there's a mysterious `-_isKVOA` method which looks to be a private method that Apple code can use to determine if an object is being subject to this dynamic subclassing.

Next we print out the implementation for `-setX:`. Using `-methodForSelector:` returns the same value for both. Since there is no override for this method in the dynamic subclass, this must mean that `-methodForSelector:` uses `-class` as part of its internal workings and is getting the wrong answer due to that.

So of course we bypass that altogether and use the Objective-C runtime to print the implementations instead, and here we can see the difference. The original agrees with `-methodForSelector:` (as of course it should), but the second is completely different.

Being good explorers, we're running in the debugger and so can see exactly what this second function actually is:

```
(gdb) print (IMP)0x96a1a550
$1 = (IMP) 0x96a1a550 <_NSSetIntValueAndNotify>
```

It's some sort of private function that implements the observer notification. By using `nm -a` on Foundation we can get a complete listing of all of these private functions:

```
0013df80 t __NSSetBoolValueAndNotify
000a0480 t __NSSetCharValueAndNotify
0013e120 t __NSSetDoubleValueAndNotify
0013e1f0 t __NSSetFloatValueAndNotify
000e3550 t __NSSetIntValueAndNotify
0013e390 t __NSSetLongLongValueAndNotify
0013e2c0 t __NSSetLongValueAndNotify
00089df0 t __NSSetObjectValueAndNotify
0013e6f0 t __NSSetPointValueAndNotify
0013e7d0 t __NSSetRangeValueAndNotify
0013e8b0 t __NSSetRectValueAndNotify
0013e550 t __NSSetShortValueAndNotify
0008ab20 t __NSSetSizeValueAndNotify
0013e050 t __NSSetUnsignedCharValueAndNotify
0009fcd0 t __NSSetUnsignedIntValueAndNotify
0013e470 t __NSSetUnsignedLongLongValueAndNotify
0009fc00 t __NSSetUnsignedLongValueAndNotify
0013e620 t __NSSetUnsignedShortValueAndNotify
```

There are some interesting things to be found in this list. First, you'll notice that Apple has to implement a separate function for every primitive type that they want to support. They only need one for Objective-C objects (`_NSSetObjectValueAndNotify`) but they need a whole host of functions for the rest. And that host is kind of incomplete: there's no function for `long double` or `_Bool`. There isn't even one for a generic pointer type, such as you'd get if you had a `CFTypeRef` property. And while there are several functions for various common Cocoa structs, there obviously aren't any for the huge universe of other structs out there. This means that any properties of these types will simply be ineligible for automatic KVO notification, so beware!

KVO is a powerful technology, sometimes a little too powerful, especially when automatic notification is involved. Now you know exactly how it all works on the inside and this knowledge may help you decide how to use it or to debug it when it goes wrong.

If you plan to use KVO in your own application you may want to check out my article on Key-Value Observing Done Right.

Wrapping Up
That's it for this week. Will Mike face down the terrifying code monster? Will his IDE finish compiling in time? Tune in next week for another exciting installment! In the meantime, post your thoughts below.

Friday Q&A 2009-01-30: Code Injection

Related Articles

    Creating a Blocks-Based Object System 205

    Probing Cocoa With PyObjC...240

    Method Replacement for Fun and Profit 297

    Trampolining Blocks with Mutable Code..311

    Zeroing Weak References in Objective-C 428

    Zeroing Weak References to CoreFoundation Objects...447

Welcome back to another exciting Friday Q&A. This week I'll be taking Jonathan Mitchell's suggestion to talk about code injection, the various ways to do it, why you'd want to, and why you wouldn't want to.

What It Is

Let's start with a real easy example:

```
Fear:~/shell mikeash$ cat injectlib.c
#include <stdio.h>
void inject_init(void) __attribute__((constructor));
void inject_init(void)
{
    fprintf(stderr, "Here's your injected code!\n");
}
Fear:~/shell mikeash$ gcc -bundle -o injectlib injectlib.c
Fear:~/shell mikeash$ gdb attach `ps x|grep Safari|grep -v grep|awk '{print $1}'`
GNU gdb 6.3.50-20050815 (Apple version gdb-962) (Sat Jul 26 08:14:40 UTC 2008)
[snip]
0x93e631c6 in mach_msg_trap ()
(gdb) p (void *)dlopen("/Users/mikeash/shell/injectlib", 2)
$1 = (void *) 0x28f3b5b0
(gdb)
```

And if we look in our Console (where Safari's stderr goes), we see:

```
[0x0-0x17f97f8].com.apple.Safari[23558]: Here's your injected code!
```

And that's code injection in a nutshell. You bang into another process, load some of your own code, and get it to run. What you do there is up to you!

How to Do It
Of course, using `gdb` to inject code isn't exactly what one might call practical. For one thing, `gdb` is unlikely to be present on your users' systems, as it's a developer tool.

However there are better alternatives, some as part of Mac OS X and some as third-party tools.

Input Managers
Input Managers are intended to provide keyboard input mechanisms for allowing custom ways to translate keystrokes into text on the screen, for example a custom Chinese input method.

They aren't very useful for their stated purpose on Mac OS X because they only work in Cocoa apps, not Carbon apps. But because they work by loading the input manager directly into every Cocoa application, they're great for code injection. All you need to do is build a bundle with the right layout, put it in the right place, and suddenly you're loaded into every Cocoa app.

Of course Apple isn't too keen on code injection and they've threatened that they might take our toys away at some point. Input Managers still work on Leopard, although they've been restricted and now require root access to install them. They may or may not still be around on Snow Leopard, it's hard to say yet.

Input Managers are a bit troublesome. First, on Leopard, they have to be installed with some fairly precise permissions and that's annoying. Second, they load into every Cocoa app even if you only want to fiddle with one of them. The third-party SIMBL helps with both of these problems. It will load standard bundles placed in standard locations (although SIMBL itself still needs the special magic installation to function), and it allows plugins to provide a list of applications they want to load into.

Mach ports
In a previous edition, I briefly mentioned that mach ports allowed injecting code into other processes. This works because mach ports can allow essentially full control over other processes. If you can get your hands on the right port (and see the `task_for_pid` function for how to do that) you can do things like map new memory into the process with custom contents and create a new thread in the target process that executes that memory. Set things up right and you have code injection.

This is pretty hard to pull off, as it ends up being a pretty complex bootstrapping process. Fortunately, the third-party mach_inject does all the hard work for you.

There are, of course, some downsides. One is that you need to run as root (or as part of the `procmod` group) to be able to get the necessary task port, even if you're injecting code into another process owned by the same user. Another is that the time of injection is non-deterministic. Input Managers load at a fairly well defined point in the application startup process, but mach_inject loads whenever your process can make the call, which could be much later, and potentially earlier, before things are really set up properly yet.

APE
Application Enhancer is a third-party injection mechanism. It's kind of like a better SIMBL which can load code into any application, not just Cocoa apps, and which loads it a little earlier than SIMBL does (which is an advantage for certain kinds of code).

Once again, there are downsides. Probably the biggest downside is that APE is by far the largest offender in the code injection war. A lot of people out there know APE by name, think that APE is evil, and refuse to use it.

Another big downside is that the company which makes APE is no longer maintaining it in a timely fashion. The first non-beta release of APE that supported Leopard was made in August 2008, a year after that OS version shipped. It's currently unknown whether they even plan to support Snow Leopard at all, let alone how long it will take them to release Snow Leopard support if they do. At this point, APE is good for experimentation but I can't recommend basing an actual product on it.

Lastly, APE is non-free and requires a license fee for commercial/shareware products, although that fee is quite reasonable.

Miscellaneous
Those are the main mechanisms, but the system provides a few more, of varying utility:

1. **Contextual menu plugins.** These are Finder plugins intended to extend the contextual menu in the Finder. Of course once they're loaded, they can do whatever they want. The downside is that, as I understand it, they're loaded lazily on Leopard so you don't get your shot until and unless the user actually brings up the plugins section of the contextual menu. And of course it only gets you into the Finder.
2. **Scripting Additions.** These are meant to be used to extend the capabilities of AppleScript on the system, but they actually work by loading into an application which is responding to the appropriate Apple Event. For example, run this command in your shell: `osascript -e 'tell app "Finder" to display dialog "I just injected some code into Finder!"'` Replace that standard scripting additions command with your own and off you go.
3. **WebKit plugins.** These are rarely useful unless you really are implementing a browser plugin, but it's a way to potentially get code into Safari and other WebKit-using applications.
4. **Kernel extensions.** Not really an injection mechanism, but once you're in the kernel you rule the system and can do whatever you want to anything.
5. **Buffer overflows.** Don't laugh too hard, people have done this! One of the older iPhone jailbreaking mechanisms used a buffer overflow in Safari to get in and do

its dirty work. Of course these are absolutely not something to rely on, as vendors have this weird idea that they ought to fix them once they're discovered.

What's It Good For?

Code injection is a powerful tool for extending applications you don't control. For example, my own LiveDictionary uses the Input Manager mechanism to load into Safari so that it can monitor the user's keyboard and mouse inputs in that app, and read the text under the mouse cursor at the appropriate times. (This is something that could be done using the Accessibility API today, but at the time LiveDictionary was written it wasn't yet functional enough.)

For more examples, just take a look at Unsanity. They have a whole line of products based around APE and code injection, doing things ranging from GUI themes to mouse cursor customization to custom menus.

Basically, any time you need control over objects inside another application, and that application doesn't expose a mechanism to get at them from the outside (such as AppleScript or a plugin interface), code injection is how you do it.

How do you accomplish your task once you're inside? Well that all depends on exactly what you want to do. It's much like writing code in your own application, except you have much less control about how things work and much less information about how things are structured. It's the kind of thing where if you don't know how to write the injected code, it's probably something you shouldn't be doing in the first place. Since you're running code in a foreign process, you're in an unforgiving environment where mistakes are much more dire than usual.

What's Bad About It?

Code injection is dangerous and nasty and very special care needs to be taken when doing it.

There are two fundamental reasons for this. First, when you're in another process, you have much less control over the environment than usual. It's also easy for that process to make certain assumptions about how things work. For example, you might pop up a window, while the application assumes that all windows are ones that it created. Crash, boom, game over.

The second reason is more of a political one. It's extremely rude to crash another process. Users hate it when you crash their other programs. Developers hate it when they get crash reports and support requests caused by your code. While crashing is never a good thing, crashing somebody else's program is an order of magnitude worse than crashing your own standalone program.

Practical Advice

Given the dangers, how should you proceed? Here are some very general guidelines:

1. Avoid code injection if at all possible. Take another look at your options. Can you use Accessibility to do what you want? AppleScript? Is there an official plugin interface? Sometimes you really have no choice, but exhaust all other options first.
2. Load into as few programs as possible. If you're using a mechanism like Input Managers that loads into a lot of applications but you only want to hit a few, be sure to restrict your module to just the ones you want. This reduces the chances of affecting an application you didn't even need to be in. For Input Managers, you can use SIMBL to accomplish this.
3. Do as little in the injected code as possible. If you do a lot of complicated work in your code, move that into a background process and talk to it using Distributed Objects or another IPC mechanism. That way, if something in the background process crashes, it won't take other applications down with it. (LiveDictionary is a good example of this, the Input Manager itself basically just grabs input and text out of the target application, and all of the dictionary parsing, lookup, and display is done in an LSUIElement application.)
4. Modify your environment as little as possible. Got a handy Cocoa programming trick that involves posing as a common AppKit class? Don't do it. Need to install some category methods with common names on NSObject? Forget about it. Want to load some enormous framework that you don't *really* need? Best to avoid it if you can. Any large application is going to have hidden assumptions about the environment it runs it, often completely inadvertently. Try to modify as little as possible to avoid make it crash when you step over one of those invisible lines.
5. Program defensively. I mean *really* defensively. Check every potential failure spot thoroughly, and fail as gracefully as possible. Remember, it's much better for your injected code to stop working or disable itself but leave the application running than it is to crash the application.

Friday Q&A 2009-02-06: Profiling With Shark

Related Articles

    Multithreaded Programming and Parallelism Overview 11

    Operations-Based Parallelization...53

    The Good and Bad of Distributed Objects..56

    Holistic Optimization...60

    Multithreaded Optimization in ChemicalBurn 82

    Mac OS X Process Memory Statistics..123

    Intro to Grand Central Dispatch, Part I: Basics and Dispatch Queues 162

    Intro to Grand Central Dispatch, Part II: Multi-Core Performance 169

    Intro to Grand Central Dispatch, Part III: Dispatch Sources 174

    Intro to Grand Central Dispatch, Part IV: Odds and Ends......................................179

    GCD Practicum..183

Welcome back to Friday Q&A. This week I'm taking Jeff Johnson's idea to discuss optimization and profiling tools.

Tools

So you've progressed beyond the first rule of optimization (Don't Do It) and have decided that enough time has passed at the second rule (Don't Do It Yet). Being smart about this whole optimization business, you know that the first thing you need to do before you actually start changing code is to measure it.

Measurement breaks down into two basic categories:

1. Overall performance. This is usually defined in terms of operations per second, whatever it is that you're doing. If it's an animation, this will probably be frames per second. If it's some kind of lookup system, it might be searches per second. More exotic cases might look at CPU usage or memory consumption. No matter what it is, you need to come up with a number so that you can do before-and-after comparisons to see how much any given code change helped (or hurt).
2. Profiling. This tells you how much time the computer spent in every piece of your code. You need this so that you know which parts of the code to attack.

Overall performance measurement is pretty easy, so I'm not really going to discuss that. Much more interesting is profiling. The first question is, what tool should you use?

You may be tempted to use Instruments. It is new and shiny and Apple hypes it up a lot. Don't. When it comes to profiling, Instruments, in a word, blows. It's difficult to use, bloated, and doesn't provide enough information. As if that weren't bad enough, in threaded applications it frequently provides information which is just plain wrong. Avoid Instruments for this work.

(Actually it's pretty good at other kinds of profiling, like memory usage. But when it comes to reducing CPU usage, Instruments is worse than useless.)

There are other tools on the system, such as Activity Monitor's sample command, or the 'sample' command line tool (which Activity Monitor uses) but there's really only one worthy tool for this job: Shark.

Opinions may differ, but mine is solid: Shark is the *only* tool to even consider using here. Some of the others are decent (aside from Instruments), but Shark is pure gold. I have actually had people who have never touched a Mac before tell me that they need to buy one after I give them a 30-second demo of this program. It's that good.

Something to Optimize

Before we can talk about Shark, we need a program to use it on. I wrote a little program that just searches for substrings in the `/usr/share/dict/words` word list that ships with the operating system. Here it is:

```objc
#import <Foundation/Foundation.h>

@interface Dict : NSObject
{
    NSArray *_words;
}
- (NSArray *)find:(NSString *)toFind;
@end

@implementation Dict
- (id)init
{
    if((self = [super init]))
    {
        NSString *str = [NSString stringWithContentsOfFile:@"/usr/share/dict/words"];
        _words = [[str componentsSeparatedByString:@"\n"] copy];
    }
    return self;
}

- (void)dealloc
{
    [_words release];
    [super dealloc];
}

- (NSArray *)find:(NSString *)toFind
{
    NSMutableArray *array = [NSMutableArray array];
    for(NSString *word in _words)
    {
        if([[word lowercaseString] rangeOfString:[toFind lowercaseString]].location != NSNotFound)
            [array addObject:word];
    }
    return array;
}
@end

int main(int argc, char **argv)
{
    NSAutoreleasePool *outerPool = [[NSAutoreleasePool
```

```
    alloc] init];
    
    NSTimeInterval start = [NSDate timeIntervalSinceReferenceDate];
    NSTimeInterval lastPrinted = start;
    unsigned counter = 0;
    while(1)
    {
        NSAutoreleasePool *innerPool = [[NSAutoreleasePool alloc] init];
        Dict *dict = [[Dict alloc] init];
        [dict find:@"bob"];
        [dict release];
        counter++;
        
        NSTimeInterval now = [NSDate timeIntervalSinceReferenceDate];
        if(now - lastPrinted >= 1.0)
        {
            NSLog(@"%.1f/second", counter / (now - start));
            lastPrinted = now;
        }
        [innerPool release];
    }
    
    [outerPool release];
    return 0;
}
```

I've also made a whole package available for today's post, including this source code, the source code for the changes that I'll be making throughout the article, Shark traces for each one, and precompiled x86 binaries for each one. You should download it and follow along. Download it here.

There are a lot of pretty obvious speed problems here, but it's meant to illustrate the usage of Shark, not to be a perfect real-world example.

First, let's establish a baseline by running the program. You'll notice that I measure the number of lookups performed per second and print it out periodically. This is the overall performance number that we'll be concentrating on. On my Mac Pro, I see about 1.6/second with this code.

Let's shark it:

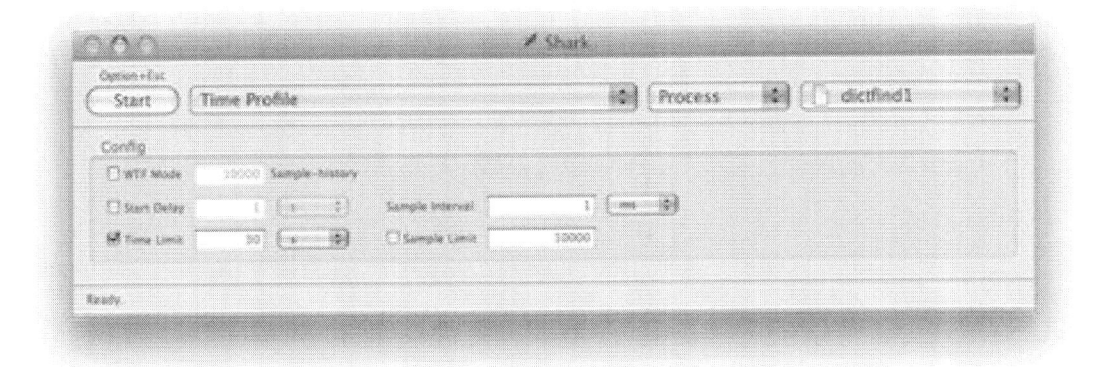

This is the opening window, where you control what Shark will do. For now we'll set it to Time Profile, Process, and give it our dictfind1 program, which we've already run in a shell. The other settings can be left alone. Then we click the Start button, wait 30 seconds, wait some more for it to process, and we can view the results:

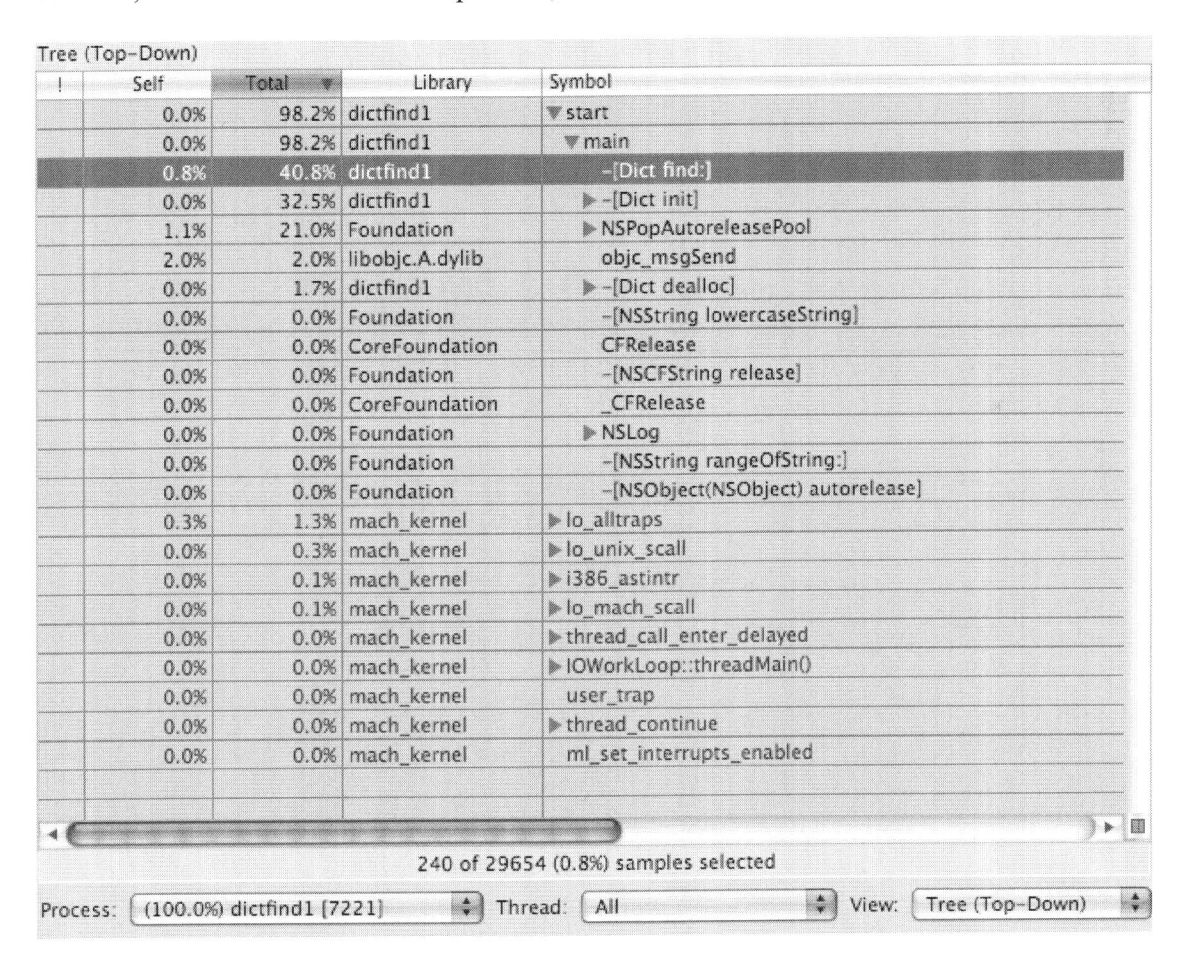

Self	Total	Library	Symbol
0.0%	98.2%	dictfind1	▼ start
0.0%	98.2%	dictfind1	▼ main
0.8%	40.8%	dictfind1	-[Dict find:]
0.0%	32.5%	dictfind1	▶ -[Dict init]
1.1%	21.0%	Foundation	▶ NSPopAutoreleasePool
2.0%	2.0%	libobjc.A.dylib	objc_msgSend
0.0%	1.7%	dictfind1	▶ -[Dict dealloc]
0.0%	0.0%	Foundation	-[NSString lowercaseString]
0.0%	0.0%	CoreFoundation	CFRelease
0.0%	0.0%	Foundation	-[NSCFString release]
0.0%	0.0%	CoreFoundation	_CFRelease
0.0%	0.0%	Foundation	▶ NSLog
0.0%	0.0%	Foundation	-[NSString rangeOfString:]
0.0%	0.0%	Foundation	-[NSObject(NSObject) autorelease]
0.3%	1.3%	mach_kernel	▶ lo_alltraps
0.0%	0.3%	mach_kernel	▶ lo_unix_scall
0.0%	0.1%	mach_kernel	▶ i386_astintr
0.0%	0.1%	mach_kernel	▶ lo_mach_scall
0.0%	0.0%	mach_kernel	▶ thread_call_enter_delayed
0.0%	0.0%	mach_kernel	▶ IOWorkLoop::threadMain()
0.0%	0.0%	mach_kernel	user_trap
0.0%	0.0%	mach_kernel	▶ thread_continue
0.0%	0.0%	mach_kernel	ml_set_interrupts_enabled

I have it in Tree (Top-Down) mode which is generally the best mode to use for profiling. This shows you the call stacks that were profiled from the top down. Here you can see that `start` called `main` which then called `-[Dict find:]`, `-[Dict init]`, and a bunch of others.

The Self and Total columns are important here. The Self column shows how much CPU time was spent in that function. The Total column shows how much time was spent in that function and in all of its descendants. We can see here that `-[Dict find:]` is responsible for 40.8% of all CPU time. However we can see that only 0.8% of the time is spent in `-[Dict find:]` itself. The other 40% of the time is spent in things being called from there. This tells us that we may be able to optimize that method by changing what it calls, but we won't gain much by trying to make the code right in `-[Dict find:]` go faster.

There's one obvious bit of slowness here, which was probably obvious just from looking at the code and is even more clear once we have the profile to look at: this code reinitializes the dictionary every time through the loop! If we imagine that our real case is going to be looking up a lot of words for each run, this is foolish. Let's create a single instance of `Dict` before the loop and just reuse it for each pass. You'll find this modified code in `dictfind2.m` in the package.

Compile and run. Result: 2.7/second. Not bad! That's about a 70% speedup over the original code, just from moving two lines of code around.

Of course this is still pretty slow, so let's see what else we can do. Profiling this version, we see that about 70% of the time is spent in `-[Dict find:]` and about 26% in `NSPopAutoreleasePool`. The latter is an indication that we're creating too many temporary objects. If we pop open `-[Dict find:]` we can immediately see why: half the time is spent calling `-[NSString lowercaseString]`, and that of course produces a temporary object each time which then needs to be destroyed. So we can guess that about 75% of this program's time is due to the two calls to that method.

Easy fix, though: NSString allows case insensitive searching. Instead of comparing lowercase strings, we'll just compare the original strings with the case insensitive option set. `dictfind3` in the package contains this change.

Compile and run. Result: 17.5/second. This is a 6.5x speedup over `dictfind2`, roughly in line with what we would expect. (Removing code that takes up 75% of the time should result in a 4x speedup, and the numbers are imprecise enough that this is well within the fudge factor.) It's an 11x speedup over the original code. Not too bad at all.

But still, under 20 lookups per second kind of sucks. Let's profile this version too. What we find is that 90% of the time is spent in `-[NSString rangeOfString:options:]`. We don't control that code, and it's hard to imagine that we could write a faster custom version. Optimizing the rest of the code will win us at best 10%. So now we're stuck.

If we can't speak up -[NSString rangeOfString:options:], maybe we can call it less frequently. Let's start to think of an algorithmic improvement. Every time we do a search, we do a linear search through the entire dictionary. Can we reduce that?

It's tricky, because we're doing a substring search, so something easy like sticking everything in an NSDictionary won't do. Neither will a classic binary search. A modified binary search will do it, if we pay a memory price. Instead of storing each word in the array to search, we'll store *pairs*. The first part of a pair will be a suffix of the word, and the second part will be the entire word. Then if we binary search on the suffixes, we can rapidly find all words that contain the search term. The memory cost will be substantial: a 10-character word will result in 10 entries in the array instead of just 1, and with all those suffix strings floating around in memory. But if we really want speed, the tradeoff may be worth it.

dictfind4 contains the binary search version. Dictionary initialization is now substantially more complex, building up all the substrings. In the find routine, we take advantage of CoreFoundation toll-free bridging and use the CFArrayBSearchValues function.

Compile and run. Result: initialization takes *forever*, over 10 seconds on my computer. But once that's done, the reward is enormous, at about 24500/second. This is a 1400x speedup over the last version, and a 15000x speedup over the original.

Let's profile this one too just for fun. We find that 22.5% of the time is spent just in -[NSCFArray addObject:]. This code spends nearly a quarter of its time just adding the results to the array after it finds them! There are no doubt further optimizations to be had here, but at this point we hit diminishing returns. We already got a fifteen-thousand-times speedup over the original slow version, and that's good enough for me.

Before we quit for the day, let's flip Shark into "Heavy (Bottom-Up)" mode:

!	Self ▼	Total	Library	Symbol
	24.7%	24.7%	libobjc.A.dylib	objc_msgSend
	9.9%	9.9%	CoreFoundation	▶ CFStringFindWithOptionsAndLocale
	8.2%	8.2%	CoreFoundation	▶ _CFArrayReplaceValues
	4.5%	4.5%	CoreFoundation	▶ CFStringGetCStringPtr
!	4.3%	4.3%	libobjc.A.dylib	▶ 0xffff0088 [unknown]
	3.3%	3.3%	Foundation	▶ -[NSString rangeOfString:options:range:locale:]
	2.7%	2.7%	dictfind4	▶ -[Dict find:]
	2.7%	2.7%	CoreFoundation	▶ CFStringGetCharactersPtr
	2.3%	2.3%	CoreFoundation	▶ _CFStringGetLength2
	2.0%	2.0%	CoreFoundation	▶ CFStringCompareWithOptionsAndLocale
	1.9%	1.9%	libSystem.B.dylib	▶ OSAtomicCompareAndSwapPtr
	1.8%	1.8%	CoreFoundation	▶ CFStringGetLength
	1.7%	1.7%	Foundation	▶ -[NSString rangeOfString:options:]
	1.7%	1.7%	CoreFoundation	▶ _CFArrayCheckAndGetValueAtIndex
	1.4%	1.4%	CoreFoundation	▶ CFArrayGetCount
	1.4%	1.4%	dictfind4	▶ 0x2ca0 [13.3KB]
	1.4%	1.4%	CoreFoundation	▶ CFRetain
	1.4%	1.4%	Foundation	▶ -[NSCFArray addObject:]
	1.2%	1.2%	CoreFoundation	▶ -[NSObject isKindOfClass:]
	1.0%	1.0%	CoreFoundation	▶ _CFRelease
	1.0%	1.0%	Foundation	▶ dyld_stub_objc_msgSend

7335 of 29659 (24.7%) samples selected

This essentially flips everything around. Instead of showing the top of each stack, and then showing what each entry called underneath, it shows you the bottom first. It then shows what functions called it, what functions called those functions, and so forth. This is generally less useful than the top-down mode, but sometimes it's really handy, because occasionally you have an important bottleneck which is called from many locations scattered around your code.

This is a great illustration of just one of those cases. We see that `objc_msgSend` is taking up 25% of our time now. Of course we can't very well improve on libobjc, but if we were after even more speed we might start taking measures to make fewer message sends.

Friday Q&A 2009-02-13: Operations-Based Parallelization

Related Articles

    Multithreaded Programming and Parallelism Overview 11

    Profiling With Shark 45

    The Good and Bad of Distributed Objects..56

    Holistic Optimization..60

    Multithreaded Optimization in ChemicalBurn 82

    Mac OS X Process Memory Statistics 123

    Intro to Grand Central Dispatch, Part I: Basics and Dispatch Queues 162

    Intro to Grand Central Dispatch, Part II: Multi-Core Performance 169

    Intro to Grand Central Dispatch, Part III: Dispatch Sources 174

    Intro to Grand Central Dispatch, Part IV: Odds and Ends......................................179

    GCD Practicum..183

Welcome back to Friday Q&A, which this week is also Friday the Thirteenth! Be especially careful, as this is the first of two consecutive Friday the Thirteenths. For this first Friday the Thirteenth I'm going to talk about parallel software design using an "operations" approach (think NSOperation), as suggested by Nikita Zhuk way back when I first started this whole thing.

What It's For
Parallel processing is becoming more and more important. Right now, good parallelization can result in perhaps a factor of eight speedup to your application compared to a non-parallel implementation, on high-end hardware and with the right sort of computation. More realistically you'll probably see less than that, but even a 50% speedup is nothing to sneeze at, and it's not that hard to get significantly more on a Mac Pro. The future looks to be just more and more cores too, so today's 50% speedup on a dual-core machine might become much more on tomorrow's 32-core monster.

Splitting a program into discretely-executable chunks, or operations, is a good way to parallelize it. Apple introduced this idea on Mac OS X with NSOperationQueue, which provides a nice API for it. Unfortunately, they totally screwed up the implementation so you might not want to use it now, but the concept is still very useful, whether you're waiting for Apple to fix NSOperationQueue, using a similar API like RAOperationQueue or are just doing multithreading the old fashioned way. [Note: NSOperationQueue was fixed in 10.5.7 and is now a viable API to use in production code.]

Design Approaches
First, think about your program and what it does. A single-threaded program is a

serialized list of actions, performed in order. Sometimes they're performed in order because the second action depends on the results of the first. But sometimes it's simply because the program has to do two things, and if you're single-threaded then you need to pick one to do first.

Try to find those unrelated actions where order doesn't matter. Loops are often a good candidate for this sort of thing. Imagine something like this:

```
for(NSImage *image in images) {
    [self rotate:image];
    [self scale:image];
    [self save:image];
}
```

There are no dependencies between those images, so each one can go into a separate operation. On the other hand, each individual method call within the loop depends on the previous one, so those can't be split out beneficially.

It can go beyond loops, too. Imagine some code like this:

```
[self loadImage];
[self parseDictionary];
[self setupNetworkListener];
[self getDirectoryListing];
```

If these methods have no interdependencies, as their names imply, then they too can be broken out into separate operations for parallel execution.

One question to ask here is whether you *should* break them out. Is it a win?

The answer to that question will depend greatly on how long it takes to complete the operation. There's always going to be extra overhead for a parallel operation, and you don't want that overhead to overwhelm the gains you get. As a *general* guideline (very general, overhead will vary a lot depending on what you're using to do parallel processing), figure that if your operation finishes in less than a millisecond it's probably not worth it. As always when it comes to performance optimization, measure before and after to see if you achieved a speedup, and profile to make sure you're hitting the parts that will do the most good.

It will also depend on exactly what your operations are doing. For example, if you have one I/O-bound operation (reading a bunch of stuff from a disk) and a bunch of CPU-bound operations, you'll benefit from having that I/O-bound operation sit in the background and let the CPU-bound operations get on with their tasks. You'll also benefit from running the CPU-bound operations simultaneously to benefit from multi-core machines. On the other hand, if all you have is a bunch of I/O bound operations, you're likely to make your performance *worse* if you try to run many of them in parallel, due to disk contention.

The key to this style of parallel programming is functional programming. By that I mean programming in the style of mathematical functions. The key attrtibute of mathematical functions is that they always give the same result if you give them the same argument. For example, if f(3) = 5 then f(3) will *always* give you 5. This essentially means that there are no side effects. Side effects are deadly for parallel programming. Side effects means dealing with external data, which means *shared* data, which means synchronization, locks, and all pain that brings. It's much better if you can write your operations in terms of computing a function based on some arguments but nothing else.

Wrapping Up
Parallel programming is challenging and rewarding, and has many complicating factors, but I hope this gives you some ideas to start with. While I don't recommend using NSOperationQueue in any shipping product [note: as mentioned at the beginning of the article, NSOperationQueue was fixed in 10.5.7 and is now safe to use], it can be a good learning tool, and if you're starting on something new that can require Snow Leopard it's probably a good bet. Even if you can't use it, doing your own custom multithreading in such a way as to deal with discrete operations like this can be a big help in avoiding the locking and concurrency hell that plagues so many multithreaded programs.

That wraps it up. Come back next week for the exciting conclusion, including what happened to the horse, where they hid the loot, and why are there so many pigeons in there anyway?

Friday Q&A 2009-02-20: The Good and Bad of Distributed Objects

Related Articles

    Multithreaded Programming and Parallelism Overview 11

    Thread Safety in OS X System Frameworks 24

    Interprocess Communication 29

    Profiling With Shark 45

    Operations-Based Parallelization 53

    Holistic Optimization 60

    Multithreaded Optimization in ChemicalBurn 82

    Mac OS X Process Memory Statistics 123

    Intro to Grand Central Dispatch, Part I: Basics and Dispatch Queues 162

    Intro to Grand Central Dispatch, Part II: Multi-Core Performance 169

    Intro to Grand Central Dispatch, Part III: Dispatch Sources 174

    Intro to Grand Central Dispatch, Part IV: Odds and Ends 179

    GCD Practicum 183

    Care and Feeding of Singletons 194

    Dangerous Cocoa Calls 236

    Probing Cocoa With PyObjC 240

    Using Accessors in Init and Dealloc 246

    NSRunLoop Internals 273

    NSNotificationQueue 284

    Implementing a Custom Slider 382

    Dealing with Retain Cycles 392

    What Every Apple Programmer Should Know 401

    Leopard Collection Classes..405

    Implementing Equality and Hashing 412

    Implementing NSCoding 459

    Defensive Programming in Cocoa 468

Welcome back to another Friday Q&A. This week I'm going to take Erik's (no last name given) suggestion from my interprocess communication post and expand a bit on Distributed Objects, what makes it so cool, and the problems that it has.

Overview

I'm not going to take a detailed look at the basics of Distributed Objects, as there are plenty of resources out there for that. But for those readers who are unfamiliar with Distributed Objects, I'll give a quick look at what it is.

Distributed Objects (DO) is a Cocoa API for interprocess communication (IPC) built on automatic proxying of messages, so that remote objects look and act mostly like local objects. The primary interface to the DO system is the `NSConnection` class. Vending an object with DO is as easy as this:

```
NSConnection *connection = [[NSConnection
connectionWithReceivePort:[NSPort port]] sendPort:nil];
[connection setRootObject:theObject];
[connection registerName:@"com.example.whatever"];
```

And accessing that vended object from another process is as easy as this:

```
id theObject = (id)[NSConnection
rootProxyForConnectionWithRegisteredName:@"com.example.whatever"
host:nil];
[theObject someMethod];
```

From this point, theObject acts as though it were local. You can send messages to it just like any other object. You can pass it local objects as arguments or get remote objects back as return values, and DO takes care of proxying or serializing the objects as appropriate. It's very cool, and there's literally nothing else that needs to be done other than the above code if you just need basic functionality.

The Good

I think this should be pretty clear from the above description, but let's quickly compare it to other IPC mechanisms:

1. **It's easy.** Just a few lines of code to set up a fully functional connection.
2. **It's transparent.** For the most part, remote objects can be passed around just like local objects. This means that little of your code needs to be DO-aware.
3. **It's flexible.** DO can be used over mach ports or sockets. It can be used to communicate between threads or between processes. It's reasonably configurable.
4. **It's robust.** Because DO works the same way as Objective-C messages, you don't have the same problems you might have trying to support two different protocol versions. Of course it's not always rosy, but if your changes involve implementing different methods, it's easy to check for what's going on using `respondsToSelector:` and the like, rather than having to give up.

All of this makes DO a very useful facility.

The Bad

So if DO is so great, why am I not a bigger fan? Part of it is simply because DO can't completely abstract away the fact that it's running over a transport layer and talking to a remote process, and part of it is because DO itself is just not as good as it could be.

One leaky abstraction is primitive types. DO needs to be able to either serialize (i.e. copy across the connection) or proxy everything that gets used as an argument or returned as a value with a "distant object". For objects, this is fine. Objects that want to be copied can implement `NSCoding`, and all other objects can use Objective-C's built-in message capturing facilities to proxy all requests across the connection.

For primitives, things get harder. For scalars and even structs, the Objective-C runtime provides enough type information that these can be copied across. But once you hit pointers, things fall apart. Imagine trying to proxy a call like this:

```
[array getObjects:objarray range:NSMakeRange(5, 13)];
```

It basically can't be done. DO would have to somehow know that the length of the `objarray` parameter is determined by the length of the range being passed in, and copy only that much memory across the connection. It would also have to know that this is a return-by-reference only, and that it shouldn't be trying to serialize or proxy the contents of `objarray` across the connection (it could be filled with junk, and an attempt to proxy that junk would crash). This particular method could be special-cased to work, but it's impossible to create a general solution that would work with arbitrary methods like this.

DO does have some interesting language-level facilities to help with this. You can specify a pointer parameter as being `in`, `out`, or `inout` so that it knows which way to serialize or proxy. But this only works with pointers to single objects. For arrays, it just can't cope.

Another leaky abstraction is that the process you're talking to could disappear at any moment. Objective-C just isn't set up to deal with this very well:

```
id obj = [self method];
[obj thing1];
[obj thing2];
```

In normal Objective-C, `obj` is either broken from the start (in which case you'll crash) or it remains valid throughout the method. But if `obj` is a distant object, suddenly things are not so clear. The remote process could disappear (or freeze up and time out) in between the call to `thing1` and `thing2`.

When that happens, DO deals with it by throwing an exception. Surprise!

Most Objective-C code is not exception safe. Although there's no particular reason that exceptions can't be used more frequently the way they are in languages like Java, convention is that exceptions in Objective-C are only used to indicate a programming error. In order to really robustly use DO, you need to write your code such that it can handle an exception being thrown by *any* interaction with a distant object. Worse yet, this includes Cocoa code, meaning that you essentially cannot pass a distant object to any Cocoa code. (Ever wonder what happens when an `NSSet` sends `-hash` to your object, and `-hash` throws an exception? Odds are fair that it leaves the `NSSet` in an inconsistent state that will lead to a crash.)

This requirement for all code touching distant objects to be exception safe is tough, and greatly limits the places in which DO can be practically used. The promise is that remote objects look like local objects, and they mostly do, but this one (absolutely necessary) detail means that they can't be used like local objects at all.

Lastly, DO is not very modular or extensible. Ideally, DO would be a fully modular system. You'd have the DO system which would sit on top of some kind of interchangeable transport class. Customizing the transport class (for example, to make it use encryption, or talk to a serial port, or use avian carriers) would simply be a matter of subclassing a public abstract class and implementing a documented set of primitive methods.

The reality is not so simple. The classes that DO uses internally are fairly tightly coupled, and there's a lot of legacy cruft. Implementing a custom NSPort subclass that works with NSConnection is so difficult that I'm only aware of one working example (Secure Distributed Objects, which appears to be a dead project now). This pretty much sinks the idea of using DO for any serious network communication, since DO doesn't encrypt the transport and it's not practical to add encryption to it.

Conclusion
Distributed Objects is a very cool system that has many uses. Unfortunately, due to both the constraints under which it works and some poor design decisions, it's not as useful as it could be. It can still be handy for doing IPC and it's a great tool to have in Cocoa, but it falls short of being a no-brainer way to talk to other processes.

Friday Q&A 2009-02-27: Holistic Optimization

Related Articles

    Multithreaded Programming and Parallelism Overview 11

    Profiling With Shark 45

    Operations-Based Parallelization 53

    The Good and Bad of Distributed Objects 56

    Multithreaded Optimization in ChemicalBurn 82

    Mac OS X Process Memory Statistics 123

    Intro to Grand Central Dispatch, Part I: Basics and Dispatch Queues 162

    Intro to Grand Central Dispatch, Part II: Multi-Core Performance 169

    Intro to Grand Central Dispatch, Part III: Dispatch Sources 174

    Intro to Grand Central Dispatch, Part IV: Odds and Ends 179

    GCD Practicum 183

Welcome back to Friday Q&A, a bit early this week since I won't be around to post it at the usual time. This week I'm going to cheat a little bit and use a topic that I "suggested" myself. I'll be talking about what I like to call "holistic optimization", which is essentially how to look at optimization within the context of your entire project, rather than bit-swizzling, loop unrolling, and other micro-optimizations.

Engineering Optimization

Let's forget about code for a moment, and talk about something completely different: aircraft design. Bear with me, we'll get back to programming in a bit.

I'm part owner of a Schleicher ASW-20C. This is a 15 meter wingspan competition glider originally designed in the mid-1970s. At the time it was at the top of its class, although of course technology has improved over the decades since. What does it take to make a top class competition glider?

Obviously it takes an expert aeronautical engineer with a great deal of experience in designing sailplanes and a factory which can actually construct the product. A top competition machine has to be highly optimized. But what does "optimized" mean in this case? What exactly was the designer optimizing when he designed this airplane?

The obvious thing to optimize is glide ratio. This is a measure of how much distance can be obtained for any given amount of altitude. Since altitude is the only source of the glider's energy this number is highly significant and it's usually the first thing a pilot looks at when he examines the numbers of a new machine. This number might range anywhere from 20:1 to 60:1. The ASW-20's glide ratio is a bit over 40:1 which at the time was exceptional in the 15 meter class.

But of course there's more to it than a single number. The best glide ratio is at a single speed, but pilots fly at lots of different speeds. Two machines might have the same best glide ratio but one might have a much better glide ratio at high speed, giving it a significant edge. The designer must not only optimize the best glide ratio, but the glide ratio over a wide range of speed.

Weight is another big consideration. Sailplanes are built extremely light, and their construction uses fiberglass and other advanced composites to achieve this. The lighter a glider is the better it can climb, so this is highly important.

Weight is also important. I just said this, but this time I mean the opposite. The heavier a sailplane is the faster it can fly on strong days. In order to achieve the goal of being both light and heavy, a system of water ballast is used, allowing the pilot to load up with water on strong days and leave it out on weak days.

But what else? Certainly it doesn't stop here. Handling is important: if the plane handles like a truck then nobody will buy it. Ease of assembly is important: many gliders are stored disassembled in a trailer and are put together before each day's flying. A glider which has a reputation for being difficult to assemble will be unpopular. Crashworthiness is, of course, significant. Cockpit ergonomics matter a great deal, since the pilot might spend five hours in a row or more sitting in the seat. Strength is key: gliders fly through rough air and need to be able to take the punishment. And last but far from least: cost. None of this does any good if nobody can afford to purchase the result.

Clearly, designing an airplane involves a huge number of different goals, even when the airplane is just a 600 pound competition glider. (Imagine the goals involved when designing a 200-*ton* 747.) Worse yet, many of these goals are conflicting. The quest for lighter weight is opposed to the quest for strength. Improvements in performance often hurt handling. Making the glider easier to assemble involves "wasted" structure which is otherwise just dead weight. And of course *everything* conflicts with the goal of lower cost.

A successful aeronautical engineer has to juggle all of these different constraints and come up with the best solution he can given his budget for both time and money. In fact, the word "aeronautical" is completely unnecessary in that sentence: any engineer faces the same problems.

Software Optimization as Engineering Optimization
Enough of that airplane business, let's get back to programming. Most people don't think of software engineers as "real" engineers, and there's a lot of truth to that. Software engineering is a young discipline, and it's missing a lot of the certainty and standardized practices that can be found in other forms of engineering. But one thing that we do have in common with other forms of engineering is this concept of tradeoffs.

Unfortunately, most software engineers aren't really aware of this whole idea. It's rarely taught in school, or formally explored elsewhere. Most have a vague idea that you can't have everything, and sometimes you have to sacrifice one thing, for example features or stability, in order to achieve another, for example a deadline, but there isn't a codified concept of making tradeoffs in order to come up with the best possible result given the resources at hand. As a result, programmers tend to think of "optimization" as being purely about performance.

Even performance optimization involves a lot of trade-offs. Just like with the competition glider, software performance is actually many different quantities which often conflict. Do you want to optimize latency or throughput? Speed or battery life? Memory usage or disk usage? Perceptual time or wall clock time?

And beyond performance there are many other goals to reach as well. I like to think of it mathematically. Imagine a fitness function, which takes the program as its input and as its output generates some number, the higher the better. This magical function takes into account all those different kinds of performance, as well as things like programmer time, money, features, reliability, ship date, and anything else that affects how "good" a program is. Optimization then involves getting the largest possible number out of this function with the resources available.

Looking at it this way, the problem of premature performance optimization becomes obvious. You have limited resources in the form of programmer time, programmer salaries, overhead, and other such things. To optimize the entire program, you have to spend those limited resources where they will do the most good. When you optimize too early, you don't know where to put those resources in order to extract the most good. If you spend all your time optimizing module A but it turns out the program spends most of its time in module B, you've just wasted all those resources. If you spend all your time optimizing both, so that you can be sure that you've covered everything, you've still wasted a lot of resources on A.

Beyond the question of performance, there are always other variables as well. Is spending resources on performance the best way to spend them? Often the answer is no. And even more often, the answer is "we don't know yet."

I'm a big advocate of the "optimize later" approach. Whenever I bring this up, people accuse me of advocating slow, bloated applications. But the fact of the matter is that "optimize later" is how you make the *fastest possible application*, given all of the other constraints. From the perspective of airplane design, what most programmers mean by "optimization" is stuff like drilling holes in panels to reduce the weight: it can be a big advantage, but if you spend all of your time drilling holes early in the game, the product as a whole is going to suffer badly.

Friday Q&A 2009-03-06: Using the Clang Static Analyzer

Related Articles

    Introduction to Valgrind 118

Welcome back to another exciting Friday Q&A. This week's topic, suggested by Ed Wynne, will be an overview of the Clang Static Analyzer and an example of how to use it.

What Is It?
Clang is part of the LLVM project. LLVM is essentially a compiler and JIT virtual machine framework. Some of the compiler bits are currently available in Mac OS X as llvm-gcc, which fits a gcc parser/front-end to the LLVM code generator/back-end. Clang aims to essentially fill in the other half, and provide a parser/front-end as part of the LLVM project itself, which will allow a pure LLVM compiler.

What's the point of this, and why not just use gcc? It's actually pretty simple: gcc is old and crufty and slow. It has a huge amount of legacy baggage and is not very easy to work with. Clang is considerably more lightweight and its code is much more modular.

That last part is important for this, because some enterprising people have taken Clang and implemented a static code analyzer with it. In essence, it's a compiler that, instead of translating your code to machine language, goes through and looks for mistakes.

The Clang Static Analyzer (which I will now abbreviate as CSA even though everybody calls it "clang", because Clang is actually the name for the entire front-end, not just CSA) is still early in development and very incomplete, but is still very useful even so. [Note: the Clang project has matured considerably since this chapter was written. The Static Analyzer is now built into Xcode, and can be run by selecting *Build->Build and Analyze*.]

Where Is It?
The main CSA web page can be found at http://clang.llvm.org/StaticAnalysis.html, and it can be downloaded using the link at the bottom right. I won't link directly to the download because it's still in very active development and so the download link updates frequently.

How To Use It
Using CSA is extremely easy. It provides a `scan-build` command which you simply invoke at the command line, passing the command to build your code as the parameters. `scan-build` will do some funky business to convince `gcc` to pass control over to CSA as it builds, allowing CSA to analyze all of your code instead of actually getting it built.

Since an example is worth a thousand words:

```
$ gcc -framework Foundation test.m
$ scan-build gcc -framework Foundation test.m
ANALYZE: test.m main
test.m:5:16: warning: Value stored to 'x' is never read
    int x = 0; x = 1;
               ^   ~
1 diagnostic generated.
scan-build: 1 bugs found.
scan-build: Run 'scan-view /var/folders/YT/
YTiq3QDl2RW4ME+BYnLyRU+++TM/-Tmp-/scan-build-2009-03-06-3'
to examine bug reports.
$
```

And there it is, found a bug. If you run the command it mentions at the end, it gives a *really* swank HTML view.

Note that the `scan-build` command can be used not only with `gcc` but also with `xcodebuild` and even `make`. Running an analysis of your Xcode project is just a single command, usually as simple as `scan-build xcodebuild` in your project's directory.

A Better Example

Let's actually look at some code. I made the following contrived buggy code:

```
#import <Foundation/Foundation.h>

static void TestFunc(char *inkind, char *inname)
{
    NSString *kind = [[NSString alloc]
initWithUTF8String:inkind];
    NSString *name = [NSString
stringWithUTF8String:inname];
    if(!name)
        return;

    const char *kindC = NULL;
    const char *nameC = NULL;
    if(kind)
        kindC = [kind UTF8String];
    if(name)
        nameC = [name UTF8String];
    if(!isalpha(kindC[0]))
        return;
    if(!isalpha(nameC[0]))
        return;

    [kind release];
    [name release];
}
```

Obviously this code doesn't actually do anything useful, but of course it's meant only for illustration. There are several bugs in this code. Instead of trying to find them by looking, let's ask CSA:

```
$ scan-build gcc -c test.m
ANALYZE: test.m TestFunc
test.m:5:23: warning: Potential leak of object allocated
on line 5 and store into 'kind'
    NSString *kind = [[NSString alloc]
initWithUTF8String:inkind];
                      ^
test.m:18:17: warning: Dereference of null pointer.
    if(!isalpha(nameC[0]))
                ^~~~~~~~
2 diagnostics generated.
scan-build: 2 bugs found.
scan-build: Run 'scan-view /var/folders/YT/
YTiq3QDl2RW4ME+BYnLyRU+++TM/-Tmp-/scan-build-2009-03-06-6'
to examine bug reports.
```

And there we are two bugs! They're both pretty subtle too. The object that's leaked does get released at the end of the method. The problem is simply that there are some return statements in the middle that can cause that code not to be reached. CSA is clever enough to trace out those code paths and find the problem. The other bug requires a similar depth of analysis to find, as the null dereference can only happen if a previous if statement isn't followed.

You may have noticed that it missed a bug, though. This function releases `name`, which points to an object that it does not own. I'm not sure why CSA missed this, but it's important to keep in mind that it's not perfect and it won't catch everything.

CSA also sometimes sees false positives. These mostly occur when doing funky cross-method memory management tricks. For example, it's common when displaying a sheet to pass an object in to the `void *context` parameter so that the receiver of the end-sheet message can get information out of it. Proper memory management here requires retaining the `context` object when making the call, and then releasing it in the callback. Previous versions of CSA would consider the initial retain a leak, since it couldn't see that it was later balanced in another method. They appear to have fixed this particular case now, but other such cases will still be around, simply because it can't be perfect.

Conclusion

The Clang Static Analyzer, although limited, is an extremely useful tool. I guarantee that if you run it for the first time on any substantial base of Cocoa code, you will be surprised and frightened at what it finds. For tracking down leaks and many other common programming errors, it is invaluable. And it's under active development as part of a project with a great deal of support from Apple, so it will only get better.

Friday Q&A 2009-03-13: Intro to the Objective-C Runtime

Related Articles

Objective-C Messaging	73
Objective-C Message Forwarding	77
Objective-C Class Loading and Initialization	115
Care and Feeding of Singletons	194
Probing Cocoa With PyObjC	240
Using Accessors in Init and Dealloc	246
Method Replacement for Fun and Profit	297
Error Returns with Continuation Passing Style	303
Comparison of Objective-C Enumeration Techniques	369
Implementing Fast Enumeration	373
Implementing Equality and Hashing	412
Zeroing Weak References in Objective-C	428
Implementing NSCoding	459
Defensive Programming in Cocoa	468

Welcome back to another Friday Q&A, on another Friday the 13th. This week I'm going to take Oliver Mooney's suggestion and talk about the Objective-C runtime, how it works, and what it can do for you.

Many Cocoa programmers are only vaguely aware of the Objective-C runtime. They know it's there (and some don't even know this!), that it's important, and you can't run Objective-C without it, but that's about where it stops.

Today I want to run through exactly how Objective-C works at the runtime level and what kinds of things you can do with it.

Note: I'll be talking only about Apple's runtime on 10.5 and later. The runtime on 10.4 and earlier is missing many APIs, instead forcing direct structure access, and the runtimes for GNU is a different beast entirely.

Objects

In Objective-C we work with objects all the time, but what *is* an object? Well, let's take a look and construct something that will tell us just what an object is.

First, we know that objects are referred to using pointers, like `NSObject *`. And we know that we create them using the `+alloc` method. The documentation for that just says that it calls `+allocWithZone:`. Following the chain of documentation a bit further, we discover `NSDefaultMallocZone` and see that they're just allocated using `malloc`. Easy!

But what do they look like when they're allocated? Let's find out:

```objc
#import <Foundation/Foundation.h>

@interface A : NSObject { @public int a; } @end

@implementation A @end

@interface B : A { @public int b; } @end

@implementation B @end

@interface C : B { @public int c; } @end

@implementation C @end

int main(int argc, char **argv)
{
    [NSAutoreleasePool new];

    C *obj = [[C alloc] init];
    obj->a = 0xaaaaaaaa;
    obj->b = 0xbbbbbbbb;
    obj->c = 0xcccccccc;

    NSData *objData = [NSData dataWithBytes:obj length:malloc_size(obj)];
    NSLog(@"Object contains %@", objData);

    return 0;
}
```

We construct a class hierarchy that just has some instance variables, then we put obvious values into each ivar. Then we extract the data in nice printable form using `malloc_size` to get the right length, and use `NSData` to print a nice hex representation. Here's what we get:

```
2009-01-27 15:58:04.904 a.out[22090:10b] Object contains
<20300000 aaaaaaaa bbbbbbbb cccccccc>
```

We can see here that the class just gets laid out sequentially in memory. First you have A's ivar, then B's, then C's. Easy!

But what's this `20300000` thing at the beginning? Well, it comes before A's ivar, so it must be NSObject's. Let's look at NSObject's definition:

```
/*********          Base class              *********/

@interface NSObject <NSObject> {
    Class         isa;
}
```

Sure enough, there's another ivar. But what's this `Class` business? If we tell Xcode to take us to the definition we find ourselves in `/usr/include/objc/objc.h` which contains:

```
typedef struct objc_class *Class;
```

And following it further we get to `/usr/include/objc/runtime.h` which contains:

69

```
struct objc_class {
    Class isa;

#if !__OBJC2__
    Class super_class                         OBJC2_UNAVAILABLE;
    const char *name                          OBJC2_UNAVAILABLE;
    long version                              OBJC2_UNAVAILABLE;
    long info                                 OBJC2_UNAVAILABLE;
    long instance_size                        OBJC2_UNAVAILABLE;
    struct objc_ivar_list *ivars              OBJC2_UNAVAILABLE;
    struct objc_method_list **methodLists     OBJC2_UNAVAILABLE;
    struct objc_cache *cache                  OBJC2_UNAVAILABLE;
    struct objc_protocol_list *protocols      OBJC2_UNAVAILABLE;
#endif

} OBJC2_UNAVAILABLE;
```

So a `Class` is a pointer to a structure which... starts with another `Class`.

Let's look at another root class, `NSProxy`:

```
@interface NSProxy <NSObject> {
    Class     isa;
}
```

It's there too. Let's look in one more place, the definition of `id`, the Objective-C type for "any object":

```
typedef struct objc_object {
    Class isa;
} *id;
```

There it is again. Clearly every single Objective-C object must start with `Class isa`, even class objects. But what is it?

As the name and type imply, the `isa` ivar indicates what class a particular object is. Every Objective-C object must begin with an isa pointer, otherwise the runtime won't know how to work with it. Everything about a particular object's type is wrapped up in that one little pointer. The remainder of an object is basically just a big blob and as far as the runtime is concerned, it is irrelevant. It's up to the individual classes to give that blob meaning.

Classes

What exactly do classes contain, then? The "unavailable" structure members give a good clue. (They're there for compatibility with the pre-Leopard runtime, and you shouldn't use them if you're targeting Leopard, but it still tells us what kind of information is there.) First comes the `isa`, which allows a class to act like an object as well. There's a pointer to the superclass, giving the proper class hierarchy. Some other basic information about the class follows. At the end is the really interesting stuff. There's a list of instance variables, a list of methods, and a list of protocols. All of this stuff is accessible at runtime, and can be modified at runtime too.

> I skipped right over the `cache` member because it's not really useful for runtime manipulation, but it's an interesting exposure of an implementation detail. Every time you send a message (`[foo bar]`) the runtime has to look up the actual code to invoke by rummaging through the list of methods in the target object's class. However, methods are stored in big linear lists by default, so this is really slow. The cache is just a hash table mapping selectors to code. The first time you send a message you'll get a slow, time-consuming lookup, but the result is put in the hash table. Subsequent calls will find the entry in the hash table, making the process go much faster.

Looking at the rest of `runtime.h` you'll see a lot of functions for accessing and manipulating these properties. Each function is prefixed with what it operates on. General runtime functions start with `objc_`, functions that operate on a class start with `class_`, and so forth. For example, you can call `class_getInstanceMethod` to get information about a particular method, like the argument/return types. Or you can call `class_addMethod` to add a *new* method to an existing class at runtime. You can even create a whole new class at runtime by using `objc_allocateClassPair`.

Practical Applications

There are tons of useful things that can be done with this kind of runtime meta-information, but here are some ideas.

1. **Automatic ivar/method searches.** Apple's Key-Value Coding does this kind of thing already: you give it a name, and it looks up a method or ivar based on that name and does some stuff with it. You can do that kind of thing yourself, in case you need to look up an ivar based on a name or something of the sort.

2. **Automatically register/invoke subclasses.** Using `objc_getClassList` you can get a list of all classes currently known to the runtime, and by tracing out the class hierarchy, you can identify which ones subclass a given class. This can let you write subclasses to handle specialized data formats or other such situations and let the superclass look them up without having to tediously register every subclass manually.
3. **Automatically call a method on every class.** This can be useful for custom unit testing frameworks and the like. Similar to #2, but look for a method being implemented rather than a particular class hierarchy.
4. **Override methods at runtime.** The runtime provides a complete set of tools for re-pointing methods to custom implementations so that you can change what classes do without touching their source code.
5. **Automatically deallocate synthesized properties.** The `@synthesize` keyword is handy for making the compiler generate setters/getters but it still forces you to write cleanup code in `-dealloc`. By reading meta-information about the class's properties, you can write code that will go through and clean up all synthesized properties automatically instead of having to write code for each case.
6. **Bridging.** By dynamically generating classes at runtime, and by looking up the necessary properties on demand, you can create a bridge between Objective-C and another (sufficiently dynamic) language.
7. **Much more.** Don't feel limited to the above, come up with your own ideas!

Wrapping Up

Objective-C is a powerful language and the comprehensive runtime API is an extremely useful part of it. While it may be a bit ugly groveling around in all that C code, it's really not that difficult to work with, and it's well worth the power it provides.

Friday Q&A 2009-03-20: Objective-C Messaging

Related Articles

    Intro to the Objective-C Runtime 67

    Objective-C Message Forwarding 77

    Objective-C Class Loading and Initialization...115

    Care and Feeding of Singletons 194

    Probing Cocoa With PyObjC..240

    Using Accessors in Init and Dealloc..246

    Method Replacement for Fun and Profit 297

    Error Returns with Continuation Passing Style 303

    Comparison of Objective-C Enumeration Techniques 369

    Implementing Fast Enumeration..373

    Implementing Equality and Hashing 412

    Zeroing Weak References in Objective-C 428

    Implementing NSCoding 459

    Defensive Programming in Cocoa 468

Welcome back to another Friday Q&A. This week I'd like to take Joshua Pennington's idea and elaborate on a particular facet last week's topic of the Objective-C runtime, namely messaging. How does messaging work, and what exactly does it do? Read on!

Definitions

Before we get started on the mechanisms, we need to define our terms. A lot of people are kind of unclear on exactly what a "method" is versus a "message", for example, but this is critically important for understanding how the messaging system works at the low level.

- **Method:** an actual piece of code associated with a class, and which is given a particular name. Example: `- (int)meaning { return 42; }`
- **Message:** a name and a set of parameters sent to an object. Example: sending "meaning" and no parameters to object `0x12345678`.
- **Selector:** a particular way of representing the name of a message or method, represented as the type `SEL`. Selectors are essentially just opaque strings that are managed so that simple pointer equality can be used to compare them, to allow for extra speed. (The implementation may be different, but that's essentially how they look on the outside.) Example: `@selector(meaning)`.
- **Message send:** the process of taking a **message** and finding and executing the appropriate **method**.

Methods

The next thing that we need to discuss is what exactly a method is at the machine level. From the definition, it's a piece of code given a name and associated with a particular class, but what does it actually end up creating in your application binary?

Methods end up being generated as straight C functions, with a couple of extra parameters. You probably know that `self` is passed as an implicit parameter, which ends up being an explicit parameter. The lesser-known implicit parameter `_cmd` (which holds the selector of the message being sent) is a second such implicit parameter. Writing a method like this:

```
- (int)foo:(NSString *)str { ...
```

Gets translated to a function like this:

```
int SomeClass_method_foo_(SomeClass *self, SEL _cmd, NSString *str) { ...
```

(The name mangling is just illustrative, and the gcc doesn't actually generate a linker-visible symbol for methods at all.)

What happens when we write some code like this?

```
int result = [obj foo:@"hello"];
```

The compiler ends up generating code that does the equivalent of this:

```
int meaning = ((int (*)(id, SEL, NSString *))objc_msgSend)(obj, @selector(foo:), @"hello");
```

What that code does is take the `objc_msgSend` function, defined as part of the Objective-C runtime, and cast it to a different type. Specifically, it casts it from a function that returns `id` and takes `id`, `SEL`, and variable arguments after that to a function that matches the prototype of the method being invoked.

To put it another way, the compiler generates code that calls `objc_msgSend` but with parameter and return value conventions matched to the method in question.

> Those readers who are really awake have now noticed that the compiler needs to know the **method**'s prototype even though all it has to work with is the **message** being sent. How does the compiler deal with this discrepancy? Quite simply, it cheats. It makes a guess at the method prototype based on the methods it can see from the declarations that it has parsed so far. If it can't find one, or there's a mismatch between the declarations it sees and the method that will actually be executed at runtime, Bad Things Happen. This is why

> Objective-C deals so poorly with multiple methods which have the
> same name but different argument/return types.

Messaging

A message send in code turns into a call to `objc_msgSend`, so what does that do? The high-level answer should be fairly apparent. Since that's the only function call present, it must look up the appropriate method implementation and then call it. Calling is easy: it just needs to jump to the appropriate address. But how does it look it up?

The Objective-C header `runtime.h` includes this as part of the (now opaque, legacy) `objc_class` structure members:

```
struct objc_method_list **methodLists;
```

That struct is in turn defined:

```
struct objc_method_list {
    struct objc_method_list *obsolete;

    int method_count;
#ifdef __LP64__
    int space;
#endif
    /* variable length structure */
    struct objc_method method_list[1];
};
```

Which is just declaring a variable-length struct holding `objc_method` structs. That one is in turn defined as:

```
struct objc_method {
    SEL method_name;
    char *method_types;
    IMP method_imp;
};
```

So even though we're not supposed to touch these structs (don't worry, all the functionality for manipulating them is provided through functions in elsewhere in the header), we can still see what the runtime considers a method to be. It's a name (in the form of a selector), a string containing argument/return types (look up the `@encode` directive for more information about this one), and an `IMP`, which is just a function pointer:

```
typedef id                            (*IMP)(id, SEL, ...);
```

Now we know enough to see how this stuff works. All `objc_msgSend` has to do is look up the class of the object you give it (available by just dereferencing it and obtaining the `isa` member that all objects contain), get the class's method list, and search through the method list until a method with the right selector is found. If nothing is there, search the superclass's list, and so on up the hierarchy. Once the right method is found, jump to the IMP of method in question.

One more detail needs to be considered here. The above procedure would work but it would be extremely slow. `objc_msgSend` only takes about a dozen CPU cycles to execute on the x86 architecture, which makes it clear that it's not going through this lengthy procedure every single time you call it. The clue to this is another `objc_class` member:

```
struct objc_cache *cache;
```

And that's defined farther down:

```
struct objc_cache {
    unsigned int mask /* total = mask + 1 */;
    unsigned int occupied;
    Method buckets[1];
}
```

This defines a hash table that stores `Method` structs, using the selector as the key. The way `objc_msgSend` *really* works is by first hashing the selector and looking it up in the class's method cache. If it's found, which it nearly always will be, it can jump straight to the method implementation with no further fuss. Only if it's not found does it have to do the more laborious lookup, at the end of which it inserts an entry into the cache so that future lookups can be fast.

Friday Q&A 2009-03-27: Objective-C Message Forwarding

Related Articles

Intro to the Objective-C Runtime	67
Objective-C Messaging	73
Objective-C Class Loading and Initialization	115
Care and Feeding of Singletons	194
Probing Cocoa With PyObjC	240
Using Accessors in Init and Dealloc	246
Method Replacement for Fun and Profit	297
Error Returns with Continuation Passing Style	303
Comparison of Objective-C Enumeration Techniques	369
Implementing Fast Enumeration	373
Implementing Equality and Hashing	412
Zeroing Weak References in Objective-C	428
Implementing NSCoding	459
Defensive Programming in Cocoa	468

Welcome back to another exciting Friday Q&A. This week I'm going to continue the series on the Objective-C runtime. Yuji Tachikawa suggested talking about how `@dynamic` properties work in CoreData and I'm going to take that and expand it to talk about message forwarding in general.

No Such Method
Last week I talked about how Objective-C messaging works, and mentioned that interesting things happen when no method is found for a given selector. Those interesting things are what make forwarding happen.

(If you aren't totally clear on what a **selector** is or what the difference is between a **method** and a **message**, you might want to go read through that article real quick, or at least re-read the Definitions section if you already read it.)

Just what is message forwarding? Simply speaking, it allows unknown messages to be trapped and reacted to. In other words, any time an unknown message is sent, it gets delivered to your code in a nice package, at which point you can do whatever you like with it.

This kind of thing is incredibly powerful and allows for doing all kinds of nifty, clever things.

> Right about now, you're probably wondering, "Why is it called *forwarding?*" There doesn't seem to be much of a link between taking arbitrary actions in response to unknown messages, and "forwarding". The reason for this is because this technique was mainly intended to allow objects to let other objects handle the message for them, thus "forwarding".

What Happens

What happens when you do `[foo bar]` and `foo` doesn't have a `bar` method? When it *does* implement such a method, it's pretty straightforward: it looks up the appropriate method, then jumps to it. When no such method can be found, a complicated sequence of events ensues:

1. **Lazy method resolution.** This is done by sending `resolveInstanceMethod:` (`resolveClassMethod:` for class methods) to the class in question. If that method returns YES, the message send is restarted under the assumption that the appropriate method has now been added.
2. **Fast forwarding path.** This is done by sending `forwardingTargetForSelector:` to the target, if it implements it. If it implements this method and it returns something other than `nil` or `self`, the whole message sending process is restarted with that return value as the new target.
3. **Normal forwarding path.** First the runtime will send `methodSignatureForSelector:` to see what kind of argument and return types are present. If a method signature is returned, the runtime creates an `NSInvocation` describing the message being sent and then sends `forwardInvocation:` to the object. If no method signature is found, the runtime sends `doesNotRecognizeSelector:`.

Lazy Resolution

As we learned last week, the runtime sends messages by looking up a method, or `IMP`, and then jumping to it. Sometimes it can be useful to dynamically plug `IMP`s into a class instead of setting them all up beforehand. Doing this allows for really fast "forwarding", because after the method is resolved, it gets invoked as part of the normal message sending process. The disadvantage is, of course, that this isn't very flexible, since you need to have an `IMP` ready to plug in, and that in turn means that you need to have already anticipated the argument and return types that will be arriving.

This kind of thing is great for stuff like `@dynamic` properties. The method signature is something you should know in advance: you'll either take one parameter with a void return, or have no parameters and return one value. The types of the values will vary, but you can cover the common cases. Since the `IMP` gets passed the selector that's been sent to the object, it can use that selector to get the name of the property and look it up dynamically. Plug it in to the class using `+resolveInstanceMethod:` and off you go.

Fast Forwarding
The next thing the runtime does is see if you want to just send the whole message unchanged to a different object. Since this is a common case of forwarding, this allows it to be done with minimal overhead.

This technique is great for faking multiple inheritence. You can write a little override like this:

```
- (id)forwardingTargetForSelector:(SEL)sel { return _otherObject; }
```

This will cause any unknown message to be sent to `_otherObject`, which will make your object appear from the outside as though it combined your object with this other object in one.

Normal Forwarding
The first two are basically just optimizations that allow forwarding to go faster. If you don't take advantage of them, the full forwarding mechanism goes into action. This creates an `NSInvocation` object which fully encapsulates the message being sent. It holds the target, the selector, and all of the arguments. It also allows full control over the return value.

Before the runtime can build the `NSInvocation` it needs an `NSMethodSignature`, so it requests one using `-methodSignatureForSelector:`. This is required due to Objective-C's C heritage. In order to bundle the arguments up in the `NSInvocation`, the runtime needs to know what kind of arguments there are, and how many of them there are. This information isn't normally provided in a C runtime environment, so it has to do an end run around the C "bag of bytes" view of the world and get that type information in another way.

Once the invocation is constructed, the runtime then invokes your `forwardInvocation:` method. From there you can do whatever you want with the invocation it hands you. The possibilities are endless.

Here's one quick example. Imagine you're tired of writing loops, so you want to be able to manipulate arrays more directly. Add this little category to `NSArray`:

```objc
@implementation NSArray (ForwardingIteration)

- (NSMethodSignature *)methodSignatureForSelector:(SEL)sel
{
    NSMethodSignature *sig = [super methodSignatureForSelector:sel];
    if(!sig)
    {
        for(id obj in self)
            if((sig = [obj methodSignatureForSelector:sel]))
                break;
    }
    return sig;
}

- (void)forwardInvocation:(NSInvocation *)inv
{
    for(id obj in self)
        [inv invokeWithTarget:obj];
}

@end
```

Then you can write code like this:

```objc
[(NSWindow *)windowsArray setHidesOnDeactivate:YES];
```

I don't recommend writing code like this. The trouble is that forwarding won't catch any methods already implemented by NSArray, so you'll end up being able to capture some but not others. A much better approach is to write a trampoline class by subclassing NSProxy.

NSProxy is basically a class that's explicitly designed for proxying. It implements a minimal subset of methods, leaving everything else up for grabs. This means that a subclass that implements forwarding can capture basically any message.

To use NSProxy for this kind of thing, you'd write an NSProxy subclass that can be initialized to point at an array, and then add a little stub method to NSArray that returns a new instance of the proxy, like so:

```objc
@implementation NSArray (ForwardingIteration)
- (id)do { return [MyArrayProxy proxyWithArray:self]; }
@end
```

Then you'd use it like this:

```
[[windowsArray do] setHidesOnDeactivate:YES];
```

This whole area of writing trampolines to capture messages and have them do interesting things has been well explored and has been given the name Higher-Order Messaging. I won't go into more detail about it in this post, but there's a lot of neat stuff out there.

Declarations
Another consequence of Objective-C's C heritage is that the compiler needs to know the full method signature of every message that you're going to send in your code, even purely forwarded ones. To make a contrived example, imagine writing a class that uses forwarding to produce integers from code, so that you can write this:

```
int x = [converter convert_42];
```

This is obviously not very useful, but you could certainly do it. More useful variants of this technique are possible.

The trouble is that the compiler doesn't know about any `convert_42` method, so it has no idea what kind of value it returns. It will give you a nasty warning, and will assume that it returns `id`. The fix to this is simple, just declare one somewhere:

```
@interface NSObject (Conversion)
- (int)convert_42;
- (int)convert_29;
@end
```

Again, this obviously isn't very useful to do, but in cases where you have a more practical forwarding situation, this can help you make peace with the compiler. For example, if you use forwarding to fake multiple inheritence, use a category to declare all of the methods of the other class as applying to the multiply-inheriting class as well. That way the compiler knows that it has both sets of methods. One set gets handled by forwarding, but that doesn't matter to the compiler.

Friday Q&A 2009-04-10: Multithreaded Optimization in ChemicalBurn

Related Articles

    Multithreaded Programming and Parallelism Overview 11

    Thread Safety in OS X System Frameworks 24

    Profiling With Shark 45

    Operations-Based Parallelization..53

    The Good and Bad of Distributed Objects...56

    Holistic Optimization..60

    Mac OS X Process Memory Statistics..123

    Intro to Grand Central Dispatch, Part I: Basics and Dispatch Queues 162

    Intro to Grand Central Dispatch, Part II: Multi-Core Performance.........................169

    Intro to Grand Central Dispatch, Part III: Dispatch Sources 174

    Intro to Grand Central Dispatch, Part IV: Odds and Ends.....................................179

    GCD Practicum...183

    Dangerous Cocoa Calls...236

Welcome to another Friday Q&A, where all the women are strong, all the men are good-looking, and all the programmers are above average. This week, Phil Holland has suggested that I dissect an interesting piece of code from one of my screensavers, so we're going to take a look at ChemicalBurn's multithreaded routing code.

Background

If you aren't familiar with ChemicalBurn, you should go check it out. Essentially, it shows a network with packages being routed through the network. The trick is that the network's performance is changed by the packages as they move, leading to an interesting dynamic system.

If you would like to follow along, the source code is also available.

The core of ChemicalBurn is the routing algorithm. At each time step, packages are generated within the system. They're given a random source and a random destination. Given all of the connections and their speeds, the system computes the optimal route. Since the connections can change at any moment, this routing is redone every time the package arrives at an intermediate node. With simple OpenGL graphics and not much else going on, the routing algorithm is easily the bottleneck of the entire screensaver.

Algorithm

The routing method is located in ChemicalBurnView. It's a bit messy owing to its heavy optimization, but it's just an implementation of the standard route finding algorithm, Dijkstra's algorithm. (For all of you jumping up and down in the back yelling about A*, ChemicalBurn is not well suited to A* due to the lack of a good heuristic.)

Follow the links for the full explanation, but the basics of this algorithm are really simple. Each node in the graph gets a cost and a predecessor. Keep a queue of nodes, initialized with the starting node. In a loop, pop the node with the cheapest cost from the queue. Enumerate through all of its connections. If the cost of getting to that node, plus the cost of the connection, is cheaper than the current cost set on that other node, set that node's cost to the sum, and set its predecessor to the node that was just popped. Once you pop the destination node, follow the predecessor links back and you have the cheapest path to the destination.

Priority Queue

The heart of this algorithm is the queue of pending nodes. My initial implementation simply stored them in an NSMutableSet. To fetch the cheapest one, I iterated through the set and looked for the one with the lowest cost. This queue can get pretty big, and since this search happens every time through the inner loop of this screensaver's major hotspot, this was really slow.

The easy answer here was to switch to using a priority queue. If you aren't familiar, this is a specialized data structure which efficiently supports adding arbitrary elements and fetching the "smallest" element according to a comparison operator. I chose to write a wrapper around the C++ STL's heap algorithm. Another good choice for this would be the CFBinaryHeap class available in CoreFoundation. This one change gave a hefty speedup.

Inline Metadata

The routing algorithm depends on having two pieces of metadata for each node. Originally, I implemented this by using two CFMutableDictionary instances that used the nodes for keys and had the cost and back pointer as values. But since these values were constantly being fetched and set inside of this very hot loop, even the normally fast dictionary lookups were getting to be slow. The solution to this was easy, and is actually a common way to implement Dijkstra's algorithm: store these two values in the nodes themselves. I just made them public instance variables, and my slow dictionary lookups were transformed to fast ivar lookups.

Multithreading

Since each package's routing is independent of the others, and since many packages needed to be routed for each frame in the compute-bound case, multithreading the route finding code was an obvious way to gain more speed.

How I implemented the multithreading itself is not all that interesting. I took an obvious and standard approach of spawning as many worker threads as the machine has processor cores, then pushing packages into a queue which the worker threads access.

There's a hitch, though. I said that each package's routing is independent of the others, but that's not true. In the original implementation it was, but the **inline metadata** optimization screws this up. The per-node values are conceptually private to each individual routing problem, but storing them in instance variables makes them globally visible, so the worker threads are bound to fight over them.

The trick to solving this problem was to store not just a single pair of values, but to store an array of values. The ChemicalBurnNode class ended up looking like this:

```objc
@class ChemicalBurnNode;
struct ChemicalBurnNodePerThread {
    unsigned            cost;
    ChemicalBurnNode*   prev;
};

@interface ChemicalBurnNode : NSObject {
    unsigned            mID;
    NSPoint             mPos;

    @public
    struct ChemicalBurnNodePerThread    mPerThread[0];
}
```

That [0] is a trick to implement a variable-length array. I didn't want to hardcode a value for the maximum number of threads, and then have some huge multi-core beast come along in a few years and not be able to take advantage. To set up the storage for the array, I overrode +allocWithZone: in the implementation to allocate some extra space:

```objc
+ allocWithZone: (NSZone *)zone
    {
        unsigned extraBytes = gProcessorCount * sizeof( struct ChemicalBurnNodePerThread );
        return NSAllocateObject( self, extraBytes, zone );
    }
```

That solves the problem of storage, but leaves the problem of how to choose an array index. Obviously each thread needs to choose a different one. And obviously each thread needs to choose a small number.

I wrote a pair of functions for this:

```
// the key parameter allows multiple independent views to
share IDs
// IDs will count up from 0 based on the unique key passed
in
int NodeGetThreadID( void *key );
void NodeThreadIDCleanup( void *key );
```

The idea being that as different threads call `NodeGetThreadID`, the returned value starts at 0 and just increments for each new thread that appears. This is accomplished by using `pthread_getspecific` to store the ID per-thread, and using a CFBag to keep track of how many threads have already requested IDs for the given key, so that each new thread gets the appropriate ID. Here's how they're implemented:

```
int NodeGetThreadID( void *key )
{
    // we store ID + 1 because NULL is used to indicate "does not exist"
    int threadID = (int)pthread_getspecific( gThreadIDKey );
    if( threadID == 0 )
    {
        pthread_mutex_lock( &gIDMutex );
        CFBagAddValue( gIDs, key );
        threadID = CFBagGetCountOfValue( gIDs, key );
        pthread_mutex_unlock( &gIDMutex );

        pthread_setspecific( gThreadIDKey, (void *)threadID );

        if( threadID > gProcessorCount )
            NSLog( @"Attempted to get ID for thread #%d, more than allowed!", threadID );
    }

    return threadID - 1;
}

static void MakeKey( void )
{
    int err = pthread_key_create( &gThreadIDKey, NULL );
    if( err )
        NSLog( @"%s: pthread_key_create returned %d", __func__, err );
}

void NodeThreadIDCleanup( void *key )
{
    while( CFBagGetCountOfValue( gIDs, key ) )
        CFBagRemoveValue( gIDs, key );
}
```

(The MakeKey function is just called once from the class's +initialize method.)

And that's all it took to get this code to play nice with multiple worker threads but still allow fast access to the two critical pieces of node metadata.

Conclusion
It's been a long time since I worked on ChemicalBurn, but my recollection is that all of

these optimizations put together resulted in something like a 100x speedup from start to finish on my 4-core Mac Pro.

All of these optimizations were relatively obvious and straightforward, but they were also extremely effective. There's a nice combination of optimization techniques here. Using a priority queue instead of a set made a huge difference in the algorithm's overall performance, since the priority queue has an $O(\log n)$ running time instead of the $O(n)$ of the set. Moving the node metadata to be ivars of the node objects is a pure micro-optimization, but one which yielded significant benefits due to how often that particular data was accessed. Finally, multithreading the routing code is an obvious way to use parallel computing to good advantage.

Friday Q&A 2009-04-17: Code Generation with LLVM, Part 1: Basics

Related Articles

    Code Generation with LLVM, Part 2: Fast Objective-C Forwarding........................96

Welcome back to another heart-pounding edition of Friday Q&A. Phil Holland and Ed Wynne both suggested that I do something with LLVM, and so I'm going to discuss how to generate and call code at runtime using LLVM. This week I'm going to talk about the basics needed to get up and running with code generation, and then next week in Part 2 I'm going to show how you can use this technique to build a fast Objective-C trampoline object.

What is LLVM?
About a month ago I talked about the Clang Static Analyzer, a really handy code analyzer which can point out all kinds of errors in your programs. The static analyzer is actually an offshoot of LLVM.

LLVM stands for Low Level Virtual Machine. As far as what this means, it's basically a compiler toolkit designed to be usable for just-in-time compilation. That makes it sound smaller than it really is, though. It's a huge project which provides a wealth of features in many compiler-related areas. For more information about everything it can do, click the magic link.

Among the many things LLVM is capable of, it allows you to construct code at runtime, compile it to native code, and then get a function pointer that you can call right from your own code. This means that you can build custom code on demand and get full native speed from it. Very cool!

Building Code
This week I'm going to walk through how to use LLVM to build two basic functions. The first function will just perform a multiply and add on its arguments, and the second one, a bit more complex, will be a recursive greatest common denominator function. Of course it would be a lot easier to just write these functions in plain old C, but the point is to illustrate the technique, not actually build something useful just yet.

I'll post code snippets as I go, but if you'd like to see the entire test program, you can get it here. To use it, you will of course have to install LLVM. Instructions for that can be found on the LLVM site, but it's pretty much like any other UNIX package.

This code is mainly cobbled together from the LLVM tutorials. However, they're a bit incomplete when it comes to the basics (the "simple" tutorial shows how to build the functions but not how to compile them) and occasionally don't quite work, so I thought it would be useful to present a complete example.

The first thing to do is to create a new `Module`. This is basically a container that functions can be put into. This little function creates a new `Module`, generates the two functions, and then returns it so that we can use it.

```
Module* makeLLVMModule()
{
    // Module Construction
    Module* mod = new Module("test");

    BuildMulAdd(mod);
    BuildGCD(mod);

    return mod;
}
```

There's really nothing interesting going on here. Those build functions are where the interesting work happens.

Let's look at `BuildMulAdd`. The purpose of this function is just to compute x*y+z, where those variables are the three parameters to the function. The first thing it does is create a new `Function` object to work with:

```
void BuildMulAdd(Module *mod)
{
    Constant* c = mod->getOrInsertFunction("mul_add",
    /*ret type*/                           IntegerType::get(32),
    /*args*/                               IntegerType::get(32),
                                           IntegerType::get(32),
                                           IntegerType::get(32),
    /*varargs terminated with null*/ NULL);

    Function* mul_add = cast<Function>(c);
    mul_add->setCallingConv(CallingConv::C);
```

The first line creates the object, which for some reason is typed `Constant`. (My understanding of the system is not quite at 100% yet.) You give it a name, and the return and argument types, and it creates the object. We cast it to the right type, and set up the calling conventions. So far, so good.

The next thing to do is extract the individual arguments so that we can use them when creating the function body. While we're at it, we'll also give them names. LLVM works by building code in what's called the LLVM intermediate representation, which acts as a

89

kind of high level, portable assembly language. That IR is then translated into machine code when required. These names are used when building the IR to make it easier to read, but are not required. Here's how to set up the arguments:

```
Function::arg_iterator args = mul_add->arg_begin();
Value* x = args++;
x->setName("x");
Value* y = args++;
y->setName("y");
Value* z = args++;
z->setName("z");
```

The next thing to do is to set up a basic block. LLVM code is organized in terms of basic blocks. A basic block is just a block of code which has no branches. In this case, since the function has no branches anyway, a single basic block takes care of the entire function:

```
BasicBlock* block = BasicBlock::Create("entry", mul_add);
```

The next thing is to create an `IRBuilder`. This is an object that helps with building the intermediate representation. It's basically a helper object. It's possible to create things more directly, but `IRBuilder` makes building code much easier:

```
IRBuilder<> builder(block);
```

The next thing is to actually create the instructions for the function body. This is nice and simple, since it's just a single multiply followed by a single add:

```
Value* tmp = builder.CreateBinOp(Instruction::Mul,
                                 x, y, "tmp");
Value* tmp2 = builder.CreateBinOp(Instruction::Add,
                                  tmp, z, "tmp2");
```

Like the arguments, the intermediate values also get names that will show up in the IR code. `tmp2` contains the desired result, so now we return it:

```
builder.CreateRet(tmp2);
}
```

And that's it! Easy enough. Of course we can't actually execute the thing yet. But before we get to that, let's look at the `BuildGCD` function.

Greatest Common Denominator

The goal is to build a `gcd` function using the standard recursive algorithm, like so:

```
int gcd(int x, int y)
{
    if(x == y)
        return x;
    else if(x < y)
        return gcd(x, y - x);
    else
        return gcd(x - y, y);
}
```

The initial setup to the function is virtually identical:

```
void BuildGCD(Module *mod)
{
    Constant *c = mod->getOrInsertFunction("gcd",

IntegerType::get(32),

IntegerType::get(32),

IntegerType::get(32),
                                                    NULL);
    Function *gcd = cast<Function>(c);

    Function::arg_iterator args = gcd->arg_begin();
    Value *x = args++;
    x->setName("x");
    Value *y = args++;
    y->setName("y");
```

Next we'll set up the basic blocks needed by the function. In this case there are five needed. We need one entry block, which will contain the first `if`. We need a block to execute the `return` for the case where the `if` is true. A third block contains the second `if` The forth and fifth blocks handle the true and false branches of that:

```
    BasicBlock *entry = BasicBlock::Create("entry", gcd);
    BasicBlock *ret = BasicBlock::Create("return", gcd);
    BasicBlock *condFalse =
BasicBlock::Create("condFalse", gcd);
    BasicBlock *condTrue = BasicBlock::Create("condTrue", gcd);
    BasicBlock *condFalse2 =
BasicBlock::Create("condTrue", gcd);
```

Next we'll build code for these blocks. Since it's all relatively straightforward, and the LLVM documentation and tutorials will explain it better than I can, I'm just going to gloss over it and dump it out here:

```
    IRBuilder<> builder(entry);
    Value *xeqy = builder.CreateICmpEQ(x, y, "tmp");
    builder.CreateCondBr(xeqy, ret, condFalse);

    builder.SetInsertPoint(ret);
    builder.CreateRet(x);

    builder.SetInsertPoint(condFalse);
    Value *xlty = builder.CreateICmpULT(x, y, "tmp");
    builder.CreateCondBr(xlty, condTrue, condFalse2);

    builder.SetInsertPoint(condTrue);
    Value *yminusx = builder.CreateSub(y, x, "tmp");
    std::vector<Value *> args1;
    args1.push_back(x);
    args1.push_back(yminusx);
    Value *recurCall1 = builder.CreateCall(gcd,
args1.begin(), args1.end(), "tmp");
    builder.CreateRet(recurCall1);

    builder.SetInsertPoint(condFalse2);
    Value *xminusy = builder.CreateSub(x, y, "tmp");
    std::vector<Value *> args2;
    args2.push_back(xminusy);
    args2.push_back(y);
    Value *recurCall2 = builder.CreateCall(gcd,
args2.begin(), args2.end(), "tmp");
    builder.CreateRet(recurCall2);
}
```

Notice how all of the intermediate variables are called `"tmp"`. This is not a very useful thing to do, but it does illustrate that LLVM will automatically change these names as needed to ensure that they don't conflict, which is useful. You'll be able to see this in the generated intermediate representation, which we'll get to in a bit.

That's how to build the functions, now let's see how to use them. First thing is to actually call the function to build the module, with the functions within:

```
int main(int argc, char**argv)
{
    Module* Mod = makeLLVMModule();
```

The next thing is to call the `verifyModule` function on the new `Module`. I'll be honest with you: I have no idea what this does, but the tutorial did it so I'm doing it too!

```
verifyModule(*Mod, PrintMessageAction);
```

Now that the module is ready, I want to print it out. This just dumps the intermediate representation that's been built for the module. This step is not required, but is interesting and can help with debugging:

```
PassManager PM;
ModulePass *pmp = createPrintModulePass(&outs());
PM.add(pmp);
PM.run(*Mod);
```

Now on to the really interesting stuff: compiling and running the code. This is done by using an `ExecutionEngine` object:

```
ExecutionEngine *engine = ExecutionEngine::create(Mod);
```

Here's the really cool part. You use `getPointerToFunction` to get a function pointer from the `ExecutionEngine`. And this is a *real* function pointer. You can call it like you would any other function. Just cast it to the right type, add parentheses and parameters, and off you go.

```
typedef int (*MulAddFptr)(int, int, int);
MulAddFptr fptr =
(MulAddFptr)engine->getPointerToFunction(Mod->getFunction("mul_add"));

typedef int (*GCDFptr)(int, int);
GCDFptr gcd =
(GCDFptr)engine->getPointerToFunction(Mod->getFunction("gcd"));

fprintf(stderr, "%p: 2*3+4 = %d\n", fptr, fptr(2, 3, 4));
fprintf(stderr, "%p: gcd(10, 25) = %d, gcd(1234, 5678) = %d\n", gcd, gcd(10, 25), gcd(1234, 5678));
```

How neat is that? That's all it takes to compile and run these functions. All that's left is cleanup:

```
    delete Mod;
    return 0;
}
```

That's the whole program. Here's what it prints:

93

```
; ModuleID = 'test'

define i32 @mul_add(i32 %x, i32 %y, i32 %z) {
entry:
    %tmp = mul i32 %x, %y                       ; <i32> [#uses=1]
    %tmp2 = add i32 %tmp, %z                    ; <i32> [#uses=1]
    ret i32 %tmp2
}

define i32 @gcd(i32 %x, i32 %y) {
entry:
    %tmp = icmp eq i32 %x, %y                   ; <i1> [#uses=1]
    br i1 %tmp, label %return, label %condFalse

return:                         ; preds = %entry
    ret i32 %x

condFalse:                      ; preds = %entry
    %tmp2 = icmp ult i32 %x, %y                 ; <i1> [#uses=1]
    br i1 %tmp2, label %condTrue, label %condTrue1

condTrue:                       ; preds = %condFalse
    %tmp3 = sub i32 %y, %x                      ; <i32> [#uses=1]
    %tmp4 = call i32 @gcd(i32 %x, i32 %tmp3)    ; <i32> [#uses=1]
    ret i32 %tmp4

condTrue1:                      ; preds = %condFalse
    %tmp5 = sub i32 %x, %y                      ; <i32> [#uses=1]
    %tmp6 = call i32 @gcd(i32 %tmp5, i32 %y)    ; <i32> [#uses=1]
    ret i32 %tmp6
}
0x1880010: 2*3+4 = 10
0x1880030: gcd(10, 25) = 5, gcd(1234, 5678) = 2
```

As you can see, the intermediate representation code is nicely readable. If something is going wrong, reading it can be a good check to make sure that you're actually generating the code that you want. After it prints the intermediate representation, miracle of miracles, it prints the correct numbers too!

Conclusion
Although it's pretty pointless to build static functions using LLVM like this, it illustrates interesting techniques. Using this as a base, you can easily take these code generation functions and make them dynamic, so that they generate code in a way that you simply couldn't do from plain C. Next week, I'll show how you can use LLVM to generate Objective-C methods on the fly and actually build something almost useful from it.

Friday Q&A 2009-04-24: Code Generation with LLVM, Part 2: Fast Objective-C Forwarding

Related Articles
>   Code Generation with LLVM, Part 1: Basics 88

It's Friday again, and that means another Friday Q&A. As promised, this week's edition will pick up where last week's left off. Last week I discussed the basics of generating code at runtime using LLVM. This week I'm going to build on that base and show how to use LLVM to perform fast forwarding in Objective-C.

Forwarding?
If you aren't familiar with forwarding, then you'll want to read over my post from a few weeks ago that talks about it. Quickie version: forwarding lets you capture a method invocation and then bend it to your will.

Forwarding is really cool and powerful. Trouble is that it's also slow. A forwarded message send is about a thousand times slower than a direct one.

This should come as no surprise. After all, you perform forwarding by implementing `-(void)forwardInvocation:(NSInvocation *)invocation` That's an object parameter, one which has to be freshly created. The arguments have to be parsed from the method signature, then marshalled and loaded into the invocation object. Then to make the call, the arguments have to be marshalled out of the invocation object and into the right places to make the call. All of this takes a significant amount of time.

Higher-Order Messaging
My LLVM demonstration will involve implementing higher-order messaging, so you'd better know what that is. Cocoadev.com has a thorough explanation. The short version is that it's a technique for nested messaging which uses the outer message as an argument to the inner one. Consider this code:

```
NSArray *result = [[array map]
stringByAppendingString:@"suffix"];
```

What this code will do is iterate through the array, invoke `stringByAppendingString:@"suffix"` on every element, and return a new array containing the results. The `map` call is the higher-order message, and `stringByAppendingString:@"suffix"` serves as its argument. This is pretty neat stuff and is an interesting demonstration of the power of Objective-C.

How does it work? It's actually quite straightforward. `map` is defined in a category on NSArray and returns an instance of an `NSProxy` subclass. That proxy then implemets

-forwardInvocation: to do the work of iterating and returning the new array. Here's the full source code for my minimal proxy that implements this:

```objc
@interface ArrayMapProxyNormal : NSProxy
{
    NSArray *_array;
}
- (id)initWithArray:(NSArray *)array;
@end
@implementation ArrayMapProxyNormal
- (id)initWithArray:(NSArray *)array
{
    _array = array;
    return self;
}
- (NSMethodSignature *)methodSignatureForSelector:(SEL)sel
{
    return [[_array lastObject] methodSignatureForSelector:sel];
}
- (void)forwardInvocation:(NSInvocation *)inv
{
    NSMutableArray *newArray = [NSMutableArray array];
    for(id obj in _array)
    {
        id retval;
        [inv invokeWithTarget:obj];
        [inv getReturnValue:&retval;];
        [newArray addObject:retval];
    }
    [inv setReturnValue:&newArray;];
}
@end
```

"Normal" here in contrast to the fancy LLVM solution that's coming up. For completeness, here's the mapNormal method on NSArray:

```objc
- (id)mapNormal
{
    return [[[ArrayMapProxyNormal alloc] initWithArray:self] autorelease];
}
```

Not too much to it.

97

But, as mentioned, forwarding is slow. How can we make it faster?

Dynamic Methods

This technique gets kind of slow because it has to go through the forwarding path, which as mentioned, is very slow by itself. `NSInvocation` is expensive to build and expensive to invoke.

For the `stringByAppendingString:` example, we could special case that and speed it up by implementing it directly:

```
- (id)stringByAppendingString:(NSString *)string
{
    NSMutableArary *newArray = [NSMutableArary array];
    for(id obj in _array)
        [newArray addObject:[obj stringByAppendingString:string]];
    return newArray;
}
```

That gets rid of the forwarding and invocation overhead. Trouble is, of course, that we'd have to anticipate and reimplement every possible method in advance. That's just not practical.

LLVM to the rescue! Using LLVM we can implement nothing, and see what gets used at runtime. The forwarding mechanism will get the first message. The proxy can then generate the appropriate method dynamically, add it to the class, and "forward" the invocation to itself. Subsequent messages will go straight through. This is what the `forwardInvocation:` implementation looks like from the LLVM proxy:

```objc
- (void)forwardInvocation:(NSInvocation *)inv
{
    SEL sel = [inv selector];
    id obj = [_array lastObject];
    Method method =
class_getInstanceMethod(object_getClass(obj), sel);
    NSParameterAssert(method);

    const char *types = method_getTypeEncoding(method);
    NSMethodSignature *sig = [NSMethodSignature
signatureWithObjCTypes:types];
    NSParameterAssert([sig methodReturnType][0] == '@');

    class_addMethod([self class],
                    sel,
                    [[self class]
_trampolineMethodForSignature:sig selector:sel],
                    types);
    [inv invoke];
}
```

Mostly straightforward stuff there. We get the metadata for the method from an object in the array, and then add a new method to our class. At the end we re-invoke the invocation, which causes it to go back to `self` and hit the newly-added method. The one tricky bit is the `_trampolineMethodForSignature:selector:` call. And that is a *very* tricky bit indeed!

Building the Code
If you'd like to see the entire program at once instead of bit by bit, you can get it here.

In order to simplify the LLVM-generated method, I'm going to push most of the iteration into Objective-C. Using fast enumeration would make things go even faster, but I'm not up to building that in LLVM intermediate code.

As such, the generated method will do the equivalent of this:

```objc
- (id)trampoline
{
    NSMutableArray *array = [NSMutableArray array];
    id obj;
    while((obj = [self _nextObject]))
        [array addObject:[obj trampoline]];
    return array;
}
```

Except that the generated method will take and pass parameters depending on what we tell it to use. By using this template, the `_nextObject` method can be written in Objective-C, simplifying the job.

There's a lot of support structure that's needed before we can actually start building methods. First, we need to create an LLVM module and execution engine:

```
static ExecutionEngine *ArrayMapProxyLLVMEngine;

// requires explicit namespace due to conflict with objc
header Module type
static llvm::Module *ArrayMapProxyLLVMModule;

+ (void)initialize
{
    ArrayMapProxyLLVMModule = new llvm::Module("ArrayMapProxyLLVMDynamic");
    ArrayMapProxyLLVMEngine = ExecutionEngine::create(ArrayMapProxyLLVMModule);
}
```

We'll also define a method for printing the module, handy for debugging:

```
+ (void)printModule
{
    PassManager PM;
    ModulePass *pmp = createPrintModulePass(&outs();
    PM.add(pmp);
    PM.run(*ArrayMapProxyLLVMModule);
}
```

Next, I define a bunch of convenience functions for creating LLVM types corresponding to `int`, `char`, and various pointer types. For `id` and `SEL` I cheated a bit and defined them as `char *`. Since they're never dereferenced it doesn't really matter.

```
static const IntegerType *intType(void)
{
    return IntegerType::get(sizeof(int) * CHAR_BIT);
}

static const IntegerType *charType(void)
{
    return IntegerType::get(CHAR_BIT);
}

static const IntegerType *intptrType(void)
{
    return IntegerType::get(sizeof(void *) * CHAR_BIT);
}

static const PointerType *idType(void)
{
    return PointerType::getUnqual(charType());
}

static const PointerType *selType(void)
{
    return PointerType::getUnqual(charType());
}
```

Another important piece of infrastructure is code to go from an Objective-C type string to an LLVM type. We get the method argument types as C strings that conform to the @encode directive, but LLVM obviously expects values of its own Type class. This function maps from the one to the other:

```
static const Type *LLVMTypeForObjCType(const char *type)
{
#define IF_ISTYPE(t) if(strcmp(@encode(t), type) == 0)
#define INT_TYPE(t) IF_ISTYPE(t) return
IntegerType::get(sizeof(t) * CHAR_BIT)
#define PTR_TYPE(t) IF_ISTYPE(t) return
PointerType::getUnqual(charType())
    INT_TYPE(char);
    INT_TYPE(short);
    INT_TYPE(int);
    INT_TYPE(long);
    INT_TYPE(long long);
    INT_TYPE(unsigned char);
    INT_TYPE(unsigned short);
    INT_TYPE(unsigned int);
    INT_TYPE(unsigned long);
    INT_TYPE(unsigned long long);
    IF_ISTYPE(float) return Type::FloatTy;
    IF_ISTYPE(double) return Type::DoubleTy;
    IF_ISTYPE(void) return Type::VoidTy;
    PTR_TYPE(char *);
    PTR_TYPE(id);
    PTR_TYPE(SEL);
    PTR_TYPE(Class);
    if(type[0] == '^') return
PointerType::getUnqual(charType());

    return NULL;
}
```

You'll note that there is absolutely no handling of any `struct` types. That was simply too involved and I didn't bother trying to implement it. It certainly could be done, but it would require considerably greater sophistication.

I need to refer to selectors and classes within the generated function, so here are convenience functions that take a `SEL` or a `Class` and generate an LLVM constant with that value:

```
static Value *PtrValue(void *ptr, IRBuilder<> &builder,
const Type *type, const char *name)
{
    Value *intv = ConstantInt::get(intptrType(),
(int64_t)ptr, 0);
    return builder.CreateIntToPtr(intv, type, name);
}

static Value *SELValue(SEL sel, IRBuilder<> &builder)
{
    return PtrValue(sel, builder, selType(),
sel_getName(sel));
}

static Value *ClassValue(Class c, IRBuilder<> &builder)
{
    return PtrValue(c, builder, idType(),
class_getName(c));
}
```

This would never fly in a "real" code generator, because those pointers aren't guaranteed to remain fixed from one run to the next. But even though we're ultimately generating real machine code, we're still operating at runtime. Since those values can't change during the lifetime of the process there's no harm in embedding those values right into the code.

One more convenience function, this one for getting an LLVM `Function *` corresponding to `objc_msgSend`. This is actually pretty simple. By creating a function with that name, LLVM will automatically look it up as a C function within the process if no function with that name exists in the LLVM module. All we have to do is declare its parameter and return types correctly, and LLVM will call out to it.

```
static Function *ObjcMsgSendFunction(void)
{
    static Function *f;
    if(!f)
    {
        std::vector<const Type *> msgSendArgTypes;
        msgSendArgTypes.push_back(idType());
        msgSendArgTypes.push_back(selType());
        FunctionType *msgSendType =
FunctionType::get(idType(), msgSendArgTypes, true);
        f = Function::Create(msgSendType,
                             Function::ExternalLinkage,
                             "objc_msgSend",
                             ArrayMapProxyLLVMModule);
    }
    return f;
}
```

That's all the infrastructure needed, now let's actually build the method.

Building the Method

So again, the generated method is supposed to look like this:

```
- (id)trampoline
{
    NSMutableArray *array = [NSMutableArray array];
    id obj;
    while((obj = [self _nextObject]))
        [array addObject:[obj trampoline]];
    return array;
}
```

Except that arguments will be added as needed to fit the method signature of the target. And of course we all know that this really is a function that looks like this:

```
id Trampoline(id self, SEL _cmd, ...)
{
    NSMutableArray *array = [NSMutableArray array];
    id obj;
    while((obj = [self _nextObject]))
        [array addObject:objc_msgSend(obj, _cmd, ...)];
    return array;
}
```

With the ... replaced by the arguments in question. With our target in mind, let's code.

We'll need method which generates the LLVM `Function *` for this function:

```
+ (Function *)_trampolineFunctionForSignature:(NSMethodSignature *)sig
selector:(SEL)sel
{
```

The first thing this method does is build a vector of argument types, using the helper function I showed earlier to translate the `NSMethodSignature` into LLVM types:

```
    std::vector<const Type *> methodArgTypes;
    for(unsigned i = 0; i < [sig numberOfArguments]; i++)
        methodArgTypes.push_back(LLVMTypeForObjCType([sig getArgumentTypeAtIndex:i]));
```

Then we'll create the `Function` object and extract the arguments, just like last week:

```
    const Type *methodReturnType = LLVMTypeForObjCType([sig methodReturnType]);
    FunctionType *trampolineType = FunctionType::get(methodReturnType, methodArgTypes, false);
    Function *trampoline = (Function *)ArrayMapProxyLLVMModule->getOrInsertFunction(
        [NSStringFromSelector(sel) UTF8String],
        trampolineType);
    trampoline->setCallingConv(CallingConv::C);

    // get the 'self' and '_cmd' args as values, and name them
    // the rest we don't care about except to pass them along
    Function::arg_iterator args = trampoline->arg_begin();
    Value *selfarg = args++;
    selfarg->setName("self");
    Value *_cmdarg = args++;
    _cmdarg->setName("_cmd");
```

The next thing to do is to set up the `BasicBlock` objects that this function will contain. That means breaking down the model C code into something a little more low level. Essentially, the function should look like this:

```
entry:
  set up selectors
  array = [NSMutableArray array];
  go to loopstart
loopstart:
  obj = [self _nextObject]
  if obj == nil then go to return
  else go to loopbody
loopbody:
  result = [obj trampoline]
  [array addObject:result];
  goto loopstart
return:
  return array
```

Thus we can see that we'll need four basic blocks:

```
    BasicBlock *entry = BasicBlock::Create("entry",
trampoline);
    BasicBlock *loopstart =
BasicBlock::Create("loopstart", trampoline);
    BasicBlock *loopbody = BasicBlock::Create("loopbody",
trampoline);
    BasicBlock *ret = BasicBlock::Create("return",
trampoline);
```

We'll also take the opportunity to do some more setup here. We need the Function object for objc_msgSend since we'll be doing several of those, and we'll also get the selectors for messaging set up:

```
    Function *msgsend = ObjcMsgSendFunction();

    IRBuilder<> builder(entry);
    Value *arraySEL = SELValue(@selector(array), builder);
    Value *addObjectSEL = SELValue(@selector(addObject:),
builder);
    Value *nextObjectSEL =
SELValue(@selector(_nextObject), builder);
```

Now we can actually start making calls. We already know how to call functions from last week. We know how an Objective-C message translates into a C function call. We have a helper function to push an Objective-C Class pointer into LLVM code. All the pieces are therefore set to make the call to [NSMutableArray array]:

```
    Value *nsmutablearray = ClassValue([NSMutableArray
class], builder);
    Value *array = builder.CreateCall2(msgsend,
nsmutablearray, arraySEL, "array");
```

Easier than I made it sound, huh? Last step, unconditionally branch to the loopstart block:

```
    builder.CreateBr(loopstart);
```

Next, fill in loopstart. This is just a message send and then an if statement, nothing we don't already know how to do. The one tricky thing here is casting the pointer to an integer before comparing it with zero. There may be a better way to do this, but this way works....

```
    builder.SetInsertPoint(loopstart);
    Value *nextObject = builder.CreateCall2(msgsend,
selfarg, nextObjectSEL, "nextObject");

    Value *nextObjectInt =
builder.CreatePtrToInt(nextObject, intptrType(),
"nextObjectInt");
    Constant *zero = ConstantInt::get(intType(), 0, 1);
    Value *nextObjectIsNil =
builder.CreateICmpEQ(nextObjectInt, zero,
"nextObjectIsNil");
    builder.CreateCondBr(nextObjectIsNil, ret, loopbody);
```

Next, loopbody. Everything is straightforward here. The only tricky bit is dynamically generating the arguments for the trampoline call. This isn't particularly hard: we just copy the original arguments vector, but put nextObject in place of self. After that, a standard call to objc_msgSend, then a branch back to loopstart:

```
    builder.SetInsertPoint(loopbody);
    Function::arg_iterator methodArgs =
trampoline->arg_begin();
    std::vector<Value *> msgsendArgs;
    msgsendArgs.push_back(nextObject); methodArgs++;
    while(methodArgs != trampoline->arg_end())
        msgsendArgs.push_back(methodArgs++);
    Value *result = builder.CreateCall(msgsend,
                                    msgsendArgs.begin(),
                                    msgsendArgs.end(),
                                    "result");
    builder.CreateCall3(msgsend, array, addObjectSEL,
result);
    builder.CreateBr(loopstart);
```

That's pretty much the whole function. Only the return block is left, and all that has to do is return the array we've built:

```
    builder.SetInsertPoint(ret);
    builder.CreateRet(array);
```

Then just return the Function:

```
    return trampoline;
}
```

In addition to this, I'm also going to introduce something else new: optimization. Turns out that running optimizations in LLVM is, like most of the rest, surprisingly easy. A FunctionPassManager object manages passes. Add some optimization passes, then run the pass manager on the function, and it's optimized:

```objc
+ (void)_optimizeFunction:(Function *)f
{
    static FunctionPassManager *fpm;
    if(!fpm)
    {
        ExistingModuleProvider *moduleProvider = new ExistingModuleProvider(ArrayMapProxyLLVMModule);
        fpm = new FunctionPassManager(moduleProvider);

        fpm->add(new TargetData(*ArrayMapProxyLLVMEngine->getTargetData()));
        fpm->add(createInstructionCombiningPass());
        fpm->add(createReassociatePass());
        fpm->add(createGVNPass());
        fpm->add(createCFGSimplificationPass());
    }

    fpm->run(*f);
}
```

Now all the pieces are in place for the really short +_trampolineMethodForSignature:selector: method:

```objc
+ (IMP)_trampolineMethodForSignature:(NSMethodSignature *)sig selector:(SEL)sel
{
    Function *f = [self _trampolineFunctionForSignature:sig selector:sel];
    [self _optimizeFunction:f];
    return (IMP)ArrayMapProxyLLVMEngine->getPointerToFunction(f);
}
```

And for completeness, the implementation of -_nextObject:

```objc
- (id)_nextObject
{
    return (_index < _count
        ? (id)CFArrayGetValueAtIndex((CFArrayRef)_array, _index++)
        : nil);
}
```

Performance Testing

In order to see how fast the LLVM version went (and make sure that it actually worked!) I built a little test harness:

```objc
@interface NSString (NOP)
- (id)nop;
- (id)nop:(int)x :(int)y :(int)z;
@end
@implementation NSString (Logging)
- (id)nop { return self; }
- (id)nop:(int)x :(int)y :(int)z
{
    NSParameterAssert(x == 1 && y == 2 && z == 3);
    return self;
}
@end


#define TIME(expr) do { \
    fprintf(stderr, "testing %s...", #expr); \
    /* let stuff happen a few times first for caching etc. */ \
    for(int i = 0; i < 10; i++) expr; \
    \
    NSTimeInterval totalTime = 0; \
    int iterations = 1; \
    while(totalTime < 5 && iterations < 2000000000) \
    { \
        iterations *= 5; \
        NSTimeInterval start = [NSDate timeIntervalSinceReferenceDate]; \
        NSAutoreleasePool *pool = [[NSAutoreleasePool alloc] init]; \
        for(int i = 0; i < iterations; i++) \
        { \
            expr; \
            if(!(i & 0xFF)) \
            { \
                [pool release]; \
                pool = [[NSAutoreleasePool alloc] init]; \
            } \
        } \
        [pool release]; \
        NSTimeInterval end = [NSDate timeIntervalSinceReferenceDate]; \
        totalTime = end - start; \
    } \
    fprintf(stderr, " %fus/call\n", totalTime * 1000000.0 / iterations); \
```

```
} while(0)

int main(int argc, char **argv)
{
    NSAutoreleasePool *pool = [NSAutoreleasePool new];

    NSArray *reallySmallTimeTestArray = [NSArray
arrayWithObject: @"0"];
    NSMutableArray *smallTimeTestArray = [NSMutableArray
array];
    for(int i = 0; i < 10; i++)
        [smallTimeTestArray addObject:[NSString
stringWithFormat:@"%d", i]];

    NSMutableArray *largeTimeTestArray = [NSMutableArray
array];
    for(int i = 0; i < 10000; i++)
        [largeTimeTestArray addObject:[NSString
stringWithFormat:@"%d", i]];

    TIME([[reallySmallTimeTestArray mapLLVM] nop]);
    TIME([[reallySmallTimeTestArray mapNormal] nop]);
    TIME([[reallySmallTimeTestArray mapLLVM] nop:1 :2 :3]);
    TIME([[reallySmallTimeTestArray mapNormal] nop:1 :2
:3]);

    TIME([[smallTimeTestArray mapLLVM] nop]);
    TIME([[smallTimeTestArray mapNormal] nop]);
    TIME([[smallTimeTestArray mapLLVM] nop:1 :2 :3]);
    TIME([[smallTimeTestArray mapNormal] nop:1 :2 :3]);

    TIME([[largeTimeTestArray mapLLVM] nop]);
    TIME([[largeTimeTestArray mapNormal] nop]);
    TIME([[largeTimeTestArray mapLLVM] nop:1 :2 :3]);
    TIME([[largeTimeTestArray mapNormal] nop:1 :2 :3]);

    [pool release];
    return 0;
}
```

Results

So how did it do? Here are the results from my Mac Pro:

```
testing [[reallySmallTimeTestArray mapLLVM] nop]...
1.450171us/call
testing [[reallySmallTimeTestArray mapNormal] nop]...
8.171945us/call
testing [[reallySmallTimeTestArray mapLLVM] nop:1 :2
:3]... 1.496475us/call
testing [[reallySmallTimeTestArray mapNormal] nop:1 :2
:3]... 9.091927us/call
testing [[smallTimeTestArray mapLLVM] nop]...
3.219738us/call
testing [[smallTimeTestArray mapNormal] nop]...
15.972872us/call
testing [[smallTimeTestArray mapLLVM] nop:1 :2 :3]...
3.471767us/call
testing [[smallTimeTestArray mapNormal] nop:1 :2 :3]...
17.267069us/call
testing [[largeTimeTestArray mapLLVM] nop]...
2263.705921us/call
testing [[largeTimeTestArray mapNormal] nop]...
8524.912024us/call
testing [[largeTimeTestArray mapLLVM] nop:1 :2 :3]...
2592.695684us/call
testing [[largeTimeTestArray mapNormal] nop:1 :2 :3]...
8722.084808us/call
```

In short, it ranges from about 6 times faster for the one-element array case to a bit over 3 times faster for really long arrays. The difference is not surprising: much of the cost of standard forwarding is in building the invocation object, something that only happens once for the entire array. For long arrays, that cost is amortized into nonexistence, and we only pay the cost of invoking the NSInvocation, which is expensive but not as much.

Both techniques also pay a cost for allocating a proxy, allocating an array, and filling that array. While this hurts both equally, it reduces the relative advantage of the LLVM solution.

Finally, the forwarding solution has the advantage of using fast enumeration. This is unimportant for the small array but hurts for the big one. Redoing the LLVM code to use fast enumeration is entirely doable, of course, but would make the code more complicated.

It's also interesting to watch how the argument marshalling cost hits traditional forwarding with the really short array. An method with 3 arguments takes over 10% longer to map onto a 1-element array than a method with no arguments. Meanwhile LLVM map pays only about 3% for the extra arguments, since they're essentially hardcoded.

Conclusion: up to a 6x speedup, pretty cool!

Limitations and Improvements

This LLVM forwarding stuff is neat, but it could be better. Here are some areas where it could use work, if you feel like tinkering:

1. **Fast enumeration:** I've probably mentioned this about sixteen times already, but it would definitely help with speed.
2. **Caching functions:** Right now, the implementation generates a new function for every selector. This is wasteful, because many selectors will have the same signature, and can reuse the same function. A cache that allows reusing functions for different selectors with the same method signature would cut down on overhead.
3. **Zero-size arrays:** This implementation simply explodes on empty arrays if the selector has never been seen before, because there's no object to get a method signature from to generate the function, but map shouldn't break just because it's used on an empty array.
4. **Struct support:** This one is a little scary, but writing some code that can properly generate an LLVM struct definition from an Objective-C type string would be nifty.

Conclusion

That wraps up my two week series on runtime code generation with LLVM. In the first week I showed how to get basic code generation up and running with LLVM, then this week you saw how to take that and actually make it do something useful within an Objective-C program.

LLVM is a tremendously cool project and this kind of runtime code generation is extremely powerful. This dynamic fast forwarding implementation barely scratches the surface of the kinds of interesting things you can do.

Friday Q&A 2009-05-22: Objective-C Class Loading and Initialization

Related Articles

    Intro to the Objective-C Runtime 67

    Objective-C Messaging..73

    Objective-C Message Forwarding 77

    Care and Feeding of Singletons 194

    Probing Cocoa With PyObjC 240

    Using Accessors in Init and Dealloc..246

    Method Replacement for Fun and Profit 297

    Error Returns with Continuation Passing Style 303

    Comparison of Objective-C Enumeration Techniques 369

    Implementing Fast Enumeration...373

    Implementing Equality and Hashing 412

    Zeroing Weak References in Objective-C 428

    Implementing NSCoding 459

    Defensive Programming in Cocoa 468

Welcome back to another cromulent Friday Q&A. After taking a few weeks off I intend to resume the regular schedule. We'll see how far that intention takes me, but I'm hopeful. This week I'm going to take Daniel Jalkut's suggestion to discuss class loading and initialization in Objective-C.

How classes actually get loaded into memory in Objective-C aren't anything that you, the programmer, need to worry about most of the time. It's a bunch of complicated stuff that's handled by the runtime linker and is long done before your code ever starts to run.

For most classes, that's all you need to worry about. But some classes need to do more, and actually run some code in order to perform some kind of setup. A class may need to initialize a global table, cache values from user defaults, or do any number of other tasks.

The Objective-C runtime uses two methods to provide this functionality: `+initialize` and `+load`.

+load

`+load` is invoked as the class is actually loaded, if it implements the method. This happens very early on. If you implement `+load` in an application or in a framework that an application links to, `+load` will run before `main()`. If you implement `+load` in a loadable bundle, then it runs during the bundle loading process.

Using +load can be tricky because it runs so early. Obviously some classes need to be loaded before others, so you can't be sure that your other classes have had +load invoked yet. Worse than this, C++ static initializers in your app (or framework or plugin) won't have run yet, so if you run any code that relies on that it will likely crash. The good news is that frameworks you link to are guaranteed to be fully loaded by this point, so it's safe to use framework classes. Your superclasses are also guaranteed to be fully loaded, so they are safe to use as well. Keep in mind that there's no autorelease pool present at loading time (usually) so you'll need to wrap your code in one if you're calling into Objective-C stuff.

An interesting feature of +load is that it's special-cased by the runtime to be invoked in categories which implement it as well as the main class. This means that if you implement +load in a class and in a category on that class, both will be called. This probably goes against everything you know about how categories work, but that's because +load is not a normal method. This feature means that +load is an excellent place to do evil things like method swizzling.

+initialize

The +initialize method is invoked in a more sane environment and is usually a better place to put code than +load. +initialize is interesting because it's invoked lazily and may not be invoked at all. When a class first loads, +initialize is not called. When a message is sent to a class, the runtime first checks to see if +initialize has been called yet. If not, it calls it before proceeding with the message send. Conceptually, you can think of it as working like this:

```
id objc_msgSend(id self, SEL _cmd, ...)
{
    if(!self->class->initialized)
        [self->class initialize];
    ...send the message...
}
```

It is of course considerably more complex than that due to thread safety and many other fun things, but that's the basic idea. +initialize happens once per class, and it happens the first time a message is sent to that class. Like +load, +initialize is always sent to all of a class's superclasses before it's sent to the class itself.

This makes +initialize safer to use because it's usually called in a much more forgiving environment. Obviously the environment depends on exactly when that first message send happens, but it's virtually certain to at least be after your call to NSApplicationMain().

Because +initialize runs lazily, it's obviously not a good place to put code to register a class that otherwise wouldn't get used. For example, NSValueTransformer or

NSURLProtocol subclasses can't use +initialize to register themselves with their superclasses, because you set up a chicken-and-egg situation.

This makes it a good place to do virtually everything else as far as class loading goes, though. The fact that it runs in a much more forgiving environment means you can be much freer with the code you write, and the fact that it runs lazily means that you don't waste resources setting your class up until your class actually gets used.

There's one more trick to +initialize. In my pseudocode above I wrote that the runtime does [self->class initialize]. This implies that normal Objective-C dispatch semantics apply, and that if the class doesn't implement it, the superclass's +initialize will run instead. That's exactly what happens. Because of this, you should always write your +initialize method to look like this:

```
+ (void)initialize
{
    if(self == [WhateverClass class])
    {
        ...perform initialization...
    }
}
```

Without that extra check, your initializations could run twice if you ever have a subclass that doesn't implement its own +initialize method. This is not just a theoretical concern, even if you don't write any subclasses. Apple's Key-Value Observing creates dynamic subclasses which don't override +initialize.

Conclusion
Objective-C offers two ways to automatically run class-setup code. The +load method is guaranteed to run very early, as soon as a class is loaded, and is useful for code that must also run very early. This also makes it dangerous, as it's not a very friendly environment to run it.

The +initialize method is much nicer for most setup tasks, because it runs lazily and in a nice environment. You can do pretty much anything you want from here, as long as it doesn't need to happen until some external entity messages your class.

Friday Q&A 2009-06-05: Introduction to Valgrind

Related Articles

> Using the Clang Static Analyzer..63

Welcome back to another late Friday Q&A. My apologies to all of my readers for missing last week's edition. Some family events beyond the scope of this blog prevented me from writing one. And I should probably point out right now that WWDC is almost certainly going to prevent me from writing one next week. This week, however, I *do* have a post, and I'm going to be talking about Valgrind as suggested by Landon Fuller.

What It Is
A few months ago I talked about the Clang Static Analyzer and how it could help you find bugs in your code. Valgrind is a similar sort of program except it checks for errors at runtime instead.

There's an entire class of bugs which are easy to write and difficult to track down in C-based languages, such as reading from uninitialized memory or writing past the end of an array. Reading from uninitialized memory just gives junk values and a lot of times those junk values actually work. Writing past the end of an array is frequently harmless since arrays are generally backed by storage that's larger than what was requested. Because of this, these code bugs might only show up as crashes rarely. For really bad ones, they never crash, but just cause bad behavior. Figuring out what piece of code is causing the misbehavior can be extremely difficult.

Thus Valgrind. The way it works is it essentially runs your program inside an emulator. By doing this, it has total control over everything your program does. Something that's undetectable when running on the processor, like reading from a memory location that was never initialized, suddenly becomes easy to see.

There are some downsides to this approach. The most obvious one is that the target program runs about an order of magnitude slower than it normally would, due to being run under emulation. A less obvious downside is that Valgrind needs to know the behavior of every syscall in order to make everything work properly, and right now on the Mac there are some missing ones. For example, QuickTime uses the `aio` family of functions which aren't currently supported by Valgrind, so QuickTime won't work. Still, lots of things *do* work, and you can run an entire Cocoa application under Valgrind.

How to Get It
Valgrind's Mac support has only recently been merged into their main code repository, and is not yet available as an official release. This means that, for now, the only way to get it is by pulling down their subversion repository:

```
$ svn co svn://svn.valgrind.org/valgrind/trunk valgrind
```

From there, building it is like any other UNIX program. Read the README or just do this:

```
$ cd valgrind
$ ./autogen.sh
$ ./configure
$ make
$ sudo make install
```

At this point you should be able to run Valgrind. You can give it a quick test by just typing `valgrind` in the shell. Note that as far as I know, Valgrind for Mac only works on Intel machines. If you have a PowerPC Mac you're probably out of luck, although there's no harm in trying.

> Note: in the course of preparing this post I discovered an unfortunate incompatibility between Valgrind and Rogue Amoeba's Instant Hijack. We're looking into a fix but for now, if you have Instant Hijack installed, you'll need to temporarily disable it before using Valgrind. (You'll know this is happening to you if Valgrind immediately crashes with a SIGTRAP.) You can do this like so:
>
> ```
> $ sudo /usr/local/hermes/bin/hermesctl unload
> ```
>
> And when you're done using Valgrind, you can re-enable it like so:
>
> ```
> $ sudo /usr/local/hermes/bin/hermesctl load
> ```

Finding Bugs

Let's take a look at this example program:

```
#include <stdlib.h>
#include <stdio.h>
#include <string.h>

char *bad_strdup(char *s)
{
    char *ret = malloc(strlen(s));
    strcpy(ret, s);
    return ret;
}

int main(int argc, char **argv)
{
    char *str = "hello world";
    char *str2 = bad_strdup(str);
    int i;
    printf("%s\n", str2);
    printf("%d\n", i);
    free(str2);
    return 0;
}
```

This program contains two bugs. One of them is really obvious: it prints the value of `i` at the end, even though that variable was never initialized. One of them is more subtle: `bad_strdup` doesn't allocate enough memory to hold the NUL byte at the end of the string. This would normally go undetected, because memory allocations are padded, and that extra byte is often available. It would only fail if the string length were a nice round number, and even then it might simply fail by overwriting something else and causing corrupted data far later.

Let's compile and run with Valgrind:

```
$ gcc -g valgrind.c
$ valgrind ./a.out
==4296== Memcheck, a memory error detector.
==4296== Copyright (C) 2002-2009, and GNU GPL'd, by Julian
Seward et al.
==4296== Using LibVEX rev 1899, a library for dynamic
binary translation.
==4296== Copyright (C) 2004-2009, and GNU GPL'd, by
OpenWorks LLP.
==4296== Using valgrind-3.5.0.SVN, a dynamic binary
instrumentation framework.
==4296== Copyright (C) 2000-2009, and GNU GPL'd, by Julian
Seward et al.
==4296== For more details, rerun with: -v
==4296==
==4296== Invalid write of size 1
==4296==    at 0x18B9E: strcpy (mc_replace_strmem.c:303)
==4296==    by 0x1F8C: bad_strdup (valgrind.c:8)
==4296==    by 0x1FB6: main (valgrind.c:15)
==4296==  Address 0x3ec35b is 0 bytes after a block of
size 11 alloc'd
==4296==    at 0x15516: malloc (vg_replace_malloc.c:193)
==4296==    by 0x1F77: bad_strdup (valgrind.c:7)
==4296==    by 0x1FB6: main (valgrind.c:15)
==4296==
==4296== Invalid read of size 1
==4296==    at 0x17BB1: strlen (mc_replace_strmem.c:275)
==4296==    by 0x268125: puts (in /usr/lib/
libSystem.B.dylib)
==4296==    by 0x1FC4: main (valgrind.c:17)
==4296==  Address 0x3ec35b is 0 bytes after a block of
size 11 alloc'd
==4296==    at 0x15516: malloc (vg_replace_malloc.c:193)
==4296==    by 0x1F77: bad_strdup (valgrind.c:7)
==4296==    by 0x1FB6: main (valgrind.c:15)
hello world
==4296==
==4296== Conditional jump or move depends on uninitialised
value(s)
==4296==    at 0x1F8E5E: __vfprintf (in /usr/lib/
libSystem.B.dylib)
==4296==    by 0x22CE66: vfprintf_l (in /usr/lib/
libSystem.B.dylib)
==4296==    by 0x251FBA: printf (in /usr/lib/
libSystem.B.dylib)
```

```
==4296==      by 0x1FD9: main (valgrind.c:18)
==4296==
==4296== Conditional jump or move depends on uninitialised value(s)
==4296==      at 0x2C9A66: __ultoa (in /usr/lib/libSystem.B.dylib)
==4296==      by 0x1FA305: __vfprintf (in /usr/lib/libSystem.B.dylib)
==4296==      by 0x22CE66: vfprintf_l (in /usr/lib/libSystem.B.dylib)
==4296==      by 0x251FBA: printf (in /usr/lib/libSystem.B.dylib)
==4296==      by 0x1FD9: main (valgrind.c:18)
...
```

I've snipped off the report here even though it goes on quite a bit longer. The important stuff is here. First, we see an invalid write past the end of the memory block. It says how big the write is, the exact stack trace where it happened, the address where it happened, how big the block really was, and where it was allocated. This is all incredibly useful stuff. Following that we get an invalid read because we then print that string and it ends up reading this same memory location.

After that you can see it successfully printing "hello world", then it tries to print the uninitialized i, which it immediately catches and complains about. Valgrind appears to cascade the uninitialized state of memory as that memory moves around, as it complains about uninitialized memory access many, many times during the course of printing (most of which I cut out for the sake of brevity). This bug manifests in an obvious way here, but it's not uncommon to have uninitialized variable reads which cause much more subtle bugs than this.

Conclusion

It's easy to write extremely difficult bugs in C and C-based languages, and Valgrind is an incredibly useful tool for discovering and tracking down these bugs, and we're fortunate to have a tool of this caliber available on the Mac.

That wraps up this edition of Friday Q&A. Come back... well, probably in two weeks for another exciting installment.

Friday Q&A 2009-06-19: Mac OS X Process Memory Statistics

Related Articles
- Multithreaded Programming and Parallelism Overview 11
- Profiling With Shark 45
- Operations-Based Parallelization...53
- The Good and Bad of Distributed Objects...56
- Holistic Optimization...60
- Multithreaded Optimization in ChemicalBurn 82
- Intro to Grand Central Dispatch, Part I: Basics and Dispatch Queues 162
- Intro to Grand Central Dispatch, Part II: Multi-Core Performance 169
- Intro to Grand Central Dispatch, Part III: Dispatch Sources 174
- Intro to Grand Central Dispatch, Part IV: Odds and Ends.....................................179
- GCD Practicum 183
- Stack and Heap Objects in Objective-C...289
- Dealing with Retain Cycles 392

Welcome back to another Friday Q&A. Now that WWDC is behind us, I'm back on track to bring you more juicy highly-technical goodness. Maybe I can even get back to doing one a week.... This week I'm going to take André Pang's suggestion of discussing process memory statistics (the stuff you see in Activity Monitor or `top`) in Mac OS X.

Memory Structure
Before I can discuss what the stats mean, I first have to discuss just how memory actually works on a modern operating system. If you already know the difference between physical memory and virtual address space, understand how file mapping works, etc., then feel free to skip ahead.

Hardware
At the hardware level, memory is physical chips accessed over a bus. Each byte of memory in those chips has a discrete physical address (although technically modern systems aren't usually byte-addressable, requiring larger chunks to be accessed).

Mediating access to the physical chips is the CPU's MMU (Memory Management Unit). The MMU is what allows for virtual memory. It maps between logical addresses coming from the CPU and physical addresses sitting out in physical RAM.

This gives the CPU a large virtual address space that doesn't necessarily correspond to the physical memory. (This space is 4GB in 32-bit, and a really big number in 64-bit.) Any given section of that address space can either be mapped to an arbitrary section of physical memory, or it can be left unmapped.

OS

What happens when a program tries to access memory that's unmapped? A hardware exception results, and the OS gets to take over.

A cleverly programmed OS (like, say, any halfway recent UNIX, or even Windows) can use this fact to do some interesting things. It could, say, maintain its own, more complicated mapping behind the scenes which says that a section of memory that's unmapped in hardware is actually mapped to a file on disk. Then when a hardware exception is raised for trying to access that section, the OS can read a chunk of the file into that spot and then let program execution continue. Now you have file mapping and (if you automatically *unmap* little-used sections of memory and write their contents out to disk) swap.

Another clever thing is to map sections of two different processes' address spaces to the same chunk of physical memory. Now you have shared memory!

These techniques can be combined. For example, shared frameworks are typically loaded by mapping them into memory (allowing the OS to load them off of disk lazily). And they're then mapped into multiple processes at once, allowing them to use the same physical RAM for all processes instead of having a bunch of copies.

Definitions

Now that we know roughly how the stuff works, let's define some memory-related terms:

- **Resident:** memory which is located in physical RAM.
- **Private:** memory which is only mapped into one process.
- **Shared:** memory which is mapped into multiple processes.
- **Address space size:** the quantity of address space occupied by a particular section of virtual memory.
- **Memory size:** the amount of actual physical memory occupied.

And with that, we can now see what the various fields in top mean, from looking at the man page and using these definitions:

- **RPRVT:** The amount of address space, local to this process, which corresponds to items currently present in physical RAM.
- **RSHRD:** The amount of address space, shared between this process and at least one other, which corresponds to items currently present in physical RAM.
- **RSIZE:** The total amount of physical RAM used by this process. (This is *not* equal to **RPRVT** + **RSHRD** because they measure address space, but this measures actual memory.)
- **VPRVT:** The amount of address space in the process mapped to items which are not shared with other processes.

- **VSIZE:** The total amount of address space in the process that's mapped to anything.

It should also be noted that these numbers are derived from an accounting system which does not always completely correspond to the true numbers, especially when distinguishing between shared and private memory. They're generally close enough to be useful, at least.

Interpretation
By this point you're probably scratching your head and wondering which number you should look at to see how much memory your program is using. Trouble is, there isn't one!

As you've seen, memory usage is highly complicated, and none of these numbers answers that question. In fact, with things like file mapping and shared memory, it's not even a question that really makes sense.

That's not to say that these numbers are useless, though. Even though nothing directly corresponds to what you'd really like to know, there are still some interesting facts you can obtain.

For 32-bit programs, **VSIZE** can be very important. This is because 32-bit programs have a hard 4GB limit on virtual address space, and in this modern world it's not all that hard to hit that limit. Once you do, memory allocations will begin to fail and your program will probably crash shortly afterwards. If your **VSIZE** is near the 4GB limit, you're chewing up too much address space on something.

(For 64-bit programs, the virtual address space is virtually unlimited, and so this column is of little use. For example, garbage collected apps in 64-bit immediately allocate a 64GB chunk of virtual address space just to make the accounting easier. This has no bearing on your actual memory usage and is completely harmless, although it tends to freak out users who go groveling around Activity Monitor.)

RPRVT can be useful as a rough indicator for watching if the total amount of memory your program has allocated is going up or down. This is dangerous to rely on, however. Because this only tracks resident memory, if your program has started to swap then your **RPRVT** will no longer increase, even though you're still allocating more and more memory. (To detect this, you can watch to see if **VPRVT** is going up, and the number of pageouts listed at the top of the screen is going up.) Conversely, the memory allocator doesn't always give memory back to the system right away, so this number may not go down if your program is freeing memory.

Overall, be careful not to rely too much on these statistics. For more precise information to track down leaks and excessive memory allocation, tools like the `leaks` command and the ObjectAlloc instrument are much better.

Conclusion

That brings us to the end of this edition of Friday Q&A. Now you should understand what all those weird numbers mean in `top` (except, potentially, for all of the ones that aren't related to memory) and how best to use and not use them.

Friday Q&A 2009-06-26: Type Qualifiers in C, Part 1

Related Articles

    Type Qualifiers in C, Part 2 131

    Type Qualifiers in C, Part 3 135

    Format Strings Tips and Tricks..141

    Writing Vararg Macros and Functions 158

Welcome back to another warm and fuzzy edition of Friday Q&A. This week I'm going to discuss the use of type qualifiers in C, a subject suggested by Nate Vander Wilt.

What They Are

The first thing is to talk about what type qualifiers actually are. In short, they're keywords which can be used to modify the properties of an arbitrary type. The most common one is `const`. Type qualifiers should not be confused with keywords which modify the *storage* of a particular variable. Those are called storage specifiers.

Let me illustrate with an example:

```
static const int *x;
```

Here, `static` is a storage specifier. It modifies the variable `x` to change how `x` is actually stored. The `const` keyword is a type qualifier, which modifies the `int` type.

By way of illustration, it makes perfect sense to use `const` in a `typedef`, like so:

```
typedef const int MyConstInt;
```

But it makes no sense to use `static` in this way, because `static` is not part of the type:

```
typedef static int MyStaticInt;
// will not compile, does not make sense!
```

The C99 language contains three type qualifiers:
- `const`
- `restrict`
- `volatile`

This week I will discuss `const` and `restrict`, and I'll finish up next week with a discussion of `volatile`.

The `const` keyword

The const qualifier is far and away the most common and the most useful of the three. Its meaning is very easy to understand: when applied to a type, `const` makes that type become read-only.

There are several places where `const` can be useful:

1. **On a function pointer parameter.** A `const` function pointer parameter means that the function won't modify the value that the pointer points to. For example, look at the standard `strchr` function. The first parameter is declared of type `const char *`, because this function only reads the string, and doesn't modify it. This is a useful thing to do with your own code as well when taking pointer parameters that won't be modified.
2. **On a function pointer return value.** Used here, `const` indicates that the data being returned is read-only and the caller is not allowed to modify it. For example, the `-[NSString UTF8String]` method in Cocoa returns a `const char *`. This means you can use the data, but you're not allowed to write to it. The data may be a pointer to some kind of internal storage or cache, and the `const` is used to enforce access to make this useful.
3. **On a local or global pointer variable.** When used here, `const` indicates that this pointer can't be used to modify its contents. This can be useful to preserve correctness when you know that your use is read-only, but is most often useful to shut up the compiler when accessing `const` return values from functions that return `const` pointers as in #2.
4. **On a local or global non-pointer variable.** This is handy to declare a compile-time constant. For example, `const int kMeaning = 42;` declares a constant. The `const` here will help prevent you from changing this value by accident, and may also allow the compiler to do some optimizations that otherwise would not be possible.

Note that this is not meant to be an exhaustive list, and there are probably other interesting places to use it as well.

Since this is a heavily Mac-centric blog, I also want to briefly discuss `const` as it applies to Objective-C. In particular, you should never declare an Objective-C object type as `const`. For example, this is *not* a good way to enforce the immutability of an `NSString`:

```
const NSString *immutableNSStringPointer;
```

What `const` means here is that you can't use `immutableNSStringPointer` to modify the memory at that location. But the immutability of an `NSString` is part of the API contract only. Nothing says that the memory of an `NSString` can't be modified, only that the *semantic* contents of the `NSString` can't be modified. For example, `NSString` might have some internal caches that get updated, but which don't affect the conceptual contents of the string. Changing those caches would violate the `const` requirement, but not the immutability of the `NSString`.

More concretely, if you declare a variable like this and then try to use it anywhere, you'll get a huge number of useless warnings about violating the `const`-ness of your variable.

What if you want a constant NSString pointer? Not a pointer to a constant NSString, but a constant pointer, one which can't be changed. The NSString equivalent of the `const int kMeaning = 42;` example from above. This can easily be done, you just have to apply the `const` to the *variable* directly, by altering its position:

```
NSString * const kConstantString = @"hello, world";
```

The `restrict` Keyword

The `restrict` keyword is new in C99. (The other two date from C89.) This one is purely for the purposes of optimization. That fact, combined with the fact that it's kind of hard to understand, means that this keyword is extremely rare to see and even more rare to actually use.

So what does `restrict` mean, exactly? It's actually pretty simple: when a pointer is declared with `restrict`, it tells the compiler that this is the only pointer which will be accessing a particular chunk of memory in that scope.

But what does that *mean*? Consider the following code:

```
char *src, *dst;
...
for(int i = 0; i < len; i++)
    dst[i] = src[i];
```

When compiling this code, the compiler will need to generate an individual memory load followed by an individual memory store for each iteration of this loop. There are techniques to make this loop run significantly faster by loading and storing larger chunks of memory at once, but the compiler can't use them. Imagine what would happen if `dst` pointed to `src + 1`. Each time the assignment is made, it also alters the value that will be used for the next iteration of the loop. Unless the compiler can rule out this possibility (which is extremely difficult to do automatically) it's forced to generate very slow code.

This is where the `restrict` keyword comes in. By declaring `src` and `dst` as `restrict`, you tell the compiler that you are personally guaranteeing that they won't point into the same block of memory, and thus that the compiler should feel free to generate nice, fast code for this loop.

It's unlikely that you'll have occasion to use `restrict` in your own code. However you may encounter it elsewhere. For example, here is the prototype for the `memcpy` function:

```
void *memcpy(void *restrict s1, const void *restrict s2,
size_t n);
```

When used on a function argument like this, it means that you must not provide overlapping pointers to this function. That's part of `memcpy`'s API contract: it only works on blocks which don't overlap. (The `memmove` function is provided for blocks which potentially do overlap.) Previously this was only expressed in the documentation, but using `restrict` it can actually be expressed right in the code.

Wrapping Up

That brings us to the end of Part 1. Now you know what `const` and `restrict` mean and how to use them. The `const` can be very useful and every C programmer should know how to use it. The `restrict` keyword is mostly useless unless you're writing certain kinds of highly optimized code, but it's still good to know the basics.

Next week I'll discuss the `volatile` keyword. It sits in an interesting middle ground in between `const` and `restrict`: not nearly as useful or common as the former, but much more widely used and marginally more useful than the latter. It's also very frequently misunderstood and misused. For all the details on what it does, how to use it, and (most importantly) how *not* to use it, check back next week.

Friday Q&A 2009-07-03: Type Qualifiers in C, Part 2

Related Articles

    Type Qualifiers in C, Part 1 127

    Type Qualifiers in C, Part 3 135

    Format Strings Tips and Tricks...141

    Writing Vararg Macros and Functions 158

Welcome to another edition of Friday Q&A. Last week I began to talk about type qualifiers in C, and discussed the meaning and use of the `const` and `restrict` qualifiers. This week I will continue with a discussion of the third qualifier, `volatile`.

Virtual Machine
To properly understand `volatile`, you first have to understand the way that the C language is defined. It may seem strange, because C is (rightly) seen as basically a high-level assembly language, but the behavior of C is actually defined in terms of a virtual machine.

Don't misunderstand. C isn't actually implemented with a virtual machine. (Well, there's probably an implementation out there somewhere that is, but it *usually* isn't.) It's purely a logical device that's used to discuss behavior.

The behavior of any given chunk of C code is written into the standard. The + operation results in performing arithmetic on the operands. The = operation causes a value to be stored into the lvalue. And so forth. However, a lot of these actions end up being unnecessary. For example, consider this code:

```
int x = 3; y = 4;
int z = x + y * 2;
z = x + y;
x = x + y;
```

There's a fair amount of redundancy here. First, the initial values of the three variables are unused. Then the expression x + y is used twice. It would be inefficient to compile all of this code literally.

The C standard has an answer to this problem. It states that the program must execute *as if* all the specified actions were executed in a virtual machine. In other words, given the code above, at the end of the day x must contain 7, y must contain 4, and z must contain 7. But how it actually gets there is entirely up for grabs. A smart compiler will just do all of the computations at compile time and generate code that dumps those final values into the variables right away, instead of doing math every time through.

Memory Model

So what's the problem? Consider a piece of code like this:

```
int *x = ...; int y;
y = *x;
*x = y;
y = *x;
*x = y;
y = *x;
```

Again, this code has a bunch of redundancies in it. The compiler would be entirely within its rights to rip out most of this and simply execute a single load from x, because there's no way that the value pointed to by x or anything else could possibly be changed by executing all the intermediate statements.

This is true according to the C standard, where memory is just another component of the virtual machine, and doesn't have to have any real relationship to the actual physical RAM that's sitting in your computer.

And what's wrong with that? Well, nothing really, except for when you go outside the idealized virtual machine of the C standard.

Device Drivers

This is what `volatile` was originally created for, and is still what it's most useful for. C is a common language for kernel programming and other bare metal tasks. When you're working at that level, memory isn't just memory anymore. Sometimes a particular address in memory will actually be a register on a physical device. For example, you could imagine reading and writing data to a serial port by hitting registers on the serial port hardware:

```
char *data = ...; int length = ...;
char *writeAddr = SerialPortWriteAddress();
for(int i = 0; i < length; i++)
    *writeAddr = data[i];

int responseLength = ...;
char response[responseLength];
char *readAddr = SerialPortReadAddress();
for(int i = 0; i < responseLength; i++)
    response[i] = *readAddr;
```

In this case, every read from readAddr would actually fetch a new character from the serial port, and every write to writeAddr would actually push a new character into it. This is called memory-mapped IO.

The trouble is that the C compiler (and the C standard) has no idea about this magical pointer that gives you a different value every time you read from it, and this other magical pointer that causes electrons to flow through a wire every time you write to it. As far as it knows, this is just memory like anything else, and the compiler may very well decide that your loops are pointless and redundant, and hoist all of the pointer reading/writing out of them so that you only do one load and one store instead of a whole bunch of redundant ones.

This would be great if this were standard memory. Free speedup! But it's a disaster here.

Thus the `volatile` keyword. By declaring these pointers as `volatile char *` we can tell the compiler that these pointers are special pointers and every interaction with them must be taken literally. Every time we dereference one, the compiler *must* actually read or write that memory location, even if it looks redundant.

At this point you might think that this is interesting but wondering why we care. After all, I've never done any kernel programming and you probably haven't either. Userland programs never get to play with funky device-mapped pointers. So what's the point?

Well, there *mostly* isn't one. `volatile` just isn't that useful in userland! However there are two things where `volatile` can make a difference in userland code.

setjmp/longjmp

Long before any C-based language had ever heard of exceptions, there was this tremendously evil pair of functions called `setjmp` and `longjmp`. In short, `setjmp` saves the register state of the machine, and `longjmp` restores it, causing program flow to jump backwards. This can be used to build an exception-handling system, and indeed Cocoa did just that for a long time.

The trouble is with those pesky registers. Variables are often stored in registers instead of memory. This means that a call to `longjmp` could actually revert values stored in registers after an assignment had taken place.

Thus one handy use for `volatile`: declare any variables that this might happen to as `volatile`, and the compiler will make sure that all assignments go to memory, and thus that their contents will survive the jump.

Again, this isn't actually all that useful. Basically nobody uses `setjmp/longjmp` anymore. And while Objective-C's exception handling is still based on them (in the 32-bit Mac runtime), the compiler takes care of marking everything that needs it as volatile behind the scenes so you don't have to.

This leaves us with the one place where `volatile` can actually be useful in userland. It's no coincidence that this is also the one place where it is terribly abused, and where people don't really understand what it does.

Threading

Threads are another thing that the C language standard simply does not cover. The standard assumes a single thread of control in the program. All threading APIs in C go beyond the standard's guarantees.

Threading is also a place where memory semantics matter, because the heap is shared between threads. Since the C standard doesn't make any guarantees about how memory is *actually* used with a non-`volatile` pointer, only that it *looks* like it was used in a certain way, and because the standard is unaware of threads, that shared memory can become very screwed up if the programmer assumes that the memory will be modified in exactly the manner and order in which his program specifies.

Threading also exposes another layer of hardware to the programmer. Suddenly the programmer has to worry about having multiple CPUs in the system. Much like the C standard, modern CPUs often treat memory access on an *as if* basis. Real memory accesses may happen in a completely different order than the program actually issued them in. The `volatile` keyword can't get around this, which diminishes its usefulness to some extent.

A full discussion of the use of `volatile` in multithreaded code is unfortunately beyond my ability to write for this week! I thought I could cram it all in but I just can't. Come back next week for Part 3, and what is hopefully our exciting conclusion.

Conclusion

Now you know the basics of what `volatile` does and what it's good for. Answer: not much. As a general guideline, if you're using `volatile` in your code then you're *probably* doing something wrong. However, there are cases where it can be useful, and most of them fall under the heading of multithreading. There are also many cases in multithreaded code where it *looks* useful but isn't. Next week, Part 3 will explore the ups and downs of `volatile` in multithreaded code.

Friday Q&A 2009-07-10: Type Qualifiers in C, Part 3

Related Articles

Type Qualifiers in C, Part 1 127
Type Qualifiers in C, Part 2 131
Format Strings Tips and Tricks...141
Writing Vararg Macros and Functions 158

Here at last is the conclusion to Friday Q&A's three-part series on C type qualifiers. The first week I discussed `const` and `restrict`. Last week I discussed the basics of `volatile` and why it's not very useful. This week I'm going to finish up by discussing the use of `volatile` in a multithreaded context.

Synchronization
Shared data is a big part of what makes multithreaded code so difficult to write. In standard multithreaded code, you must synchronize access to any pieces of shared memory, usually by using a lock.

A key piece of advice: if you're using locks on all of your shared data, you do *not* need to use `volatile` for anything.

This should give you a big clue as to when `volatile` *is* useful.

Lockless Shared Data
What happens when you access shared data without a lock? Unless you're really careful, lots of bad things can happen. Unless your data access is carefully constructed, you can easily end up with inconsistent data. For example, imagine a simple shared counter built like so:

```
int gCounter;
void Increment(void) { gCounter++; }
int GetCurrent(void) { return gCounter; }
```

If multiple threads use `Increment` then this code is not safe! On most systems, `gCounter++` will break down into multiple steps:
1. load current value into register
2. increment register
3. store register into current value

And those individual steps can be interleaved, so you can end up losing increments due to the overlap.

Note that making `gCounter` be `volatile` does not help in any way.

(If you want to learn more about lockless thread safe data structures, you may want to listen to my podcast with the Mac Developer Network.)

The problems with shared data run deeper than simple interleaving of more basic steps. Let's say that you're allocating a data structure on a thread, and want to flag when it's ready:

```
struct SharedDataStructure gSharedStructure;
int gFlag;
```

Then you create it:

```
gSharedStructure.foo = ...;
gSharedStructure.bar = ...;
gSharedStructure.baz = ...;
gFlag = 1;
```

And then you periodically check for it in another thread:

```
if(gFlag)
    UseSharedStructure(&gSharedStructure;);
```

This code is broken! Last week we discussed the "as-if" rule: the C compiler doesn't have to generate code that does exactly what you write in the exact order that you wrote it in, but rather it only has to generate code that does "as if" that happened. The standard knows nothing about multithreading, so the possibility that this shared data could be seen by other threads never enters into it: the "as if" rule applies only to threads individually.

Since `gFlag` shares no dependencies with `gSharedStructure`, the compiler is free to reorder all of those assignments. It could assign `gFlag` first, then fill out the structure. Your other thread will then see the flag as set before the structure is initialized, leading to chaos.

Easy to fix! We'll just make `gFlag` be `volatile`. This will force the compiler to make the store happen right on that line. Not so fast! This doesn't fix the problem at all. Yes, it forces the compiler to make the store happen right on that line, but it doesn't force the compiler to do anything about the struct. The C language requires that stores to `volatile` variables happen in order with respect to other `volatile` accesses, but it does *not* require anything with respect to non-`volatile` variables. Thus the compiler is free to reorder the `gSharedStructure` stores as it wishes across the `volatile` boundary.

Still easy to fix! Just make both of them be `volatile`. This does indeed fix the problem with respect to the C compiler. The stores will be guaranteed to be generated in the proper order....

But no, this doesn't work, you're still doomed!

CPU Memory Reordering

It turns out that your CPU is playing its own version of the C "as if" game. Your CPU sees a list of instructions but is only required to execute them "as if" they occurred in the proper order. Internally, your CPU will aggressively re-order things to run faster. This could result in some loads or stores occurring in a different order from what the machine code indicates. Normally this is not a problem, because the CPU guarantees that the end result is still "as if" they all happened in the original order.

It becomes a problem when you have multiple CPUs sharing the same memory, as happens when you access shared data without locks on a multi-CPU system (which is most PC-class systems these days). Although everything happens "as if" it were in the original order on one CPU, another CPU will see the true out-of-order memory accesses. If your two threads are running on two different CPUs, then you still have the potential that the reader thread will see `gFlag` as set and not see `gSharedStructure` as initialized, even with `volatile` on both of them.

Easy to fix! I'm actually serious this time. You just insert a call to the `OSMemoryBarrier` function (from `libkern/OSAtomic.h`) in between the two sections to enforce ordering at the hardware level:

```
gSharedStructure.foo = ...;
gSharedStructure.bar = ...;
gSharedStructure.baz = ...;
OSMemoryBarrier();
gFlag = 1;
```

And also in the reader:

```
if(gFlag) {
    OSMemoryBarrier();
    UseSharedStructure(&gSharedStructure;);
}
```

Now everything works correctly. Ordering is guaranteed at both the software and hardware level.

But there's a twist. At this point, you don't need the `volatile` qualifiers anymore! At least, you *probably* don't....

As If!

Once again, the "as if" rule is key to understanding all of this. The compiler has to generate code that works "as if" everything happened as written. The trick is that the compiler can't see all of the code that's running in your process. Much of it is in system

137

libraries. The moment that control jumps to code that the compiler can't see, it must make sure that all of its virtual ducks are in a row, and get all of those values to actually be in memory. For all the compiler knows, that external code may access your data, so it has to ensure that it's stored.

This means that `volatile` is definitely not needed on `gSharedStructure`. The call to `OSMemoryBarrier` in the writer forces the compiler to commit all of those stores to memory before making the call, to ensure that `OSMemoryBarrier` can see the correct values. (It won't look at them, but the compiler cannot know this.) Likewise, the call to `OSMemoryBarrier` in the reader forces the compiler to re-fetch everything from memory, because for all it knows `OSMemoryBarrier` could have modified the values.

What about `gFlag`? This is a bit more complex. Here's an example where it would definitely need to be `volatile`:

```
while(1) {
    if(gFlag) {
        OSMemoryBarrier();
        UseSharedStructure(&gSharedStructure;);
    }
}
```

As far as the compiler is concerned, nothing could possibly change `gFlag` as long as it's false, because you never hit any external code. If `gFlag` is not `volatile`, the compiler is free to read `gFlag` once, then use the cached value each time through the loop, so it would never see any change to it. Thus it must be made `volatile` for this code to be correct.

Now here's an example where it has no need to be `volatile`:

```
- (void)method {
    if(gFlag) {
        OSMemoryBarrier();
        UseSharedStructure(&gSharedStructure;);
    }
}
```

Here, the compiler must consider the caller to be foreign code, so it will re-read `gFlag` every time.

(Note: this is *largely* true if this were a function instead of an Objective-C method, but can be false in the face of inlining and whole-program optimization such as is performed by gcc-llvm and clang. Be careful!)

Here is another example where `volatile` is useful:

```
int gCount;
...
while(!done) {
    work();
    gCount++;
}
...
while(gCount < total)
    ;
```

As before, the while loop is not guaranteed to work properly unless `gCount` is marked as volatile.

At this point it's important to note that even marking it as `volatile` won't be enough if `gCount` cannot be read or written atomically by your CPU. Whether this is true depends on your individual CPU. General guidelines are that the data must be aligned to a multiple of its size (true of a global, but not always true if you're doing skanky stuff) and that for integers it must be equal to or smaller than the CPU's native size. In other words, if you declared `volatile int64_t gCount` on a 32-bit CPU this code would not necessarily work. Your program could see half-written values, with the top and bottom mismatched, which would not be a good thing.

Finally, you need to be careful with `volatile` because it's a common place to find compiler bugs. The fact that `volatile` is used so rarely and is in conflict with things like the compiler's optimizer makes it a good place for bugs to flourish. A survey of many popular compilers found that many of them miscompiled `volatile` code a large percentage of the time.

Conclusion

To break down what we've learned:

1. `volatile` is necessary when reading or writing a shared value in a loop whose body does not touch "foreign" code.
2. `volatile` is *not* sufficient when doing this on multiple pieces of dependent data when ordering is important. In order for this to work, `OSMemoryBarrier` must be used. Since this is foreign code, this *may* remove the requirement to use `volatile`, depending on the exact structure of your code.
3. `volatile` does not help in a multithreading context with variables that cannot be atomically written or read by your CPU.
4. `volatile` is neither necessary nor helpful when working with complex shared data protected by locks or using atomic operations.
5. Be wary of using `volatile` even where it's perfectly correct, as you stand a decent chance of encountering a compiler bug which defeats your correct code.

In short, `volatile` can be occasionally useful for certain types of shared data access in a lockless context. However, when in doubt, use locks! Lockless shared data is *extremely* difficult to get right. I hope that this guide gives you some idea of how `volatile` can help you get it right, and more importantly how it can't help you get it right, but unless you absolutely must not use locks in any way, it's much better to protect your shared data with a lock instead. (And if you can, avoid shared data altogether! Message passing is usually a much nicer way to do multithreading.)

Friday Q&A 2009-07-17: Format Strings Tips and Tricks

Related Articles

Type Qualifiers in C, Part 1 127
Type Qualifiers in C, Part 2 131
Type Qualifiers in C, Part 3 135
Writing Vararg Macros and Functions 158

Greetings and welcome back to Friday Q&A. This week I'm going to discuss some tips and tricks for using `printf`-style format strings in C, as suggested by Kevin Avila.

Introduction
Almost everyone doing C or Objective-C programming uses format strings. In C, they're used by the `printf` family of functions. In Cocoa, `NSLog` and `NSString` both use them. They're a powerful way to build strings, but many people only know the basics. This week I'll delve into some hidden corners to take full advantage of the power it offers. Note that if you *don't* know the basics already, this article isn't going to make a lot of sense to you, so read up on a good `printf` tutorial before continuing.

Finding the Documentation
Hopefully all my readers know this, but just in case: if you type `man printf` at your shell prompt, you will get a bunch of confusing stuff that does not appear relevant to C programming. That's because you're actually reading the documentation for the shell command `printf`, not the C function. To see documentation on the C function, you need to type `man 3 printf`. The Cocoa documentation also contains information on format strings, but since the only significant difference in Cocoa format strings is the addition of the `%@` specifier for printing the `-description` of objects, I like to just use the `printf` documentation.

Varags and Type Promotion
Format strings are always used with a function (or method) that takes variable arguments. This is important for several reasons.

First, the more obvious reason is that C doesn't provide any mechanism for the called function to know how many or what type of variable arguments it got. This means that your format string *must* exactly match the arguments you provide. Any mismatch could lead to bad output or a crash.

The less obvious reason is that C promotes types in values that get passed as variable arguments. In short, anything smaller than an `int` gets promoted to `int`, and `float` gets promoted to double. So when you pass in a char, you'll use a format specifier for int to print it, and likewise with passing a float and using a double specifier.

Types of Unknown Size
Frequently when programming in C or Cocoa you'll use a typedef whose definition is not guaranteed. Examples of this are size_t, socklen_t, NSInteger, and CGFloat.

For size_t it's easy: printf actually has a format specifier for size_t: use the z with one of the standard int specifiers.

For CGFloat it's also easy: because float gets promoted to double, the same %f specifier will work with either. No need to change anything.

For socklen_t and NSInteger you need to get a little cleverer. You can't use %d because they might be bigger than an int. You can't use %ld or %lld because they might be smaller than those, and type promotion doesn't carry over. They could even be bigger than those. What you'll want to do here is make an explicit cast to your variable to a size you know will be large enough to hold it, and then use that specifier. For example:

```
printf("%jd", (intmax_t)myNSInteger);
```

Strings of Limited Length
The %s specifier will print a C string. This is tremendously handy. However sometimes you want to print a sequence of characters that isn't necessarily a C string. For this, you can use the . (period) modifier to specify a length. For example, here is a convenient way to turn a FourCharCode into an NSString:

```
uint32_t valSwapped = CFSwapInt32HostToBig(fcc); // FCCs
are stored backwards on Intel
NSString *str = [NSString stringWithFormat:@"%.4s",
&valSwapped;];
```

The .4 tells NSString that the string is only four characters long, which keeps it from running off the end.

Sometimes you don't know the length at compile time. This used to happen a lot with Pascal strings, but they're getting pretty rare these days. For this, you can use * as your length, and then it will read the length as a separate argument. (Note that this separate argument must be of type int, so beware types of unknown size!)

Here's an example of that:

```
printf("%.*s", length, charbuffer);
```

And here's how you can use that to print a Pascal string, in case you ever run into one:

```
printf("%.*s", pstring[0], pstring + 1);
```

Printing Pointers

Printing pointers is a handy thing to do but many people don't know how to do it right. You often see code like this:

```
printf("0x%x", pointer);
```

This is wrong! Not only is the output ugly (you don't get leading zeroes) but it's not guaranteed to work at all, because you're passing a pointer but specifying an `int`.

The correct way is easy: just use the `%p` specifier. You get nice hexadecimal output and the type always matches.

Beware of NULL

This one is so commonly ignored that `gcc` and `clang` actually have a workaround just for this, but it's still interesting to know. `NULL` can legally just be a `#define` to `0`, like so:

```
#define NULL 0
```

If you then try to pass `NULL` as a pointer argument to a vararg function like `NSLog`, your code is no longer conformant, because you're really passing an `int`! For example, this is, strictly speaking, wrong:

```
printf("%p", NULL);
```

(Note that the same goes for `nil`.)

This is easy to fix: if you ever need to do this sort of thing, you can just cast the `NULL` to a pointer type like so:

```
printf("%p", (void *)NULL);
```

Note that this problem is most commonly encountered in functions which need a `NULL`-terminated list of arguments, like `-[NSArray arrayWithObjects:]` or `execl`. Yes, that means all of the code out there which looks like this is, strictly speaking, wrong:

```
[NSArray arrayWithObjects:a, b, c, nil];
```

How do we get away with it? The compiler helps. As I mentioned before, `gcc` and `clang` have a workaround for this. They `#define NULL` to be a magic symbol which

143

has either pointer or integer type depending on the context in which it's used, so the correct pointer value is passed into the function.

Always Constant Format Strings
I see far too much code which does this:

```
NSLog(someString);
```

This works most of the time, but what if `someString` contains the character sequence %@, or another format specifier? Then you probably crash.

It gets worse. What if you do this with `printf` or similar instead, and `someString` comes from a source outside your control, like off the internet? Then horrible things can occur.

One of the format specifiers supported by `printf` (but not Cocoa) is the `%n` specifier. This is very different from the other specifiers, in that it actually gives you a value back instead of taking one from you. It wants an `int *` argument, and will write the number of characters written so far into that argument. For example:

```
printf("%d%n%d", a, &howmany, b);
```

After this executes, `howmany` will contain the width of the first integer being printed.

If an attacker has control over the format string, then they can use the `%n` specifier to write an arbitrary value to a location in memory! This can then be used to take over your program. This attack is not theoretical.

In general, you should not pass anything other than a constant string as a format string. Every so often it is useful to build a format string dynamically first, but think hard before you do this whether you can accomplish your goal without that, and if you do it, then take extra care to ensure that your string will always be valid.

Random Access Arguments
Typical format string usage is straight through start to finish. The first specifier uses the first argument, the second specifier uses the second argument, etc. However this is not mandatory! You can actually have any specifier use any argument. This is done by adding `n$` to the format specifier, where `n` is the argument number to print. Arguments count from 1. For example, this prints the two arguments in reverse order:

```
printf("a = %2$d  b = %1$d", b, a);
```

You can even reuse the same argument more than once. This can be handy when writing out a long string and you need to use the same variable string, for example a name, multiple times.

```
printf("%1$s could not be accessed, error %d. Try
rebooting %1$s.", name, err);
```

Note that if you do this, you *must not* skip any arguments. For example, this is invalid:

```
printf("a = %2$d", b, a);
```

The reason for this is revealed in the fact that C does not tell the called function about the arguments. It has to retrieve all type information and argument counts from the format string itself. Here you're giving it incomplete information. It knows there are two arguments, but it has no idea of the type of the first argument. This means that it cannot know how to access the second argument, so the result of making this call is undefined.

Conclusion
That wraps up this week's Friday Q&A. There's a lot more to what format strings can do than what I discussed today. Read the man page and take a look at how you can control precision, padding, output formats, and more.

Friday Q&A will be going on hiatus for at least one week and probably two due to various things which are going to keep me busy in that time.

Friday Q&A 2009-08-14: Practical Blocks

Related Articles

    Blocks in Objective-C 14

    Creating a Blocks-Based Object System 205

    Error Returns with Continuation Passing Style 303

    Trampolining Blocks with Mutable Code 311

    Futures 330

    Compound Futures 342

    Background Timers 419

Welcome back to another edition of Friday Q&A. I'm back from my break and ready to bring you more programming goodies. This week I want to take Landon Fuller's suggestion to write a followup to my original Friday Q&A on blocks now that the design is finalized and code available for them.

Although Apple has yet to ship blocks with any of their developer tools [editor's note: blocks support is now available from Apple on both Mac and iOS when targeting Mac OS X 10.6+ or iOS 4.0+], they have released code for their blocks implementation due to their participation in the open-source compilers gcc and clang. Landon has used this code to put together PLBlocks, which allows building and running blocks-based code on Mac OS X 10.5. While there are no blocks-based APIs on 10.5 (aside from the very basics which are part of the runtime), they can still be used to great effect.

I'm not going to cover the installation or basic use of PLBlocks here, as the PLBlocks page covers this in great detail. If you want to follow along, go there and follow the directions. For more information about how blocks work, see Clang's blocks language spec and implementation spec.

I'm also going to assume that you know the basics of block syntax and usage, as covered in my last Friday Q&A on the subject. Today's is essentially Part II of that one. If you haven't already, go read that one first.

Fundamentals

Blocks are Objective-C objects. A block literal written in code is an expression that has an object type, much like the @"..." constant string syntax gives you an object. You can then use this object like you would any other Objective-C object, by sending it messages that it responds to, putting it into containers, passing it as a parameter, returning it, etc.

There is a major difference from the constant string syntax. Unlike constant strings, blocks are not exactly the same each time through a piece of code. This is because blocks capture their enclosing scope, and that scope is different every time they're called. In short, each time code execution hits a ^{...} construct, a new object is created.

Allocating a new object every time would be kind of slow, so blocks take an unusual approach: the object you get from a ^{...} construct is a *stack object*. This means that it has the same lifetime as local variables, and will be destroyed automatically upon leaving the current scope. Weird, huh?

It's frequently useful for a block to outlive the scope where it was created. For example, you may want to return a block, or save it for later. For this to work, you must copy the block. You can do this like any other Objective-C object by sending it the `-copy` message. And like any other Objective-C object, if you aren't running under Garbage Collection then you own the resulting object and must eventually dispose of it using `-release` or `-autorelease`.

This, then, is an example of returning a block from a method:

```
- (void (^)(void))block { return [[^{ ... } copy] autorelease]; }
```

Note that external variable capture gives const copies of those variables by default. In other words, this is not legal:

```
int i;
^{ i++; };
```

The way to work around this is to use the `__block` keyword, like so:

```
__block int i;
^{ i++; };
```

The reason for requiring explicit marking of local variables like this is because `__block` variables are significantly more costly than the regular kind, and have different semantics when applied to Objective-C object pointers (more details on that later), so rather than figure out a one-size-fits-all policy, the blocks guys decided it was better to just let the programmer choose.

Examples

I'm going to be showing a bunch of examples for how to use blocks with PLBlocks on 10.5. [Editor's note: all of these examples apply equally well to Apple's official blocks support.] Those of you who want to follow along may wish to look at the example project I built, which you can get out of my public subversion repository here:

```
svn co http://www.mikeash.com/svn/PLBlocksPlayground/
```

If you just want to browse the code you can just click on the link in that command.

Custom APIs

That's the basic idea of how they work, now let's see what we can do with them.

As I mentioned in my first blocks post, blocks essentially allow you to build new control constructs without needing to modify the language. Before we get into it, I want to introduce a little typedef to keep things simple. Most control-construct blocks are blocks which take no parameters and return no value. As such, it's nice to have that type wrapped up in something a little nicer to write:

```
typedef void (^BasicBlock)(void);
```

As a really simple example, let's take a fairly common task in Cocoa: that of running some code with an inner autorelease pool to keep your high water mark low. Normally this would look like:

```
NSAutoreleasePool *pool = [[NSAutoreleasePool alloc] init];
...
[pool release];
```

This is not all that bad, but it's a little verbose. We could write a macro to do this, but macros are fairly evil, and often have hidden gotchas. Instead, let's write a little function to do this, using blocks:

```
void WithAutoreleasePool(BasicBlock block)
{
    NSAutoreleasePool *pool = [[NSAutoreleasePool alloc] init];
    block();
    [pool release];
}
```

And then we can use it like so:

```
for(id obj in array)
    WithAutoreleasePool(^{
        [self createLotsOfTemporaryObjectsWith:obj];
    });
```

That's quicker and easier than writing it out manually, and just as readable at the end. Nice!

Let's attack something a little more complicated. It's common in Cocoa programs to need to run some code after a short delay, using

`-performSelector:withObject:afterDelay:`. Often we'll use a zero delay to mean "run this code immediately after returning to the runloop". The trouble with this is that it requires an object and a separate method, and getting the relevant context over can be painful. Let's write a quickie blocks function instead:

```
void RunAfterDelay(NSTimeInterval delay, BasicBlock block)
{
    [[[block copy] autorelease] performSelector:
@selector(my_callBlock) withObject: nil afterDelay: delay];
}
```

Notice how we have to do a copy/autorelease on the block so that the object stays alive until the perform is complete. This makes use of a small category on NSObject to actually invoke the block, taking advantage of the fact that blocks are NSObjects too:

```
@implementation NSObject (BlocksAdditions)

- (void)my_callBlock
{
    void (^block)(void) = (id)self;
    block();
}

@end
```

Then we can use it like so:

```
NSString *something = ...;
RunAfterDelay(0, ^{
    NSLog(@"%@", something);
    [self doWorkWithSomething: something];
});
```

This is a lot easier to work with than the typical Cocoa pattern for anything more complex.

Another thing that we frequently write is a critical section of code protected by a lock. Normally this would look like:

```
[lock lock];
/* do stuff */
[lock unlock];
```

However this can be somewhat error prone. For example if you forget to unlock the lock in one code path, or return from the middle, or throw an exception, then your application will deadlock. The safest way to write the above is to use a `@try/@finally` block like so:

```
[lock lock];
@try
{
    ...do stuff...
}
@finally
{
    [lock unlock];
}
```

Which is sort of cumbersome. We can turn this idiom into a blocks-based method on NSLock to handle locking and unlocking completely automatically:

```
@implementation NSLock (BlocksAdditions)

- (void)whileLocked: (BasicBlock)block
{
    [self lock];
    @try
    {
        block();
    }
    @finally
    {
        [self unlock];
    }
}

@end
```

This isn't exactly the same. For example, with the explicit `@try/@finally` you can return a value from the method from within the `@try` block and it works, whereas doing this from inside the block will simply error, because you'll be returning a value from the block instead, which will make the block's type incompatible. This can be worked around by using a `__block` qualified variable to hold the return value. In my opinion this is superior, as it helps discourage tricky behavior inside the critical section, where the potential for bugs is high.

A Stylistic Note
There are two interesting choices in the above code, both due to the same reason. The first choice is that these are functions, not methods. Since blocks are NSObjects, category methods on NSObjects can be used for them. Rather than a `RunAfterDelay` function,

150

we could write a -runAfterDelay: method on NSObject. The second choice is to always put the block parameter last, even though it's the most significant parameter and would make more sense to go first.

The reason for both of these is that you want the block to come absolutely last so that your code remains readable when the block is split onto multiple lines. For example, imagine some nested blocks code using the above functions recast using methods instead:

```
[^{
    for(id obj in array)
        [^{
            [self doImportantWork:obj];
        } withAutoreleasePool];
} runAfterDelay: 0];
```

This is significantly less readable. The code appears first, and what's being done with it only comes at the end, which can come much later. When nested, you have to read everything in LIFO order. For this reason, it's a bad idea to write control constructs using methods, and when taking a block as a parameter, always put the block last.

Collections

Using blocks with collections can make for powerful looping constructs. Let's start out with this really simple substitute for a for loop, as a method on NSArray:

```
- (void)do: (void (^)(id obj))block
{
    for(id obj in self)
        block(obj);
}
```

This is not really all that interesting. It ends up being just like a for/in loop, but without the ability to statically type the objects. (It would have been nice to have before Apple introduced for/in, at least, illustrating the idea of adding your own control constructs using blocks.) Example use:

```
NSArray *array = ...;
[array do: ^(id obj){ NSLog(@"%@", obj); }];
```

Not too exciting. Here's one that's more interesting. This uses a block to map one array to a new array:

```
- (NSArray *)map: (id (^)(id obj))block
{
    NSMutableArray *new = [NSMutableArray array];
    for(id obj in self)
    {
        id newObj = block(obj);
        [new addObject: newObj ? newObj : [NSNull null]];
    }
    return new;
}
```

This shows how you could use it to construct an array of name strings from an array of people:

```
NSArray *people = ...;
NSArray *names = [people map: ^(id person){
    return [NSString stringWithFormat: @"%@ %@", [person firstName], [person lastName]];
}];
```

This is much nicer than manually writing the loop encapsulated in the -map: method. By passing blocks around, we only have to write that loop once, then reuse it many times.

One more example, this allows filtering an array:

```
- (NSArray *)select: (BOOL (^)(id obj))block
{
    NSMutableArray *new = [NSMutableArray array];
    for(id obj in self)
        if(block(obj))
            [new addObject: obj];
    return new;
}
```

An example of using it to filter out strings that are too short:

```
NSArray *longStrings = [strings select: ^ BOOL (id obj) {
return [obj length] > 5; }];
```

Note the explicit return value. The result from C comparison operators is int, not BOOL, so allowing the compiler to infer the return value would produce a block of incompatible type. An alternative would be to cast the expression used in the return statement.

Here's an example of a use in a GUI application, for getting all the text fields inside a particular view:

```
NSArray *textFields = [[view subviews] select: ^(id obj){
return [obj isKindOfClass: [NSTextField class]]; }];
```

Callbacks

Callbacks-based APIs are a place where blocks really shine. Instead of passing a selector/delegate pair, or a function pointer/context pointer pair, pass a block. It makes it much easier to pass context around (since the block packages up all needed context automatically) and keeps all of the code nearby.

An obvious example of a callback is notifications. While there's often a benefit to having separated methods for notifications, the implementation is easy and it can sometimes make for nicer code:

```
@implementation NSNotificationCenter (BlocksAdditions)

- (void)addObserverForName: (NSString *)name object:
(id)object block: (void (^)(NSNotification *note))block
{
    [self addObserver: [block copy] selector:
@selector(my_callBlockWithObject:) name: name object:
object];
}

@end
```

The `my_callBlockWithObject:` method is implemented in a category on `NSObject`, much like the `my_callBlock` method seen earlier, except that it takes a parameter and passes that parameter on to the block.

You can use it like so:

```
[[NSNotificationCenter defaultCenter] addObserverForName:
NSApplicationDidBecomeActiveNotification
                                                object:
nil
                                                 block:
^(NSNotification *note){ NSLog(@"Did become active"); }];
```

Note that there is no mechanism provided for deactivating the notification block. This could be added, but would require additional state to be managed by the caller. Such a mechanism is left as an exercise for the reader.

Sheets are a good example of a painful callbacks-based API in Cocoa. You have to implement a callback method, then cram all of the state associated with the sheet, which is often large, either into the single `void *` context parameter provided, or into instance variables. Neither way is particularly nice.

Here is a small category which translates this API to use blocks instead:

```objc
@implementation NSApplication (SheetAdditions)

- (void)beginSheet: (NSWindow *)sheet
modalForWindow:(NSWindow *)docWindow didEndBlock: (void (^)(NSInteger returnCode))block
{
    [self beginSheet: sheet
        modalForWindow: docWindow
         modalDelegate: self
        didEndSelector: @selector(my_blockSheetDidEnd:returnCode:contextInfo:)
           contextInfo: [block copy]];
}

- (void)my_blockSheetDidEnd: (NSWindow *)sheet returnCode: (NSInteger)returnCode contextInfo: (void *)contextInfo
{
    void (^block)(NSInteger returnCode) = contextInfo;
    block(returnCode);
    [block release];
}

@end
```

Now you can simply provide a block inline, right in with the rest of your code, and access all of the necessary context directly.

Another example of a similarly painful API is `NSURLConnection`. It provides two modes: synchronous and asynchronous. The synchronous mode can only be used from a secondary thread which can be blocked for arbitrarily long amounts of time, since any network operation can take a long time to complete. The asynchronous mode requires writing a lot of boilerplate code. Let's write a method that adds an asynchronous mode that simply makes a single call to a block when it's done to hand over the data, the response metadata, and the error, if any. To do this, we'll just use the synchronous API in a background thread. This code uses two functions, `RunInBackground` and `RunOnThread`, which are blocks-based APIs for spawning a new thread and running a block on an existing thread, respectively. These functions are pretty straightforward to implement and I won't duplicate them here, but you can get them in the sample project if you need.

Here's what the code looks like:

```
@implementation NSURLConnection (BlocksAdditions)

+ (void)sendAsynchronousRequest: (NSURLRequest *)request
            completionBlock: (void (^)(NSData *data,
NSURLResponse *response, NSError *error))block
{
    NSThread *originalThread = [NSThread currentThread];

    RunInBackground(^{
        WithAutoreleasePool(^{
            NSURLResponse *response = nil;
            NSError *error = nil;
            NSData *data = [self sendSynchronousRequest:
request returningResponse: &response error: &error;];
            RunOnThread(originalThread, NO, ^{ block(data,
response, error); });
        });
    });
}

@end
```

There are a couple of notable features here. First, notice how the current thread is saved into a local variable, then later on accessed inside a block which will be executed on a different thread. This shows how blocks can be used to easily pass context around in callbacks. Notice then how the block passed to `RunInBackground` ends with a call to `RunOnThread` which uses another block to call back to the originating thread. This kind of nested block messaging is handy for making asynchronous callbacks in a concise manner.

Here's an example of using this API:

```
NSURLRequest *request = [NSURLRequest requestWithURL:
[NSURL URLWithString: @"http://www.google.com/"]];
[NSURLConnection sendAsynchronousRequest: request
                completionBlock: ^(NSData *data,
NSURLResponse *response, NSError *error){
    NSLog(@"data: %ld bytes  response: %@  error: %@",
(long)[data length], response, error);
}];
```

This is very nice! The equivalent using the asynchronous APIs would require implementing several methods, and possibly a whole new class. Using the synchronous

API explicitly, and doing all the work of managing the secondary thread, and calling back to the main thread when done, passing along all of the objects that were received, would require many more lines of code than this does.

Caveats
It should be no surprise that there are some things to look out for when working with blocks.

When blocks are copied, any local object variables they refer to get automatically retained. They are then automatically released when the block is destroyed. This is convenient to ensure that the references remain valid. Any reference to `self` is a reference to a local object variable, causing `self` to be retained. Any reference to an instance variable is an implicit reference to `self` and causes the same thing. However, this makes it easy to cause a retain cycle in some instances. Imagine using a more fleshed-out version of that blocks-based notification API which allows unregistering the notification. If your block refers to `self` in any way, and you do the standard Cocoa thing of unregistering the notification in `-dealloc`, your object will leak because the block will hold a reference to your object.

A simple workaround to this lies in the fact that `__block` variables are *not* retained. This is because such variables are mutable, and automatic memory management of them would require each mutation to generate memory management code behind the scenes. This was seen as too intrusive and difficult to get right, especially since the same block may be executing from multiple threads simultaneously. Thus you can avoid the retain cycle like so:

```
__block MyClass *blockSelf = self;
^{
    [blockSelf message];
    [blockSelf->ivar message];
};
```

CoreFoundation types need to be retain/released when captured in non-`__block` variables, just like Objective-C objects, since they really are Objective-C objects as well. However, the compiler doesn't see them this way. To help with this, the compilers have added an attribute, `__attribute__((NSObject))`, which causes struct pointers to be treated like Objective-C objects as far as their block retain/release semantics. We can assume that Apple will be applying this attribute to all `CFTypes` on 10.6. While we're stuck in 10.5, however, they won't have this attribute, and so CoreFoundation objects will not be correctly memory managed when captured by blocks. To avoid problems, either avoid capturing CoreFoundation objects in blocks (declaring the variables to be of the equivalent Objective-C toll-free bridged type instead will convince the compiler to retain/release them) or ensure that the lifetime of the CF objects is at least as long as the lifetime of the block.

Another pitfall with blocks is due to the fact that they are stack objects. Using the
^{...} syntax is essentially the same, behind the scenes, as declaring a local variable
and then taking its address for something. The address can be passed around, but as soon
as you leave the scope in which the local variable was declared, it's no longer valid. Thus,
something as innocent as this ends up being broken code:

```
BasicBlock block;
if(condition)
    block = ^{...};
else
    block = ^{...};
```

The body of the `if` statement (and the `else` clause) is a separate scope from the main
body which is destroyed as soon as control flow exits the `if`/`else` clause. The block
reference which is being stored in `block` is invalid as soon as control flow returns to the
main body! It's simple to fix this just by copying the blocks:

```
BasicBlock block;
if(condition)
    block = [[^{...} copy] autorelease];
else
    block = [[^{...} copy] autorelease];
```

The main danger with this isn't that it's hard to fix (it's not) but that it's not necessarily
easy to notice when you do it.

Conclusion

That wraps up this week's Friday Q&A. You've seen how to get blocks up and running
with your current tool chain, a few examples of how they can be used in a useful manner,
and some problems to watch out for. Now you're ready to start using blocks in your 10.5
apps today, no need to wait for 10.6 to ship.

Questions about blocks? Have your own ideas for how best to use them? Post below.

Friday Q&A 2009-08-21: Writing Vararg Macros and Functions

Related Articles

    Type Qualifiers in C, Part 1 127

    Type Qualifiers in C, Part 2 131

    Type Qualifiers in C, Part 3 135

    Format Strings Tips and Tricks..141

Welcome to another Friday Q&A, where all references are strong and all values are above average. This week I'm going to talk about how to write macros and functions that take variable arguments in C, as suggested by Damien Sorresso.

Vararg Macros

Writing a vararg macro is pretty simple in principle. Note that unlike functions, vararg macros are new as of C99, so they won't work with earlier dialects. You create one by putting ... at the end of the macro's argument list, like so:

```
#define vararg_macro(a, b, c, ...)
```

And then you access them by using __VA_ARGS__, which just expands to the arguments provided, separated by commas just like they were provided.

Here's an example of a debug logging macro using this technique:

```
#define DEBUG_LOG(...) do { \
    if(gDebugLoggingEnabled) { \
        fprintf(stderr, "Debug log:" __VA_ARGS__); \
        fprintf(stderr, "\n") \
    } \
} while(0)
```

If you haven't seen it before, the do/while construct is a common way to construct a multi-statement macro which is actually a single statement. The worth of this can be seen in this hypothetical code:

```
if(!condition)
    DEBUG_LOG("condition was false!");
else
    do_something_important();
```

If this macro were written without the do/while wrapping, this code would fail in hilarious ways.

Now let's say we wanted to add logging of the file name and line number where the log is, using the `__FILE__` and `__LINE__` macros. We could do this by adding a third `fprintf` line, but imagine we want to combine it into the first line instead. This is easy enough to do:

```
#define DEBUG_LOG(fmt, ...) do { \
    if(gDebugLoggingEnabled) \
        fprintf(stderr, "Debug log, %s:%d: " fmt "\n", __FILE__, __LINE__, __VA_ARGS__); \
} while(0)
```

This works, but it has a problem: it requires at least one argument besides the format string. You can't just do `DEBUG_LOG("condition was false!")` anymore, because that leaves a dangling comma at the end.

The easiest solution to this is to take advantage of a gcc-specific extension. Putting `##` in between the comma and the `__VA_ARGS__` will remove the comma when `__VA_ARGS__` is empty:

```
#define DEBUG_LOG(fmt, ...) do { \
    if(gDebugLoggingEnabled) \
        fprintf(stderr, "Debug log, %s:%d: " fmt "\n", __FILE__, __LINE__, ## __VA_ARGS__); \
} while(0)
```

Now everything works as expected! Of course this code is not strictly C99 compliant anymore, so beware.

Vararg Functions

Vararg functions aren't that much harder. The declaration is pretty much the same as for a macro: put `...` at the end of the argument list. One important difference can be seen here: the `...` *must not* be the only parameter the function takes. In other words, a vararg function must take at least one fixed parameter.

In the body of the function, you'll want to make sure to do `#include <stdarg.h>` to get the appropriate declarations, then you can use some simple functions to work with the argument list. The `va_list` type describes a variable argument list. Then you call `va_start` on it to initialize it. To do your actual work, call `va_arg` in a loop to pop arguments, and when you're all done you call `va_end` to terminate processing.

Note that these are the only three operations supported. It's not possible to query the argument list for length, for type, or anything else like that. You must take care of these things yourself by arranging a convention with the caller.

Let's write a quick example. Imagine that for some reason you find yourself frequently needing to post several `NSNotification`s at a time. To cut down on the work required, we can write a vararg function that takes a number of notifications as the parameters. This is what the declaration will look like:

```
void PostNotifications(id obj, NSString
*firstNotificationName, ... /* terminate with nil */)
```

Notice how I just document that the caller must terminate the list with `nil`. Since I can't query for the length of the list, that's how we'll know when to stop. Also notice how `firstNotificationName` is a fixed parameter. This will make the following code a little simpler.

Next, we'll set up the `va_list`:

```
{
    va_list args;
    va_start(args, firstNotificationName);
```

To call `va_start` we have to tell it what the last fixed parameter is. This is why there needs to be at least one fixed parameter.

Next, we'll run a loop to post the notifications:

```
    NSString *notificationName = firstNotificationName;
    while(notificationName)
    {
        [[NSNotificationCenter defaultCenter]
postNotificationName:notificationName object:obj];
        notificationName = va_arg(args, NSString *);
    }
```

Then clean up:

```
    va_end(args);
}
```

Now we can use it like so:

```
PostNotifications(self, FirstNotificationName,
SecondNotificationName, ThirdNotificationName, nil);
```

Easy!

This is kind of fragile, because you'll crash if the caller forgets to terminate the list, and anything could happen if he passes in something of the wrong type (like a `float`) by accident, but that's just how vararg functions work in C.

Conclusion

That wraps up this week's Friday Q&A. Vararg macros and functions are a little strange but they can be handy, and once you know the basics they're not too hard to make at all.

Friday Q&A 2009-08-28: Intro to Grand Central Dispatch, Part I: Basics and Dispatch Queues

Related Articles

- Multithreaded Programming and Parallelism Overview 11
- Profiling With Shark 45
- Operations-Based Parallelization 53
- The Good and Bad of Distributed Objects 56
- Holistic Optimization 60
- Multithreaded Optimization in ChemicalBurn 82
- Mac OS X Process Memory Statistics 123
- Intro to Grand Central Dispatch, Part II: Multi-Core Performance 169
- Intro to Grand Central Dispatch, Part III: Dispatch Sources 174
- Intro to Grand Central Dispatch, Part IV: Odds and Ends 179
- GCD Practicum 183
- A GCD Case Study: Building an HTTP Server 256
- Background Timers 419

Welcome back to Friday Q&A. This week's edition lines up with Apple's release of Snow Leopard, so I'm going to take this opportunity to open up the discussion on previously NDA'd technologies and talk about some of the cool stuff now available in Snow Leopard. For this week I'm going to start what I plan to be an ongoing series on Grand Central Dispatch, a topic suggested by Chris Liscio.

What Is It?
Grand Central Dispatch, or GCD for short, is a low level API which introduces a new way to perform concurrent programming. For basic functionality it's a bit like NSOperationQueue, in that it allows a program's work to be divided up into individual tasks which are then submitted to work queues to run concurrently or serially. It's lower level and higher performance than NSOperationQueue, and is not part of the Cocoa frameworks.

In addition to the facilities for parallel execution of code, GCD also provides a fully integrated event handling system. Handlers can be set up to respond to events on file descriptors, mach ports, and processes, to timers and signals, and to user-generated events. These handlers are executed through the GCD facilities for concurrent execution.

GCD's API is heavily based around blocks, which I talked about in previous Friday Q&A's, first to introduce the basics of blocks and then to discuss the practical aspects of using blocks in real-world code. While GCD can be used without blocks, by using the traditional C mechanism of providing a function pointer and a context pointer, it's vastly easier to use and ultimately more capable, from a practical standpoint, when used with blocks.

For documentation on GCD, start with `man dispatch` on a Snow Leopard machine.

Why Use It?
GCD offers many advantages over traditional multi-threaded programming:

1. **Ease of use:** GCD is much easier to work with than threads. Because it's based around work units rather than threads of computation, it can take care of common tasks such as waiting for work to finish, monitoring file descriptors, executing code periodically, and suspending work. The blocks-based APIs make it extremely easy to pass context between different sections of code.
2. **Efficiency:** GCD is implemented in a lightweight manner which makes it practical and fast to use GCD in many places where creating dedicated threads is too costly. This ties into ease of use: part of what makes GCD so easy to use is that for the most part you can just use it, and not worry too much about using it efficiently.
3. **Performance:** GCD automatically scales its use of threads according to system load, which in turn leads to fewer context switches and more computational efficiency.

Dispatch Objects
Although pure C, GCD is built in an object-oriented style. GCD objects are called dispatch objects. Dispatch objects are reference counted, much like Cocoa objects. The `dispatch_retain` and `dispatch_release` functions can be used to manipulate the reference count of dispatch objects for the purposes of memory management. Note that unlike Cocoa objects, dispatch objects do *not* participate in garbage collection, so you will have to manage GCD objects manually even if you have GC enabled.

Dispatch queues and dispatch sources (more on what these are later) can be suspended and resumed, can have an arbitrary context pointer associated with them, and can have a finalizer function associated with them. For more information on these facilities, see `man dispatch_object`.

Dispatch Queues
A fundamental concept in GCD is that of the dispatch queue. A dispatch queue is an object which accepts jobs and which executes them in the order in which they arrive. A dispatch queue can either be concurrent or serial. A concurrent queue will execute many jobs simultaneously, as appropriate for system load, much like NSOperationQueue. A serial queue will only execute a single job at a time.

There are three main types of queues in GCD:

1. **The main queue:** Analogous to the main thread. In fact, jobs submitted to the main queue execute on the main thread of the process. The main queue can be

obtained by calling `dispatch_get_main_queue()`. Since the main queue is inherently tied to the main thread, it is a serial queue.

2. **Global queues:** Global queues are concurrent queues shared through the entire process. Three global queues exist: a high, a default, and a low priority queue. Global queues can be accessed by calling `dispatch_get_global_queue` and telling it which priority you want.

3. **Custom queues:** Custom queues (GCD does not call them this, but doesn't have a specific name for these, so I call them "custom") are queues created with the `dispatch_queue_create` function. These are serial queues which only execute one job at a time. Because of this, they can be used as a synchronization mechanism, much like a mutex in a traditional threaded program.

Creating Queues

If you want to use a custom queue, you'll have to create one. To do this, just call `dispatch_queue_create`. The first parameter is a label, which is purely for debugging purposes. Apple recommends using reverse-DNS naming to give the queue a unique name, like `"com.yourcompany.subsystem.task"`. These names show up in crash logs and can be queried from the debugger and will help a lot when trying to see where things went wrong. The second argument is an attribute argument which is currently unsupported, so pass `NULL`.

Submitting Jobs

Submitting a job to a queue is easy: call the `dispatch_async` function, and pass it a queue and a block. The queue will then execute that block when it's that block's turn to execute. Here is an example of executing some long-running job in the background using a global queue:

```
dispatch_async(dispatch_get_global_queue(DISPATCH_QUEUE_PRIORITY_DEFAULT, 0), ^{
    [self goDoSomethingLongAndInvolved];
    NSLog(@"Done doing something long and involved");
});
```

`dispatch_async` returns immediately, and then the block will execute asynchronously in the background.

Of course, it's not really very useful to perform an `NSLog` when the work is done. In a typical Cocoa application, you probably want to update a part of your GUI, and that in turn means running code on the main thread. You can easily accomplish this by using nested dispatches, with the outer one performing the background work, and then from within the background block dispatching onto the main queue, like this:

```
dispatch_async(dispatch_get_global_queue(DISPATCH_QUEUE_PRIORITY_DEFAULT,
0), ^{
    [self goDoSomethingLongAndInvolved];
    dispatch_async(dispatch_get_main_queue(), ^{
        [textField setStringValue:@"Done doing something long and involved"];
    });
});
```

There is also a `dispatch_sync` function, which does the same thing but which waits for the block to complete before returning. In conjunction with the `__block` type qualifier, this can be used to get a value back from the executing block. For example, you may have some code running on a background thread (or better yet, a non-main dispatch queue) which needs to get a value from a GUI control. You can do this easily by using `dispatch_sync` and `dispatch_get_main_queue`:

```
__block NSString *stringValue;
dispatch_sync(dispatch_get_main_queue(), ^{
    // __block variables aren't automatically retained
    // so we'd better make sure we have a reference we can keep
    stringValue = [[textField stringValue] copy];
});
[stringValue autorelease];
// use stringValue in the background now
```

It can be better to use a more asynchronous programming style, however. Rather than block background processing to fetch the GUI value, you can use nested blocks to terminate background processing, execute your fetch on the main thread, and then simply submit further processing back in the background. You can write code like this instead:

```
dispatch_queue_t bgQueue = myQueue;
dispatch_async(dispatch_get_main_queue(), ^{
    NSString *stringValue = [[[textField stringValue] copy] autorelease];
    dispatch_async(bgQueue, ^{
        // use stringValue in the background now
    });
});
```

Depending on your needs, `myQueue` could be a custom queue or it could just be one of the global queues.

Replacing Locks
Custom queues can be used as a synchronization mechanism in place of locks. In

traditional multi-threaded programming, you might have an object which is designed to be usable from multiple threads. In order to accomplish this, it protects all accesses to shared data using a lock, which you might find in an instance variable:

`NSLock *lock;`

Then accesses look like this:

```
- (id)something
{
    id localSomething;
    [lock lock];
    localSomething = [[something retain] autorelease];
    [lock unlock];
    return localSomething;
}

- (void)setSomething:(id)newSomething
{
    [lock lock];
    if(newSomething != something)
    {
        [something release];
        something = [newSomething retain];
        [self updateSomethingCaches];
    }
    [lock unlock];
}
```

Using GCD, you can replace the instance variable with a queue:

`dispatch_queue_t queue;`

In order to be used as a synchronization mechanism, the queue must be a custom queue, not a global queue, so you would initialize it using `dispatch_queue_create`. You would then wrap all code accessing shared data in `dispatch_async` or `dispatch_sync`:

```
- (id)something
{
    __block id localSomething;
    dispatch_sync(queue, ^{
        localSomething = [something retain];
    });
    return [localSomething autorelease];
}

- (void)setSomething:(id)newSomething
{
    dispatch_async(queue, ^{
        if(newSomething != something)
        {
            [something release];
            something = [newSomething retain];
            [self updateSomethingCaches];
        }
    });
}
```

Note that dispatch queues are extremely lightweight so it's entirely reasonable to use them just as often as you would use a lock.

At this point you may be asking, this is all well and good, but what's the point? I just switched code from one mechanism to another mechanism that looks pretty much the same. Why would you do this?

There are actually several advantages to the GCD approach:

1. **Parallelism:** Notice how -setSomething: uses dispatch_async in the second version of the code. This means that the call to -setSomething: will return right away, and then the bulk of the work will happen in the background. This could be a significant win if updateSomethingCaches is a costly operation and the caller will be doing something processor intensive as well.
2. **Safety:** It's impossible to accidentally write a code path that doesn't unlock the lock using GCD. In normal locked code it's not unusual to inadvertently put a return statement in the middle of the lock, or conditionalize the exit, or something equally unfortunate. With GCD, the queue always continues to run and you can't help but return control to it normally.
3. **Control:** It's possible to suspend and resume dispatch queues at will, which cannot easily be done with a locks-based approach. It's also possible to point a custom queue at another dispatch queue, making it inherit the attributes of that other dispatch queue. Using this, the priority of the queue can be adjusted by

making it point to the different global queues, and the queue can even be made to execute code on the main thread if this were required for some reason.
4. **Integration:** The GCD event system integrates with dispatch queues. Any events or timers that the object needs to use can be pointed at the object's queue, causing the handlers to automatically run on that queue, making them automatically synchronized with the object.

Conclusion

Now you know the basics of Grand Central Dispatch, how to create dispatch queues, how to submit jobs to dispatch queues, and how to use queues as a substitute for locks in multithreaded programs. Next week I'll show you techniques for using GCD to write code which performs parallel processing to extract more performance out of multi-core systems. And in the coming weeks, I'll discuss more of GCD in depth, including the event system and queue targeting.

Friday Q&A 2009-09-04: Intro to Grand Central Dispatch, Part II: Multi-Core Performance

Related Articles

    Multithreaded Programming and Parallelism Overview 11

    Profiling With Shark 45

    Operations-Based Parallelization 53

    The Good and Bad of Distributed Objects 56

    Holistic Optimization 60

    Multithreaded Optimization in ChemicalBurn 82

    Mac OS X Process Memory Statistics 123

    Intro to Grand Central Dispatch, Part I: Basics and Dispatch Queues 162

    Intro to Grand Central Dispatch, Part III: Dispatch Sources 174

    Intro to Grand Central Dispatch, Part IV: Odds and Ends 179

    GCD Practicum 183

    A GCD Case Study: Building an HTTP Server 256

    Background Timers 419

Welcome back to Friday Q&A. Last week I discussed the basics of Grand Central Dispatch, an exciting new technology in Snow Leopard. This week I'm going to dive deeper into GCD and look at how you can use GCD to take advantage of multi-core processors to speed up computation. This post assumes that you've read last week's edition, so be sure to do that if you haven't already.

Concepts

In order to take advantage of multiple CPU cores within a single process, it's necessary to use multiple threads. (I'm ignoring multi-process concurrency, because it's unrelated to GCD.) This is just as true in the GCD world as it is in the purely threaded world. At the low level, GCD global dispatch queues are just abstractions around a pool of worker threads. Blocks on those queues get dispatched onto the worker threads as they become available. Blocks submitted to custom queues end up going through global queues and into that same pool of worker threads. (Unless your custom queue is targeted at the main thread, but you would never do that for speed purposes!)

There are essentially two ways to extract multi-core performance out of GCD: by parallelizing a single task or a group of related tasks onto one of the global queues, and by parallelizing multiple unrelated or loosely related tasks onto multiple custom queues.

Global Queues
Imagine the following loop:

```
for(id obj in array)
    [self doSomethingIntensiveWith:obj];
```

Assume that -doSomethingIntensiveWith: is thread safe and can be run in parallel with other uses of that same method. If this is true, and array regularly contains more than one object, it's easy to use GCD to parallelize this code:

```
dispatch_queue_t queue =
dispatch_get_global_queue(DISPATCH_QUEUE_PRIORITY_DEFAULT,
0);
for(id obj in array)
    dispatch_async(queue, ^{
        [self doSomethingIntensiveWith:obj];
    });
```

Easy as that, you're running on multiple cores.

Of course code isn't always this nice. Sometimes you have code which manipulates an array like this, but then has to perform some work with the result:

```
for(id obj in array)
    [self doSomethingIntensiveWith:obj];
[self doSomethingWith:array];
```

The use of dispatch_async in the GCD example means that this doesn't work. And you can't solve it just by switching to dispatch_sync, because that will cause each individual iteration to block, destroying all parallelism.

One way to solve this problem is by using dispatch groups. A dispatch group is a way to group together multiple blocks, and either wait for them to complete or be notified once they complete. They are created using dispatch_group_create, and the dispatch_group_async function allows submitting a block to a dispatch queue and also adding it to the group. We could then rewrite this code to use GCD like so:

```
dispatch_queue_t queue =
dispatch_get_global_queue(DISPATCH_QUEUE_PRIORITY_DEFAULT,
0);
dispatch_group_t group = dispatch_group_create();
for(id obj in array)
    dispatch_group_async(group, queue, ^{
        [self doSomethingIntensiveWith:obj];
    });
dispatch_group_wait(group, DISPATCH_TIME_FOREVER);
dispatch_release(group);

[self doSomethingWith:array];
```

If this work can be performed asynchronously relative to the calling code, then we can get even fancier than this, and run `-doSomethingWith:` in the background instead of waiting. To do this, we'll use `dispatch_group_notify` to set a block to run when the group completes:

```
dispatch_queue_t queue =
dispatch_get_global_queue(DISPATCH_QUEUE_PRIORITY_DEFAULT,
0);
dispatch_group_t group = dispatch_group_create();
for(id obj in array)
    dispatch_group_async(group, queue, ^{
        [self doSomethingIntensiveWith:obj];
    });
dispatch_group_notify(group, queue, ^{
    [self doSomethingWith:array];
});
dispatch_release(group);
```

Now not only will all of the work on the array objects run in parallel, but the final work will also run asynchronously with respect to the rest of the application, giving even more parallelism. Note that if `-doSomethingWith:` needed to run on the main thread, for example to manipulate the GUI, all you need to do is pass the main queue to `dispatch_group_notify` instead of a global queue.

For the synchronous case, GCD provides a nice shortcut with the `dispatch_apply` function. This function calls a single block multiple times in parallel and waits for it to complete, just like what we wanted:

```
dispatch_queue_t queue =
dispatch_get_global_queue(DISPATCH_QUEUE_PRIORITY_DEFAULT,
0);
dispatch_apply([array count], queue, ^(size_t index){
    [self doSomethingIntensiveWith:[array
objectAtIndex:index]];
});
[self doSomethingWith:array];
```

This is nice, but what about the asynchronous case? There's no asynchronous version of `dispatch_apply` that we can use. But we're using an API built around asynchronous invocation! We can just use `dispatch_async` to push the whole thing into the background:

```
dispatch_queue_t queue =
dispatch_get_global_queue(DISPATCH_QUEUE_PRIORITY_DEFAULT,
0);
dispatch_async(queue, ^{
    dispatch_apply([array count], queue, ^(size_t index){
        [self doSomethingIntensiveWith:[array
objectAtIndex:index]];
    });
    [self doSomethingWith:array];
});
```

Easy!

The key to this approach is identifying code which is performing identical work on many different pieces of data at once. If you ensure that the work performed is done in a thread safe manner (beyond the scope of this post) then you can replace your loops with calls to GCD in order to achieve parallelism.

In order to see a performance gain, you need to be performing a fairly substantial amount of work. GCD is lightweight and low-overhead compared to threads, but it's still somewhat costly to submit a block to a queue. The block has to be copied and enqueued, and the appropriate worker thread somehow notified. Submitting a block for every pixel in an image is probably not going to be a win. On the other hand, submitting a block for each image when converting a collection of images is probably going to be a win. The point where GCD ceases to be profitable falls somewhere in the middle. When in doubt, experiment. Parallelizing applications is an optimization, and as such you should always measure before and after to make sure that your changes helped. (And to make sure that you're making the changes in the right place!)

Subsystem Parallelism

The previous section talked about taking advantage of multiple cores in a single subsystem of your application. It can also be useful to do this across multiple subsystems.

For example, imagine an application which opens a document containing metadata. The document data itself must be parsed and converted into model objects for display, as must the metadata. However, the document data and the metadata don't interact. You could create a dispatch queue for each one, then run both in parallel. The code for each piece of data parsing would be entirely serial within itself, and thread safety is not a concern (as long as you don't have shared data between them), but they will still run in parallel.

Once the document is open, the program needs to perform tasks in response to user actions. For example, it may need to perform spell checking, syntax highlighting, word counting, autosave, and other such things. If each one of these tasks is implemented using a separate dispatch queue, they will all run in parallel with respect to each other without many of the difficulties of multithreaded programming.

By using dispatch sources, something I'll cover next week, you can have GCD deliver events directly to a custom dispatch queue. A part of your program that monitors a network socket, for example, could be given its own dispatch queue which will then allow it to run in parallel with respect to the rest of the application. And again, by using a custom queue, this module will run serially with respect to itself, simplifying programming.

Conclusion

This week we saw how to use GCD to increase the performance of your applications and take advantage of modern multi-core systems. Although care must still be taken when writing parallel applications, GCD makes it easier than ever to take advantage of all available computing power.

Friday Q&A 2009-09-11: Intro to Grand Central Dispatch, Part III: Dispatch Sources

Related Articles

    Multithreaded Programming and Parallelism Overview 11

    Profiling With Shark 45

    Operations-Based Parallelization...53

    The Good and Bad of Distributed Objects...56

    Holistic Optimization...60

    Multithreaded Optimization in ChemicalBurn 82

    Mac OS X Process Memory Statistics 123

    Intro to Grand Central Dispatch, Part I: Basics and Dispatch Queues 162

    Intro to Grand Central Dispatch, Part II: Multi-Core Performance 169

    Intro to Grand Central Dispatch, Part IV: Odds and Ends 179

    GCD Practicum..183

    A GCD Case Study: Building an HTTP Server..256

    Background Timers..419

Welcome back to another Friday Q&A. This week I continue the discussion of Grand Central Dispatch from the past two weeks. In the last two weeks I mainly focused on dispatch queues. This week I'm going to examine dispatch sources, how they work, and how to use them.

Note that I assume you've already read the first two posts in this series. The first post is particularly important, the second one less so. If you have not, go read them now.

Before I go any further, there's been some great news this week: GCD has been open sourced! This is a very nice move on Apple's part. The source is relatively clean and very interesting to read through.

What Are Dispatch Sources
In short, a dispatch source is an object which monitors for some type of event. When the event occurs, it automatically schedules a block for execution on a dispatch queue.

That's kind of vague. What kind of events are we talking about?

Here is the full list of events supported by GCD in 10.6:

1. Mach port send right state changes.
2. Mach port receive right state changes.
3. External process state change.

4. File descriptor ready for read.
5. File descriptor ready for write.
6. Filesystem node event.
7. POSIX signal.
8. Custom timer.
9. Custom event.

That's a lot of useful stuff. It's basically everything kqueue supports, plus mach ports, plus built-in support for timers (instead of having to build your own using the timeout parameter), plus custom events.

Custom Events

Most of these events are pretty much self explanatory, but you may be wondering what a custom event is. In short, this is an event which you signal yourself by calling the dispatch_source_merge_data function.

This is a bit of an odd name for a function that signals an event. The reason it's named this way is because GCD will automatically coalesce multiple events that happen before the event handler has a chance to run. You can "merge" data into the dispatch source as many times as you want, and if the dispatch queue was busy for this whole period, GCD will only invoke the event handler once.

Two types of custom events are available, DISPATCH_SOURCE_TYPE_DATA_ADD and DISPATCH_SOURCE_TYPE_DATA_OR. A custom event source has an unsigned long data attribute, and you also pass an unsigned long to dispatch_source_merge_data. When using the _ADD variant, events are coalesced by adding all of the numbers together. When using the _OR variant, events are coalesced by doing a logical or. When the event handler executes, it can access the current value using dispatch_source_get_data, and the data is then reset to 0.

Let's look at a scenario where this could be useful. Imagine some asynchronous code performing some work that needs to update a progress bar. Since the main thread is just another dispatch queue to GCD, we can push the GUI work onto the main queue. However, there may be a lot of events, and we don't want to make redundant updates to the GUI; it's much better to coalesce all of the changes as much as possible if the main thread is busy with other work.

Dispatch sources are perfect for this, using the DISPATCH_SOURCE_TYPE_DATA_ADD type. We can merge the amount of work done, and then the main thread code can find out how much work has been performed since the last event, and update the progress indicator by that amount.

Enough talk, here's some code:

```
dispatch_source_t source =
dispatch_source_create(DISPATCH_SOURCE_TYPE_DATA_ADD, 0,
0, dispatch_get_main_queue());
dispatch_source_set_event_handler(source, ^{
    [progressIndicator
incrementBy:dispatch_source_get_data(source)];
});
dispatch_resume(source);

dispatch_apply([array count], globalQueue, ^(size_t index)
{
    // do some work on data at index
    dispatch_source_merge_data(source, 1);
});
```

(I want to make one note about this code, about something that stymied me to no end when I first started working with dispatch sources. It bothered me enough that I'm going to put it in bold. **Dispatch sources always start out suspended! You must resume them after creating them if you want events to be delivered!**)

Assuming you've configured the progress indicator to have the correct min/max value, this will all work perfectly. The data will be processed in parallel. As each chunk of data finishes, it signals the dispatch source and adds 1 to the dispatch source data, which we treat as the number of work units completed. The event handler increments the progress indicator by the number of work units that have been completed since the last time it ran. If the main thread is idle and work units complete slowly, the event handler will be called for every work unit completion, giving real time results. If the main thread is busy or work units complete quickly, completion events will be coalesced and the progress indicator will only be updated one time each time the main thread becomes available to process it.

At this point you may be thinking, this all sounds great, but what if I don't *want* my events to be coalesced? Sometimes you just want every signal to cause an action, without any smarts going on behind the scenes. Well, this is actually really easy, you just need to think a bit outside the box. If you want every signal to cause an action, use `dispatch_async` instead of a dispatch source. That's what it does, after all: schedules a block to be executed on the queue in question. In fact, the only reason to use a dispatch source instead of `dispatch_async` is to take advantage of coalescing.

Built-In Events

That's how to use a custom event, how about a built-in event? Let's look at an example of reading from standard input using GCD:

```
dispatch_queue_t globalQueue =
dispatch_get_global_queue(DISPATCH_QUEUE_PRIORITY_DEFAULT,
0);
dispatch_source_t stdinSource =
dispatch_source_create(DISPATCH_SOURCE_TYPE_READ,
STDIN_FILENO, 0, globalQueue);
dispatch_source_set_event_handler(stdinSource, ^{
    char buf[1024];
    int len = read(STDIN_FILENO, buf, sizeof(buf));
    if(len > 0)
        NSLog(@"Got data from stdin: %.*s", len, buf);
});
dispatch_resume(stdinSource);
```

This is pretty easy! Since we used a global queue, the handler automatically runs in the background, in parallel to the rest of the application, meaning an automatic parallel speed boost if the application is doing anything else at the time the event comes in.

This also has a nice benefit over the standard UNIX way of doing things in that there's no need to write a loop. With typical calls to `read`, you always have to be wary because it can return less data than requested, and can also suffer from transient "errors" like `EINTR` (interrupted system call). With GCD, you can just bail out in those cases and not do anything. If you leave unread data on the file descriptor, GCD will just invoke your handler a second time.

For standard input it's not a problem, but for other file descriptors you need to consider how to clean up once you're done reading from (or writing to) the descriptor. You must not close the descriptor while the dispatch source is still active. If another file descriptor is created (perhaps from another thread) and happens to get the same number, your dispatch source will suddenly be reading from (or writing to) something it shouldn't be. This will not be fun to debug.

The way to properly implement cleanup is to use `dispatch_source_set_cancel_handler` and give it a block which closes your file descriptor. You can then use `dispatch_source_cancel` to cancel the dispatch source, causing the handler to be invoked and the file descriptor to be closed.

Using other dispatch source types is much the same. In general, you give the identifier of the source (mach port, file descriptor, process ID, etc.) as the dispatch source handle. The mask argument is usually unused, but for `DISPATCH_SOURCE_TYPE_PROC` indicates what kind of process events you're interested in receiving. Then just provide a handler, resume the source, and off you go. These dispatch sources also provide source-specific data which can be accessed using the `dispatch_source_get_data` function. For example, file descriptors will give the rough number of bytes available on the descriptor as the dispatch source data. Process sources will give a mask of events which occurred since the last call. For a complete listing of what the data means for each type of source, see the man page.

Timers

Timer events are a bit different. They don't use the handle/mask arguments, but instead use a separate function, `dispatch_source_set_timer`, to configure the timer. This function takes three separate parameters to control when the timer fires:

The `start` parameter controls when the timer first fires. This parameter is of type `dispatch_time_t`, which is an opaque type that you can't manipulate directly. The functions `dispatch_time` and `dispatch_walltime` can be used to create them, and the constants `DISPATCH_TIME_NOW` and `DISPATCH_TIME_FOREVER` can be used if those are the values you're after.

The `interval` argument is an integer and is self explanatory. The `leeway` argument is an interesting one. This argument tells the system how much precision you want on your timer firing. Timers are never guaranteed to be absolutely 100% precise, but this argument lets you tell the system how hard you want it to try. If you want a timer to fire every 5 seconds and be as exact as possible, you would pass 0. On the other hand, consider a periodic task like checking for new e-mail. You want to check every 10 minutes, but this doesn't have to be exact. You might pass a leeway of 60 seconds, telling the system that you'll accept the timer running up to 60 seconds later than the scheduled time.

What's the point of this? In short, reduced power consumption. It's more energy efficient if the OS can let the CPU sleep for as long as possible, and then accomplish a bunch of things at once when it wakes up, rather than cycling between sleep and wake constantly to accomplish tasks in a spread-out manner. By giving a large leeway to your timer, you allow the system to lump your timer with other actions in order to group tasks together like this.

Conclusion

Now you know how to use GCD's dispatch source facilities to monitor file descriptors, run timers, coalesce custom events, and other similar activities. Because dispatch sources are fully integrated with dispatch queues, you can use any dispatch queue you have available. You can have a dispatch source run its handler on the main thread, in parallel on one of the global queues, or serialized with respect to a particular module of your program by using a custom queue.

Friday Q&A 2009-09-18: Intro to Grand Central Dispatch, Part IV: Odds and Ends

Related Articles

    Multithreaded Programming and Parallelism Overview 11

    Profiling With Shark 45

    Operations-Based Parallelization 53

    The Good and Bad of Distributed Objects 56

    Holistic Optimization 60

    Multithreaded Optimization in ChemicalBurn 82

    Mac OS X Process Memory Statistics 123

    Intro to Grand Central Dispatch, Part I: Basics and Dispatch Queues 162

    Intro to Grand Central Dispatch, Part II: Multi-Core Performance 169

    Intro to Grand Central Dispatch, Part III: Dispatch Sources 174

    GCD Practicum 183

    A GCD Case Study: Building an HTTP Server 256

    Background Timers 419

It's that time of the week again. Over the past three weeks I've introduced you to the major pieces of Grand Central Dispatch, an exciting new API for parallel processing and event handling in Snow Leopard. The first week I covered basic concepts and dispatch queues. The second week I discussed how to use dispatch queues for parallel processing on multi-core computers. The third week I covered GCD's event handling system. This week I'm going to cover various odds and ends which I didn't get to before: dispatch queue suspension and targeting, semaphores, and one-time initialization.

As with the previous weeks, I will assume that you've read all of the previous articles before reading this one, and are thus familiar with all aspects of GCD discussed up to this point. If you have not already read those articles, please do so now.

Dispatch Queue Suspension
Dispatch queues can be suspended and resumed at will. To suspend, use the `dispatch_suspend` function, and to resume, use `dispatch_resume`. These work pretty much the way you'd expect them to. Note that they also work on dispatch sources.

One caveat to dispatch queue suspension is that suspension is block-granular. In other words, suspending a queue does *not* suspend the currently executing block. Instead what happens is that the block is allowed to run to completion, and then no further blocks are allowed to run until the queue (or source) is resumed.

One final note, straight from the man page: you *must* resume a queue/source before destroying it if you have previously suspended it.

Dispatch Queue Targeting
All custom dispatch queues have the concept of a target queue. In essence, a custom dispatch queue doesn't actually execute any work, but passes work to its target queue for execution. Normally the target queue of a custom queue is the default-priority global queue.

The target queue of a custom queue can be set by using the `dispatch_set_target_queue` function. You can pass it any other dispatch queue, even another custom queue, so long as you never create a cycle. This function can be used to set the priority of a custom queue by simply setting its target queue to a different global queue. If you set your custom queue's target to be the low priority global queue, all work on your custom queue will execute with low priority, and the same with the high priority global queue.

Another potential use of this is to target a custom queue to the main queue. This will cause all blocks submitted to that custom queue to run on the main thread. The advantage of doing this instead of simply using the main queue directly is that your custom queue can be independently suspended and resumed, and could potentially be retargeted onto a global queue afterwards, although you'll have to be careful to ensure that all blocks which run after that point can tolerate being away from the main thread!

Yet another potential use is to target custom queues to other custom queues. This will force multiple queues to be serialized with respect to each other, and essentially creates a group of queues which can all be suspended and resumed together by suspending/resuming the queue that they target. For a way that this could be used, imagine an application which is scanning a set of directories and loading the files within. In order to avoid disk contention, you want to make sure that only one file loading task is active for each physical disk. However, multiple files can be read from physically separate disks simultaneously. To make this happen, all you have to do is build a dispatch queue structure which mirrors your disk structure.

First, you would scan the system and find the disks, and create a custom dispatch queue for each one. Then you would scan the filesystems and create a custom queue for each one of those as well, pointing their target queues at the queue of the appropriate disk. Finally, each directory scanner can have its own queue as well, pointing the target at the filesystem on which the directory resides. The directory scanners can enumerate their directories and submit a block for each file directly to their own queue. Due to how the system is set up, this will inherently serialize all access to each physical disk while allowing parallel access to separate disks, all without any manual intervention beyond the initial queue setup process.

Semaphores

Dispatch semaphores work just like any other semaphore and if you're familiar with semaphores from other multithreading systems, this will look entirely familiar to you.

A semaphore is basically an integer which has an initial count and supports two operations: signal and wait. When a semaphore is signaled, the count is incremented. When a thread waits on a semaphore, it will block, if necessary, until the count is greater than 0, and then decrement the count.

Dispatch semaphores are created using `dispatch_semaphore_create`, signaled using `dispatch_semaphore_signal`, and waited on using `dispatch_semaphore_wait`. The man page for these functions shows two good examples of how to use semaphores, one involving synchronizing work completion and one involving controlling access to a finite resource. Rather than make up my own, inferior examples, I encourage you to simply read the man page to see some potential uses for these objects.

One-Time Initialization

GCD also has support for one-time initialization, which if you're familiar with pthreads is pretty much the same as the `pthread_once` call. The main advantage of the GCD approach is that it uses blocks instead of function pointers, allowing for a more natural flow of code.

A major use of this is for lazily initializing singletons or other shared data in a thread-safe manner. The typical singleton initialization technique looks like this, for singletons that need to be thread safe:

```
+ (id)sharedWhatever
{
    static Whatever *whatever = nil;
    @synchronized([Whatever class])
    {
        if(!whatever)
            whatever = [[Whatever alloc] init];
    }
    return whatever;
}
```

This is fine, but expensive; every call to `+sharedWhatever` incurs the expense of taking a lock, even though that lock is basically only needed once. There are fancier ways to approach this, using things like double-checked locking or atomic operations, but they're difficult and extremely error-prone.

Using GCD you can rewrite the above method using `dispatch_once` like so:

```
+ (id)sharedWhatever
{
    static dispatch_once_t pred;
    static Whatever *whatever = nil;
    dispatch_once(&pred, ^{
        whatever = [[Whatever alloc] init];
    });
    return whatever;
}
```

This is actually slightly simpler than the @synchronized method, and GCD makes sure to do these checks in a fast manner. It ensures that the code in the block will have run before any threads can pass beyond the call to dispatch_once, but doesn't force code to take the hit of synchronization every time it uses this function. In fact, if you look at the header where this function is declared, you'll discover that the current implementation is actually a macro which performs the initial test inline, meaning that you don't even incur *function call* overhead, much less synchronization overhead, for the common case.

Conclusion

That wraps up this series on Grand Central Dispatch. This week you saw how to suspend, resume, and retarget dispatch queues, and some uses for these facilities. You also saw how to use dispatch semaphores and one-time initialization facilities. In previous weeks you saw how to manage dispatch objects, how to create/access and use the different types of dispatch queues available for different tasks, strategies for taking advantage of multi-core systems, and how to monitor for events using GCD's events system. Now you have the complete picture of how GCD operates and how to use it, so go out there and write some great new software with it!

Friday Q&A 2009-09-25: GCD Practicum

Related Articles
- Multithreaded Programming and Parallelism Overview 11
- Profiling With Shark 45
- Operations-Based Parallelization 53
- The Good and Bad of Distributed Objects 56
- Holistic Optimization 60
- Multithreaded Optimization in ChemicalBurn 82
- Mac OS X Process Memory Statistics 123
- Intro to Grand Central Dispatch, Part I: Basics and Dispatch Queues 162
- Intro to Grand Central Dispatch, Part II: Multi-Core Performance 169
- Intro to Grand Central Dispatch, Part III: Dispatch Sources 174
- Intro to Grand Central Dispatch, Part IV: Odds and Ends 179
- A GCD Case Study: Building an HTTP Server 256
- Background Timers 419

Welcome back to another Friday Q&A. I'm off to C4 today (hope to see you there!) but I've prepared this in advance so everyone stuck at home (or worse, work) can at least have something interesting to read. Over the past four weeks I've introduced Grand Central Dispatch and discussed the various facilities it provides. Part I talked about the basics of GCD and how to use dispatch queues. Part II discussed how to use GCD to extract more performance from multi-core machines. Part III discussed GCD's event dispatching mechanism, and Part IV took care of various odds and ends that I hadn't covered before. This week I'm going to examine a practical application of using GCD to speed up the production of thumbnails for a large quantity of images, a topic suggested by Willie Abrams.

Overview
I'm going to walk through the parallelization of this program in four steps. The first step will be the basic serialized program, and the following steps work through building it into a fully parallel program using GCD. If you'd like to follow along, you can get the full source code for all four steps. Don't run `imagegcd2.m` though. You'll see why in a bit.

The Original Program
The program that we're going to work with is a simple thing that goes through the contents of `~/Pictures` and generates thumbnails for everything inside. It's a pure command-line program, albeit using Cocoa to do most of the work. This is what its main function looks like:

```
int main(int argc, char **argv)
{
    NSAutoreleasePool *outerPool = [NSAutoreleasePool new];
    
    NSApplicationLoad();
    
    NSString *destination = @"/tmp/imagegcd";
    [[NSFileManager defaultManager] removeItemAtPath: destination error: NULL];
    [[NSFileManager defaultManager] createDirectoryAtPath: destination
                                  withIntermediateDirectories: YES
                                                   attributes: nil
                                                        error: NULL];
    
    
    Start();
    
    NSString *dir = [@"~/Pictures" stringByExpandingTildeInPath];
    NSDirectoryEnumerator *enumerator = [[NSFileManager defaultManager] enumeratorAtPath: dir];
    int count = 0;
    for(NSString *path in enumerator)
    {
        NSAutoreleasePool *innerPool = [NSAutoreleasePool new];
        
        if([[[path pathExtension] lowercaseString] isEqual: @"jpg"])
        {
            path = [dir stringByAppendingPathComponent: path];
            
            NSData *data = [NSData dataWithContentsOfFile: path];
            if(data)
            {
                NSData *thumbnailData = ThumbnailDataForData(data);
                if(thumbnailData)
                {
                    NSString *thumbnailName = [NSString stringWithFormat: @"%d.jpg", count++];
```

```
                NSString *thumbnailPath = [destination
stringByAppendingPathComponent: thumbnailName];
                [thumbnailData writeToFile:
thumbnailPath atomically: NO];
            }
          }
       }

       [innerPool release];
    }

    End();

    [outerPool release];
}
```

For the full listing including all of the auxiliary functions, please refer to the companion source code download. This program is `imagegcd1.m`. The important parts are all here, though. `Start` and `End` are just simple timing functions using `gettimeofday`. `ThumbnailDataForData` uses Cocoa to load the data into an image, shrink it proportionally to be no larger than 320x320, and then encodes the result as JPEG.

Naïve Parallelization

At first glance this looks pretty easy to parallelize. Each iteration through the loop can be pushed onto a GCD global queue. We can wait for them all to finish at the end by using a dispatch group. One last trick: to ensure that each iteration still gets a unique number for its filename, we'll use `OSAtomicIncrement32` to atomically increment `count`. This is what the new code looks like:

```
dispatch_queue_t globalQueue = 
dispatch_get_global_queue(0, 0);
dispatch_group_t group = dispatch_group_create();
__block uint32_t count = -1;
for(NSString *path in enumerator)
{
    dispatch_group_async(group, globalQueue,
BlockWithAutoreleasePool(^{
        if([[[path pathExtension] lowercaseString] 
isEqual: @"jpg"])
        {
            NSString *fullPath = [dir 
stringByAppendingPathComponent: path];
            
            NSData *data = [NSData dataWithContentsOfFile: 
fullPath];
            if(data)
            {
                NSData *thumbnailData = 
ThumbnailDataForData(data);
                if(thumbnailData)
                {
                    NSString *thumbnailName = [NSString 
stringWithFormat: @"%d.jpg", 
OSAtomicIncrement32(&count;)];
                    NSString *thumbnailPath = [destination 
stringByAppendingPathComponent: thumbnailName];
                    [thumbnailData writeToFile: 
thumbnailPath atomically: NO];
                }
            }
        }
    });
}
dispatch_group_wait(group, DISPATCH_TIME_FOREVER);
```

This one is imagegcd2.m. But *don't run it!*

If you ignored my warning and ran it anyway, you're probably just reloading this page after rebooting your computer. If you haven't run it, what happens (if you have a lot of pictures, at least) is that your computer locks up and you probably can't fix it unless you wait much longer than you'd really like to.

The Problem

What's causing all this trouble? The problem lies in GCD's smarts. GCD runs tasks on a global thread pool whose size is scaled in response to system load. For example, my computer has four cores, and so if I load up GCD with work, GCD will run four worker threads to load every core. If something else on my computer starts doing work, GCD will scale back a bit to give the other task some room.

However, GCD can also *increase* the number of active threads. It will do this if one of the worker threads blocks. Imagine these four worker threads running and then suddenly one of them does something like, oh, let's say, read a file. It goes off to wait for the disk, and your cores are being under-utilized. GCD will see this situation and spawn another worker thread to fill the gap.

Now, think about what happens here. The main loop is pushing jobs onto the global queue extremely quickly. GCD will start off with a few worker threads and start popping jobs off the queue. These jobs perform a trifling amount of work up front and then immediately they go off and read a file from the disk. The slow, spinning disk.

And let's not forget another important property of the disk: unless you have an SSD or a fancy RAID, *they get substantially slower under contention.*

These first four jobs all hit the disk at the same time, which goes crazy trying to fill all four requests at once. GCD, which only looks at CPU usage, sees that the CPU cores are sitting mostly idle and starts spawning more worker threads. These threads also slam into the disk wall, causing GCD to spawn yet more threads, etc.

Eventually the file reads begin to complete. Now, instead of four threads for the four cores, there are hundreds. GCD will scale back if there are too many worker threads using CPU time, but it's limited in when it can scale back. It can't kill worker threads in the middle of a job, and can't even pause them. It has to wait until an entire job has completed before it can kill the thread that job is on. All of these pending in-flight jobs prevent GCD from reducing the worker thread count.

All these hundreds of threads start to finish reading their image data and begin to process. They get in each other's way on the CPU as well, although the CPU handles contention much better than the disk. The trouble is, the first thing these threads do once they have the file data is decode it. If you have a lot of JPEGs, this image data is going to expand by a factor of 10 or more. With hundreds of these things in flight, you'll start to blow out your memory. What happens when you run out of physical RAM? More disk usage!

Now you have a vicious feedback cycle. Disk contention causes more worker threads, which causes more memory usage, which causes more disk contention. The process runs away until GCD hits its limit of 512 worker threads. With typical picture sizes, 512 in-flight jobs is more than enough to send your system into swap hell from which it will take a long time to recover. Quite likely you won't even be able to kill the job for quite some time.

This is something you really have to watch out for when using GCD. GCD is great for limiting the number of concurrent jobs for CPU usage, but it will do nothing about contention over other resources. If your jobs do IO or anything else that could block for a while, you need to beware of this problem.

The Fix
The root of this whole problem was IO contention leading to runaway feedback. Remove the contention, remove the problem.

GCD makes this easy with custom queues. Custom queues are inherently serialized. If we create a custom queue just for IO and put all file reading/writing onto that queue, then the disk will only be hit up for one file at a time and the contention disappears.

Here's the main loop of our program redone to use an IO queue:

```
dispatch_queue_t globalQueue =
dispatch_get_global_queue(0, 0);
dispatch_queue_t ioQueue =
dispatch_queue_create("com.mikeash.imagegcd.io", NULL);
dispatch_group_t group = dispatch_group_create();
__block uint32_t count = -1;
for(NSString *path in enumerator)
{
    if([[[path pathExtension] lowercaseString] isEqual:
@"jpg"])
    {
        NSString *fullPath = [dir
stringByAppendingPathComponent: path];

        dispatch_group_async(group, ioQueue,
BlockWithAutoreleasePool(^{
            NSData *data = [NSData dataWithContentsOfFile:
fullPath];
            if(data)
                dispatch_group_async(group, globalQueue,
BlockWithAutoreleasePool(^{
                    NSData *thumbnailData =
ThumbnailDataForData(data);
                    if(thumbnailData)
                    {
                        NSString *thumbnailName =
[NSString stringWithFormat: @"%d.jpg",

OSAtomicIncrement32(&count;)];
                        NSString *thumbnailPath =
[destination stringByAppendingPathComponent:
thumbnailName];
                        dispatch_group_async(group,
ioQueue, BlockWithAutoreleasePool(^{
                            [thumbnailData writeToFile:
thumbnailPath atomically: NO];
                        }));
                    }
                }));
        }));
    }
}
dispatch_group_wait(group, DISPATCH_TIME_FOREVER);
```

And this one is `imagegcd3.m`. It's great how easy GCD makes it to push different parts of a task onto different queues with some simple nesting. This one will behave fairly well... most of the time.

The problem is that it's inherently unstable because the different parts are not synchronized. The flow of data in this code looks like this:

```
Main Thread            IO Queue              Concurrent Queue

find paths   ------>   read     ------------>  process
                                                 ...
                       write    <-----------   process
```

The arrows in that diagram are *non-blocking* and will simply buffer the objects being moved around.

Now imagine a machine where the disk is fast enough to read files faster than the CPU can process them. This isn't all that hard to imagine: although the CPU is much faster, it's also doing *much* more work. The data read from the disk begins to pile up in the queue. This data takes up memory, possibly substantial amounts of memory if you have a lot of big pictures.

Then you run out of physical RAM and begin to swap.

This can lead to another runaway feedback loop like the first one. If anything causes a worker thread to block, GCD will spin off a new one, which will immediately start trying to allocate a bunch of memory and block because of the ongoing memory pressure. GCD will spin off more jobs, causing more memory pressure, and you're back in swap hell.

What's interesting about this feedback is that, unlike the first GCD attempt, it's self-regulating to some extent. As IO contention goes through the roof, the IO queue will come to a halt, and won't make any significant progress until the situation has regained sanity. Once it does, you're back to low memory usage and good throughput until the buffered data builds up too far again.

End result: the program alternates between smooth processing and being bogged down.

Note that if the disk is slower the same problem can still occur because the thumbnails will be buffered at the end of the run, but it's likely to be much less severe because the quantity of data is so much smaller.

Really Fixing the Problem
Since the problem with the last attempt was a lack of synchronization between the different phases of the operation, let's synchronize them. The simple way to do this is to use a semaphore to limit the number of jobs in flight at any given time.

One question remains: how many jobs should we allow?

Obviously it should scale with the number of CPU cores in the system, because we want to take advantage of whatever is available. Simply limiting to the number of CPU cores is a bad idea, though, because much of each job is IO. And it can't be too high, because then we'll run out of memory.

I decided on having twice the number of jobs as CPU cores. My reasoning is that this will scale up to the point where IO takes as long as processing. If IO takes longer than processing, then IO will be the bottleneck anyway, and so there's no sense in having more concurrent jobs than this. If IO takes significantly less time than processing, then GCD will automatically keep the number of worker threads low enough to ensure minimal contention on the CPU.

This is what the main loop now looks like:

```
dispatch_queue_t ioQueue =
dispatch_queue_create("com.mikeash.imagegcd.io", NULL);

int cpuCount = [[NSProcessInfo processInfo]
processorCount];
dispatch_semaphore_t jobSemaphore =
dispatch_semaphore_create(cpuCount * 2);

dispatch_group_t group = dispatch_group_create();
__block uint32_t count = -1;
for(NSString *path in enumerator)
{
    WithAutoreleasePool(^{
        if([[[path pathExtension] lowercaseString]
isEqual: @"jpg"])
        {
            NSString *fullPath = [dir
stringByAppendingPathComponent: path];

            dispatch_semaphore_wait(jobSemaphore,
DISPATCH_TIME_FOREVER);

            dispatch_group_async(group, ioQueue,
BlockWithAutoreleasePool(^{
                NSData *data = [NSData
dataWithContentsOfFile: fullPath];
                dispatch_group_async(group, globalQueue,
BlockWithAutoreleasePool(^{
                    NSData *thumbnailData =
ThumbnailDataForData(data);
                    if(thumbnailData)
                    {
                        NSString *thumbnailName =
[NSString stringWithFormat: @"%d.jpg",
OSAtomicIncrement32(&count;)];
                        NSString *thumbnailPath =
[destination stringByAppendingPathComponent:
thumbnailName];
                        dispatch_group_async(group,
ioQueue, BlockWithAutoreleasePool(^{
                            [thumbnailData writeToFile:
thumbnailPath atomically: NO];

dispatch_semaphore_signal(jobSemaphore);
```

```
            }));
        }
        else
dispatch_semaphore_signal(jobSemaphore);
            }));
        }));
        }
    });
}
dispatch_group_wait(group, DISPATCH_TIME_FOREVER);
```

And now we finally have a program which runs smoothly and processes quickly.

Benchmarking

I obtained the following runtimes, on a library of 7913 pictures:

Program	Time (seconds)
imagegcd1.m	984
imagegcd2.m	did not run
imagegcd3.m	300
imagegcd4.m	279

Note that, because I am lazy, I did not shut off all other programs before I ran this, so the program was not able to completely monopolize the CPUs. Given this, the total speedup of 3.5 is quite good for my 4 CPU cores.

It's interesting that version 3 performed as well as it did. I did observe it exhibiting the cycling behavior I discussed, but not too often. Most likely this is because my machine has 15GB of RAM. On a less well endowed system it's likely to perform substantially worse. I observed it using up to 10GB of RAM at one point. If I compile it as 32-bit then it rapidly runs out of virtual memory and crashes. Version 4 never uses any significant amout of RAM.

Conclusion

GCD is a fantastic piece of technology and does a lot of useful things, but it can't do everything for you. In particular, concurrent jobs which perform IO and have the potential to use a lot of memory must be managed carefully. Even so, the facilities that GCD provides make it easy to construct a system which will not overwhelm the computer's resources.

Friday Q&A 2009-10-02: Care and Feeding of Singletons

Related Articles

Thread Safety in OS X System Frameworks	24
The Good and Bad of Distributed Objects	56
Intro to the Objective-C Runtime	67
Objective-C Messaging	73
Objective-C Message Forwarding	77
Objective-C Class Loading and Initialization	115
Dangerous Cocoa Calls	236
Probing Cocoa With PyObjC	240
Using Accessors in Init and Dealloc	246
NSRunLoop Internals	273
NSNotificationQueue	284
Method Replacement for Fun and Profit	297
Error Returns with Continuation Passing Style	303
Comparison of Objective-C Enumeration Techniques	369
Implementing Fast Enumeration	373
Implementing a Custom Slider	382
Dealing with Retain Cycles	392
What Every Apple Programmer Should Know	401
Leopard Collection Classes	405
Implementing Equality and Hashing	412
Zeroing Weak References in Objective-C	428
Implementing NSCoding	459
Defensive Programming in Cocoa	468

It's time for another Friday Q&A. I hope everyone who had a chance to go to C4 had a good time and is back home safe and sound. This week I'm going to discuss singletons, both how to make them and when to use them, as suggested by Jon Trainer.

What Is It?
Most of you probably know this already, but for the sake of completeness, a singleton is an object which is restricted to be the only instance of its class. In other words, within any given process, you have the concept of *the* Foo, rather than *a* Foo.

Benefits
Why would you use a singleton instead of a regular class? There are a few basic reasons:

1. **Global access:** A singleton is essentially shared throughout the entire program, making it easier to coordinate activities. A major example of this in Cocoa is `NSNotificationCenter`.
2. **Resource management:** Having a single instance of a class is appropriate if that class represents an entity which is inherently singular. An example of this in Cocoa is `NSApplication`.
3. **Grouping functionality:** Sometimes you have a lot of similar functionality that logically goes together but which doesn't necessarily fit into the object model because there's no long-term state. By using a singleton you simplify access to this functionality. `NSWorkspace` is an example of this usage of a singleton in Cocoa.
4. **Lazy initialization:** Properly-written singleton classes aren't instantiated until something asks for them, meaning that the resources occupied by the singleton aren't allocated until they're needed.

Downsides

Singletons aren't always appropriate. (In fact, they're almost always not appropriate. Just look at the proportion of singletons to normal classes in any given program.) In general you should not use one unless you need it, but there are some specific pitfalls to look out for:

1. **Shared global state:** Singletons are inherently globally accessible, which means that any state which exists as part of the singleton can be accessed and potentially changed from any part of the program. Good encapsulation of singleton state can help with this a lot, but if you're not careful then the problem can be much like that of global variables. This can be particularly vicious in a multithreaded environment. Many Cocoa singletons suffer from not being thread safe and their global accessibility makes them inherently limited to only being used from the main thread.
2. **Over-specialized code:** You thought there would only be one, so you made a singleton around it. Now there are two. All of your code assumes that there is only one. Time for a big, painful rewrite.

How to Make One

At its most basic, a singleton is implemented like this:

```
+ (id)sharedFoo
{
    static Foo *foo = nil;
    if(!foo)
        foo = [[self alloc] init];
    return foo;
}
```

That's it! You're done!

Right about now, a bunch of people are thinking back to a certain Apple document on singletons which shows a much more complicated implementation. There are basically two advantages to Apple's version which this doesn't have.

1. **Thread safety:** Apple's version correctly deals with the case where multiple threads try to access the singleton before it's been created.
2. **Programmer safety:** Apple's version tries to cover for a lot of dumb mistakes a programmer might make, like incorrectly releasing a singleton.

Thread safety is useful but not always necessary. Programmer safety is, in my opinion, counterproductive. Apple's approach, of building a singleton which can't be destroyed by accident and which intercepts attempts to allocate a second instance, covers up errors rather than fixing them. It's much better to trap and eliminate the bad code rather than render it harmless. For example, instead of overriding `release` to do nothing, override `dealloc` to log an error and abort the program.

Furthermore, it's not always necessary to really strictly enforce singleton-ness. `NSFileManager` is a good example of this from Cocoa. Through 10.4 it was a singleton, and not thread safe and thus could only be used on the main thread. Starting in 10.5, Apple allowed the creation of separate instances which could then be safely used on other threads. Your code might well want to do the same thing. Often, providing the shared globally-accessible instance is the major benefit of having a singleton, and there's no need to prohibit other instances being created on the side.

This brings up one tip I want to mention regarding singletons: *always implement a dealloc method and keep it up to date*. With a singleton, it's tempting to forget about releasing resources because it will live for the life of the program. But it's much easier to write code to release resources as you write the rest of the code than it is to add it in later, and you'll be glad you did if you ever decide to make your singleton no longer be single.

Thread Safe Singletons

What about when thread safety *is* necessary?

One really simple way to deal with this is to simply toss in a lock, like so:

```
+ (id)sharedFoo
{
    static Foo *foo = nil;
    @synchronized([Foo class])
    {
        if(!foo)
            foo = [[self alloc] init];
    }
    return foo;
}
```

Now your singleton can be safely accessed from multiple threads.

Note: this makes it safe to retrieve the shared singleton from multiple threads, but does not automatically make it safe to *use* it. Making the singleton's code thread safe is up to you!

This code is kind of slow, though. Taking a lock is somewhat expensive. Making it more painful is the fact that, the vast majority of the time, the lock is pointless. The lock is only needed when `foo` is `nil`, which basically only happens once. After the singleton is initialized, the need for the lock is gone, but the lock itself remains.

One fix for this is to take advantage of the Objective-C runtime and use the `+initialize` method instead:

```
static Foo *gSharedFoo;

+ (void)initialize
{
    if(self == [Foo class])
        gSharedFoo = [[self alloc] init];
}

+ (id)sharedFoo
{
    return gSharedFoo;
}
```

The runtime takes care of all the nasty locking stuff for you, and ensures that `+initialize` always runs before `+sharedFoo` can execute. The only downside to this approach is that `+initialize` will run if *any* message is sent to your class, possibly initializing the singleton earlier than necessary.

Double-Checked Locking
If you search on the above phrase you'll find a bunch of web pages talking about how this technique is a bad idea. And it is, for platform-independent code. However, if you can assume some knowledge of your target platform (and hey, we're all doing OS X development here) then it can be done safely.

The basic concept of double-checked locking is to have two copies of the if statement that checks to see if the singleton has been initialized. An outer if statement checks to see if the singleton is initialized. If it is, then return it, no lock taken. If it's not, then take the lock *and check the singleton again*. This ensures that all threads which might try to initialize the singleton are synchronized via the lock.

The problem with this approach is out-of-order memory access, either generated by the compiler or performed by the CPU. For more information on this, you can read my article on using the `volatile` keyword in a multithreaded context.

The solution to the CPU side is to insert a memory barrier when writing and when reading. Memory barriers enforce in-order access to memory locations by the CPU. In OS X, a memory barrier function is available in the `libkern/OSAtomic.h` header, called `OSMemoryBarrier`. The solution to the compiler side is to use `volatile` on the shared variable.

Thus our double-checked locking singleton method looks like this:

```
+ (id)sharedFoo
{
    static Foo * volatile foo = nil;
    if(!foo)
    {
        @synchronized([Foo class])
        {
            if(!foo)
            {
                Foo *tmpFoo = [[self alloc] init];
                OSMemoryBarrier();
                foo = tmpFoo;
            }
        }
    }
    OSMemoryBarrier();
    return foo;
}
```

This is better than taking a lock every time, but we still have to pay for the memory barrier. It probably doesn't matter at all, and this smacks of premature optimization, but it grates to have that in there.

Grand Central Dispatch

If you can target 10.6+, Grand Central Dispatch provides an extremely fast one-time initialization API which is perfect for a singleton. Not only is it fast, but it's also extremely easy to use. It's a win all around!

Here's what the GCD solution looks like:

```
+ (id)sharedFoo
{
    static dispatch_once_t pred;
    static Foo *foo = nil;
    
    dispatch_once(&pred, ^{ foo = [[self alloc] init]; });
    return foo;
}
```

The `dispatch_once` function takes care of all the necessary locking and synchronization. It's actually a macro which expands to something much like the double-checked locking solution above. However, using some extremely underhanded trickery, it doesn't even need to take the hit of a memory barrier. In the common case, this code is a single if check followed by a return. Aside from the fact that it's examining two variables instead of one (an extremely small cost) it's as fast as the non-thread-safe version I started out with, and very nearly as simple. Nice!

Advanced Topics

There are a couple of interesting advanced techniques with singletons that I want to cover briefly. I won't go over how to build them, but think of them as exercises for the reader.

One such thing is an automatic singleton class. This would be a class which you subclass and which automatically provides all the necessary infrastructure to provide a singleton of that class. The superclass would have a method which returns (and creates, if necessary) the singleton instance of the subclass on which it was invoked. Managing the singletons would probably involve a global dictionary mapping classes to their singleton instances.

Another interesting variant, which I've never actually seen implemented, is a destroyable singleton. Rather than create a single shared instance which lives forever, the singleton accessor would not take ownership of the singleton object, and would allow it to be destroyed when all other code gives up ownership of it. In Cocoa, this would be accomplished by returning an autoreleased singleton, or when programming with garbage collection, by using a `__weak` global to store it. Making this thread safe, to ensure that duplicates aren't created but that old ones aren't resurrected as they're being destroyed, would be a challenge.

Conclusion

That wraps up this week's edition. Now you know all about singletons, probably far more than you wanted to know.

Friday Q&A 2009-10-09: Defensive Programming

Related Articles

    Defensive Programming in Cocoa 468

It's that time of the week again. This week I'm going to discuss defensive programming, a topic suggested by Ed Wynne.

Evolution of the Programmer
If you're like most programmers, your first enemy when learning to program was the compiler. You'd type in a perfectly good program, but the thing would spit out these cryptic errors at you. You'd go poring over the code looking for that missing semicolon or misspelled variable.

Eventually, you tamed the compiler. Your programs maybe didn't compile right away, but writing syntactically acceptable code became routine. Your goal then moved on to writing programs that behaved correctly. You put in 2+2 and it gave you 5, oops. Once you found the broken code and it gave you 4, you were overjoyed.

A lot of programmers stop here. There are plenty of refinements to be had at this level. They learn algorithms, data structures, and design patterns to help with the task of building a correct program. Writing correct programs, while not always easy, at least becomes more or less routine.

But there's one more level, one which many programmers aren't even really aware of. At that level, the goal is to write programs *which fail gracefully*. This takes even more thought and care than making programs which behave correctly, and this is what I want to address today.

What Happens If It Fails?
This question is the key to writing programs which fail gracefully. Let's take a fairly common line that you might find in any average Cocoa program:

```
NSData *data = [NSData dataWithContentsOfFile: path];
```

Cocoa makes this so easy that we can be lulled into a false sense of security. How much can go wrong from one line of code?

Actually, quite a lot:

1. **The file is unreadable:** Maybe the file doesn't exist at that path, maybe it exists but the permissions don't allow you to read it, etc.

2. **The file is truncated or empty:** Maybe the file got trashed by another program. Or by yours!
3. **The file contains an unexpected data format:** Especially possible for files outside your app bundle.
4. **The file contains unexpected data in the format you want:** Ditto.
5. **The file contains an enormous amount of data:** 2TB drives can be had for well under $200 now, and a single file could be enormous. What happens if the file you're pointing at is 2TB long?
6. **The file takes an unreasonable amount of time to read:** Network filesystems like AFP are extremely common these days, and networks can be slow.

How many of these failure modes does a typical Cocoa program actually handle in any sort of explicit fashion? Generally zero. Depending on the context, these failures could lead to a freeze, a crash, weird behavior, or nothing going wrong at all.

Even extremely mundane code can "fail". For example:

```
int x = y + z;
```

What happens if the sum of y + z is greater than INT_MAX, or less than INT_MIN? The result, while not a "failure" in the sense of a freeze or crash, may not be what the code expects.

Ways to Fail

There are a lot of ways that a program can respond to a failure. Ranked from worst to best:

1. Corrupt/delete user data
2. Crash/freeze
3. Fail silently
4. Display an error
5. Work around the failure

It should be obvious why #1 is the worst. No matter how much your program crashes or fails to do its job, the worst it can do is be useless. But if you destroy your user's data, then your program can actually acquire *negative* value. When he discovers the culprit, the user will wish he had never tried your program, and he will tell all of his friends about this.

Everything after #1 is acceptable to some degree. Working around the failure isn't always possible; what if the user is opening a file and the file isn't readable? Ideally, displaying an error is the worst that would ever happen. In reality, it's not practical to trap every failure so that you can display an error message.

Working Around Failures

How and whether this is possible will depend entirely on what you're doing, so I can't say much beyond generalities.

If there are multiple ways to accomplish the same task, then you can write code to try each way in sequence. It's pointless to do this if all the different ways funnel through the same mechanism in the end; there's little reason to fall back to `open`/`read` if your `NSData` file reader fails, for example. For a case where it's worthwhile, imagine saving a file with some user-provided metadata. You use that metadata to synthesize a useful filename. However, the synthesized filename may contain characters which are illegal on your target filesystem, and there's no way to know which characters are allowed in advance. Thus, if the file write fails, try it again with a more simplified filename.

Another example is when connecting to a network server. It's common for a server to advertise multiple addresses through a normal DNS entry or through ZeroConf. If your first attempt fails, try the other addresses before giving up. It's incredibly common, especially in a LAN environment with mixed IPv4/IPv6 addresses and ZeroConf advertisements, for half of a server's addresses to produce failures of some kind, and for the other half to work fine.

Occasionally it can be useful to simply retry the same operation more than once. Networking is a prime example of this. I can't count how many times I've loaded up Twitterrific on my iPhone and had it tell me that it couldn't connect to Twitter, only to have it work perfectly fine when I told it to try again. It would be great if it would try several times on its own before giving up.

Above all, make sure you test these fallback and retry paths! Many errors are rare, and it's not uncommon to have an error path which has never been executed. This can be fine, and even common, where your handler is just a log statement, but it's a very bad policy if you're actually doing real work there. If at all possible, set up unit tests to expose the error handling path. Even if you can't, be sure to at least manually test it after writing it to make sure that it works the way you want. An error handler which misbehaves is worse than one which simply logs the relevant information and gives up.

Displaying Errors
There's nothing complex here, it's just a bunch of annoying grunt work. Detect every useful error you can think of, and make it display an alert of some kind. Not much fun, and not much thought needed. The trick is that you can only do this for errors you anticipate, so you're limited.

Providing Diagnostics
When you're unable to work around the failure or display an error, you've gone beyond the realm of helping the user, but that doesn't mean that there's nothing else to do. Once you reach the point of crashing, freezing, or failing without an error message, you should consider how easy your code will be to debug.

As illustration, consider these two scenarios.

1. Your application crashes in a dealloc method called from NSPopAutoreleasePool called from the main event loop. No messages are logged.
2. Your application crashes in `abort()` after logging:
   ```
   Warning: couldn't read file /some/path: error: Error
   Domain=NSCocoaErrorDomain Code=260
   UserInfo=0x100605690 "The file "path" couldn't be
   opened because there is no such file." Underlying
   Error=(Error Domain=NSPOSIXErrorDomain Code=2 "The
   operation couldn't be completed. No such file or
   directory"
   assertion failure in -[SomeClass someMethod] line 42:
   fileData != nil, aborting
   ```

Your response to #1 is likely that nameless dread that we get when seeing a really difficult bug. Your response to #2 is, "Oh, I guess I should put a more intelligent handler in `someMethod`."

There are two big tricks to making your app be more like #2.

First, always check for errors. I'll say it again: *always check for errors*. You don't have to handle them intelligently, but at least log them when you get one that's unexpected, and consider aborting, depending on the circumstances.

I'll make an exception to this for calls which do adequate logging on their own, such as `malloc`. There's no point in trying to recover from a `malloc` failure on OS X, because by the time you detect the failure and try to recover, your process is likely to already be doomed. There's no need to do your own logging, because `malloc` itself does a good job of that. And finally there's no real need to even explicitly abort, because any `malloc` failure is virtually guaranteed to result in an instantaneous crash with a good stack trace.

Some of you may have heard of Steinbach's Rule, which goes: "Never test for an error condition you don't know how to handle." This rule is tongue in cheek, but is partially correct. You should always *check* for errors, but if you don't know how to handle them, then don't try. It's much better to have a program which produces clear logs and an obvious crash when something really unexpected happens than to have a program run a bunch of poorly thought out and poorly tested code to try to handle the error "properly" when you don't have a clear idea of what that actually means.

The second trick is to be liberal with asserts. The trick with asserts is that they should be used with conditions that you *know* must be true, but which are somehow doubtful. Don't use an assert for something that could definitely fail unless there's absolutely no way to continue execution afterwards. For example, this is not a good way to go:

```
int fd = open(...);
assert(fd >= 0);
```

You can easily have `open` fail, and you'll want better handling than just asserting and blowing up. This is the sort of thing you should be able to get back to the user in the form of a real error message somehow, even if it's not a very useful one. If the error message can't be useful, and the failure isn't considered "normal", consider logging more thorough information right at the site of failure so that the console logs will at least be informative to you.

On the other hand, this is a good way to use asserts:

```
void DoSomethingWithFileDescriptor(fd)
{
    assert(fd >= 0);
    ...
}
```

Many failures are not due to external events, like files being unavailable, but are simply an internal clash of assumptions or outright bugs. By sprinkling asserts around on the conditions you know to be true, you ensure that your program will fail in an informative fashion when it turns out that your assumptions have been violated somehow.

Conclusion
While these techniques are all useful for defensive programming, overall it's largely a matter of attitude. You need to get used to asking the question, "What if it fails?" It's easy to get fixated on simply making sure that the code works. After all, that's hard enough as it is. But as you're writing the code, take the time to ask, "What if it fails?" The result will be a more robust program that behaves better, crashes less, and is easier to debug.

Friday Q&A 2009-10-16: Creating a Blocks-Based Object System

Related Articles

    Blocks in Objective-C 14

    Code Injection 40

    Practical Blocks 146

    Method Replacement for Fun and Profit 297

    Error Returns with Continuation Passing Style 303

    Trampolining Blocks with Mutable Code 311

    Futures 330

    Compound Futures 342

    Background Timers 419

    Zeroing Weak References to CoreFoundation Objects 447

It's Friday again, and that means another Friday Q&A. This week, Guy English proposed talking about a blocks-based object system, and that is what I will do. The system I've developed is a rudimentary system for doing object-oriented programming in pure C (plus blocks), and I'll discuss how it works and how to use it.

Warning
This system is weird and fairly impractical. The purpose of this article is to explore the system and think about what lessons might be learned from it that could transfer into more realistic situations. It is *not* meant to be something that you would actually go out and use.

Source Code
For those of you who would like to follow along at home, you can get the full source code to my rudimentary blocks-based object system, plus a small example class and some testing code, from my public subversion repository.

C Object Orientation
C has seen a number of object systems over the years, and not just the ones with language extensions like C++ and Objective-C. A common way to program in C is to use opaque structs and provide functions that operate on them. CoreFoundation is a good example of this. Here's what such a thing looks like:

```
typedef struct MyFakeClass *MyFakeClassRef;

MyFakeClassRef NewMyFakeClass(void);
void DoSomethingInterestingWithFakeClass(MyFakeClassRef
obj, int foo);
void DestroyMyFakeClass(MyFakeClassRef obj);
```

This gives you many of the advantages of object-oriented programming without ever having to leave C. You get encapsulated data (other code doesn't know what the contents of a MyFakeClass are), a strong link between a data structure and the code that operates on it, better organization, etc.

Of course it's missing some key features of object orientation as well, like inheritance. You might remedy that by making the "methods" actually be members of the struct:

```
struct MyFakeClass
{
    void (*doSomethingInteresting)(struct MyFakeClass *obj, int foo);
    void (*destroy)(struct MyFakeClass *obj);
};
```

The trouble with this is that it gets a little redundant, using the object both to find the function pointer and then having to pass it as a parameter too:

```
struct MyFakeClass *obj = ...;
obj->doSomethingInteresting(obj /* UGLY! */, 42);
```

And then you need a reference to the object's data somewhere, and the most natural place to put it is in the struct next to all of the function pointers, right in plain view.

Enter Blocks

Apple's new blocks extension to C gives us something much like function pointers, but with implicit context. When you call a block, it can automatically access whatever data is necessary without the caller needing to pass that data explicitly. The struct then looks like this:

```
struct MyFakeClass
{
    void (^doSomethingInteresting)(int foo);
    void (^destroy)(void);
};
```

And you'd call things on it like this:

```
struct MyFakeClass *obj = ...;
obj->doSomethingInteresting(42);
```

Not bad at all!

This system allows overriding existing "methods" by simply putting in a new block, and having that block call through to the one that used to be there. Defining entirely new methods for a "subclass" gets a little trickier, but it's not bad. Define the subclass to contain the parent:

```
struct MyFakeSubclass
{
    struct MyFakeClass parent;

    void (^additionalMethod)(void);
};
```

Then callers can call parent methods like this:

```
struct MyFakeSubclass *obj = ...;
obj->parent.doSomethingInteresting(42);
```

That `parent` is not ideal, but it's workable. As a bonus, this technique separates the ideas of overriding an existing method and implementing a new method with the same name. In most OO systems it's impossible to implement a new method with the same name, as it's automatically an override. Here, they're two separate actions.

By putting `parent` at the front, this allows subtype polymorphism. By casting an instance of `MyFakeSubclass` to a `struct MyFakeClass *`, the result is still a valid object which continues to work as an instance of its parent class, but with any overridden behavior given by its subclass.

Building the System

That's the theory. Let's go ahead and actually build it now.

The first question is what objects will actually look like. We'll define them as structs containing blocks pointer members, and possibly a pointer to a parent struct/class. These are our methods. The struct contains nothing else: any per-object data is done using local variables which get captured by the method blocks.

We can then define a root object like this:

```
struct RootObject
{
    void (^retain)(void);
    void (^release)(void);
    void (^dealloc)(void);

    struct String *(^copyDescription)(void);
    int (^isEqual)(struct RootObject *);
};
```

We need a function to create new instances of the root object. We'll call it `NewRootObject`. It takes one parameter: the size of the object to allocate. Subclasses may be bigger, and the memory needs to be contiguous, so `NewRootObject` needs to know how much to allocate.

To ease the task of creating new objects (and figuring out how much memory to allocate), we'll create a convention that new objects are always created using a function called New*ClassName* which takes a single size parameter. We can then create a little macro for creating new objects:

```
#define Alloc(classname) New ## classname(sizeof(struct classname))
```

Using this, you'd allocate a new instance of the root class like so:

```
struct RootObject *obj = Alloc(RootObject);
```

Now, what does `NewRootObject` actually look like?

The first thing it needs are the "instance variables", which in this case are just `__block` qualified local variables.

```
struct RootObject *NewRootObject(size_t size)
{
    // "ivars"
    __block int retainCount = 1;
```

Next, it needs to actually allocate memory:

```
    // make the object
    struct RootObject *self = calloc(size, 1);
```

Then it can start filling out methods. It does this by just declaring blocks and assigning them to the slots. One wrinkle: since these blocks need to outlive their enclosing scope, we need to call `Block_copy` on them:

```
    // "methods"
    self->retain = Block_copy(^{ retainCount++; });
    self->release = Block_copy(^{
        retainCount--;
        if(retainCount <= 0)
            self->dealloc();
    });
```

Of course, that means that we eventually need to `Block_release` them. Having to go through and manually release every method in `dealloc` would be really tedious and error-prone, though. To work around this problem, the `dealloc` method can just scan the entire object for block pointers and release them all automatically. Since the only data in the object struct itself is block pointers, we can just scan one pointer-sized chunk at a time to get them all. Since we used `calloc` to allocate the object, we know that any memory "off the end" that got allocated due to `malloc` allocating more memory than necessary will be zeroed, and so any NULL pointer will be a signal to stop. This is what the dealloc method looks like:

```
    self->dealloc = Block_copy(^{
        size_t size = malloc_size(self);
        for(void **methodPtr = (void **)self;
            *methodPtr && ((intptr_t)methodPtr +
sizeof(*methodPtr) - 1 - (intptr_t)self) < size;
            methodPtr++)
            Block_release(*methodPtr);
        free(self);
    });
```

Finally, we define the `copyDescription` method (using a method of the as-yet-unseen `String` class) and return the new object:

```
    self->copyDescription = Block_copy(^{
        return Alloc(String)->initWithFormat("<Object %p>", self);
    });

    return self;
}
```

Creating New Classes

Now that we've done all of that, how do we make a subclass? Let's go ahead and create the `String` class, since the root class depends on it anyway.

As mentioned before, a subclass gets a `struct` for its parent at the top, and then follows with its own methods, like so:

```
struct String
{
    struct RootObject parent;
    
    struct String *(^initWithFormat)(char *fmt, ...);
    const char *(^cstring)(void);
};
```

Then it just needs a `NewString` function to create one. As with `NewRootObject`, the first part of the function is for "instance variables":

```
struct String *NewString(size_t size)
{
    __block char *str = NULL;
```

And next, just like before, we allocate the object. Only this time, instead of allocating raw memory, we call through to the parent's `New` function to allocate the object.

```
    struct String *self = (void *)NewRootObject(size);
```

Next up, we want to override a couple of methods from the root object. The first one we want to override is `copyDescription`. Since we don't want to call through to the original implementation, we can just release the old block, then assign a new one:

```
    Block_release(self->parent.copyDescription);
    self->parent.copyDescription = Block_copy(^{
        self->parent.retain();
        return self;
    });
```

Next, we need to override `dealloc` to free the `str` variable. This is a little trickier, though, because we need to call through to the old implementation once we're done. To do this, we'll save off the old implementation into a local variable, and call through to it. We also have to take care of releasing the old implementation:

```
    void (^superdealloc)(void) = self->parent.dealloc;
    self->parent.dealloc = Block_copy(^{
        free(str);
        superdealloc();
    });
    Block_release(superdealloc);
```

This is some tricky memory management business. At first blush this looks good, but if you look deeper you'll realize that `Block_release(superdealloc)` is being called too early! The body of the new `dealloc` block won't run until the object is destroyed, but the `Block_release` runs while the object is still being created.

This actually ends up working perfectly fine, because the compiler automatically does a `Block_copy` on the `superdealloc` instance variable when it gets captured by the new block referencing it. There's a bit of automatic reference counting going on behind the scenes, and this ensures that the block stays alive for as long as it's needed.

Finally, we'll define the `String`-specific methods and return the new object:

```
    self->initWithFormat = Block_copy(^(char *fmt, ...){
        va_list args;
        va_start(args, fmt);
        vasprintf(&str, fmt, args);
        va_end(args);

        return self;
    });
    self->cstring = Block_copy(^{ return (const char *)str; });

    return self;
}
```

We now have a fully functioning, albeit simplistic and a bit verbose, object system.

Custom Classes Let's create one more class just to reinforce how it's done. We'll call this one `MyObject`, and it will just hold two numbers. Here's the class struct:

```
struct MyObject
{
    struct RootObject parent;

    struct MyObject *(^initWithNumbers)(int a, int b);
};
```

And here's the function to create a new one:

211

```
struct MyObject *NewMyObject(size_t size)
{
    __block int numbers[2];

    struct MyObject *self = (void *)NewRootObject(size);

    // override parent methods
    Block_release(self->parent.copyDescription);
    self->parent.copyDescription = Block_copy(^{
        return Alloc(String)->initWithFormat("<MyObject %d %d>", numbers[0], numbers[1]);
    });

    self->initWithNumbers = Block_copy(^(int a, int b){
        numbers[0] = a;
        numbers[1] = b;
        return self;
    });

    return self;
}
```

Finally, here's some example code that actually uses it:

```
struct MyObject *myobj = Alloc(MyObject);
myobj->initWithNumbers(42, 65535);
description = myobj->parent.copyDescription();
printf("myobj is %s\n", description->cstring());
description->parent.release();
myobj->parent.release();
```

Which produces the output you'd expect:

```
myobj is <MyObject 42 65535>
```

To summarize, here's what you need to do to create a new class using this system:

1. Define a new struct with the appropriate name.
2. As the first member of the struct, add a struct for the parent class.
3. For subsequent members of the struct, add block pointers for each method.
4. Pause for breath.
5. Define an appropriately-named New function.
6. At the top, define any "instance variables" you need using the __block qualifier.
7. Allocate the object by calling through to the superclass's New function.

8. Override any parent methods by releasing the original block pointer and reassigning it. If you need to call through to the old implementation, save it into a local variable, and release that local variable after the reassingnment.
9. Initialize any new methods by assigning to them.

Advantages and Disadvantages

This is an unusual object system. To be clear, this is *not* what Objective-C (or C++ or Java or...) is doing behind the scenes. (For information on what Objective-C *is* doing behind the scenes, check out my series on the Objective-C runtime.) It more closely resembles the prototype-based object systems found in languages like JavaScript.

Some of these differences are good, and some are bad. Let's take the bad first. There are a lot of them.

- It's pretty ugly and verbose. Almost everything is defined by convention, not syntax. Calling through to an overridden superclass implementation is particularly bad, but overall there's a lot of redundancy in there. A carefully crafted set of macros could help this.
- The per-object memory footprint is large. In a language like Objective-C, an object is a single chunk of memory containing a pointer to its class followed by any instance-specific data that object's class requires. An object's size grows only with the amount of data it contains. In this system, an object is a chunk of memory containing one pointer per method implemented by the object's class. Each of those points to a new chunk of memory which is not shared with other objects of that class. Finally, they all point to chunks of shared storage for the object's class's "instance variables", and for each superclass's "instance variables". That's a lot of memory allocations, and their quantity and size dwarfs what you'd find in a language like Objective-C.
- Object creation and destruction is very slow. All of these allocations need to be created and filled out.
- The hierarchy of a class is forcibly exposed to client code because of how superclass methods are accessed. If `MyObject` starts to inherit from `String` instead of `RootObject`, any calls to `myobj->parent.release()` would have to be replaced with `myobj->parent.parent.release()`.
- There's absolutely no metadata or introspection available.
- The result of the pointer casting stuff going on to achieve subtype polymorphism does not actually have a defined result in the C language, although it works in almost any real implementation you'll find.

In my defense, this object system was not meant to be practical, and I built it in about an hour.

Despite all of this, there are some advantages to it:

- It works in plain old C (with Apple's blocks extension), no need for Objective-C or C++ or anything like that.

- Since it's a single struct member load followed by a block call (which is just another struct member load followed by a function pointer invocation), invoking a method should be faster than in Objective-C.
- Methods can be dynamically replaced on individual objects at any time. For example, this is how I tested to make sure that the `dealloc` method really is invoked when an object's retain count reaches zero:

```
obj = Alloc(RootObject);
void (^olddealloc)(void) = obj->dealloc;
obj->dealloc = Block_copy(^{
    printf("dealloc was called!\n");
    olddealloc();
});
obj->release();
Block_release(olddealloc);
```

This sort of thing is much more difficult to accomplish in Objective-C.
- Overriding a parent method is a completely separate action from implementing a new method in a child class, eliminating accidental overrides and allowing a child to implement a completely separate method which happens to have the same name.
- The whole object system fits in a page and can be readily understood in a short time.

Again, I don't recommend actually using this object system for anything practical, but it's an interesting construct just the same.

Conclusion

We now have a fully functional, albeit strange, object system based on blocks, and one that's less than 100 lines long. This object system, while not entirely practical, is an interesting illustration of the sort of power that blocks add to the language.

Friday Q&A 2009-10-23: A Preview of Coming Attractions

Related Articles
- Generators in Objective-C 216
- A GCD Case Study: Building an HTTP Server 256

I'm afraid that I ran out of time this week and wasn't able to put together a real Friday Q&A. However, as a preview of what I'll be talking about next week, check out the MAGenerator project in my public subversion repository.

MAGenerator is a library for building generators in Objective-C. These are much like the generators found in Python, although with a slightly different interface. They are essentially functions which remember state between invocations, such that when you call them a second time, all local variables have the same value they did at the end of the first call, and execution resumes where it was when it returned from the first call.

There's complete, if terse, documentation found in the `MAGenerator.h` header, and some examples in the `GeneratorTests.m` file. I plan to release the code under an MIT license if you'd actually like to use it somewhere. Unlike my blocks-based object system from last week, I think this code could actually be used in a practical sense, even though the implementation is still pretty much evil.

Friday Q&A 2009-10-30: Generators in Objective-C

Related Articles

    A Preview of Coming Attractions..215

    A GCD Case Study: Building an HTTP Server..256

It's Friday again and time for another Friday Q&A. This week I'm going to discuss a framework for creating generators in Objective-C. I'm indulging myself a bit with this, because nobody suggested it, but nothing in my suggestion bank inspired me this time around, so I decided to go with something of my own.

Generators

A generator is essentially a function which remembers its state between invocations. In a normal function, the second time you call it is just like the first. Execution starts over at the top, local variables reset their values, etc. With a generator, execution starts where it left off, and local variables remember their values.

In Python, a simple generator looks like this:

```python
def countfrom(n):
    while True:
        yield n
        n += 1
```

The `yield` statement takes the place of the `return` statement that you'd find in a normal function. When execution hits `yield`, the value is returned but the function's state is also saved. The net result is that successive calls return successively increasing numbers.

Things aren't actually quite this simple in Python. A call to `countfrom` doesn't start returning numbers, but rather returns an object. Calling the `next` method on the object it returns will return the successive numbers.

Using my MAGenerator, things are much the same. The generator is considerably more wordy and uglier, but this should be so surprise considering that it's C, and that this is basically hacked on support rather than a language feature. The example counter generator using `MAGenerator` would look like this:

```
GENERATOR(int, CountFrom(int start), (void))
{
    __block int n;
    GENERATOR_BEGIN(void)
    {
        n = start;
        while(1)
        {
            GENERATOR_YIELD(n);
            n++;
        }
    }
    GENERATOR_END
}
```

Much like in Python, calling `CountFrom` doesn't start returning numbers. Instead, it returns a block. Calling the block will then start returning numbers. Here's an example of how you'd actually use this generator:

```
int (^counter)(void) = CountFrom(42);
for(int i = 0; i < 10; i++)
    NSLog(@"%d", counter());
```

This will log 42, 43, 44, 45, 46, 47, 48, 49, 50, 51.

Basic Implementation

The basic concept behind how `MAGenerator` works was inspired by Simon Tatham's Coroutines in C. His coroutines are considerably more limited due to the fact that C without blocks can't really handle what's needed, but there's a great deal of cleverness in the implementation.

There are two major problems that need to be solved. The first problem is that of resuming execution where it left off. This is solved using a switch statement. The individual `case` labels give places to resume execution. In C, `case` labels can be put practically anywhere, even inside other control constructs, and they still work

The second problem is that of preserving state. Tatham solved this one by simply using `static` variables instead of locals. While this works, it has the severe limitation of only allowing one instance of the function to be active. Using blocks, we can work around this much more nicely using variables captured from the enclosing scope. Thus, here is the basic idea of what our `CountFrom` function would look like if we implemented it directly instead of with the help of macros:

```
// this crazy thing is how you declare a function that
returns a block
int (^CountFrom(int start))(void)
{
    __block int state = 0;
    __block int n;
    int (^block)(void) = ^{
        switch(state)
        {
            case 0:
                n = start;
                while(1)
                {
                    state = 1;
                    return n;
                    case 1: ; // yes, this is legal!
                    n++;
                }
        }
    };
    return [[block copy] autorelease];
}
```

As you can see, the call to CountFrom returns a block, which captures the start parameter as well as the state and n local variables. Those are qualified with __block so that they can be mutated from within the block.

The state variable is where the magic happens. When you call the block, execution always begins at the top, just like with a function. However, the first thing it encounters is a switch statement. By setting the state variable to correspond to the location of the return statement, this switch statement causes execution to resume immediately after it. Since all of our variables are captured from the enclosing scope, they remember their contents across calls.

Cleanup

Let's consider a little string builder generator. This generator will take path components and build a complete path out of them. Here's a first stab at it:

```
NSString *(^PathBuilder(void))(NSString *component)
{
    __block int state = 0;
    __block NSString *path;
    NSString *(^block)(NSString *component) = ^{
        switch(state)
        {
            case 0:
                path = @"/";
                while(1)
                {
                    path = [path stringByAppendingPathComponent: component];
                    state = 1;
                    return path;
            case 1: ;
                }
        }
    };
    return [[block copy] autorelease];
}
```

This works, but is dangerous. The danger comes because `__block` variables don't retain what they point to. Our `path` variable points to an unowned string. If the caller happens to pop an autorelease pool in between calls to the path builder generator, that will destroy the string, leave a dangling pointer in `path`, and cause a crash at the next call.

We could fix this by copying the string, like so:

```
NSString *(^PathBuilder(void))(NSString *component)
{
    __block int state = 0;
    __block NSString *path;
    __block NSString *newPath;
    NSString *(^block)(NSString *component) = ^{
        switch(state)
        {
            case 0:
                path = @"/";
                while(1)
                {
                    newPath = [path stringByAppendingPathComponent: component];
                    [path release];
                    path = [newPath copy];
                    state = 1;
                    return path;
            case 1: ;
                }
        }
    };
    return [[block copy] autorelease];
}
```

This has a new problem: it will leak the last string assigned to `path`.

The proper solution is to create a cleanup block which gets executed when the main block is destroyed. This can be accomplished by using the fact that blocks *do* automatically manage the memory of captured non-`__block` object pointer variables. We can create an object:

```
NSString *(^PathBuilder(void))(NSString *component)
{
    id cleanupObj = ...;
```

Reference it in a meaningless way so that it gets captured by the block:

```
    ...
    NSString *(^block)(NSString *component) = ^{
        [cleanupObj path];
    ...
```

Then have that object call the cleanup block when it's destroyed:

```
[cleanupObj callBlockWhenDeallocated: ^{ ... }];
```

This could be done using a custom class, but for the sake of simplicity, I opted instead to use a `CFMutableArray` with custom callbacks set up so that the retain callback would copy the object, and the release callback would cast it to the appropriate block pointer, call it, and then release it. By adding the cleanup block to the array, it will be automatically invoked when the array (and the generator block) is destroyed.

Assuming `MAGeneratorMakeCleanupArray` does the job of setting up the appropriate `CFMutableArray` (and casting it to an `NSMutableArray`) then the final code, with cleanup, looks like this:

```
NSString *(^PathBuilder(void))(NSString *component)
{
    __block int state = 0;
    __block NSString *path;
    __block NSString *newPath;
    NSMutableArray *cleanupArray = MAGeneratorMakeCleanupArray();
    NSString *(^block)(NSString *component) = ^{
        [cleanupArray self]; // meaningless reference to capture it
        switch(state)
        {
            case 0:
                path = @"/";
                while(1)
                {
                    newPath = [path stringByAppendingPathComponent: component];
                    [path release];
                    path = [newPath copy];
                    state = 1;
                    return path;
                case 1: ;
                }
        }
    };
    [cleanupArray addObject: ^{ [path release]; }];
    return [[block copy] autorelease];
}
```

Now everything works as expected.

221

Macroization

Much of the above, while workable, is tremendously annoying to write. To help, I turned all the boilerplate parts into macros.

To start with, the GENERATOR macro takes care of the function declaration as well as a variable to hold the cleanup block. It also declares a GENERATOR_zeroReturnValue variable, which is used to quiet compiler warnings about failing to return a value at the end of the block. Unfortunately, this trick means you can't use these macros to create a generator which returns void. However, since you can just declare another type (like int) and ignore the value in the caller, this is not a big problem. Here's what it looks like:

```
#define GENERATOR(returnType, nameAndCreationParams, perCallParams) \
    returnType (^nameAndCreationParams) perCallParams \
    { \
        returnType GENERATOR_zeroReturnValue; \
        bzero(&GENERATOR;_zeroReturnValue, sizeof(GENERATOR_zeroReturnValue)); \
        returnType (^GENERATOR_cleanupBlock)(void) = nil;
```

Local variables can be declared immediately after GENERATOR.

The GENERATOR_DECL works the same as the GENERATOR macro, but only produces the prototype, making it suitable for a declaration in a header file.

```
#define GENERATOR_DECL(returnType, nameAndCreationParams, perCallParams) \
    returnType (^nameAndCreationParams) perCallParams
```

Next comes GENERATOR_BEGIN, which takes the generator's parameters again. This declares the state variable (called GENERATOR_where), the cleanup array, and starts off the block:

```
#define GENERATOR_BEGIN(...) \
    __block int GENERATOR_where = -1; \
    NSMutableArray *GENERATOR_cleanupArray = MAGeneratorMakeCleanupArray(); \
    id GENERATOR_mainBlock = ^ (__VA_ARGS__) { \
        [GENERATOR_cleanupArray self]; \
        switch(GENERATOR_where) \
        { \
            case -1:
```

The generator code can follow this macro. Within the generator code, you want to return values, so you do this using the GENERATOR_YIELD macro. This macro does exactly the same thing as the sequence we wrote manually above. The one trick here is that we need a unique number to identify the state value for this yield. Previously we could just write 1, 2, 3, 4, etc., in the code. We could make this macro take another parameter for the state value, but it's annoying to have to keep track of them all. Instead, as Tatham did, I chose to use the __LINE__ macro, which gets replaced by the line number of the current line of code.

```
#define GENERATOR_YIELD(...) \
        do { \
            GENERATOR_where = __LINE__; \
            return __VA_ARGS__; \
        case __LINE__: ; \
        } while(0)
```

This works great, with the exception that you must never place two GENERATOR_YIELDs on the same line.

Next we also want to be able to define a cleanup block using a GENERATOR_CLEANUP macro. This macro gets a little funky, because the macros are designed to work whether GENERATOR_CLEANUP is present or not. GENERATOR_END, which will end the definition of the generator, needs to work properly whether it follows GENERATOR_CLEANUP or GENERATOR_BEGIN. This is done in this macro by adding a superfluous set of curly braces to the cleanup block:

```
#define GENERATOR_CLEANUP \
        } \
        GENERATOR_where = -1; \
        return GENERATOR_zeroReturnValue; \
    }; \
    GENERATOR_cleanupBlock = ^{{
```

The return statement shuts up the compiler about missing return statements, and also provides a safety net if you let execution fall off the end. Finally we come to the end. Again, this macro has to work whether GENERATOR_CLEANUP is present or not. Thus, it has the same return statement, which works in both contexts. Finally it checks to see if a cleanup block has been set, adds it to the cleanup array if so, and then returns the newly created generator block.

```
#define GENERATOR_END \
            } \
            GENERATOR_where = -1; \
            return GENERATOR_zeroReturnValue; \
        }; \
        if(GENERATOR_cleanupBlock) \
            [GENERATOR_cleanupArray addObject: ^{
GENERATOR_cleanupBlock(); }]; \
        return [[GENERATOR_mainBlock copy] autorelease]; \
    }
```

Note that in order to accommodate the return statement in the cleanup block, the cleanup block needs to have the same return type as the generator block. Since the array has no way to figure out the proper block type to invoke, we wrap the cleanup block in a nice void/void block that it can deal with.

Results

These macros are pretty scary, but the results are quite nice. This is the same example that I showed at the beginning:

```
GENERATOR(int, CountFrom(int start), (void))
{
    __block int n;
    GENERATOR_BEGIN(void)
    {
        n = start;
        while(1)
        {
            GENERATOR_YIELD(n);
            n++;
        }
    }
    GENERATOR_END
}
```

More complicated generators look nice too. I previously showed a PathBuilder generator written without macros. Here's the same generator written with these macros:

```
GENERATOR(NSString *, PathBuilder(void), (NSString
*component))
{
    __block NSString *path;
    __block NSString *newPath;
    GENERATOR_BEGIN(NSString *component)
    {
        path = @"/";
        while(1)
        {
            newPath = [path
stringByAppendingPathComponent: component];
            [path release];
            path = [newPath copy];
            GENERATOR_YIELD(path);
        }
    }
    GENERATOR_CLEANUP
    {
        [path release];
    }
    GENERATOR_END
}
```

Certainly this is not 100% natural, but all in all it's amazingly reasonable and readable considering that the language has no support for this sort of thing.

Caveats

As with all blasphemous crimes against nature, MAGenerator has a few caveats.

1. **Local variables must be declared at the top, before GENERATOR_BEGIN.** Local variables declared within the generator block will not remember their state between invocation. You can get away with this with carefully structured code, but it's best not to try.
2. **This includes the implicit locals generated by using a for/in loop.** You cannot safely use for/in loops (other loop constructs are fine) unless the body contains no invocations of GENERATOR_YIELD.
3. **You can't put two invocations of GENERATOR_YIELD on the same line.** This is not a big hardship: just separate them with a carriage return. Thankfully, this one will generate a compiler error, not a difficult runtime error.
4. **switch statements used within the generator must not contain any invocations of GENERATOR_YIELD.** Because the generator's execution state is resumed using a switch statement, and because GENERATOR_YIELD creates case labels, using GENERATOR_YIELD inside your own switch statement

will cause confusion, because the generated case labels will belong to the inner `switch` rather than the macro-generated one.

5. **Object lifetime must be managed carefully if it crosses GENERATOR_YIELD.** You can't assume that the caller will keep an autorelease pool around for you until you're done. GENERATOR_CLEANUP takes care of this, but it's still harder than it is in normal code.

These are all unfortunate, and I wish they weren't there, but all in all they aren't deal breakers by any stretch of the imagination.

Potential Uses

I'm fairly new to the world of generators, and of course everybody is new to the world of generators in Objective-C, but I have some ideas of how they could be productively used.

Lazy Evaluation

A major use of generations in Python is to lazily evaluate enumerated values. The generator creates new values on demand rather than requiring them all to be precomputed. MAGenerator includes a convenience function, `MAGeneratorEnumerator`, which takes a generator with no per-call parameters and an `id` return type, and returns an object conforming to `NSFastEnumeration` which enumerates by successively calling the generator.

As an example, here's a generator which will find files with a certain extension in a certain path:

```
GENERATOR(id, FileFinder(NSString *path, NSString *extension), (void))
{
    NSDirectoryEnumerator *enumerator = [[NSFileManager defaultManager] enumeratorAtPath: path];
    __block NSString *subpath;
    GENERATOR_BEGIN(void)
    {
        while((subpath = [enumerator nextObject]))
        {
            if([[subpath pathExtension] isEqualToString: extension])
                GENERATOR_YIELD((id)[path stringByAppendingPathComponent: subpath]);
        }
    }
    GENERATOR_END
}
```

You could just write a function that returns an array, but that requires enumerating over the entire contents of the directory, which is slow if the caller doesn't actually need them all. You could write an `NSEnumerator` subclass which wraps the `NSDirectoryEnumerator`, but that requires a lot more code. You could write code which takes a block as a parameter and invokes it for each one it finds, but that's less natural. Here's what it looks like to use this generator:

```
for(NSString *path in MAGeneratorEnumerator(FileFinder(@"/Applications", @"app")))
    NSLog(@"%@", path);
```

It doesn't get any easier than that.

Replacing State Machines

Code frequently requires state machines. Imagine something like a network protocol parser. The natural way to write this is to write code that flows from top to bottom. Read a character, act on it. Read the next character, act on it. Have loops for reading strings, read individual characters to skip over separators, etc.

Then asynchronous programming appears and suddenly this doesn't seem like a good idea. Every one of those read calls could block. You could put it in a separate thread, but that has its own problems. You look into doing callback-based networking, using `NSStream` or GCD, but suddenly you have to deal with buffers, keep around a bunch of explicit state about where you are in the protocol parsing, etc.

By virtue of their inside-out approach to programming, generators allow you to invert control flow while preserving the nice linear code that you get from the synchronous approach.

As an example, consider a very simple RLE decoder, which reads pairs of `{ count, value }` bytes. Normally the decoder, if asynchronous, would have to keep track of what state it's in so that it knows whether the next byte it receives is a count or a value. However, using a generator, that state information disappears, replaced with the implicit generator state:

```
GENERATOR(int, RLEDecoder(void (^emit)(char)), (unsigned
char byte))
{
    __block unsigned char count;
    GENERATOR_BEGIN(unsigned char byte)
    {
        while(1)
        {
            count = byte;
            GENERATOR_YIELD(0);

            while(count--)
                emit(byte);
            GENERATOR_YIELD(0);
        }
    }
    GENERATOR_END
}
```

This code is more straightforward and easier to understand than a non-generator asynchronous version would be.

For a much more complicated example, here's an HTTP response parser written as a generator. It takes several blocks as parameters to use as callbacks for when it finishes parsing the various components of the response.

```
GENERATOR(int, HTTPParser(void
(^responseCallback)(NSString *),
                            void
(^headerCallback)(NSDictionary *),
                            void (^bodyCallback)(NSData *),
                            void (^errorCallback)(NSString
*)),
                            (int byte))
{
    NSMutableData *responseData = [NSMutableData data];
    
    NSMutableDictionary *headers = [NSMutableDictionary
dictionary];
    __block NSMutableData *currentHeaderData = nil;
    __block NSString *currentHeaderKey = nil;
    
    NSMutableData *bodyData = [NSMutableData data];
    
    GENERATOR_BEGIN(char byte)
    {
        // read response line
        while(byte != '\r')
        {
            AppendByte(responseData, byte);
            GENERATOR_YIELD(0);
        }
        responseCallback(SafeUTF8String(responseData));
        GENERATOR_YIELD(0); // eat the \r
        if(byte != '\n')
            errorCallback(@"bad CRLF after response line");
        GENERATOR_YIELD(0); // eat the \n
        
        // read headers
        while(1)
        {
            currentHeaderData = [[NSMutableData alloc]
init];
            while(byte != ':' && byte != '\r')
            {
                AppendByte(currentHeaderData, byte);
                GENERATOR_YIELD(0);
            }
            
            // empty line means we're done with headers
            if(byte == '\r' && [currentHeaderData length]
```

```
== 0)
                break;
            else if(byte == '\r')
                errorCallback(@"No colon found in header line");
            else
            {
                GENERATOR_YIELD(0);
                if(byte == ' ')
                    GENERATOR_YIELD(0);
                
                currentHeaderKey = [SafeUTF8String(currentHeaderData) copy];
                [currentHeaderData release];
                
                currentHeaderData = [[NSMutableData alloc] init];
                while(byte != '\r')
                {
                    AppendByte(currentHeaderData, byte);
                    GENERATOR_YIELD(0);
                }
                
                NSString *currentHeaderValue = SafeUTF8String(currentHeaderData);
                [currentHeaderData release];
                
                [headers setObject: currentHeaderValue forKey: currentHeaderKey];
                [currentHeaderKey release];
            }
            GENERATOR_YIELD(0);
            if(byte != '\n')
                errorCallback(@"bad CRLF after header line");
            GENERATOR_YIELD(0); // eat the \n
        }
        headerCallback(headers);
        
        // read body
        while(byte != -1)
        {
            AppendByte(bodyData, byte);
            GENERATOR_YIELD(0);
        }
```

```
        bodyCallback(bodyData);
    }
    GENERATOR_CLEANUP
    {
        [currentHeaderData release];
        [currentHeaderKey release];
    }
    GENERATOR_END
}
```

To use it, code would simply create a new parser like so:

```
int (^httpParser)(int) = HTTPParser( /* callbacks go here */ );
```

It would then store this object somewhere. Whenever new data became available from the remote end, it would just call it:

```
httpParser(newByte);
```

When the connection is closed, it signals the end of the stream:

```
httpParser(-1);
```

And everything else just happens automatically. Any time `newByte` provides enough information for the parser to have parsed a new component of the response, the appropriate callback block is invoked.

This generator is declared to return `int` since MAGenerator doesn't support `void` generators. The return value is simply ignored in this case. Execution begins at the top, with the first character from the data stream stored in `byte`. Each time it invokes `GENERATOR_YIELD`, the effect is to get a new `byte` from the caller. Parsing thus flows naturally from top to bottom, even though this code is in fact heavily asynchronous.

It should be noted that these parsers are not very efficient, because they require a block call (a function call plus additional overhead) for every single byte. This could be easily remedied if necessary, however. Modify the generator to take a buffer instead of a single byte. Then, instead of blind invocation of `GENERATOR_YIELD`, the code would advance a cursor in the buffer, and only invoke `GENERATOR_YIELD` when the buffer is empty and needs to be refilled. This would get you down to one call per buffer instead of one per byte.

Wrapping Up

Now you know how to build generators in Objective-C using blocks, and have at least some ideas of how to use them productively. Of course you shouldn't be building them manually, but rather you should use my MAGenerator library! MAGenerator is open source. You can get the source by checking it out from my subversion repository:

    `svn co http://www.mikeash.com/svn/MAGenerator/`

Or browse it by just clicking on the URL above. It's available under the MIT license, so you can use it in pretty much any project you like. The project includes everything needed to write generators, as well as a bunch of examples/test cases.

I'm sure there are improvements that could be made, and patches are welcome. Depending on the change you're making I can't guarantee that I'll accept it, but of course you're always welcome to fork it if I don't.

Friday Q&A 2009-11-06: Linking and Install Names

It's another Friday, and thus another Friday Q&A. I have recovered from the confusion of the Daylight Saving Time transition and am now ready to talk about Mac OS X linking, install names, `@executable_path`, and friends. Before getting into the meat of the article, I want to quickly go over the different kinds of libraries and the basics of how they work.

Static Libraries
These are so simple they barely need discussion. When you link against a static library, the contents of that library are copied into your application when you build. From that point on, the code acts just like the code you wrote yourself.

Dynamic Libraries
When you link against a dynamic library, things are less straightforward. The linker basically makes a note that various symbols you reference are to be found in this library, and that your binary depends on that library. Then at runtime, when your application is loaded, the dynamic linker also loads that library.

The big question for today is, how does the dynamic linker know where to find it?

Install name
The answer to that question varies greatly from one OS to another, but on the Mac, the answer is install names.

An install name is just a pathname embedded within a dynamic library which tells the linker where that library can be found at runtime. For example, `libfoo.dylib` might have an install name of `/usr/lib/libfoo.dylib`. This install name gets copied into the application at link time. When the dynamic linker goes looking for `libfoo.dylib` at runtime, it will fetch the install name out of the application and know to look for the library in `/usr/lib`.

Frameworks are just dynamic libraries with a funny wrapper, so they work the same way. `Foo.framework` might have an install name of `/Library/Frameworks/Foo.framework/Versions/A/Foo`, and that's where the dynamic linker will search for it.

`@executable_path`
Absolute paths are annoying. Sometimes you want to embed a framework into an application instead of having to install the framework into `/Library` or a similar location.

The Mac's solution to this is `@executable_path`. This is a magic token that, when placed at the beginning of a library's install name, gets expanded to the path of the executable that's loading it, minus the last component. For example, let's say that `Bar.app` links against `Foo.framework`. If `Bar.app` is installed in `/Applications`, `@executable_path` will expand to `/Applications/Bar.app/Contents/MacOS`. If you intend to embed the framework in `Contents/Frameworks`, then you can just set `Foo.framework`'s install name to `@executable_path/../Frameworks/Foo.framework/Versions/A/Foo`. The dynamic linker will expand that to `/Applications/Bar.app/Contents/MacOS/../Frameworks/Foo.framework/Version` and will find the framework there.

@loader_path

Finding the executable isn't always good enough. Imagine that you ship a plugin or a framework which embeds another framework. Say, `Foo.framework` embeds `Baz.framework`. Even though `Foo.framework` is the one requesting the load, the dynamic linker will still go off of `Bar.app`'s location when figuring out what `@executable_path` refers to, and this won't work right.

Starting in 10.4, Apple provided `@loader_path` which does what you want here. It expands to the full path, minus the last component, of whatever is actually causing the target library to be loaded. If it's an application, then it's the same as `@executable_path`. If it's a framework or plugin, though, then it's relative to that framework or plugin, which is much more useful.

@rpath

While the above is sufficient for anything in theory, it can be troublesome in practice. The problem is that a single copy of a library can only be used in one way. If you want `Foo.framework` to work when embedded in an application or when installed to `/Library/Frameworks`, you have to provide two separate copies with two different install names. (Or manually tweak install names later on using `install_name_tool`.) This is doable, but annoying.

Starting in 10.5, Apple provides `@rpath`, which is a solution to this. When placed at the front of an install name, this asks the dynamic linker to search a list of locations for the library. That list is embedded in the application, and can therefore be controlled by the application's build process, not the framework's. A single copy of a framework can thus work for multiple purposes.

To make this work, `Foo.framework`'s install name would be set to `@rpath/Foo.framework/Versions/A/Foo`. An application that intends to embed `Foo.framework` would then pass `-rpath @executable_path/../Frameworks` to the linker at build time, which tells the dynamic linker to search for @rpath frameworks there. An application that intends to install the framework would pass -rpath /Library/Frameworks, telling the dynamic linker to search there. An application that for some reason doesn't want to commit to one or the other at build time can just pass both sets of parameters, which will cause the dynamic linker to try both locations.

Conclusion

Now you hopefully know a little bit more about how dynamic linking works on Mac OS X and how the dynamic linker finds your libraries, including how to embed frameworks in applications, in plugins, and in other frameworks.

Friday Q&A 2009-11-13: Dangerous Cocoa Calls

Related Articles

    Multithreaded Programming and Parallelism Overview 11

    Thread Safety in OS X System Frameworks 24

    The Good and Bad of Distributed Objects..56

    Multithreaded Optimization in ChemicalBurn 82

    Care and Feeding of Singletons 194

    Probing Cocoa With PyObjC...240

    Using Accessors in Init and Dealloc..246

    NSRunLoop Internals 273

    NSNotificationQueue...284

    Implementing a Custom Slider 382

    Dealing with Retain Cycles 392

    What Every Apple Programmer Should Know 401

    Leopard Collection Classes...405

    Implementing Equality and Hashing 412

    Implementing NSCoding 459

    Defensive Programming in Cocoa 468

It's another Friday, and so time for another Friday Q&A. This week, Quentin Carnicelli (one of the guys who signs my paychecks) suggested that I talk about dangerous API calls in Cocoa.

First, let me clarify what I mean by a dangerous call. I don't mean something that is obviously dangerous, like `-[NSFileManager removeFileAtPath:handler:]`. That call is dangerous because you could use it to wipe the user's entire hard drive, but it's not interesting, because it's obvious that it can do this. Instead, I'm going to cover calls which are *subtly* dangerous, things which you might easily use in an innocent manner, only to discover later that bad things can occur.

Without further ado, here are my dangerous calls:

`-[NSTask launch]`

This call is dangerous because it throws exceptions when it fails, and it can fail for completely mundane problems, like trying to execute a file that doesn't have the executable bit set. Because the Cocoa tradition is to only throw exceptions for programmer errors, this can cause trouble for the unwary programmer who doesn't wrap this in a `@try` block.

-[NSTask waitUntilExit]
This one looks tremendously innocent. The problem is that, if the task is still running, it will run the runloop to wait for the task to exit. Even that would not be a problem, except that *it runs the runloop in the default mode*. Because of this, all timers, callbacks, etc., that are installed in the default mode will continue to run, but will be running in a context they did not expect. This call looks like a simple blocking call, but it can potentially lead to the invocation of random timers or other callbacks. This in turn can easily lead to deadlocks or data corruption.

+[NSTimer scheduledTimerWithTimeInterval:target:selector:userInfo:repeats:]
This returns a timer whose memory management is difficult to get right. Many people simply stash the return value in an instance variable. This is legitimate, because the runloop is documented to retain the timer. However, the runloop will release it as soon as it's invalidated, which will happen once a non-repeating timer fires, and also upon explicit invalidation. It's easy to get this wrong and end up with a dangling reference, and a lot of code has this problem. To make things even more fun, the timer retains its target, so if you retain the timer, you're likely to set up a retain cycle.

NSHost
Yes, this entire class is dangerous, and should not be used. Why? It's an unfortunate confluence of two otherwise unrelated properties of the class.

The first property is that NSHost has a blocking API. It accesses network resources, and as such any call to it can take an indefinite amount of time. This is fine by itself.

The second property is that NSHost returns shared objects, but NSHost is not thread safe. This means that it can only be safely used on the main thread.

Put the two together, and you have a class which can block any time you use it, but which can only be used on the main thread. Since it's unacceptable to indefinitely block the main thread of an application, this basically means that you can't use NSHost.

NSBundle
This one has half of the problems of NSHost. NSBundle returns shared objects, but is not thread safe, so it's main-thread only. It's still safe to use from the main thread. The reason I mark it as dangerous is because the fact that it's unsafe to use from secondary threads is not really documented, but rather has to be inferred from the fact that it's not thread safe and the fact that the instances are shared, and it can be tempting to use it from other threads.

-[NSBundle unload]
Because it's very easy to make references to memory within a bundle's code (e.g. by creating instances of an Objective-C class defined within the bundle, or by referring to literal strings defined within the bundle), and extremely difficult to make sure that all

such references are gone, it's generally not safe to unload code on Mac OS X. If any such dangling references remain, your application will crash.

-[NSImage imageNamed:], followed by mutation

This call is very convenient, but it returns a shared object. A lot of code will make this call, and then immediately start resizing or drawing into the object that it returns. This can mess up the shared image for any other code that uses it. If you're going to modify the image, then you need to copy it first, but this isn't immediately obvious.

-[NSDate timeIntervalSinceReferenceDate] used for elapsed time

How many of you have written code like this?

```
BOOL success;
NSTimeInterval start = [NSDate
timeIntervalSinceReferenceDate];
do
    success = [self trySomething];
while(!success && [NSDate timeIntervalSinceReferenceDate]
- start <= kTimeoutInterval);
```

I'm guilty of it myself. It's a pretty natural way to write a timeout loop. There are many other circumstances where you might use this sort of thing too, not with an explicit loop, but in something more asynchronous.

So what's the problem? -timeIntervalSinceReferenceDate uses the system clock, *which can be changed!* Imagine that your program enters this loop, but before it can exit it, the system clock is set back by a day. Your timeout has now gone up to a day! Or imagine the opposite, that the system clock is suddenly set forward. Your timeout will suddenly become zero.

Mac OS X tries to make time adjustments smooth. For example, if the NTP client discovers that your clock is a few seconds out of whack, it will gradually pull it back in rather than making the adjustment all at once. However, sudden adjustments are still possible, even if rare, and your code should be robust against them. Even the gradual adjustments will cause your timeouts to change duration, albeit not by a huge amount.

The bad news is that Cocoa doesn't make it easy to do this right. You want to use a consistent, non-adjustable clock for elapsed time, but Cocoa has no APIs for such a thing. The OS does, so you just have to drop down a level.

My preferred API for this task is mach_absolute_time. However, this returns a value that's in terms of arbitrary timebase units, not something comfortable like seconds or nanoseconds. It's not hard to convert, but requires some work. Apple has two examples of how to convert the return value into something sensible.

Two other reasonable alternatives are the Carbon calls `Microseconds` and `UpTime`.

Distributed Objects

I've said it before, but Distributed Objects need special care and attention. The trouble is that DO looks like a completely transparent way to access objects in other processes, but it doesn't entirely succeed at this. It can still be a good way to do IPC, but it requires more care than you might think from reading through the documentation on it. For details on why that's so, my original post on the subject covers it all.

Friday Q&A 2009-11-20: Probing Cocoa With PyObjC

Related Articles

Thread Safety in OS X System Frameworks	24
Code Injection	40
The Good and Bad of Distributed Objects	56
Intro to the Objective-C Runtime	67
Objective-C Messaging	73
Objective-C Message Forwarding	77
Objective-C Class Loading and Initialization	115
Care and Feeding of Singletons	194
Dangerous Cocoa Calls	236
Using Accessors in Init and Dealloc	246
NSRunLoop Internals	273
NSNotificationQueue	284
Method Replacement for Fun and Profit	297
Error Returns with Continuation Passing Style	303
Comparison of Objective-C Enumeration Techniques	369
Implementing Fast Enumeration	373
Implementing a Custom Slider	382
Dealing with Retain Cycles	392
What Every Apple Programmer Should Know	401
Leopard Collection Classes	405
Implementing Equality and Hashing	412
Zeroing Weak References in Objective-C	428
Zeroing Weak References to CoreFoundation Objects	447
Implementing NSCoding	459
Defensive Programming in Cocoa	468

It's another Friday and time for another Friday Q&A. This week, fellow Amoeba Jeff Johnson suggested talking about using Cocoa from the command line using Python and PyObjC.

I assume everybody reading this knows what Cocoa is, but may not know what the other two parts are:

- **Python:** A clean, fairly modern "scripting" language. Its object model is much like Smalltalk, in that pretty much everything is an object and there are no

primitives, but the syntax is more C-like. Significantly, for the purposes of this article, Python provides a nice, friendly command-line interpreter that you can access by typing `python` into your nearest terminal window.
- **PyObjC:** A language bridge between Python and Objective-C. It will translate or proxy objects from one language into objects in the other language, bi-directionally. Allows you to write Cocoa apps partly or entirely in Python, and also lets you poke at Cocoa from Python's interpreter.

Basics

PyObjC gets implicitly loaded whenever you load one of the Python modules that need it. Most system frameworks have a corresponding Python module. To load such a module, you can enter `import FrameworkName` at the Python command line. However, since Python supports namespaces, this requires putting `FrameworkName.` before any symbol inside that framework that you want to use. This is usually a good thing for "real" code, but if we're just going to experiment with things from the command line, it's better to avoid that. You can tell Python to import everything in the framework into the top-level namespace instead with `from FrameworkName import *`. Then you can use symbols from the framework directly. Example:

```
>>> from Foundation import *
>>> NSFileManager
<objective-c class NSFileManager at 0x7fff7101eb18>
```

And then you can send messages to these classes using Python's C++/Java-ish syntax:

```
>>> NSFileManager.defaultManager()
<NSFileManager: 0x100257900>
```

PyObjC automatically translates common object types across, such as strings, so you can just write normal string literals in Python and have it work. To pass a parameter, you have to deal with the syntax mismatch, because Python has a single method name, whereas Objective-C interleaves method name components with parameters. To translate to Python, glue all of the method's components together, then replace the colons with underscores. Examples:

```
>>> NSFileManager.defaultManager().displayNameAtPath_('/')
u'Fear'
>>> NSFileManager.defaultManager().fileAttributesAtPath_traverseLink_('/',
True)
{
    NSFileCreationDate = "2006-08-18 08:33:34 -0400";
    NSFileExtensionHidden = 0;
    NSFileGroupOwnerAccountID = 80;
    NSFileGroupOwnerAccountName = admin;
    NSFileModificationDate = "2009-11-16 23:58:45 -0500";
    NSFileOwnerAccountID = 0;
    NSFileOwnerAccountName = root;
    NSFilePosixPermissions = 1021;
    NSFileReferenceCount = 38;
    NSFileSize = 1360;
    NSFileSystemFileNumber = 2;
    NSFileSystemNumber = 234881026;
    NSFileType = NSFileTypeDirectory;
}
```

Note that, while basic Python objects like strings and dictionaries will get converted to their Cocoa equivalents when passing through the bridge, they are not instances of their Cocoa equivalents if they stay in Python-land. In other words, if you have a Python string, you can't just go and use NSString methods with it:

```
>>> 'abc'.length()
Traceback (most recent call last):
  File "<stdin>", line 1, in <module>
AttributeError: 'str' object has no attribute 'length'
```

Instead, you can do a simple pass into Cocoa first to get it to work:

```
>>> NSString.stringWithString_('abc').length()
3
```

(Of course in this specific example, you could just use the built in Python way of getting the length, with `len('abc')`.)

Errors

Cocoa methods that return `NSError` instances by reference get special treatment by PyObjC. Python cleanly supports returning multiple values from a method, but doesn't cleanly support return-by-reference, so PyObjC translates the `NSError` return by reference into a multiple return. You just assign two variables to the result of the method, and then pass `None` (Python's version of `nil` for the `NSError` argument. Example:

```
>>> string, error =
NSString.stringWithContentsOfFile_encoding_error_('/',
NSUTF8StringEncoding, None)
>>> string
>>> error.description().encode('utf8')
'Error Domain=NSCocoaErrorDomain Code=257
UserInfo=0x11994b610 "The file
\xe2\x80\x9cFear\xe2\x80\x9d couldn\xe2\x80\x99t be opened
because you don\xe2\x80\x99t have permission to view it."
Underlying Error=(Error Domain=NSPOSIXErrorDomain Code=13
"The operation couldn\xe2\x80\x99t be completed.
Permission denied")'
```

I have to engage in a bit of trickery to print the error object at the end because of the non-ASCII characters it contains. If I just try to print `error` directly, Python will complain that its description can't be converted to ASCII, so I have to manually get the description and convert it to UTF-8 for printing.

Arrays and Dictionaries

A Python array can be written like this:

```
['a', 'b', 'c']
```

And PyObjC will convert it to an NSArray as it crosses the bridge. This makes it trivial to pass arrays to Cocoa methods which take them:

```
>>> data, error =
NSPropertyListSerialization dataFromPropertyList_format_errorDescription_
'world'], NSPropertyListXMLFormat_v1_0, None)
>>> NSString.alloc().initWithData_encoding_(data,
NSUTF8StringEncoding)
u'<?xml version="1.0" encoding="UTF-8"?>\n<!DOCTYPE plist
PUBLIC "-//Apple//DTD PLIST 1.0//EN" "http://www.apple.com/
DTDs/PropertyList-1.0.dtd">\n<plist
version="1.0">\n<array>\n\t<string>hello</string>\n\t<string>world</strin
```

Dictionaries are written like this:

```
{ 'key' : 'value', 'key2' : 'value2' }
```

And likewise they get translated across the bridge:

```
>>> data, error =
NSPropertyListSerialization dataFromPropertyList_format_errorDescription_
    'key' : 'value', 'key2' : 'value2' },
    NSPropertyListXMLFormat_v1_0, None)
>>> NSString.alloc().initWithData_encoding_(data,
NSUTF8StringEncoding)       u'<?xml version="1.0"
encoding="UTF-8"?>\n<!DOCTYPE plist PUBLIC "-//Apple//DTD
PLIST 1.0//EN" "http://www.apple.com/DTDs/
PropertyList-1.0.dtd">\n<plist
version="1.0">\n<dict>\n\t<key>key</key>\n\t<string>value</string>\n\t<ke
```

Custom Frameworks

A fun thing with PyObjC is that it's not limited to system frameworks. You can load your own frameworks! It's trivial to do, because you can do it exactly as you would do it in a Cocoa program: just use NSBundle to load the framework and start getting and manipulating classes. Here's an example of doing this with a system framework, but it works just the same for your own:

```
>>> bundle = NSBundle.bundleWithPath_('/System/Library/
Frameworks/WebKit.framework')
>>> bundle.principalClass()
<objective-c class WebPlaceholderModalWindow at
0x7fff7095cc40>
>>> bundle.classNamed_('WebView').alloc().init()
<WebView: 0x100212490>
```

Once you have framework classes and objects, you can manipulate them just as you would Cocoa classes and objects.

Note that on 10.6 and 64-bit capable machines, Python loads as 64-bit by default, so if your framework is 32-bit only then this won't work. You can load Python in 32-bit mode by starting it with the following command (assuming you use the default bash shell):

```
VERSIONER_PYTHON_PREFER_32_BIT=yes python
```

AppKit

So far we've just been working with Foundation-like objects, but PyObjC supports AppKit as well:

```
>>> from AppKit import *
```

And it's trivial to get a little window up on the screen from there:

```
>>> NSApplicationLoad()
True
>>> window = NSWindow.alloc().init()
>>> window.makeKeyAndOrderFront_(None)
```

Where this really comes in handy is with things like NSImage. This lets you easily manipulate images using classes you already know. For example:

```
>>> image = NSImage.alloc().initWithContentsOfFile_('brakes.jpg')
>>> image
<NSImage 0x1198b6f70 Size={483, 450} Reps=(
    "NSBitmapImageRep 0x1198bcfa0 Size={483, 450}
ColorSpace=(not yet loaded) BPS=8 BPP=(not yet loaded)
Pixels=483x450 Alpha=NO Planar=NO Format=(not yet loaded)
CurrentBacking=nil (faulting) CGImageSource=0x1198bc220"
)>
>>> scaledImage = NSImage.alloc().initWithSize_((32, 32))
>>> scaledImage.lockFocus()
>>> image.drawInRect_fromRect_operation_fraction_(((0, 0), (32, 32)), NSZeroRect, NSCompositeCopy, 1.0)
>>> scaledImage.unlockFocus()
>>> scaledImage.TIFFRepresentation().writeToFile_atomically_('/tmp/brakes_thumb.tiff', True)
True
```

Conclusion

This article barely scratches the surface of what's possible with PyObjC, but it should get you started. You can manipulate QuickTime movies, put up windows, test frameworks, and even write full-blown applications. For further reading, check out the PyObjC documentation and the Python documentation. This is a valuable tool to have in your kit, whether for testing, rapid prototyping, or just trying things out.

Friday Q&A 2009-11-27: Using Accessors in Init and Dealloc

Related Articles

    Thread Safety in OS X System Frameworks 24

    The Good and Bad of Distributed Objects..56

    Intro to the Objective-C Runtime 67

    Objective-C Messaging...73

    Objective-C Message Forwarding 77

    Objective-C Class Loading and Initialization..115

    Care and Feeding of Singletons 194

    Dangerous Cocoa Calls..236

    Probing Cocoa With PyObjC...240

    NSRunLoop Internals 273

    NSNotificationQueue..284

    Method Replacement for Fun and Profit 297

    Error Returns with Continuation Passing Style 303

    Comparison of Objective-C Enumeration Techniques 369

    Implementing Fast Enumeration...373

    Implementing a Custom Slider 382

    Dealing with Retain Cycles 392

    What Every Apple Programmer Should Know 401

    Leopard Collection Classes...405

    Implementing Equality and Hashing 412

    Zeroing Weak References in Objective-C 428

    Implementing NSCoding 459

    Defensive Programming in Cocoa..468

It's Black Friday, and that means it's time for another Friday Q&A. Today I'm going to talk about the use of accessors in Objective-C init/dealloc methods, a topic suggested by Jon Trainer.

Introduction
There has been a change in the Cocoa community in the past few years, where the use of accessors in `init/dealloc` is frowned upon, recommend against, and outright considered to be wrong. Proponents of this position say that it is better to directly access instance variables instead. In other words, the recommendation is to write code like this:

```
- (id)initWithWhatever: (id)whatever
{
    if((self = [self init]))
    {
        _whatever = [whatever retain];
    }
    return self;
}

- (void)dealloc
{
    [_whatever release];

    [super dealloc];
}
```

The alternative is to use accessors, like this:

```
- (id)initWithWhatever: (id)whatever
{
    if((self = [self init]))
    {
        [self setWhatever: whatever];
    }
    return self;
}

- (void)dealloc
{
    [self setWhatever: nil];

    [super dealloc];
}
```

Pros of Accessors

The pros of using accessors in init/dealloc are pretty much the same as the pros of using them anywhere else. They decouple the code from your implementation, and in particular help you with memory management. How many times have you accidentally written code like this?

```
- (id)init
{
    _ivar = [NSArray arrayWithObjects:...];
    return self;
}
```

247

I expect the answer will vary quite a bit (I haven't made this particular error in quite a long time) but using an accessor will make sure you don't make this mistake:

```
- (id)init
{
    [self setIvar: [NSArray arrayWithObjects:...]];
    return self;
}
```

Furthermore, you might have ancillary state, like caches, summaries, etc. that need to be set up and torn down when the object value changes. Correct use of accessors can ensure that all of this happens as it needs to when the object is created and destroyed without duplicate code.

Cons of Accessors

The downside to using accessors in this way can be summed up in one short sentence: accessors can have side effects. Sometimes these side effects are undesirable for `init/dealloc`.

When writing a setter, it needs to behave correctly if you're going to call it from `init/dealloc`. This means dealing with a partially constructed object.

Worse, if you ever override a setter in a subclass, you need to write it to handle the case where the superclass is using that setter to initialize or destroy its ivars. For example, this bit of innocuous-looking code is potentially dangerous:

```
- (void)setSomeObj: (id)obj
{
    [anotherObj notifySomething];
    [super setSomeObj: obj];
}

- (void)dealloc
{
    [anotherObj release];
    [super dealloc];
}
```

If the superclass uses the accessor to destroy `someObj`, then the override will execute after `dealloc` has already executed, causing the override to access a dangling reference to `anotherObj`, probably causing a nice crash.

It's not hard to fix this code to handle the situation gracefully. Simply assign `anotherObj = nil` after releasing it in `dealloc`, and everything works again. In general it's not difficult to make sure that your overrides behave properly, but if you're going to use accessors like this then you must remember to, and that is the difficult part.

Key-Value Observing
A topic which is frequently brought up in these discussions is key-value observing, because KVO is a common way for accessors to have side effects. Like other cases, if KVO side effects are triggered when the object is partially initialized or destroyed, and that code isn't written to tolerate such an object, bad things will occur. I personally think that it's mostly a red herring.

The reason it's mostly a red herring is because 99% of the time, KVO is not set up on an object until after it's already fully initialized, and is ceased before an object is destroyed. It is *conceivable* for KVO to be used such that it activates earlier or terminates later, but it's unlikely in practice.

It's not possible for outside code to do anything with your object until it's fully initialized, unless your initializer itself is passing pointers around to outside objects. And likewise, it's not possible for outside code to keep a KVO reference to your object as it's executing its `dealloc` method, because it's too late for it to remove it, unless your `dealloc` triggers something that allows it to do so. Superclass code does execute in these timeframes, but superclass code is extremely unlikely to do anything to cause external objects to observe properties that the superclass itself doesn't even have.

Conclusion
Now you know the pros and cons; should you use accessors in `init` and `dealloc`? In my opinion, it can go either way. The advantages aren't generally that great. The downsides are minor. I don't use accessors for the vast majority of my instance variables, but there are certain cases where the advantages become significant because I'm doing something special with an ivar, and in that case I don't hesitate to let the accessors save me some headache.

Friday Q&A 2009-12-04: Building Standalone iPhone Web Apps

Welcome to another edition of Friday Q&A. This week I'm going to talk about building standalone iPhone web apps, web apps that have an icon on the home screen, and which start a separate program when tapped, just like native apps, a topic suggested by Mike Shields.

iPhone web apps have been in the news a fair bit lately as a way to bypass Apple's troublesome review process. While web apps aren't as capable as native apps, and almost certainly never will be, they're still interesting to work with simply because they're so much simpler to develop and deploy.

Neven Mrgan's Pie Guy is perhaps the most prominent example. It's a complete Pac-Man look-alike built as a standalone web app, albeit one which, because it's all HTML and JavaScript, requires a 3GS to run smoothly.

While the ability to build apps like this is well known, I haven't seen anything that gathers all the requisite parts in one place and walks through how to build one, so that's my intent today. I cribbed much of this information from dissecting how Pie Guy does it, so don't think for a moment that I discovered any of this stuff myself.

Getting Started
In this post I'll walk through the process of creating a basic standalone web app. My example app simply queries the JavaScript location object and displays your latitude and longitude. You can try the completed app, or get its source with Subversion:

```
svn co http://mikeash.com/svn/PhoneWebApp
```

The scope of this post is simply building the parts that are special to iPhone standalone web apps. The actual HTML and JavaScript for the app functionality itself is beyond the scope of the discussion, but there are of course a wide range of resources out there for them.

Separate Program The first thing that you want in a standalone web app is for it to start as its own program, rather than loading into Safari, when the user taps your icon on the home screen. To make this happen, you simply add a `<meta>` tag to your `<head>` setting `apple-mobile-web-app-capable` to `yes`, like so:

```
<meta name="apple-mobile-web-app-capable" content="yes">
```

While you're in there, it can be useful to set the viewport of your web page to achieve 1x zoom instead of the default (which is around ⅓x zoom), and to disallow the user from changing the zoom factor. This helps make your web page act more like a real app. You can do this by adding another `<meta>` tag:

```
<meta name="viewport"
    content="width=device-width; height=device-height;
initial-scale=1.0; maximum-scale=1.0; user-scalable=no;">
```

Icons and Startup Images

Another thing that's a must for real iPhone apps is to have an actual icon and a startup image that's displayed while the app is loading. You can specify an icon by referencing it in a `<link>` tag with `apple-touch-icon-precomposed` set as the relationship, and you can specify a startup image with `apple-touch-startup-image`:

```
<link rel="apple-touch-icon-precomposed" href="icon.png">
<link rel="apple-touch-startup-image" href="default.png">
```

The images themselves need to be 57x57 for the icon and 320x460 for the startup image.

`<head>`

Putting the above together, and with the page title and link to the app's JavaScript code, the entire `<head>` tag looks like this:

```
<head>
    <title>PhoneWebApp</title>
    <meta name="apple-mobile-web-app-capable" content="yes">
    <meta name="viewport" content="width=device-width; height=device-height; initial-scale=1.0; maximum-scale=1.0; user-scalable=no;">

    <link rel="apple-touch-icon-precomposed" href="icon.png">
    <link rel="apple-touch-startup-image" href="default.png">

    <script src="main.js" type="text/javascript" />
</head>
```

Body

The body of the page is, of course, where you put all the stuff for your web app to interact with the user. Beyond the basic functionality of your app, you'll also want some iPhone-specific sections. You'll want to display a different page to users who view the app on a non-iPhone browser, to tell them to reload it with an iPhone. You'll also want to display a different page to users who view the app on an iPhone, but who have not yet installed it, to tell them how to install it.

251

For this particular app, I also have three more pages. One is a "loading" page, which is visible on initial load and gives the computer something to display until the JavaScript kicks in. One is a page to display in case navigation services aren't available for some reason. And finally, I have the real page that displays the navigation data.

Each conceptual "page" is actually a `<div>`. All but the initial "loading" page are set to be hidden, so that they can then be selectively un-hidden from JavaScript after things load.

With all of that, here's what the `<body>` tag looks like:

```
<body onload="load()">
    <div id="loading" style="position: absolute; left: 0; top: 0;">
        Loading....
    </div>

    <div id="noiphone" style="visibility: hidden; position: absolute; left: 0; top: 0;">
        This is an iPhone web app. Load this page on an iPhone!
    </div>

    <div id="notinstalled" style="visibility: hidden; position: absolute; left: 0; top: 0;">
        To install this web app, tap the + button at the bottom of the page, then select "Add to Home Screen".
    </div>

    <div id="nonavigation" style="visibility: hidden; position: absolute; left: 0; top: 0;">
        Location services aren't available for some reason.
    </div>

    <div id="navigation" style="visibility: hidden; position: absolute; left: 0; top: 0;">
        Longitude: <span id="longitude">N/A</span>
        <br>
        Latitude: <span id="latitude">N/A</span>
    </div>
</body>
```

Scripting

With the HTML out of the way, it's time to start scripting. The `<body>` tag references a load() function which will get called once the page is loaded. The first thing it does is hide the "loading" page:

```
function load()
{
    document.getElementById("loading").style.visibility = "hidden";
```

Then it has to decide which of the other four pages to display. First, it checks for a non-iPhone browser:

```
    // no iPhone
    if(navigator.appVersion.indexOf('iPhone OS ') < 0)
    {
document.getElementById("noiphone").style.visibility = "visible";
    }
```

Next, it checks to see if it's on an iPhone but not running standalone:

```
    else if(!window.navigator.standalone)
    {
document.getElementById("notinstalled").style.visibility = "visible";
    }
```

Then a check to see if navigation services are available:

```
    else if(!hasNavigation())
    {
document.getElementById("nonavigation").style.visibility = "visible";
    }
```

If all of these checks fail, then the app is running standalone on an iPhone and navigation services are available, so it can start doing normal app tasks:

253

```
        else
        {
            // we're on a phone, and installed standalone
            // "real" app init code goes here
    document.getElementById("navigation").style.visibility =
    "visible";


    navigator.geolocation.watchPosition(positionWatcher);
        }
    }
```

For the above code to work, it needs a function to check for the availability of navigation services, which is easy:

```
function hasNavigation()
{
    return (typeof navigator.geolocation != "undefined");
}
```

And another function to respond to position updates by updating the GUI:

```
function positionWatcher(location)
{
    document.getElementById("longitude").textContent =
location.coords.longitude;
    document.getElementById("latitude").textContent =
location.coords.latitude;
}
```

That's it!

Caching

The above code will work great to build a simple little web app that acts like a native app, with one significant exception: native apps work even when you have no data service, and this does not.

Even this problem can be solved, though. Specify a manifest file in the `<html>` tag at the top of the HTML file:

```
<html manifest="cache.manifest">
```

The manifest file itself must start with a line saying `CACHE MANIFEST`, and then subsequent lines refer to the files that the app needs to access, one per line. The manifest file for this app looks like this:

```
CACHE MANIFEST

index.html
main.js
default.png
icon.png
```

One more trick: the manifest file *must* be served with a content type of `text/cache-manifest`, otherwise iPhone Safari won't recognize it. The Subversion repository includes a `.htaccess` file which declares that MIME type, but beware that if you're trying to test it with OS X's personal web sharing, you have to do some configuration hacking to enable `.htaccess` support, which is beyond the scope of this post.

With the manifest in place, the iPhone will cache all resources locally when the user adds the bookmark, and the app will launch and function even when no data access is available. (Try enabling Airplane Mode to test it.)

While developing the app, the cache manifest can be really annoying, so it's a good idea to remove it from the `<html>` tag while you're working on it. Apple says that the browser will reload everything if there are any changes in the manifest file (like adding a blank line), but while working on this example I found this to be frustratingly unreliable.

Conclusion

iPhone web apps don't behave as well as native apps, and probably never will, but with these few simple tips you can bridge the gap much more closely than with just a simple web page, and create an app that completely bypasses the App Store. Building an interesting and useful app with HTML and JavaScript once you're in is, of course, up to you!

For further reading, Apple's Safari Web Content Guide documents all of the special tags I used here, and has a lot of other useful information as well. Also, I linked to this at the beginning but it merits a second mention, Neven Mrgan's Pie Guy is a great example of these tehcniques that you can examine to see how it ticks on the inside.

Friday Q&A 2009-12-11: A GCD Case Study: Building an HTTP Server

Related Articles

>Intro to Grand Central Dispatch, Part I: Basics and Dispatch Queues 162
>Intro to Grand Central Dispatch, Part II: Multi-Core Performance 169
>Intro to Grand Central Dispatch, Part III: Dispatch Sources 174
>Intro to Grand Central Dispatch, Part IV: Odds and Ends 179
>GCD Practicum...183
>A Preview of Coming Attractions..215
>Generators in Objective-C 216
>Background Timers...419

It's time for another wintry edition of Friday Q&A. From the comfort of your toasty-warm homes, you can read about building an HTTP server using Grand Central Dispatch, a topic suggested by Steven Degutis.

Techniques
An HTTP server obviously does a lot of networking, and GCD is great for managing I/O. It's quick and easy to set up a dispatch source that triggers when a file descriptor is available for reading and writing, which makes it straightforward to write a server that supports many connections simultaneously without inefficient techniques like using a dedicated thread for each connection, and without having to write your own dispatching loop or deal with messy runloop sources.

The desire for asynchronous I/O also makes this a perfect use case for generators. Using a generator allows code to be written in a natural top-down manner while still being completely asynchronous and not occupying a thread until completion. This makes it great for incrementally parsing an HTTP request as it comes down the wire, or incrementally sending the response.

This web server is meant more to illustrate techniques and be easy to understand than to be high performance. The primary source of inefficiency is that it reads and writes a single character at a time, which causes a great deal of overhead, but which simplifies the code substantially. A real server should read and write large buffers at once, and also pass those large buffers to and from the generators in use.

Source
If you want to follow along at home, the source code is available in my public subversion repository.

It also depends on MAGenerator, so if you want to build it you'll need to build `MAGenerator.m` as well, and make sure that `MAGenerator.h` is in your include path.

Due to the heavy use of generators, you'll need to know what those are and how `MAGenerator` works. If you haven't already, read my article on `MAGenerator` before you go further.

main

I'm going to take a top-down approach to this server, so the logical place to start is `main`. The program is intended to be run with one argument, the port number, so the first thing it does is check for the proper number of arguments, and then extract that port number if it's correct:

```
int main(int argc, char **argv)
{
    if(argc != 2)
    {
        fprintf(stderr, "usage: %s <port>\n", argv[0]);
        return 1;
    }

    int port = atoi(argv[1]);
```

Next, it will set up sockets to listen on that port (one socket each for IPv4 and IPv6), then call `dispatch_main` to let GCD start doing its thing:

```
    SetupSockets(port);

    LOG("listening on port %d", port);

    dispatch_main();

    return 0;
}
```

Setup

The code to set up the sockets is straightforward sockets code, and I won't go into details on that. If you're unfamiliar with sockets, there are lots of references out there. Note that the `CHECK` macro is just something that tests for a `-1` return value and prints an error and exits the program if so.

```
static void SetupSockets(int port)
{
    int listenSocket4 = CHECK(socket(PF_INET, SOCK_STREAM, 0));
    int listenSocket6 = CHECK(socket(PF_INET6, SOCK_STREAM, 0));

    struct sockaddr_in addr4 = { sizeof(addr4), AF_INET, htons(port), { INADDR_ANY }, { 0 } };
    struct sockaddr_in6 addr6 = { sizeof(addr6), AF_INET6, htons(port), 0, IN6ADDR_ANY_INIT, 0 };

    int yes = 1;
    CHECK(setsockopt(listenSocket4, SOL_SOCKET, SO_REUSEADDR, (void *)&yes, sizeof(yes)));
    CHECK(setsockopt(listenSocket6, SOL_SOCKET, SO_REUSEADDR, (void *)&yes, sizeof(yes)));
    CHECK(bind(listenSocket4, (void *)&addr4, sizeof(addr4)));
    CHECK(bind(listenSocket6, (void *)&addr6, sizeof(addr6)));

    SetupListenSource(listenSocket4);
    SetupListenSource(listenSocket6);
}
```

The SetupListenSource function is where things start to get interesting. This first calls listen on the socket to make it start listening for connections. It then creates a new dispatch_source_t to handle events on the socket. Note that, just as with select, GCD treats a new connection on a listening socket as a read event, so that's the type of dispatch source that this function creates:

```
static void SetupListenSource(int s)
{
    CHECK(listen(s, 16));

    dispatch_source_t source = NewFDSource(s, DISPATCH_SOURCE_TYPE_READ, ^{
        AcceptConnection(s);
    });
    dispatch_resume(source);

    // leak it, it lives forever
}
```

The `NewFDSource` function is just a simple wrapper for a couple of GCD calls:

```
static dispatch_source_t NewFDSource(int s,
dispatch_source_type_t type, dispatch_block_t block)
{
    dispatch_source_t source =
dispatch_source_create(type, s, 0,
dispatch_get_global_queue(DISPATCH_QUEUE_PRIORITY_DEFAULT,
0));
    dispatch_source_set_event_handler(source, block);
    return source;
}
```

Reading

When a new connection arrives, `AcceptConnection` is called to set up the connection. The first thing it does is call `accept` to get the socket for that specific connection:

```
static void AcceptConnection(int listenSock)
{
    struct sockaddr addr;
    socklen_t addrlen = sizeof(addr);
    int newSock = CHECK(accept(listenSock, &addr,
&addrlen;));
    LOG("new connection on socket %d, new socket is %d",
listenSock, newSock);
```

Next, it creates a new `Connection` structure:

```
    struct Connection *connection = NewConnection(newSock);
```

I initially thought that I could get away with not having such a structure at all, and let everything about a connection be managed as implicit block/generator state. However, there's a wrinkle. It starts with this text on the `dispatch_source` man page:

```
Important: a cancellation handler is required for file
descriptor and
mach port based sources in order to safely close the
descriptor or
destroy the port. Closing the descriptor or port before the
cancellation
handler has run may result in a race condition: if a new
descriptor is
allocated with the same value as the recently cosed[sic]
```

259

```
descriptor while the
source's event handler is still running, the event handler may read/write
data to the wrong descriptor.
```

The trick is that a socket is bidirectional, and the server will ultimately have *two* dispatch sources monitoring it, one for reading and one for writing. Neither one can safely close the socket in its cancellation handler, because it's unknown which one will be cancelled first. Thus, the `Connection` structure simply holds the socket as well as a reference count which starts out at 2. Each cancellation handler decrements the refcount, and then closes the socket if it's the last one out.

The next step is to create a request reader, which is a generator that parses the incoming HTTP request:

```
int (^requestReader)(char) = RequestReader(connection);
```

Next, it creates a dispatch source to look for available data on the new socket. The event handler reads a single character from the socket, then passes that character off to the request reader. On `EOF`, it writes out an error response if the request wasn't complete enough to generate a normal response, then cancels the handler. Since this is an HTTP 1.0 server, not a 1.1 server, the connection is not reusable for subsequent requests, but rather the client must open a new one each time.

```
    __block BOOL didSendResponse = NO;
    __block dispatch_source_t source;
    // gcc tosses a spurious error if this is an initializer for some reason
    source = NewFDSource(newSock, DISPATCH_SOURCE_TYPE_READ, ^{
        char c;
        LOG("reading from %d", newSock);
        int howMuch = read(newSock, &c, 1);
        LOG("read from %d returned %d (errno is %d %s)", newSock, howMuch, errno, strerror(errno));

        BOOL isErr = NO;
        if(howMuch == -1 && errno != EAGAIN && errno != EINTR)
        {
            LOG("read returned error %d (%s)", errno, strerror(errno));
            isErr = YES;
        }
        if(howMuch > 0)
        {
            int ret = requestReader(c);
            if(ret)
                didSendResponse = YES;
        }
        if(howMuch == 0 || isErr)
        {
            if(!didSendResponse)
                Write(connection, ErrCodeWriter(400));
            dispatch_source_cancel(source);
        }
    });
```

Note that after reading a byte, the handler simply falls off the end. As long as data is available, GCD will keep invoking the event handler, so GCD essentially functions as the outer loop to this code.

The cancel handler simply releases the connection and the dispatch source:

```
    dispatch_source_set_cancel_handler(source, ^{
        ReleaseConnection(connection);
        dispatch_release(source);
    });
```

And as its last act, `AcceptConnection` "resumes" the source so that it can start processing:

```
    dispatch_resume(source);
}
```

The request reader generator simply accepts a character at a time as a parameter, and parses the HTTP request. The big advantage of using a generator can be seen here, where the parser is written completely top-down, and yet is fully asynchronous. It returns an integer to indicate to the caller whether it sent a response or not, so that the caller can know whether it needs to send its own fail-safe error response. If it hits a parse error at any point, it responds with an error and bails out, otherwise it makes a call to `ProcessResource` and tells it which resource it's supposed to process. This parser completely ignores any headers sent by the client, so once the method and resource have been read, it simply enters a loop and skips over any remaining input.

```
GENERATOR(int, RequestReader(struct Connection
*connection), (char))
{
    NSMutableData *buffer = [NSMutableData data];
    GENERATOR_BEGIN(char c)
    {
        // read the request method
        while(c != '\r' && c != '\n' && c != ' ')
        {
            [buffer appendBytes: &c length: 1];
            GENERATOR_YIELD(0);
        }

        // if the line ended before we got a space then we don't understand the request
        if(c != ' ')
        {
            LOG("Got a bad request from the client on %d", connection->sock);
            Write(connection, ErrCodeWriter(400));
            GENERATOR_YIELD(1); // signal that we got enough for a response
        }
        else
        {
            // we only support GET
            if([buffer length] != 3 || memcmp([buffer bytes], "GET", 3) != 0)
            {
                LOG("Got an unknown method from the client on %d", connection->sock);
                Write(connection, ErrCodeWriter(501));
                GENERATOR_YIELD(1); // signal that we got enough for a response
            }
            else
            {
                // skip over the delimeter
                GENERATOR_YIELD(0);

                // read the resource
                [buffer setLength: 0];
                while(c != '\r' && c != '\n' && c != ' ')
                {
                    [buffer appendBytes: &c length: 1];
```

```
                GENERATOR_YIELD(0);
            }
            
            LOG("Servicing request from the client on %d", connection->sock);
            NSString *s = [[[NSString alloc] initWithData: buffer encoding: NSUTF8StringEncoding] autorelease];
            if(!s)
                Write(connection, ErrCodeWriter(400));
            else
                ProcessResource(connection, s);
            GENERATOR_YIELD(1); // signal that we got enough for a response
        }
    }
    
    // we just ignore anything else sent by the client
    while(1)
        GENERATOR_YIELD(0);
    }
    GENERATOR_END
}
```

Responding

The `ProcessResource` function is extremely simple. It simply gets a content generator for the resource in question, and writes it:

```
static void ProcessResource(struct Connection *connection, NSString *resource)
{
    Write(connection, ContentGeneratorForResource(resource));
}
```

`ContentGeneratorForResource` just checks for known resources and returns the appropriate handler if it finds one, otherwise returning a "not found" handler. If you wanted to add more handlers, this is where they would go:

```
static NSData *(^ContentGeneratorForResource(NSString
*resource))(void)
{
    if([resource isEqual: @"/"])
        return RootHandler(resource);
    if([resource isEqual: @"/listing"])
        return ListingHandler(resource);

    return NotFoundHandler(resource);
}
```

The Write function is basically the inverse of the read handler shown above. It takes the content generator, and wraps it in a byte generator which generates one byte at a time. It then writes those bytes until no more remain, or an error occurs, at which point it shuts down the write side of the socket and releases the connection and dispatch source:

```
static void Write(struct Connection *connection, NSData *(^contentGenerator)(void))
{
    int (^byteGenerator)(void) = ByteGenerator(contentGenerator);
    __block dispatch_source_t source;
    source = NewFDSource(connection->sock, DISPATCH_SOURCE_TYPE_WRITE, ^{
        int byte = byteGenerator();
        BOOL err = NO;
        if(byte != -1) // EOF
        {
            unsigned char buf = byte;
            int howMuch;
            do
            {
                howMuch = write(connection->sock, &buf, 1);
            }
            while(howMuch == -1 && (errno == EAGAIN || errno == EINTR));
            if(howMuch == -1)
            {
                err = YES;
                LOG("write returned error %d (%s)", errno, strerror(errno));
            }
        }
        if(byte == -1 || err)
        {
            LOG("Done servicing %d", connection->sock);
            dispatch_source_cancel(source);
        }
    });
    dispatch_source_set_cancel_handler(source, ^{
        CHECK(shutdown(connection->sock, SHUT_WR));
        ReleaseConnection(connection);
        dispatch_release(source);
    });
    dispatch_resume(source);
}
```

As you can see from the declaration, a content generator is a generator that returns NSData instances. The idea is that it can return its response in nice manageable chunks, but not have to build up the entire response in memory ahead of time. However, to simplify writing, the server writes only one byte at a time. The ByteGenerator

generator takes an NSData generator and returns the individual bytes, one by one. Since it needs to be able to signal when it reaches the end, it actually returns an int, using -1 as the EOF signal and positive numbers for byte values:

```
GENERATOR(int, ByteGenerator(NSData
*(^contentGenerator)(void)), (void))
{
    __block NSData *data = nil;
    __block NSUInteger cursor = 0;
    GENERATOR_BEGIN(void)
    {
        do
        {
            if(cursor < [data length])
            {
                const unsigned char *ptr = [data bytes];
                GENERATOR_YIELD((int)ptr[cursor++]);
            }
            else
            {
                [data release];
                data = [contentGenerator() retain];
                cursor = 0;
            }
        } while(data);
        GENERATOR_YIELD(-1);
    }
    GENERATOR_CLEANUP
    {
        [data release];
    }
    GENERATOR_END
}
```

With this, the server is essentially complete except for the handlers.

Resource Handlers

The first handler is an error code writer. Give it a code, it dumps out an appropriate error response. This is used in the request parsing code to handle errors there:

```
GENERATOR(NSData *, ErrCodeWriter(int code), (void))
{
    GENERATOR_BEGIN(void)
    {
        if(code == 400)
            GENERATOR_YIELD(Data(@"HTTP/1.0 400 Bad Request"));
        else if(code == 501)
            GENERATOR_YIELD(Data(@"HTTP/1.0 501 Not Implemented"));
        else
            GENERATOR_YIELD(Data(@"HTTP/1.0 500 Internal Server Error"));
        
        NSString *str = [NSString stringWithFormat:
            @"\r\n"
            @"Content-type: text/html\r\n"
            @"\r\n"
            @"The server generated error code %d while processing the HTTP request",
            code];
        GENERATOR_YIELD(Data(str));
    }
    GENERATOR_END
}
```

Next, the "not found" handler simply generates a typical 404 error page:

```
GENERATOR(NSData *, NotFoundHandler(NSString *resource), (void))
{
    GENERATOR_BEGIN(void)
    {
        NSString *str = [NSString stringWithFormat:
            @"HTTP/1.0 404 Not Found\r\n"
            @"Content-type: text/html\r\n"
            @"\r\n"
            @"The resource %@ could not be found",
            HTMLEscape(resource)];
        GENERATOR_YIELD(Data(str));
    }
    GENERATOR_END
}
```

The root handler just displays a little welcome page with a link to a more interesting handler:

```
GENERATOR(NSData *, RootHandler(NSString *resource),
(void))
{
    GENERATOR_BEGIN(void)
    {
        NSString *str = @"HTTP/1.0 200 OK\r\n"
                        @"Content-type: text/html\r\n"
                        @"\r\n"
                        @"Welcome to GCDWeb. There isn't much here. <a href=\"listing\">Try the listing.</a>";
        GENERATOR_YIELD(Data(str));
    }
    GENERATOR_END
}
```

Finally there's a listing handler, which serves to illustrate the asynchronous nature of this server. It just lists the full contents of /tmp using an NSDirectoryEnumerator. The server architecture allows the response to be generated incrementally and sent to the client as the response is created, rather than buffering it all and sending it in one big chunk, and yet the response handler code is, once again, completely straightforward top-to-bottom:

```
GENERATOR(NSData *, ListingHandler(NSString *resource),
(void))
{
    __block NSEnumerator *enumerator = nil;
    GENERATOR_BEGIN(void)
    {
        NSString *str = @"HTTP/1.0 200 OK\r\n"
                        @"Content-type: text/html; charset=utf-8\r\n"
                        @"\r\n"
                        @"Directory listing of <tt>/tmp</tt>:<p>";
        GENERATOR_YIELD(Data(str));

        NSFileManager *fm = [[NSFileManager alloc] init];
        // +defaultManager is not thread safe
        enumerator = [[fm enumeratorAtPath: @"/tmp"] retain];
        [fm release];

        NSString *file;
        while((file = [enumerator nextObject]))
        {
            GENERATOR_YIELD(Data(file));
            // note: file is no longer valid after this point!

            GENERATOR_YIELD(Data(@"<br>"));
        }
    }
    GENERATOR_CLEANUP
    {
        [enumerator release];
    }
    GENERATOR_END
}
```

And that's all of the significant code in the server. There are a couple of helpers, and the code to manage the `Connection` structure, which I won't go over here, but you can always read the source if you want to see them.

Conclusion
The combination of GCD and generators makes for a relatively simple asynchronous server architecture. 400 lines of code gives us a fairly complete, if not very featureful,

web server which is fully multithreaded to handle multiple connections simultaneously, and which automatically uses thread pools to distribute work.

However, this server is not very efficient due to reading and writing single bytes. A better technique would be to manage buffers. Doing so would not make the code too much more complex, and would eliminate a great deal of overhead. This would, I think, push this server into the realm of being reasonable to use for real-world situations.

Another interesting thing to consider is that the response side of the server is only asynchronous in one direction. Resource handlers commonly read files, but the architecture of this server does not allow for asynchronous reading of files in the resource handler, only asynchronous writing of the data. Although probably not a problem in normal situations (the file read can simply block for a bit, and it won't cause trouble except for holding on to a worker thread until it's done) it would be cleaner and potentially more efficient to make the server asynchronous in both directions.

Accomplishing this would be a fair amount of work. The write side would need to use two dispatch sources, one for the write socket and one for the file, and would have to suspend and resume them in a complicated fashion to stop GCD from calling the event handler of one source while waiting for the other source to open up. It could be done, and wouldn't be enormously complicated, but is well beyond the scope of this demonstration server.

Friday Q&A 2009-12-18: Highlights From a Year of Friday Q&A

It's hard to believe that it's been a full year (minus a day) since my first Friday Q&A. It's become more successful than I thought possible, and many kind and obviously deluded people have said great things about it to me. Since I'm feeling lazy this week, I thought I'd pull up some highlights from the past year rather than write anything new.

The most popular article was Mac OS X Process Memory Statistics, probably because it was accessible and relevant enough to be of interest to the average user, plus Daring Fireball linked to it. That link drove a huge amount of traffic, and that article got well over 10,000 hits to it that weekend.

The most popular article among developers, as measured by the number of comments left on it, was my early introduction to blocks (written before I had the idea of giving each one a title), which racked up an impressive 42 comments (so far).

Blocks remained a popular topic, with Practical Blocks coming once blocks were mature enough to use them in real code.

Blocks are the natural ally of Grand Central Dispatch, which I covered in a four-part series, talking about Basics and Dispatch Queues, Multi-Core Performance, Dispatch Sources, Odds and Ends, and finally capping it all off with a Practicum.

I did more than just talk about blocks. I did a three-part series on the Objective-C runtime, built an absolutely insane message forwarding system with LLVM, and created a nutty blocks-based generator framework.

There are, of course, a lot more posts. I very nearly succeeded in doing one post each week for the whole year, only missing a few weeks here and there. Thanks to my recent addition of tags support to my blog, you can view the full list of Friday Q&A posts.

It's been a great year, and I'm looking forward to the next one. I'll be taking next week off, but I'll be back in two weeks with another one.

Friday Q&A 2010-01-01: NSRunLoop Internals

Related Articles
- Thread Safety in OS X System Frameworks 24
- The Good and Bad of Distributed Objects..........56
- Care and Feeding of Singletons 194
- Dangerous Cocoa Calls..........236
- Probing Cocoa With PyObjC..........240
- Using Accessors in Init and Dealloc..........246
- NSNotificationQueue..........284
- Implementing a Custom Slider 382
- Dealing with Retain Cycles 392
- What Every Apple Programmer Should Know 401
- Leopard Collection Classes..........405
- Implementing Equality and Hashing 412
- Implementing NSCoding 459
- Defensive Programming in Cocoa..........468

It's the first Friday of the new year, and that means it's time for the first Friday Q&A of 2010. This week, I'm taking Dave DeLong's suggestion of talking about NSRunLoop internals.

If you want to understand something as thoroughly as possible, you should build one yourself. That's a little too much for a blog post, so rather than build a complete implementation of NSRunLoop, I'm going to take the second-best route and plan out the key features of its internals in pseudocode.

CoreFoundation
On the Mac, NSRunLoop sits on top of its CoreFoundation equivalent, CFRunLoop. Most of the smarts are there, and the Cocoa side of things is mostly a wrapper. For this discussion, I am going to ignore this layering, and examine NSRunLoop as a single, standalone entity. From this perspective, CFRunLoop can be considered to be an implementation detail.

Autorelease Pools
One of the basic things that NSRunLoop does is to manage autorelease pools, both for itself and for any code that it calls. Since autorelease pools are fairly straightforward compared to the rest, and will just serve to clutter things up, I will ignore this aspect of NSRunLoop's functionality.

Fundamentals

Most of the mysteriousness in `NSRunLoop` is in its various `run` methods. What goes on in there? How does it all work?

The `-run` method is pretty simple, since the documentation describes it in terms of `-runMode:beforeDate::`

```
If no input sources or timers are attached to the runloop,
this method exits immediately; otherwise, it runs the
receiver in the NSDefaultRunLoopMode by repeatedly invoking
runMode:beforeDate:.
```

Its implementation must therefore look something pretty close to:

```
- (void)run
{
    while([self hasSourcesOrTimers])
        [self runMode: NSDefaultRunLoopMode beforeDate:
[NSDate distantFuture]];
}
```

The `-runUntilDate:` method is similar:

```
If no input sources or timers are attached to the runloop,
this method exits immediately; otherwise, it runs the
receiver in the NSDefaultRunLoopMode by repeatedly invoking
runMode:beforeDate: until the specified expiration date.
```

Its implementation would then be like this:

```
- (void)runUntilDate: (NSDate *)limitDate
{
    while([self hasSourcesOrTimers])
    {
        [self runMode: NSDefaultRunLoopMode beforeDate:
limitDate];

        // check limitDate at the end of the loop to
ensure that
        // the runloop always runs at least once
        if([limitDate timeIntervalSinceNow] < 0)
            break;
    }
}
```

That was easy enough. How about `-runMode:beforeDate:`, then? Well, that's where all the complication lies.

Input Sources

As described in Apple's Run Loops programming guide, a runloop contains two types of sources: inputs and timers. An input source is basically some kind of external signal from outside the runloop itself.

In Mac OS X, input sources are mach ports. While things like NSFileHandle and CFFileDescriptor may give the appearance of connecting non-mach-port things into the runloop, this is actually fake! They monitor their file descriptor sources on a dedicated thread, then signal back to the runloop over a mach port.

(This may have changed in 10.6, which now has APIs which are capable of monitoring both mach ports and file descriptors at the same time. However, the fundamental fact remains that mach ports are the major input source used on OS X.)

Most people's eyes glaze over when they hear about mach ports. They're not very well known, nor well documented. And personally, I don't know them all that well myself. Because of this, I'm going to explore an alternate `NSRunLoop` which uses file descriptors as its input sources instead. The fundamentals are the same, and file descriptors are more readily understandable to most people.

Quick refresher: what is a file descriptor, or FD for short? An FD is an object (not in the Objective-C sense, but in the conceptual sense) which you can either read from, write to, or both read and write. An FD can have data available for reading, space available for writing, or neither. This particular state of an FD can change over time. For example, imagine an FD which represents a socket communicating with another application. When that other application writes to the socket, the FD in your application will have data available for reading. If that FD is an input source for a runloop, that runloop will wake up and process that source. Likewise, if the other application reads from the socket, the FD in your application will have space available for writing, and this will also wake up the runloop and process that source. This is one of the fundamental tasks of a runloop.

A runloop needs to monitor multiple input sources at a time. There are several APIs for doing this on OS X, but the one I'm going to use here is `select(2)`.

I won't go into details on how to use `select` (pseudocode, remember?), but the basics are pretty easy: you give it three sets of FDs, which you want to monitor for reading, writing, and errors. It then returns whenever there's activity, and the three sets contain those FDs which have had that sort of activity on them.

Thus, we can see the first pass at how `-runMode:beforeDate:` would work. I'm going to simplify things a bit further and ignore the fact that `select` takes three different sets of FDs, and just use one. The idea is just that we're interested in activity on these input sources.

And remember, I'm doing pseudocode, so don't expect this to look 100% like real Objective-C.

The first thing is to check if there are any sources. According to the documentation, this method immediately returns NO if not:

```
- (BOOL)runMode: (NSString *)mode beforeDate: (NSDate *)limitDate
{
    if(![self hasSourcesOrTimers])
        return NO;
```

Next, create an empty FD set:

```
fd_set fdset;
FD_ZERO(&fdset);
```

Then, set each input source's FD within the set. I assume that the input source class has a `-fileDescriptor` method that returns the FD it wants to monitor:

```
for(inputSource in [self inputSources])
    FD_SET([inputSource fileDescriptor], &fdset);
```

Now call `select`. Remember, to simplify, I'm pretending that it only takes one file descriptor set rather than three. I'm also ignoring all error checking:

```
select(fdset, NULL);
```

Once it returns, check each input source to see if it's ready for processing now. I iterate over a copy of the input sources because the code that the input source executes may modify the set of input sources:

```
for(inputSource in [[[self inputSources] copy] autorelease])
    if(FD_ISSET([inputSource fileDescrptor], &fdset))
        [inputSource fileDescriptorIsReady];
```

The documentation states that this method returns YES if the runloop was run in any way, so that's the last thing to do here:

```
    return YES;
}
```

Modes

So far so good, but it has a way to go. This method completely ignores its parameters! First, we'll look at the mode parameter.

Just what is the mode parameter, anyway? A mode is essentially a grouping of input and timer sources. Different sources are active in different modes. NSRunLoop has NSDefaultRunLoopMode, which as the name would expect is where most sources are added. In Cocoa, you also have secondary modes like NSEventTrackingRunLoopMode, which is used when the mouse is held down on a control. By switching to this mode, sources which were only added to the default mode will not fire, which prevents unwanted code from running while the user is in the middle of making a menu selection or moving a slider. Sources which need to fire during event tracking can be added to that mode. Sources which need to fire in both circumstances can be added to both.

You can then imagine NSRunLoop containing an instance variable for input sources like this:

```
// maps modes to NSMutableSets
NSMutableDictionary *_inputSources;
```

NSRunLoop's method to add an input source is called -addPort:forMode:, and its implementation would then look like this:

```
- (void)addPort: (NSPort *)aPort forMode: (NSString *)mode
{
    NSMutableSet *sourcesSet = [_inputSources objectForKey: mode];
    if(!sourcesSet)
    {
        // this is the first time anything has used this mode
        // so create a new set for it
        sourcesSet = [NSMutableSet set];
        [_inputSources setObject: sourcesSet forKey: mode];
    }
    [sourcesSet addObject: aPort];
}
```

Similarly for the removal method:

```
- (void)removePort: (NSPort *)aPort forMode: (NSString *)mode
{
    NSMutableSet *sourcesSet = [_inputSources objectForKey: mode];
    [sourcesSet removeObject: aPort];

    // this isn't strictly necessary, but keeps us from leaking
    // sets if the caller uses a lot of one-time "throwaway" modes
    // (which it probably never would)
    if(![sourcesSet count])
        [_inputSources removeObjectForKey: mode];
}
```

And then the run method needs to be changed to match:

```
- (BOOL)runMode: (NSString *)mode beforeDate: (NSDate *)limitDate
{
    if(![self hasSourcesOrTimersForMode: mode])
        return NO;

    fd_set fdset;
    FD_ZERO(&fdset);

    for(inputSource in [_inputSources objectForKey: mode])
        FD_SET([inputSource fileDescriptor], &fdset);

    select(fdset, NULL);

    for(inputSource in [[[_inputSources objectForKey: mode] copy] autorelease])
        if(FD_ISSET([inputSource fileDescrptor], &fdset))
            [inputSource fileDescriptorIsReady];

    return YES;
}
```

Timeout

This code still ignores one parameter, `limitDate`. The purpose of this parameter is to force the method to return even if no input sources were ready. It functions as a timeout. To make this work, the code simply computes the timeout and passes it as the last parameter to `select` (which in reality requires a more complicated timeout structure, not just an `NSTimeInterval`, but remember, pseudocode!):

```
- (BOOL)runMode: (NSString *)mode beforeDate: (NSDate *)limitDate
{
    if(![self hasSourcesOrTimersForMode: mode])
        return NO;

    fd_set fdset;
    FD_ZERO(&fdset);

    for(inputSource in [_inputSources objectForKey: mode])
        FD_SET([inputSource fileDescriptor], &fdset);

    NSTimeInterval timeout = [limitDate timeIntervalSinceNow];
    select(fdset, timeout);

    // if the timeout was hit, there may not be
    // any active input sources, but this loop
    // will simply do nothing if that's the case
    for(inputSource in [[[_inputSources objectForKey: mode] copy] autorelease])
        if(FD_ISSET([inputSource fileDescrptor], &fdset))
            [inputSource fileDescriptorIsReady];

    return YES;
}
```

Timer Sources

This implementation deals with input sources and the timeout parameter well enough, but completely ignores timers.

As with input sources, I'll assume an instance variable which holds timers. And like input sources, timers are grouped into modes:

```
// maps modes to NSMutableSets
NSMutableDictionary *_timerSources;
```

I'll skip over the implementation of `-addTimer:forMode:`, as it should be pretty obvious and is basically identical to `-addPort:forMode:`.

Adding timer support to the above code is relatively straightforward. The list of timers can be consulted to find the one that fires earliest. If that time is earlier than `limitDate`, then it gets to be the timeout instead of `limitDate`. After `select` runs, check the list of timers to see if any of them are ready to fire, and fire the ones that are.

There's one wrinkle, which is that a timer firing does *not* make `-runMode:beforeDate:` return. If a timer fires, it should be processed, and then control should return back to `select`. This continues until an input source fires. If an input source does fire, the method still needs to check the list of timers and fire any that are ready, because otherwise a busy input source could prevent timers from ever running.

Given all of that, here's what the code looks like with timer support:

```objc
- (BOOL)runMode: (NSString *)mode beforeDate: (NSDate *)limitDate
{
    if(![self hasSourcesOrTimersForMode: mode])
        return NO;

    // with timer support, this code has to loop until an input
    // source fires
    BOOL didFireInputSource = NO;
    while(!didFireInputSource)
    {
        fd_set fdset;
        FD_ZERO(&fdset);

        for(inputSource in [_inputSources objectForKey: mode])
            FD_SET([inputSource fileDescriptor], &fdset);

        // the timeout needs to be set from the limitDate
        // and from the list of timers
        // start with the limitDate
        NSTimeInterval timeout = [limitDate timeIntervalSinceNow];

        // now run through the list of timers and set the
        // timeout to the smallest one found in them and
        // in the limitDate
        for(timer in [_timerSources objectForKey: mode])
            timeout = MIN(timeout, [[timer fireDate] timeIntervalSinceNow]);

        // now run select
        select(fdset, timeout);

        // process input sources first (this choice is arbitrary)
        for(inputSource in [[[_inputSources objectForKey: mode] copy] autorelease])
            if(FD_ISSET([inputSource fileDescrptor], &fdset))
            {
                didFireInputSource = YES;
                [inputSource fileDescriptorIsReady];
            }
```

```
        // now process timers
        // responsibility for updating fireDate for
repeating timers
        // and for removing the timer from the runloop for
non-repeating timers
        // rests in the timer class, not in the runloop
        for(timer in [[[_timerSources objectForKey: mode]
copy] autorelease])
            if([[timer fireDate] timeIntervalSinceNow] <=
0)
            [timer fire];

        // see if we timed out, if so, abort!
        // this is checked at the end to ensure that
timers and inputs are
        // always processed at least once before returning
        if([limitDate timeIntervalSinceNow] < 0)
            break;
    }
    return YES;
}
```

And that covers all of the necessary functionality. The final code is pretty straightforward and understandable.

Conclusion

What does this exercise tell us? We have to be careful not to take *too* much away from this pseudocode, as there's no guarantee that it matches Apple's. In fact, I know of one case that recently bit me where it does not: Apple's implementation will only fire *one* pending timer for each pass through the runloop, even if multiple timers are ready to fire, whereas this code will fire all pending timers once before returning. And of course there's the major difference that Apple's code uses mach ports, not file descriptors, although their semantics are similar.

Despite this problem, a lot can be learned from this sort of exercise. For example, runloop modes are a common point of confusion among Cocoa programmers, and writing all of this stuff out helps to make it clear just what a mode is and how it works.

It can also inform speculation about the implementation of other parts of Cocoa. For example, we can deduce how the -performSelector:withObject:afterDelay: method works on the inside. Since a runloop only handles sources and timers, it must use one of those two. Since it activates after a delay, it must use a timer. Watching how it behaves in the debugger will confirm this to be correct. As another example, we can conclude that

`-performSelectorOnMainThread:withObject:waitUntilDone:` must use a mach port, since it can't manipulate a timer on the main thread from a secondary thread. (`NSRunLoop` is not thread safe.)

All in all, this kind of technique is really useful in general. I don't usually take it as far as writing out detailed pseudocode like this, but thinking about *how* some Apple code might be implemented can really help further understanding of how it works and what the documentation says, as well as what it implies but does not say directly. You have to be careful to ensure that your conclusions are ultimately based on documentation and real-world constraints, and not the peculiarities of your particular idea of how it might work, but that just takes a bit of care.

It's also helpful just to demystify a class. It's easy to get into magical thinking, where you see a class as being incomprehensible and elevated above the mortal plane. The fact is, while the particular implementations of some of these classes can be pretty sophisticated (the `CFRunLoop` source will make your eyes bleed), the basics of what they do and how they do it are usually very straightforward. For 99.9% of the APIs in Cocoa, they aren't there because they're doing something amazing that you could never achieve, but rather they simply exist to save you the time and trouble of having to write it all yourself.

Friday Q&A 2010-01-08: NSNotificationQueue

Related Articles

> Thread Safety in OS X System Frameworks 24
> The Good and Bad of Distributed Objects... 56
> Care and Feeding of Singletons 194
> Dangerous Cocoa Calls.. 236
> Probing Cocoa With PyObjC 240
> Using Accessors in Init and Dealloc 246
> NSRunLoop Internals 273
> Implementing a Custom Slider 382
> Dealing with Retain Cycles 392
> What Every Apple Programmer Should Know 401
> Leopard Collection Classes.. 405
> Implementing Equality and Hashing 412
> Implementing NSCoding 459
> Defensive Programming in Cocoa 468

It's that time of the week again. No, it's not just time to go get drunk, but time for Friday Q&A! This week's topic, suggested by Christopher Lloyd of Cocotron (a really neat open source project that lets you write Objective-C/Cocoa code for non-Mac platforms like Windows), is `NSNotificationQueue`, a little-known, poorly-understood, but handy Foundation class.

Runloops
`NSNotificationQueue` works in close concert with `NSRunLoop`. If you haven't already, it might be a good idea to read my post from last week on NSRunLoop internals.

(No) Threading
Many people, upon confronted with `NSNotificationQueue`, immediately think that it allows posting notifications across threads. (Well, I did, anyway.) In fact, `NSNotificationQueue` is completely unrelated to threads! Like `NSRunLoop`, there exists a single `NSNotificationQueue` per thread, and that per-thread instance can't be used from other thread.

So What *Is* It?
Simply put, the primary mission of `NSNotificationQueue` is to delay posting of a notification, and to allow coalescing of notifications.

Delayed Notifications
Sometimes you don't want to post a notification immediately. This is especially true if you want to coalesce multiple identical notifications; you can't do that unless you delay

posting the first one. It can be useful for other scenarios as well, such as wanting to give calling code a chance to run before the notification's observers run. (In this respect, it's very similar to passing zero delay to `performSelector:withObject:afterDelay:` in order to have some code run at the next runloop cycle.)

`NSNotificationQueue` provides three posting styles for notifications:

```
NSPostWhenIdle = 1,
NSPostASAP = 2,
NSPostNow = 3
```

Let's take them bottom to top.

`NSPostNow` is the easiest to understand. This has the same semantics as posting the notification directly to the `NSNotificationCenter`, in that the notification is posted immediately and observers are notified before control returns to the caller. The only reason to use this instead of `NSNotificationCenter` is because it can be used to coalesce previously enqueued notifications before posting.

`NSPostASAP` is much like a zero-delay timer. The notification is not posted immediately, but will be posted as soon as control returns to the runloop. The usage scenarios are much like for a zero-delay timer.

`NSPostWhenIdle` will wait until the runloop is idle, then post the notification. You can think of this as using a zero-delay timer with low priority. As long as the runloop has other work to do, the notification will not be posted. Once the runloop runs out of stuff to do, the notification will be posted. This is useful if you want to wait until your program has not only finished the currently executing code, but has nothing else to do. For example, imagine tracking mouse movement and performing an expensive update on the basis of that movement. Performing that update with every movement will make the program unresponsive, but you still want to update as often as possible within reason. Using `NSPostWhenIdle` will accomplish this. As long as more mouse movement events are pending, the notification will not be posted. If the user pauses for a moment, the runloop will clear out and the notification will be posted. If the user has a really fast computer, or the computation takes less time than expected, the runloop may have time to idle in between mouse moved events, and your update will then happen more frequently.

Coalescing

The real power of `NSNotificationQueue` is in coalescing. What does that mean?

When posting with `NSPostASAP` or `NSPostWhenIdle`, the notification is not posted immediately, but rather is queued. Coalescing means that if a notification is posted which matches one already in the queue, the two are merged, so that only a single notification is posted to observers.

This behavior can be really handy. Imagine a loop modifying a bunch of objects which posts notifications that cause other parts of the application to update their idea of the world. If they only need one notification at the end of all the modifications, coalescing will allow that other code to avoid a lot of needless computation that would occur if every modification caused a separate notification.

`NSNotificationQueue` provides three types of coalescing.

- `NSNotificationNoCoalescing` means that no coalescing is performed.
- `NSNotificationCoalescingOnName` means that coalescing is performed if two notifications share the same name.
- `NSNotificationCoalescingOnSender` means that coalescing is performed if two notifications share the same sender object.

These are bitwise flags, so you can combine them. Writing `NSNotificationCoalescingOnName | NSNotificationCoalescingOnSender` means that coalescing is performed if two notifications share both the same name and the same sender object. (Most of the time when coalescing, this is what you want, and it's what `-enqueueNotification:postingStyle:` implicitly uses.)

With coalescing, the semantics of `NSPostNow` make more sense. By using `NSPostNow` with `NSNotificationQueue`, any matching enqueued notifications will be coalesced with the one being posted before it's posted, essentially clearing them out and posting the coalesced notification earlier than would have otherwise happened.

These coalescing flags can also be used to remove notifications from the queue without posting them, using the `-dequeueNotificationsMatching:coalesceMask:` method.

Examples

`NSNotificationQueue` is pretty straightforward to use. Rather than standard code using `NSNotificationCenter`, you more or less drop in `NSNotificationQueue`. As a concrete example, imagine you have an `NSSlider` set to be "continuous", so that it sends its action message every time the mouse is moved, even while it's down:

```
- (IBAction)sliderMoved: (id)sender
{
    [self updateWithNewSliderValue: [sender doubleValue]];
```

But you also have some updates that you only want to run once the mouse has been released. Since the runloop is run in `NSEventTrackingRunLoopMode` while the mouse is down, you can just post a notification using `NSPostASAP` onto the `NSNotificationQueue`, and the notification will be posted only once the mouse is released. By coalescing, this code ensures that only one notification is posted when the mouse is released, even though this action message may be called many times:

```
    NSNotification *note = [NSNotification
notificationWithName: SliderDoneMovingNotification object:
self];
    [[NSNotificationQueue defaultQueue]
enqueueNotification: note postingStyle: NSPostASAP];
```

Imagine that you also want to update a value while the slider is moving, but that this update is expensive to perform, so you want to keep the application responsive. Using NSPostWhenIdle and NSEventTrackingRunLoopMode will allow this:

```
    note = [NSNotification notificationWithName:
ExpensiveSliderUpdate object: self];
    NSArray *modes = [NSArray arrayWithObject:
NSEventTrackingRunLoopMode];
    [[NSNotificationQueue defaultQueue]
enqueueNotification: note

postingStyle: NSPostWhenIdle

coalesceMask: NSNotificationCoalescingOnName |
NSNotificationCoalescingOnSender
                                                forModes:
modes];
}
```

To avoid a pending notification waiting around a long time if the mouse is immediately released after this code executes, you'll want to observe SliderDoneMovingNotification and remove ExpensiveSliderUpdate from the queue:

```
- (void)sliderDoneMoving: (NSNotification *)note
{
    NSNotification *note = [NSNotification
notificationWithName: ExpensiveSliderUpdate object: self];
    [[NSNotificationQueue defaultQueue]
dequeueNotificationsMatching: note

coalesceMask: NSNotificationCoalescingOnName |
NSNotificationCoalescingOnSender];
}
```

Conclusion

`NSNotificationQueue` may not be well known in general, but now you know how it works, what it's good for, and have some ideas for how to put it to work.

That's it for this week. Come back next week for another exciting edition. (A warning: I'm going to be making a long trip not long before next Friday, and so there's some possibility that I'll miss next week's edition. In that event, my instructions to you, the reader, are to panic as thoroughly as possible until the following Friday.)

Friday Q&A 2010-01-15: Stack and Heap Objects in Objective-C

Related Articles
- Mac OS X Process Memory Statistics 123
- Dealing with Retain Cycles 392

Welcome to another Friday Q&A. I survived my travel and am (just barely) ready to write another exciting edition. This week's topic comes from Gwynne, who asked why Objective-C only uses heap objects, and no stack objects.

Before we get into that, let's define our terms.

Stack
The stack is a region of memory which contains storage for local variables, as well as internal temporary values and housekeeping. On a modern system, there is one stack per thread of execution. When a function is called, a *stack frame* is pushed onto the stack, and function-local data is stored there. When the function returns, its stack frame is destroyed. All of this happens automatically, without the programmer taking any explicit action other than calling a function.

Heap
The heap is, essentially, everything else in memory. (Yes, there are things other than the stack and heap, but let's ignore that for this discussion.) Memory can be allocated on the heap at any time, and destroyed at any time. You have to explicitly request for memory to be allocated from the heap, and if you aren't using garbage collection, explicitly free it as well. This is where you store things that need to outlive the current function call. The heap is what you access when you call `malloc` and `free`.

Stack vs Heap Objects
Given that, what's a stack object, and what's a heap object?

First, we must understand what an object is in general. In Objective-C (and many other languages), an object is simply a contiguous blob of memory with a particular layout. (If you're interested in just what it contains and how it's laid out, check out my intro to the Objective-C runtime.)

The precise location of that memory is less important. As long as you have some memory somewhere with the right contents, it's a working Objective-C object. In Objective-C, objects are usually created on the heap:

```
NSObject *obj = [[NSObject alloc] init];
```

The storage for the `obj` variable itself is on the stack, but the object it points to is in the heap. The `[NSObject alloc]` call allocates a chunk of heap memory, and fills it out to match the layout needed for an `NSObject`.

A stack object is just an object where the memory for that object is allocated on the stack. Objective-C doesn't have any support for this directly, but you can construct one manually without too much trouble:

```
struct {
    Class isa;
} fakeNSObject;
fakeNSObject.isa = [NSObject class];

NSObject *obj = (NSObject *)&fakeNSObject;
NSLog(@"%@", [obj description]);
```

This works fine, although you shouldn't depend on it, as it depends on replicating the internal layout of the class.

Advantages of Stack Objects

It's obviously possible to have stack objects in general. Aside from the above hack, real languages like C++ have language support for stack objects. In C++, you can create objects on the stack or the heap:

```
std::string stackString;
std::string *heapString = new std::string;
```

Why allow both?

Stack objects have two compelling advantages:

1. **Speed:** Allocating memory on the stack is really fast. All of the bookkeeping is done by the compiler when you build your program. At runtime, the function prolog just carves out the amount of space it needs for all local variables, and the code knows what goes where because it was all computed in advance. Stack allocations are essentially free, whereas heap allocations can be quite expensive.
2. **Simplicity:** Stack objects have a defined lifetime. You can never leak one, because it always gets destroyed at the end of the scope where it was declared.

Disadvantages of Stack Objects

The strictly defined lifetime of a stack object is a disadvantage as well, and a major one. In Objective-C (and C++, and many other languages), it is impossible to move an object after it's created. The reason for this is because there may be many pointers to that object, and those pointers are not tracked. They would all need to be updated to track the move, but there's no way to accomplish this.

(Note: it's not an impossibility in general, and many languages move objects around as a matter of course, often as part of garbage collection schemes. However, this requires more runtime smarts and a stricter type system than you get in Objective-C.)

As used in Cocoa, Objective-C uses a reference counting system for memory management. The advantage of this system is that any single object can have multiple "owners", and the system won't allow the object to be destroyed until all owners have relinquished ownership.

Stack allocated objects inherently have a single owner, the function which created them. If Objective-C had stack objects, what would happen if you passed it to some other code which then tried to keep it around by `retain`ing it? There's no way to prevent the object from being destroyed when the function which created it returns, so the `retain` can't work. The code which tries to keep the object around will fail, end up with a dangling reference, and will crash.

Another problem is that stack objects are not very flexible. It's not uncommon in Objective-C to implement an initializer which destroys the original object and returns a new one instead. How could you do that with a stack object? You really couldn't. Much of the runtime flexibility of Objective-C depends on having heap objects.

Actual Stack Objects in Objective-C
It turns out that Objective-C does have stack objects, truly and officially, as of 10.6!

Don't get too excited, though. It's only supported for a single kind of object: blocks. When you write a block inside a function using the `^{}` syntax, the result of that expression is a stack object!

But what about those problems I discussed above?

The problem with runtime dynamism doesn't exist with blocks. Blocks have a layout which is fixed by the language, and which can't be changed without destroying binary compatibility. The size of the block object can be computed at compile time, and in fact the whole object is built by compiler-generated code, so the possibility of writing an initializer that does tricky things simply doesn't exist.

The problem of object lifetime *does* exist with blocks, but is less severe. The reason for this is simply because blocks are a new kind of object that never existed in the language before, and any code that deals with a block will know that it needs to `copy` a block (which creates a copy on the heap, if it's not there already, and returns a pointer to that), rather than `retain` it, if it wants to keep a reference.

The stack nature of blocks does have some pitfalls, though. For example, this code is broken:

```
void (^block)();
if(x)
{
    block = ^{ printf("x\n"); };
}
else
{
    block = ^{ printf("not x\n"); };
}
block();
```

Block stack objects are only valid through the lifetime of their enclosing scope, and here, their enclosing scopes cease to exist before the call to `block()` at the end. Other gotchas can happen when you pass blocks to code that doesn't know that they're blocks:

```
[dictionary setObject: ^{ printf("hey hey\n"); } forKey: key];
```

The dictionary will `retain` that block object rather than `copy` it, leading to a dangling reference.

The speed and simplicity of stack objects are a great boon for blocks, but it also creates a whole new class of bugs for unwary programmers.

Friday Q&A 2010-01-22: Toll Free Bridging Internals

Related Articles

    Zeroing Weak References to CoreFoundation Objects............................447

It's been a week, and once again, it's time for a Friday Q&A. For this week's edition, I'm going to talk about how toll-free bridging works, a topic suggested by Jonathan Mitchell.

What It Is
I hope that everyone reading this already knows what toll-free bridging is, but if you don't, here's a summary.

Toll-free bridging, or TFB for short, is a mechanism which allows certain Objective-C classes to be interchangeable with certain CoreFoundation classes. For example, `NSString` and `CFString` are bridged, which means that you can treat any `NSString` as if it were a `CFString` and vice versa. Example:

```
CFStringRef cfStr = SomeFunctionThatReturnsCFString();
NSUInteger length = [(NSString *)cfStr length];

NSString *nsStr = [self someString];
CFIndex length = CFStringGetLength((CFStringRef)nsStr);
```

Most (but not all!) classes which exist in both Cocoa and CoreFoundation are bridged in this way. A bridged class will mention the bridging in its documentation.

Bridging From CF to ObjC
The way that classes are bridged from CoreFoundation to Objective-C (how a `CFString` can act like an `NSString`) is fairly straightforward.

Every bridged class is actually a class cluster, which means that the public class is abstract, and core functionality is implemented in private subclasses. The CoreFoundation class is given a memory layout that matches one of these private subclasses, which is built just for the job of being the Objective-C counterpart to the CoreFoundation class. Other Objective-C classes, independent of the bridged class, may also exist in the class cluster. From the outside, they all look and work the same, because they all share the same interface.

To put it concretely, look at `NSString`. `NSString` is an abstract class. Every time you create one, you actually get an instance of one of its subclasses.

One of those subclasses is `NSCFString`. This is the direct counterpart to `CFString`. The first field of a `CFString` is an `isa` pointer which points to the `NSCFString` class, which allows it to function as an Objective-C object.

`NSCFString` implements methods to work properly as an `NSString`. There are two ways that it can do this. One way is to implement every method as a stub which just calls through to its CoreFoundation counterpart. Another way is to implement every method to match what its CoreFoundation counterpart does. In reality, the code is probably a mix of the two.

For this direction, the mechanism of bridging is so simple it's almost not there at all. `CFString` objects just happen to be instances of `NSCFString`, which is a subclass of `NSString`, and which implements the methods needed to act like one. Many of those implementations just happen to call through to CoreFoundation to get their work done.

Bridging from ObjC to CF

Bridging in the opposite direction gets a bit more complicated. This is because any given instance of a TFB Objective-C class could be an instance of any of its subclasses, even custom classes created within the application. Just write a subclass of `NSString` and you have such a custom class. And yet these custom classes still work transparently with CoreFoundation function calls. You can call `CFStringGetLength` on an instance of your custom `NSString` subclass and it will invoke your `-length` method and return the result to the caller.

As it turns out, there's no particular magic to make this work. It's just pure brute force. The implementation of `CFStringGetLength` looks like this:

```
CFIndex CFStringGetLength(CFStringRef str) {
    CF_OBJC_FUNCDISPATCH0(__kCFStringTypeID, CFIndex, str, "length");

    __CFAssertIsString(str);
    return __CFStrLength(str);
}
```

The first line is an ugly macro that hides the secret to how TFB works on this side of things. It checks the `isa` of the object to see if it matches `NSCFString`. If it doesn't, then it's not a "real" `CFString`, but just some other Objective-C class. In that case, the CoreFoundation code doesn't know how to look up the length, so it just sends the `length` message to the object and returns the result. This is how custom subclasses work. If it *is* a "real" `CFString`, then it simply calls `__CFStrLength` which does the actual work of looking up the length of the string within the `CFString` structure, and returns that value.

In short: every CoreFoundation function for a TFB class first checks to see if the object being passed in is a "real" CoreFoundation object or a pure Objective-C class. If it's pure Objective-C, it simply calls through to the Objective-C side, and it's done. Otherwise, it proceeds normally. This is why I said it's pure brute force: every single function call has one of these checks at the top in order to make TFB work.

This implementation has an interesting consequence. Consider for a moment what would happen if you messed up and passed, say, a `CFArray` to `CFStringGetLength`. The `isa` check would show that it's not an `NSCFString`, so it would go for the Objective-C dispatch. The end result is that you get an error like this:

```
-[NSCFArray length]: unrecognized selector sent to
instance 0x100108e50
```

That's an Objective-C error coming from pure CoreFoundation code!

Bridging Basic Behavior
That's how classes which are explicitly bridged work. But there's one more interesting aspect to TFB: basic behaviors shared by all objects are also bridged for all classes. In essence, `NSObject` is bridged to `CFType`. As one of the most common examples, it's possible to `CFRetain` any Objective-C object, and `retain` any CoreFoundation object. Just like the other bridging, if you've overridden `retain` in your Objective-C code, `CFRetain` will call that override. A really useful implication of this is that you can use `autorelease` on any CoreFoundation object. This works not only for memory management, but for any `CFType` function, like `CFCopyDescription`, and for any `NSObject` method, like `performSelector:withObject:afterDelay:`.

For the bridging to Objective-C, the first field of any CoreFoundation object points to an Objective-C class. For bridged classes it points to the Objective-C counterpart class, and for non-bridged classes it points to a special `__NSCFType` class. All of these classes are subclasses of `NSObject` (most of them indirectly), so naturally they inherit all of NSObject's behavior. For methods which map to CoreFoundation counterparts, these classes simply override them and call through to the CoreFoundation side as necessary.

For bridging to CoreFoundation, the mechanism is just like the specific bridging. The first line of `CFRetain` and all the other `CFType` functions checks to see if the object is a "real" CoreFoundation object or if it's some random Objective-C class. If it's a "real" CF object, then it does its normal job. Otherwise, it dispatches through to Objective-C and lets that side of things handle all the work.

Creating Bridged Classes
I hope the title of this section didn't get anybody's hopes up, because the simple answer to this is: you can't. Now that we know how bridging works, it should be obvious why. You can't bridge an existing, unbridged CoreFoundation class because doing so requires massive cooperation on the CoreFoundation side. Every single function call needs to

have a line at the top which checks the class of the object being passed in and dispatches to Objective-C if necessary, and you can't add that if it's not already there. And you can't create a new bridged CoreFoundation class because you can't create new CoreFoundation classes, period. That's capability that Apple keeps for itself, and doesn't expose to the outside world. (And really, would you want to pepper class checks into every function you write? Just write a pure Objective-C class, it's simpler and prettier.)

Conclusion

Now you know the basics of how toll-free bridging works. If you're interested in the deeper technical details of just what the dispatching code looks like and how it works, check out ridiculous_fish's article on bridging.

Friday Q&A 2010-01-29: Method Replacement for Fun and Profit

Related Articles

    Code Injection 40

    Intro to the Objective-C Runtime 67

    Objective-C Messaging 73

    Objective-C Message Forwarding 77

    Objective-C Class Loading and Initialization 115

    Care and Feeding of Singletons 194

    Creating a Blocks-Based Object System 205

    Probing Cocoa With PyObjC 240

    Using Accessors in Init and Dealloc 246

    Error Returns with Continuation Passing Style 303

    Trampolining Blocks with Mutable Code 311

    Comparison of Objective-C Enumeration Techniques 369

    Implementing Fast Enumeration 373

    Implementing Equality and Hashing 412

    Zeroing Weak References in Objective-C 428

    Zeroing Weak References to CoreFoundation Objects 447

    Implementing NSCoding 459

    Defensive Programming in Cocoa 468

It's that time of the week again. For this week's Friday Q&A Mike Shields has suggested that I talk about method replacement and method swizzling in Objective-C.

Overriding Methods
Overriding methods is a common task in just about any object oriented language. Most of the time you do this by subclassing, a time-honored technique. You subclass, you implement the method in the subclass, you instantiate the subclass when necessary, and instances of the subclass use the overridden method. Everybody knows how to do this.

Sometimes, though, you need to override methods that are in objects whose instantiation you don't control. Subclassing doesn't suffice in that case, because you can't make that code instantiate your subclass. Your method override sits there, twiddling its thumbs, accomplishing nothing.

Posing
Posing is an interesting technique but, alas, is now obsolete, since Apple no longer supports it in the "new" (64-bit and iPhone) Objective-C runtime. With posing, you

subclass, then pose the subclass as its superclass. The runtime does some magic and suddenly the subclass is used everywhere, and method overrides become useful again. Since this is no longer supported, I won't go into details.

Categories

Using a category, you can easily override a method in an existing class:

```
@implementation NSView (MyOverride)

- (void)drawRect: (NSRect)r
{
    // this runs instead of the normal -[NSView drawRect:]
    [[NSColor blueColor] set];
    NSRectFill(r);
}

@end
```

However, this really only works if you want to override a method implemented in a superclass of the class you're targeting. When the method in question exists in the class where you want to override it, using a category to perform the override results in two problems:
1. It's impossible to call through to the original implementation of the method. The new implementation replaces the original, which is simply lost. Most overrides want to add functionality, not completely replace it, but it's not possible with a category.
2. The class in question could implement the method in question in a category too, and the runtime doesn't guarantee which implementation "wins" when two categories contain methods with the same name.

Swizzling

Using a technique called method swizzling, you can replace an existing method from a category without the uncertainty of who "wins", and while preserving the ability to call through to the old method. The secret is to give the override a different method name, then swap them using runtime functions.

First, you implement the override with a different name:

```
@implementation NSView (MyOverride)

- (void)override_drawRect: (NSRect)r
{
    // call through to the original, really
    [self override_drawRect: r];

    [[NSColor blueColor] set];
    NSRectFill(r);
}

@end
```

Notice how calling through to the original is done by calling the *same* method, in what looks like a recursive call. This works because the method gets swapped with the original implementation. At runtime, the method called `override_drawRect:` is actually the *original*!

To swap the method, you need a bit of code to move the new implementation in and the old implementation out:

```
void MethodSwizzle(Class c, SEL origSEL, SEL overrideSEL)
{
    Method origMethod = class_getInstanceMethod(c, origSEL);
    Method overrideMethod = class_getInstanceMethod(c, overrideSEL);
```

To be completely general, this code has to handle two cases. The first case is when the method to be overridden is *not* implemented in the class in question, but rather in a superclass. The second case is when the method in question does exist in the class itself. These two cases need to be handled a bit differently.

For the case where the method only exists in a superclass, the first step is to add a new method to this class, using the override as the implementation. Once that's done, then the override method is replaced with the original one.

The step of adding the new method can also double as a check to see which case is actually present. The runtime function `class_addMethod` will fail if the method already exists, and so can be used for the check:

```
    if(class_addMethod(c, origSEL,
method_getImplementation(overrideMethod),
method_getTypeEncoding(overrideMethod)))
    {
```

If the add succeeded, then replace the override method with the original, completing the (conceptual) swap:

```
        class_replaceMethod(c, overrideSEL,
method_getImplementation(origMethod),
method_getTypeEncoding(origMethod));
    }
```

If the add failed, then it's the second case; both methods exist in the class in question. For that case, the runtime provides a handy function called method_exchangeImplementations which just swaps the two methods in place:

```
        else
        {
            method_exchangeImplementations(origMethod,
overrideMethod);
        }
}
```

You'll notice that the `method_exchangeImplementations` call just uses the two methods that the code already fetched, and you might wonder why it can't just go straight to that and skip all of the annoying stuff in the middle.

The reason the code needs the two cases is because `class_getInstanceMethod` will actually return the `Method` for the *superclass* if that's where the implementation lies. Replacing that implementation will replace the method for the wrong class!

As a concrete example, imagine replacing `-[NSView description]`. If NSView doesn't implement `-description` (which is probable) then you'll get NSObject's `Method` instead. If you called `method_exchangeImplementations` on that `Method`, you'd replace the `-description` method on NSObject with your own code, which is not what you want to do!

(When that's the case, a simple category method would work just fine, so this code wouldn't be needed. The problem is that you can't know whether a class overrides a method from its superclass or not, and that could even change from one OS release to the next, so you have to assume that the class may implement the method itself, and write code that can handle that.)

Finally we just need to make sure that this code actually gets called when the program starts up. This is easily done by adding a `+load` method to the `MyOverride` category:

```
+ (void)load
{
    MethodSwizzle(self, @selector(drawRect:),
@selector(override_drawRect:));
}
```

Direct Override

This is a bit complicated, though. The swizzling concept is a little weird, and especially the way that you call through to the original implementation tends to bend the mind a bit. It's a pretty standard technique, but I want to propose a way that I believe is a little simpler, both in terms of being easier to understand and easier to implement.

It turns out that there's no need to preserve the method-ness of the original method. The dynamic dispatch involved in `[self override_drawRect: r]` is completely unnecessary. We know which implementation we want right from the start.

Instead of moving the original method into a new one, just move its implementation into a global function pointer:

```
void (*gOrigDrawRect)(id, SEL, NSRect);
```

Then in +load you can fill that global with the original implementation

```
+ (void)load
{
    Method origMethod = class_getInstanceMethod(self,
@selector(drawRect:));
    gOrigDrawRect = (void
*)method_getImplementation(origMethod);
```

(I like to cast to `void *` for these things just because it's so much easier to type than long, weird function pointer types, and thanks to the magic of C, the `void *` gets implicitly converted to the right pointer type anyway.)

Next, replace the original. Like before, there are two cases to worry about, so I'll first add the method, then replace the existing one if it turns out that there is one:

```
    if(!class_addMethod(self, @selector(drawRect:),
(IMP)OverrideDrawRect, method_getTypeEncoding(origMethod)))
        method_setImplementation(origMethod,
(IMP)OverrideDrawRect);
}
```

Finally, implement the override. Unlike before, it's now a function, not a method:

```
static void OverrideDrawRect(NSView *self, SEL _cmd,
NSRect r)
{
    gOrigDrawRect(self, _cmd, r);
    [[NSColor blueColor] set];
    NSRectFill(r);
}
```

A bit uglier, certainly, but I think it's simpler and easier to follow.

The Obligatory Warning
Overriding methods on classes you don't own is a dangerous business. Your override could cause problems by breaking the assumptions of the class in question. Avoid it if it's at all possible. If you must do it, code your override with extreme care.

Conclusion
That's it for this week. Now you know the full spectrum of method override possibilities in Objective-C, including one variation that I haven't seen discussed much elsewhere. Use this power for good, not for evil!

Friday Q&A 2010-02-05: Error Returns with Continuation Passing Style

Related Articles

- Blocks in Objective-C 14
- Intro to the Objective-C Runtime 67
- Objective-C Messaging..73
- Objective-C Message Forwarding 77
- Objective-C Class Loading and Initialization 115
- Practical Blocks 146
- Care and Feeding of Singletons 194
- Creating a Blocks-Based Object System 205
- Probing Cocoa With PyObjC 240
- Using Accessors in Init and Dealloc 246
- Method Replacement for Fun and Profit 297
- Trampolining Blocks with Mutable Code...311
- Futures..330
- Compound Futures...342
- Comparison of Objective-C Enumeration Techniques 369
- Implementing Fast Enumeration...373
- Implementing Equality and Hashing 412
- Background Timers...419
- Zeroing Weak References in Objective-C 428
- Implementing NSCoding 459
- Defensive Programming in Cocoa 468

The Earth has moved 6.9 degrees around the Sun since my last post, which means it's time for another edition of Friday Q&A. This 6.9-degree segment, Guy English has suggested that I talk about the use of continuation passing style to simplify error returns in Objective-C code.

NSError **

The standard Cocoa convention for signalling errors to a caller is to return the error by way of an extra parameter pointing to a `NSError *` variable, like so:

```
NSError *error;
NSString *string = [[NSString alloc]
initWithContentsOfFile: path encoding:
NSUTF8StringEncoding error: &error];
if(!string)
    // do something with error
```

This works, but is a bit painful to type. It's also painful to implement, because the code needs to set the error and return `nil` as two separate steps. The error parameter is also optional, so the method needs to do a NULL check for every error case, like so:

```
if(failure)
{
    if(error)
        *error = [NSError errorWith...];
    return nil;
}
```

Other languages handle this quite a bit nicer. For example, the equivalent in Python is:

```
string, error = someFunction(...)
```

And the return is equally easy:

```
if failure:
    return None, createErrorObject(...)
```

This is because Python has built-in support for returning multiple values from a function, whereas Objective-C doesn't. How can we get the Objective-C side to be equally nice?

Exceptions

For languages without support for multiple return values (and often for those that do support it), the common solution for error returns is exceptions. In Objective-C, using this technique would look like this for the caller:

```
@try
{
    NSString *string = [[NSString alloc] init...];
    // use string
}
@catch(NSException *exception)
{
    // handle exception
}
```

This is still a bit verbose, however that is often compensated by the fact that multiple calls can be placed in the same `@try` block, and share the same `@catch` handler.

The other end of it is nice and simple:

```
if(failure)
    @throw [NSException exceptionWith...];
```

It also allows chaining errors very easily. If you have a method that calls another method and the inner method can error, then allowing the outer method to also error is simply a matter of not catching the exception. With other techniques, you need to explicitly check for errors at every call and propagate them up the call chain.

However, exceptions have their own problems. If a method can return an error and you ignore it, then you just lose out on some diagnostic information. If a method can throw an exception and you fail to catch it, then it can cause inconsistent states and even crashes as the exception is thrown through code that's not written to handle it. Writing exception-safe code requires more thought and care.

These problems aren't insurmountable. Exceptions are often used in other languages for this sort of thing. However, they're not traditionally used in Objective-C, which means that even if you want to use them, it can be tough to deal with all the code out there that isn't aware of them. For routine errors, it will also make it difficult to debug your programs when you end up having a serious error where an exception shouldn't be thrown at all, but is. It's very common to simply break on `objc_exception_throw` to, for example, figure out just where an exception is being thrown from within some Cocoa calls, but that technique becomes unusable if your application frequently throws exceptions as part of its routine operations.

If you don't want to use exceptions, but want something better than `NSError **`, what can you do?

Continuation Passing Style
Continuation Passing Style, or CPS, is a style of programming using anonymous functions to replace return statements. Instead of returning a value, a function will take another function as a parameter. Then, when it gets to the point where it would have returned a value, it calls the passed-in function with the value as a parameter instead. In Objective-C, we now have anonymous functions in the form of blocks, so CPS can be achieved using blocks.

Here's an example of how CPS looks. This is the standard-style code:

```
NSString *string = [obj stringWhatever];
// use string
```

And here it is converted to CPS:

```
[obj stringWhatever: ^(NSString *string) {
    // use string
}];
```

CPS has many different uses, such as providing a convenient interface for asynchronous operations. Here, however, I want to use CPS to take advantage of a convenient fact: although Objective-C methods can only return one value, Objective-C blocks can trivially take two parameters.

Thus, the annoying error return-by-reference style can be converted into a cleaner CPS version, like this:

```
[NSString stringWithContentsOfFile: path encoding:
NSUTF8StringEncoding continuation: ^(NSString *string,
NSError *error) {
    if(error)
        // handle error
    else
        // use string
}];
```

This is nice and straightforward. As a bonus, Xcode will automatically complete the basic outline of the block for you if you hit return while on the argument placeholder.

On the other side it's pretty simple to deal with as well:

```
+ (void)stringWithContentsOfFile: (NSString *)path
encoding: (NSStringEncoding)encoding continuation: (void
(^)(NSString *, NSError *))continuation
{
    // create string from path

    if(failure)
        continuation(nil, [NSError errorWith...]);
    else
        continuation(string, nil);
}
```

Handing errors "up the stack" is pretty easy too. Imagine a method which does its own error reporting using this CPS technique, and which calls that NSString method. If it errors, it just wants to report the error up the chain:

```objc
- (void)computeObject: (id)obj continuation: (void (^)(id, NSError *))continuation
{
    [NSString stringWithContentsOfFile: path encoding: NSUTF8StringEncoding continuation: ^(NSString *string, NSError *error) {
        if(error)
            continuation(nil, error);
        else
        {
            // continue processing with string
            id result = ...;
            continuation(result, nil);
        }
    }];
}
```

Two-Block Variant

Since the first action of the continuation is almost certain to be to check and do something different if an error occurred, it would be reasonable to split up the continuation into two parts. This moves the check into the called method (which probably needs to have such a check anyway) and simplifies the caller. You pass an error block and a normal block, and the method will then call the appropriate one. This variant would look like this:

```objc
[NSString stringWithContentsOfFile: path encoding: NSUTF8StringEncoding
    errorHandler: ^(NSError *error) {
        // handle error
    }
    continuation: ^(NSString *string) {
        // use string
    }];
```

This style also simplifies handing errors "up the stack", because the caller's error handler can just be passed straight in as the error handler for the next level:

```
- (void)computeObject: (id)obj errorHandler: (void
(^)(NSError *))errorHandler continuation: (void
(^)(id))continuation
{
    [NSString stringWithContentsOfFile: path encoding:
NSUTF8StringEncoding errorHandler: errorHandler
continuation: ^(NSString *string) {
        // continue processing with string
        continuation(string);
    }];
}
```

Interfacing Between CPS and Normal Code

Using CPS for error returns isn't all roses. A problem comes at the interface between CPS code and normal-style code. In other words, where you have a method which needs to return a value, but which calls CPS methods. The problem arises because using the `return` statement inside a block returns a value from the block, not from the enclosing function:

```
- (NSString *)contentsOfFile: (NSString *)path
{
    [NSString stringWithContentsOfFile: path encoding:
NSUTF8StringEncoding
        errorHandler: ^(NSError *error) {
            [NSApp reportError: error];
        }
        continuation: ^(NSString *string) {
            return string; // fails! returns string from
the block, not the method!
        }];
}
```

In order to get around this problem, you need to move the value outside of the continuation using a `__block`-qualified local variable, then return from within the main function body:

```
- (NSString *)contentsOfFile: (NSString *)path
{
    __block NSString *returnValue = nil;
    [NSString stringWithContentsOfFile: path encoding: NSUTF8StringEncoding
        errorHandler: ^(NSError *error) {
            [NSApp reportError: error];
        }
        continuation: ^(NSString *string) {
            // string is retained here in case there are any inner autorelease pools
            // in the NSString method that's calling this continuation
            // retaining it will keep it alive even if there is one and it is popped
            // the retain is balanced by an autorelease in the method body
            returnValue = [string retain];
        }];
    return [returnValue autorelease];
}
```

This is not a huge inconvenience, but it is mildly annoying, and certainly removes some of the elegance of using CPS here.

A bigger downside is that, well, Cocoa doesn't do CPS error returns, it does return-by-reference. It's not too hard to write adapter methods:

```
typedef void (^ErrorHandler)(NSError *error);

@implementation NSString (CPSErrors)

+ (void)stringWithContentsOfFile: (NSString *)path
encoding: (NSStringEncoding)encoding errorHandler:
(ErrorHandler)errorHandler continuation: (void
(^)(NSString *string)continuation
{
    NSError *error;
    NSString *string = [self stringWithContentsOfFile:
path encoding: encoding error: &error];
    if(string)
        continuation(string);
    else if(errorHandler)
        errorHandler(error);
}

@end
```

But obviously the annoyance of having to write adapters makes for a big hit to the niceness of using CPS for error handling.

Conclusion

The addition of blocks to Objective-C enables some completely new ways of doing things, including a new way to deal with errors. The practicality of this approach remains to be seen, but it certainly does produce nicer-looking code than the traditional Cocoa way.

Friday Q&A 2010-02-12: Trampolining Blocks with Mutable Code

Related Articles

Blocks in Objective-C 14
Code Injection 40
Practical Blocks 146
Creating a Blocks-Based Object System 205
Method Replacement for Fun and Profit 297
Error Returns with Continuation Passing Style 303
Futures 330
Compound Futures 342
Background Timers 419
Zeroing Weak References to CoreFoundation Objects 447

Welcome to another edition of Friday Q&A, where deep technical talk and complete insanity combine! This week, I'm going to take a quick break from my usual reader-driven format and talk about a little toy I built earlier in the week, an adapter between blocks and more traditional function-pointer-based callback systems.

Background

Blocks are really great, but not all APIs on the Mac have caught up to them yet. Lots of APIs still use older-style callbacks that take function pointers. And while you can adapt those APIs to use blocks by building small adapter functions, it's annoying to have to do that every time you want to use one, especially since each one works a little bit differently.

The toy project I've built allows a block to be transformed into a function pointer which, when called, invokes the block. This function pointer can then be passed to any API which takes a function pointer callback, and it will call your block and be none the wiser about it.

Warning

The code which I'm about to discuss is an *extreme hack*. It relies on intimate details of low-level platform calling conventions, so much so that I haven't bothered to make it work for any architecture other than x86_64. Even there it has important limitations. The purpose of this post is *not* to present a practical library, but rather to explore some interesting but impractical low-level hacking. Do not, under any circumstances, use this code.

Code

Now that that's out of the way, let's talk about the code! It can be found in the usual place if you want to follow along with the entire codebase:

```
svn co http://mikeash.com/svn/BlockFptr/
```

Concept

Before I get into specifics, let's talk quickly about how this whole thing is supposed to work, anyway. So I don't have to repeat this a thousand times later, let me state up front that every platform-specific detail I discuss is about x86_64, and may not necessarily apply to other platforms, not even necessarily the other platforms that OS X runs on.

If you're still used to thinking of a 32-bit world, keep in mind that this means pointers are *eight* bytes long.

First, a quick reminder of what a function pointer is: it's just a plain old pointer to the beginning of a function. To call it, the compiler generates code that sets up the stack and registers to pass parameters and save temporary values, and then simply jumps to that location in memory. Execution continues from there.

Blocks work similarly, but are somewhat more complex. A block is an *Objective-C object*, meaning it's a region of memory whose first eight bytes contain an isa pointer. The remainder of the block contains various other data useful to the block, like captured local variables. One of those pieces of data is a function pointer to the block's actual implementation. In order to call a block, the compiler generates code which simply fetches this function pointer, then calls it just like any other function pointer.

The major differentiator between function pointers and blocks at runtime is *context*. Function pointers are pure code, with no data associated. Whenever you encounter a function pointer callback API, you will invariably see a *context pointer* that goes with it. This is typically just a void * pointing to arbitrary data. It's a way for the caller to get *context* to the function pointer through the API, so that the function pointer can know what's going on. A pure function pointer with no context can really only access the parameters given to it and global variables. With a context pointer, it can refer back to the object that set up the callback, data from the particular invocation it's working on, etc.

Blocks automatically carry context. The function pointer which points to their implementation takes, as a hidden first parameter, a pointer to the block object itself. Through this, blocks are able to access captured local variables, giving them access to all the context they want, and with no extra work by the programmer.

The goal for my code is to bridge this context gap. The way I decided to do it is to build a *trampoline*. This is a small piece of code which has a block's address embedded in it. When the trampoline executes, it loads the block's address and the block's function pointer, then jumps to it with the block passed as the first parameter. By embedding the block's address directly in the code, this solves the problem of *context*, because now a single pointer will get you to both code and data.

In order to embed the address of a specific block into the code, that code needs to be copied and modified, which is the *really* fun part of all of this.

Trampoline Factory

Yes, you can copy, modify, and then execute code. It's not even all that hard! You do need to ensure that the code in question will tolerate being modified (doesn't include any PC-relative references that won't be valid after it's moved), but that's easy if you write it in assembly, which I'm going to have to do anyway in order to do the parameter mangling and tail-calling that this trampoline requires.

Code can be accessed by just doing a memory copy starting with its pointer. A small assembler trick lets you figure out where the end is. Once you've copied it onto the heap, you can modify its contents at will. Once you're done with that, and you're ready to run it, then you can call `mprotect()` to make the data executable, and at that point you can call it.

However, this process is expensive. The call to `mprotect()` is a system call. Plus, it only works on full pages of memory (4096 bytes), but the trampoline itself is only a couple of dozen bytes, so there's a lot of wasted space. In order to make this cheaper, I want a way to construct trampolines in bulk, and to reuse them *without* modifying their code after the initial construction.

As such, my architecture adds an additional level of indirection. The code contains a pointer to another region of memory. That bit of memory in turn contains a pointer to a block. Want to re-point the trampoline to a new block? Easy, just modify that extra bit of memory. This way, I can fill an entire 4096-byte page full of trampoline copies, then fill out their block pointers later on.

If this is confusing (and how could it not be?), here's a diagram:

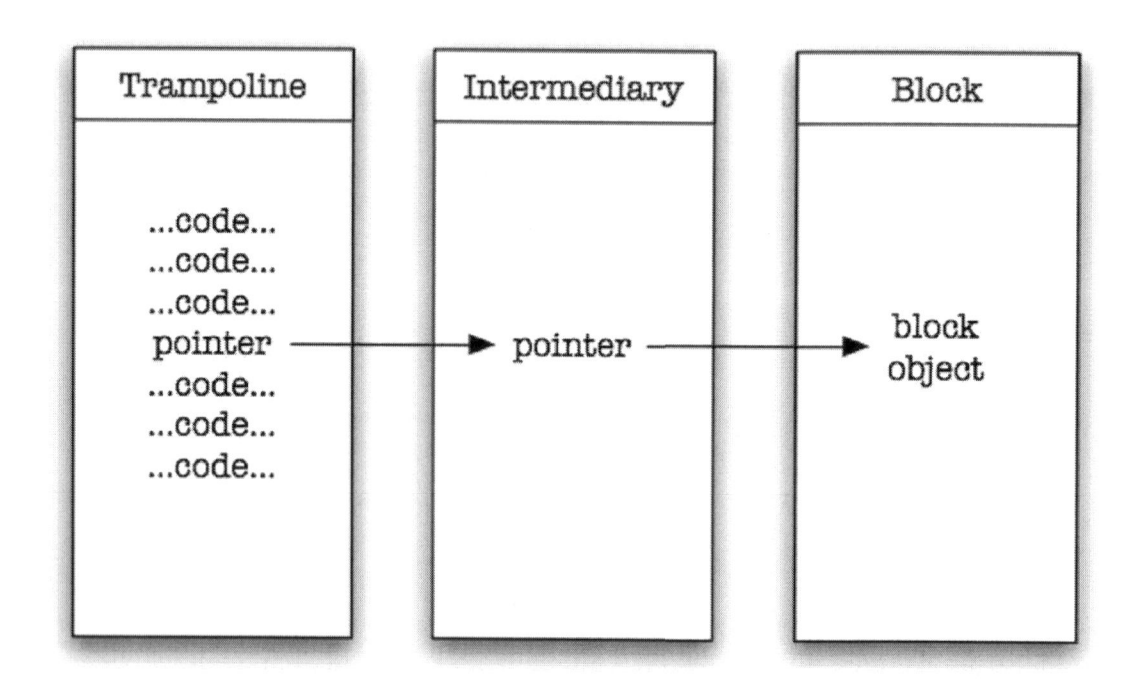

```
  Trampoline        Intermediary        Block

  ...code...
  ...code...
  ...code...                             block
   pointer  ─────▶   pointer  ─────▶    object
  ...code...
  ...code...
  ...code...
```

Assembly

Enough jabber, let's get to some code.

The trampoline needs to do four things. First, load the intermediary pointer into a register. The particular register in question is %r11, a designated scratch register whose value is not expected to survive across the function call:

movabsq $0xdeadbeefcafebabe, %r11

Second, load the block pointer from the intermediary into %rdi, the register which holds the first parameter to a function:

mov (%r11), %rdi

Third, extract the function pointer from the block into %r11, the scratch register:

mov BLOCK_FUNCTION_POINTER_OFFSET(%rdi), %r11

(BLOCK_FUNCTION_POINTER_OFFSET is just a macro #defined to 16.)

Fourth, jump to the address contained in %r11:

jmp *%r11

The pointer value `0xdeadbeefcafebabe` used in the first instruction is literal in the code. I use a recognizable pattern so that it can be searched for later on by the code that modifies this code, so that I don't have to hardcode the offset to the pointer value.

Finding the Address

The code to search for `0xdeadbeefcafebabe` is simple. First, we start out with a couple of extern definitions which allow the compiler to find the assembly code:

```
extern char Trampoline;
extern char TrampolineEnd;
```

These correspond to labels used in the assembly. The first is the trampoline function itself, and the second is a label placed just after it so that the end can easily be identified.

Notice that these aren't pointers. When the program is linked, `Trampoline` ends up being on the first byte of the trampoline function. In order to get a pointer to the trampoline, we write `&Trampoline`, and likewise write `&TrampolineEnd` to get the end. The `char` type is fairly incidental, but makes it easy to do pointer arithmetic on the resulting pointers, because `char` is by definition one byte long.

Given that, the code to find the magic value is pretty simple: just loop through, trying each memory location, until it's found or you run off the end. And of course I can't help but throw in a little Grand Central Dispatch to make this value be computed lazily:

```
static int TrampolineAddrOffset(void)
{
    static int addrOffset;
    static dispatch_once_t pred;
    dispatch_once(&pred, ^{
        uint64_t magic = 0xdeadbeefcafebabeULL;
        for(addrOffset = 0; addrOffset <= &TrampolineEnd - &Trampoline - sizeof(uint64_t); addrOffset++)
            if(*((uint64_t *)(&Trampoline + addrOffset)) == magic)
                break;
    });
    
    return addrOffset;
}
```

Right about now, you might be wondering, but what if the code *just so happens* to contain the bit pattern `0xdeadbeefcafebabe` at some spot before the magic pointer value itself, and this gets the wrong offset?

315

Well, it's extremely unlikely (and probably impossible, if you look at what instruction sequences that could possibly represent), but ultimately it doesn't matter even if it did. The beauty of writing the trampoline in assembly is that it gives you the exact same output every time it's built. It's not like writing C code, where the compiler might generate different code depending on optimization levels, other code, the compiler version, the phase of the moon, etc. Thus, if this code returns the correct value once, it'll do it every time. Likewise, if it fails, it'll fail immediately. The only risk is after changing the trampoline, so you just have to test it out real quick to make sure that this piece is still functional.

Intermediary

The intermediary is pretty simple, but a bit more complex than strictly needed just for the trampoline. The reason for this is that I want to reuse these values, and that means holding onto them in a cache after they're done being used. For maximum thread safety and speed, the cache takes the form of an OSQueue. That in turn requires that the intermediary have two fields (one for the queue's internal `next` pointer, and one to reference back to the trampoline it's associated with so we can fetch it) even though the trampoline only needs one. This is the definition of the intermediary:

```
struct Intermediary
{
    // when in the queue, the first field is the required 'next' pointer
    // when in use, the first field is the block pointer
    void *nextPtrOrBlock;

    // when in the queue, the second field is to the associated trampoline
    // when in use, the second field is unused
    void *trampoline;
};
```

Creating the Trampoline

Now we're ready to actually copy the trampoline onto the heap and point it to its intermediary. Given a location in the heap, a length (computed from `Trampoline` and `TrampolineEnd`), an offset (from `TrampolineAddrOffset`, and an intermediary pointer), the code to do the copy and modification is easy. First, copy the code:

```
static void CreateTrampoline(void *destination, int length, int addrOffset, struct Intermediary *intermediary)
{
    memcpy(destination, &Trampoline, length);
```

Fill out the intermediary:

```
        intermediary->nextPtrOrBlock = NULL;
        intermediary->trampoline = destination;
```

(The intermediary block pointer isn't being assigned yet, because we do that later, when a block is actually on hand. I set it to NULL here just for safety.)

Finally, point the newly minted trampoline back at the intermediary:

```
        *((void **)(destination + addrOffset)) =
    &intermediary->nextPtrOrBlock;
    }
```

Creating the Trampoline Factory

That's how you create an individual trampoline, but the plan was to build them in bulk to amortize the cost of that mprotect() call. To do that, I built a function which creates a page full of them, and then enqueues them all onto the OSQueue so they can be fetched later.

The first thing to do is to figure out the trampoline's length, the offset of the intermediary address, the system's page size, and how many trampolines will fit into that page size:

```
    void CreateNewFptrsAndEnqueue(void)
    {
        int trampolineLength = &TrampolineEnd - &Trampoline;
        int addrOffset = TrampolineAddrOffset();

        int pageSize = getpagesize();
        int howmany = pageSize / trampolineLength;
```

Next, allocate a page for the trampolines (using valloc, to ensure that the resulting address is actually page-aligned) and a block of memory for the intermediaries:

```
        void *page = valloc(pageSize);

        struct Intermediary *intermediaries = malloc(howmany *
    sizeof(*intermediaries));
```

Next, loop through and create all the trampolines:

```
        for(int i = 0; i < howmany; i++)
        {
            void *destination = page + i * trampolineLength;
            CreateTrampoline(destination, trampolineLength,
    addrOffset, &intermediaries[i]);
        }
```

Then mark the page executable:

```
    int err = mprotect(page, pageSize, PROT_READ | PROT_EXEC);
    if(err)
        perror("mprotect");
```

Finally, push them all onto the trampoline cache:

```
    for(int i = 0; i < howmany; i++)
    {
        void *trampoline = page + i * trampolineLength;
        EnqueueCachedFptr(trampoline);
    }
}
```

Next up, we need a bit of code that will dequeue a trampoline off that global cache, and set the intermediary to point to a block:

```
static void *DequeueCachedFptr(id block)
{
    struct Intermediary *intermediary = OSAtomicDequeue(&gFptrCache, 0);
    if(!intermediary)
        return NULL;
    
    intermediary->nextPtrOrBlock = [block copy];
    return intermediary->trampoline;
}
```

Finally, we can put it all together, with a public-facing function that returns a trampoline. It first tries the cache. If the cache is empty, it creates a page full of trampolines, then tries the cache again. In the unlikely event that the cache is *still* empty (other threads used all the trampolines before it could get any), then it creates another page and tries again, and keeps doing this until it gets one:

```
void *CreateBlockFptr(id block)
{
    void *fptr;
    while(!(fptr = DequeueCachedFptr(block)))
        CreateNewFptrsAndEnqueue();
    return fptr;
}
```

Finally, the returned argument can be used to actually call a block like a function pointer:

```
void (*fptr)(void) = CreateBlockFptr(^{ printf("hello,
world!\n"); });
fptr();
```

This will print out, `hello, world!`

Argument Shifting

If you were to run this code, you'd find that it works fine for the case where the block takes no arguments, but not so well for blocks that do take arguments. The problem is that the function signatures don't match: since the block implementation takes the block pointer as an implicit first argument, all of the other arguments get shifted down. Since the trampoline doesn't touch the arguments that were in place when it got called, the result is that the first argument is obliterated by the block pointer, and the remaining arguments all end up shifted down.

There's some bad news here: in the general case, without knowing the full function signature ahead of time (this trampoline is intended to work with arbitrary function pointers), it is *impossible* to reliably shift the arguments down by one in the x86_64 ABI.

To be more specific: under the x86_64 ABI, the first six INTEGER type parameters (which are basically integers and pointers, with some interesting things that happen to smaller structs composed of multiple integer/pointer types) get stored into six general-purpose registers, which are, in order: %rdi, %rsi, %rdx, %rcx, %r8, and %r9. Past six, they get spilled onto the stack. The problem is that a lot of other arguments can get spilled onto the stack as well, and the order in which that happens depends on the precise nature and ordering of all the arguments that the function takes.

The trampoline needs to shift all of those registers down by one (move %rdi to %rsi, %rsi to %rdx, etc.) *and* spill the contents of %r9 onto the stack. However, it's impossible to know where to spill it, or even whether it's necessary to do so.

Just because we can't solve this in the general case doesn't mean we can't solve enough to be useful, though. If we skip the step of spilling %r9 onto the stack, the result will fail for functions which take more than five INTEGER types, but most callbacks won't be affected by that. Simply shifting the registers down by one will be enough. This can be done by putting a series of mov instructions at the beginning to shuffle all of the arguments down, then proceeding with the remainder of the trampoline as shown previously. The final result looks like this:

```
.globl _Trampoline
_Trampoline:
    // shuffle integer argument registers down by one
    // to make room for the implicit block ptr argument
    mov %r8, %r9
    mov %rcx, %r8
    mov %rdx, %rcx
    mov %rsi, %rdx
    mov %rdi, %rsi

    // move ptr-to-block-ptr into r11, dummy value is replaced at runtime
    movabsq $0xdeadbeefcafebabe, %r11
    // dereference ptr-to-block-ptr, move block ptr into %rdi
    mov (%r11), %rdi
    // extract block implementation function pointer into %r11
    mov BLOCK_FUNCTION_POINTER_OFFSET(%rdi), %r11
    // jump to block implementation
    jmp *%r11
.globl _TrampolineEnd
_TrampolineEnd:
    .long 0
    .long 0
```

Since the trampoline copying/modifying code is already fully generalized and just searches for the magic pointer value, it doesn't need to be changed at all to accommodate the new trampoline. If you try this, you'll find that it works with arguments... as long as you don't exceed five INTEGER-type arguments.

Examples

That was fun to build, but how about *using* it?

These examples make use of an AutoBlockFptr function which basically wraps CreateBlockFptr to create an "autoreleased" block trampoline which is automatically destroyed when the enclosing NSAutoreleasePool is popped. I won't go into details of how it works (I didn't even cover how trampolines are recycled at all, for that matter) but you can check it out in the code if you want to see.

The pthread API is a classic one that deals with function pointers. You create a new thread with pthread_create, but it takes a function pointer and a context pointer, and that's always a pain. Of course, pthread is perhaps a bit less useful now that we have Grand Central Dispatch, but there are still lots of places where it comes in handy. Let's use this new code to adapt a block instead of dealing with function pointers:

```
pthread_t thread;
pthread_create(&thread, NULL, AutoBlockFptr(^(void
*ignore) {
    printf("hello, world from a pthread!\n");
}), NULL);
pthread_join(thread, NULL);
```

This works just as you'd expect. The `pthread` API was never so easy!

How about some Objective-C runtime hackery?

```
int captured = 99;
class_addMethod([NSObject class], @selector(printInt:),
CreateBlockFptr(^(id self, SEL _cmd, int x) {
    printf("in object %p, the captured integer is %d, the passed integer is %d\n", self, captured, x);
}), "v@:i");
NSObject *obj = [[NSObject alloc] init];
[obj printInt: 42];
[obj printInt: -11];
[obj release];
```

Again, works perfectly:

```
in object 0x1002003d0, the captured integer is 99, the passed integer is 42
in object 0x1002003d0, the captured integer is 99, the passed integer is -11
```

CoreFoundation is a place where function pointers are common. How about creating a `CFArray` with custom callbacks, all written inline?

```
CFArrayCallBacks callbacks = {
    0,
    AutoBlockFptr(^(CFAllocatorRef allocator, const void *value) {
        NSLog(@"retain %@", value);
        return value;
    }),
    AutoBlockFptr(^(CFAllocatorRef allocator, const void *value) {
        NSLog(@"release %@", value);
    }),
    AutoBlockFptr(^(CFAllocatorRef allocator, const void *value) {
        NSLog(@"description of %@", value);
        return [(id)value description];
    }),
    AutoBlockFptr(^(CFAllocatorRef allocator, const void *value1, const void *value2) {
        NSLog(@"equality %@ %@", value1, value2);
        return (Boolean)[(id)value1 isEqual: (id)value2];
    })
};

CFMutableArrayRef array = CFArrayCreateMutable(NULL, 0, &callbacks);
CFArrayAppendValue(array, @"first object");
CFArrayAppendValue(array, @"second object");
CFArrayRemoveAllValues(array);
```

When run, produces this:

```
2010-02-11 00:21:51.238 BlockFptr[9201:a0f] retain first object
2010-02-11 00:21:51.241 BlockFptr[9201:a0f] retain second object
2010-02-11 00:21:51.242 BlockFptr[9201:a0f] release first object
2010-02-11 00:21:51.243 BlockFptr[9201:a0f] release second object
```

That's all there is to it!

Caveats

I already mentioned that this code is dangerous and that you should never use it, but wanted to repeat that warning a second time. There are a *lot* of limitations:

1. Does not work with more than five `INTEGER` arguments.
2. Does not work with `struct` returns at all, if the `struct` is big enough to trigger the special `struct` return calling conventions. Large structs are essentially returned by reference, by passing a pointer as an implicit first argument to the function. The trampoline will put the block pointer there instead, leading to hilarity. This could be worked around by adding a second trampoline just for `struct` returns.
3. Managing the lifetime of a trampoline can be difficult. For one-shot uses, like with `pthread_create`, you can destroy the trampoline as soon as your block has started running. For uses which persist for the lifetime of the process, like adding a permanent method to an Objective-C object, you can just create it and leave it be. It's when it might be called multiple times but you eventually want to clean it up that it gets tricky, because normal code just assumes that any function pointer will last forever. The `CFArray` example is a good example of this: there's no easy way to link the lifetime of the trampolines to the lifetime of the `CFArray`. (The best way to do it is probably to use the Objective-C associated object API, but that's pretty ugly.)
4. Most importantly: even if you fit within all these limitations, the trampoline only exists for `x86_64`. While it could be ported to other architectures, the argument and return-type limitations are likely to be different on those other architectures, breaking previously working code. (On iPhone OS, Apple doesn't even allow this sort of runtime generation of code at all.)

Despite these problems, it's still a good learning experience and a fun toy to play with.

Conclusion

This sort of low-level assembly hacking can be tricky and, as you can see, the result isn't always completely practical. However, it's a lot of fun, and a great way to learn about how the system is put together at the bottom.

Friday Q&A 2010-02-19: Character Encodings

It's another Friday and another Friday Q&A. For this week's post, Joshua Pokotilow has suggested that I talk about character encodings, so I want to give a basic tour of just what a character encoding is, how it works, and useful details about common encodings.

What's a Character Encoding?
To define a character encoding, I first need to define a character. This is probably intuitively obvious to most of you, but there is great value in a more formal definition, especially since intuitive ideas will vary.

The trouble is that the formal definition is vague. Essentially, a **character** is the fundamental conceptual unit of textual information. Letters and numbers are characters, but that's not all characters are. Symbols are characters, but there are non-symbolic characters, such as the space character.

Now that we (sort of) know what a character is, a **character encoding** is some technique for mapping conceptual sequences of characters into actual sequences of bytes, and for mapping a sequence of bytes back to a sequence of characters.

There are many different kinds of encodings, but there are two basic kinds that are of primary interest here:

- **8-bit encodings:** These encodings maintain a one-to-one mapping between a byte and a character. Each character gets encoded to a single byte, and each byte represents one character. For obvious reasons, 8-bit encodings can't represent more than 256 characters.
- **Variable-length encodings:** These encodings can map a single character to multiple bytes, and the number of bytes varies depending on the character. This allows the encoding to represent more than 256 characters, essential if you're dealing with languages such as Chinese which have far more than this.

ASCII
The most common and fundamental character encoding used today is ASCII. ASCII is a small and simple 7-bit character encoding, which means that it defines 128 characters and maps them to the byte values 0-127. As used on modern systems, ASCII can be thought of as an 8-bit encoding where the values 128-255 go unused.

ASCII encodes all of the letters used in English, as well as common punctuation and other symbols. ASCII also encodes various control characters. Some of these, like newline and tab, are commonly used in text for formatting purposes. Some, like Record Separator and Start of Header, are basically obsolete. A full listing of all ASCII characters can be seen by typing `man ascii` into your local Terminal window.

ASCII works great for most English writing, but is inadequate for the vast majority of other languages in the world.

ASCII compatibility
The notion of ASCII compatibility is a key concept when discussing other encodings. Because of ASCII's early dominance, and the fact that it left half of the values unused on computers with 8-bit bytes, many other encodings sprouted up which maintained compatibility with ASCII, taking advantage of the unused values in order to represent more characters. Being ASCII compatible makes it much easier to use old code with a new encoding, and ensures that software will have a common denominator for communication even if they disagree on encodings.

There are two different kinds of ASCII compatibility. The first kind is full ASCII compatibility. This means that if you take a sequence of ASCII bytes and decode them using the encoding in question, the result is still the ASCII characters that they represent. It also means that if you encode a sequence of characters using this encoding, any ASCII bytes in the output represent the corresponding ASCII character. In short, ASCII gets encoded to ASCII, and anything that looks like ASCII is ASCII.

There's also partial compatibility. Some encodings will correctly read an ASCII string, but can produce bytes in the range 0-127 for non-ASCII characters which take up more than one byte. Any sort of text processing with such encodings requires a strong understanding of how the encoding works, because, for example, searching for the letter Z within the text using a raw byte-by-byte search could end up finding the byte 0x5A that just happens to be part of a multi-byte character. For this sort of encoding, it will interpret ASCII strings correctly, but may produce ASCII-looking byte sequences where no such thing is intended.

Some encodings are simply not ASCII-compatible at all. These assign different meanings to byte values 0-127 in all contexts.

Latin-1
Latin-1, is perhaps the most common 8-bit encoding, so it deserves special mention. Latin-1 is a mostly ASCII compatible encoding whose purpose is to work better with common Western European languages. As such, it uses many of the values left unused by ASCII to represent accented characters and certain letters not in ASCII, as this is the major thing lacking from ASCII for these languages. It also includes other characters useful to these languages, such as currency symbols and punctuation, and some symbols that are just useful in general, like copyright/trademark symbols.

There are actually three somewhat different encodings which can all be described as "Latin-1", which is wonderfully confusing. There's ISO 8859-1, Windows-1252, and ISO-8859-1 (the first and last names are identical except for a single hyphen). ISO 8859-1 is not ASCII compatible because it does not define characters for the ranges occupied by ASCII control characters. It does leave ASCII values intact for the rest of that range, and the other two are fully ASCII compatible. ISO-8859-1 is so frequently confused with Windows-1252 (which encodes additional human-readable characters in a space that ISO-8859-1 uses for control characters) that many documents state their encoding as ISO-8859-1 when they actually use Windows-1252. As best I can tell, in Cocoa, the `NSISOLatin1StringEncoding` constant refers to ISO-8859-1, but this is by no means clear. (The documentation doesn't say precisely what it is. When passed through `CFStringConvertNSStringEncodingToEncoding`, it comes out as `kCFStringEncodingISOLatin1`. The documentation says that encoding is ISO 8859-1. However, `CFStringConvertEncodingToIANACharSetName` returns `iso-8859-1` and that's probably the one to believe.)

MacRoman
Since this is a Mac-centric blog, MacRoman deserves special mention as well. It's roughly the Mac-specific equivalent of Latin-1. Like Latin-1, MacRoman is ASCII-compatible and fills in a lot of useful letters and symbols for Western European languages. However, the code points that it uses and the characters that it covers don't match Latin-1.

MacRoman has one nice property (which is shared by ISO-8859-1 but not the other two "Latin-1" encodings) that it defines a unique character for every possible byte value. This means that any sequence of bytes is a valid MacRoman string, and that roundtripping through MacRoman (decoding with MacRoman, then re-encoding) will always preserve the data with no changes.

Unicode
Unicode is a fantastically large and complicated system of character encodings whose full nature is too involved to explain here. However, there are a few relevant points which are valuable to know.

Unicode defines a large range of characters (in Unicode terminology, "code points") which encompass virtually every character defined in other character encodings, and thus virtually every character in use for written communication. All in all, Unicode defines about a million characters. Unicode is able to represent nearly any written text without having to worry about different encodings. This is really handy.

Once you reach the level of Unicode, an important distinction makes itself obvious. The distinction is the difference between a *character* and a *glyph*. A *character* is a logical semantic unit, and a *glyph* is a visual unit that you actually see on screen. Although many English speakers (and plenty of non-English speakers) consider these ideas to be the same, they are not. It is possible to have a character which has no glyph (for example, the space character), two characters which combine to a single glyph (Unicode defines "combining marks", like accent marks, which modify a plain letter), and it's even possible for a single character to produce multiple glyphs (like an accented character transforming into a plain letter plus a separate, appropriately positioned accent mark glyph).

All of this means that you can't just slice up Unicode text in arbitrary places without really understanding how Unicode works, or at least knowing that your text only contains characters that behave nicely. The `NSString` method `-rangeOfComposedCharacterSequenceAtIndex:` can help a lot with this.

Unicode defines characters, but does not define a single character *encoding* to map those characters to sequences of bytes. Instead, it defines several different encodings, which all have different tradeoffs and different uses.

The original Unicode was a 16-bit encoding where every character occupied exactly two bytes. This encoding is now referred to as UCS-2. UCS-2 was later expanded to be able to work with more than 65,535 characters, and this new encoding became UTF-16. UTF-16 uses two-byte code units, but uses two such code units (four bytes in total) to represent characters which don't fit into the original two bytes. (UTF-16 code units are what `NSString` puts into the `unichar` type, for things like `-characterAtIndex:`.)

Another encoding is called UTF-32, which as the name suggests uses four bytes per character. Every Unicode character fits into four bytes, so this is a fixed-length encoding, but tends to waste a lot of space so it doesn't get much use.

UTF-8

The trouble with these Unicode encodings is that they are completely incompatible with all software which works with individual bytes and assumes that ASCII is king. This, plus the fact that UCS-2 and UTF-16 double the size of plain ASCII text, with little perceived benefit for English speakers, hurt Unicode's adoption.

UTF-8 was created to solve these problems. As the name suggests, the basic code unit in UTF-8 is a single byte. These bytes are chained together in sequences up to four bytes long to encode each Unicode character.

The most important property of UTF-8 is that it's *fully ASCII compatible*. Put ASCII in, get ASCII out, every time. All non-ASCII characters are encoded using a sequence of bytes in the range 128-255. This means that software which expects ASCII but can leave the top half of the byte value range alone will generally work pretty well with UTF-8.

For non-ASCII characters, UTF-8 uses a clever variable-length encoding scheme that's very easy to work with. Any byte in a UTF-8-encoded byte stream will fall into one of five categories:

bit pattern (x is wildcard)	meaning
0xxxxxxx	single ASCII character
110xxxxx	lead byte of two-character sequence
1110xxxx	lead byte of three-character sequence
11110xxx	lead byte of four-character sequence
10xxxxxx	trailing byte in multi-character sequence

As you can see, the byte stream is self-describing. For any given character, you can see which category it falls into. If it's a trailing byte, then you can read forward (or backwards) in the stream until you come to the next lead byte. From there, you can easily tell how many trailing bytes will follow that lead byte, which characters are ASCII, etc. While Unicode is complicated and UTF-8 can't hide that fact, UTF-8 does make it relatively easy to pass arbitrary text around while still being able to parse the ASCII bits. And if you need to deal with the Unicode bits as well, it's easy to convert UTF-8 into something more useful, like an `NSString`, which knows more about Unicode.

Because of all of the useful properties that UTF-8 has, I want to leave you with this piece of advice: **when storing or transmitting text, always use UTF-8 for your character encoding**.

This obviously doesn't apply if you're writing for a protocol or format which already exists and which mandates a different encoding, but any time you have a choice, your choice should be UTF-8.

Fallbacks

Sometimes you receive textual data and you don't know in advance what the encoding is. This is ultimately a problem that's impossible to solve with complete accuracy. However, it's possible to make some useful guesses which will be right much of the time, in most contexts.

When this happens to me, I like to use code like this:

```
NSString *string = [[NSString alloc] initWithData: data
encoding: NSUTF8StringEncoding];
if(!string)
    string = [[NSString alloc] initWithData: data
encoding: NSISOLatin1StringEncoding];
if(!string)
    string = [[NSString alloc] initWithData: data
encoding: NSMacOSRomanStringEncoding];
```

The first attempt is with UTF-8. This is not just because it's a useful and common encoding, but also because UTF-8 has a rigid syntactical structure which is extremely unlikely to be reproduced by accident. In other words, if your data is a valid UTF-8 string, the odds are extremely high that it was actually intended to be UTF-8. It's difficult to find meaningful text that can be encoded with a different encoding and still produce a valid UTF-8 string.

If it's not UTF-8, then the next attempt is with Latin-1, because it's so common. If that fails (depending on which version of Latin-1 Cocoa means by this constant, it might not define characters for all possible byte values), then the final fallback is MacRoman. Since MacRoman defines characters for every byte value, this last attempt will always work, although it may not produce the correct output. And because MacRoman is ASCII-compatible, and most other encodings are at least somewhat ASCII-compatible, this step is likely to give you the correct values for any ASCII characters in the string, even if you get bad characters for the rest.

Note that there is no case for `NSASCIIStringEncoding`. It's not necessary, because any ASCII text will be correctly decoded by the `NSUTF8StringEncoding` step.

Depending on your context, you may want to try a different sequence of encodings. For example, if you expect to see mostly Japanese text, then you may want to try `NSJapaneseEUCStringEncoding` or `NSShiftJISStringEncoding` instead of, or perhaps before, `NSISOLatin1StringEncoding`.

The key elements are to first try UTF-8, because it has an extremely low false positive rate, then try any specific encodings which make sense for your scenario, and finally, if necessary, fall back to an encoding like MacRoman which will always produce some kind of sensible output.

Conclusion

That's it for this week. I hope that now you understand a little more about character encodings, what they are, how they work, and how to use them. If you learn only one lesson from this post, let it be this: use UTF-8!

Friday Q&A 2010-02-26: Futures

Related Articles

    Blocks in Objective-C 14

    Practical Blocks 146

    Creating a Blocks-Based Object System 205

    Error Returns with Continuation Passing Style 303

    Trampolining Blocks with Mutable Code 311

    Compound Futures 342

    Background Timers 419

Welcome back to another shiny edition of Friday Q&A. Guy English suggested taking a look at implementing futures in Objective-C using blocks, and for this week's post I'm going to talk about the futures implementation that I built.

Futures

A future is, in short, an object which hides a calculation. When a future is *resolved*, the resolution blocks until the calculation has finished. My code involves *implicit* futures: a future is a proxy for the calculated result and, when messaged, transparently resolves the future and then passes the message on to the result. To code which uses it, a future is essentially indistinguishable from the object that it represents.

In Objective-C, it's natural to represent the calculation using a block. Futures are created by simply calling a function which takes a block representing the calculation. They return a proxy object which captures messages sent to that object and resolves the future as needed. My code has two kinds of futures.

Background futures begin the calculation immediately on a background thread as soon as the future is created. When the future is resolved, if the calculation is not yet complete, the call blocks until it's done. If the calculation finishes first, then resolution completes immediately. Background futures provide a way to write parallel code without needing to worry about details of synchronization. For example, if you're going to pass an `NSData` to another object that won't actually use that `NSData` for a while, you can use a background future to allow other code to run concurrently with the disk access with very little effort:

```
NSString *filename = ...;
NSData *future = MABackgroundFuture(^{ return [NSData dataWithContentsOfFile: filename]; });
[object doSomethingLaterWithData: future];
```

Lazy futures do not begin the calculation until the future is resolved. If the future is never resolved, then the calculation is never performed. Lazy futures make it possible to provide an object immediately to an API which may or may not actually make use of it, and not pay the cost of creating that object until and unless it's actually requested. For example, you could use a lazy future to defer the reading of a file until and unless it's needed:

```
NSString *filename = ...;
NSData *future = MALazyFuture(^{ return [NSData dataWithContentsOfFile: filename]; });
[object doSomethingOrNotWithData: future];
```

Getting the Code
As usual, I'm just going to cover the highlights of the code here, but the library is available from my subversion repository:

```
svn co http://mikeash.com/svn/MAFuture/
```

A Custom Proxy Class
When building object proxies, Cocoa provides a convenient root proxy class to subclass in the form of NSProxy. The idea is that NSProxy provides a minimal implementation, which allows almost all messages to be captured and proxied.

Unfortunately, NSProxy doesn't quite live up to its promise. It implements a whole bunch of unnecessary methods, including important ones like -hash and -isEqual:. This is a problem because I don't want NSProxy's implementations of these, I want the implementations in the proxied object. To make that happen, I'd have to either manually override these methods, or play runtime tricks to make them hit the forwarding path. Neither alternative is particularly appealing.

Instead, I chose a third route: implement my own proxy class. MAProxy is a true minimalistic proxy class. It implements memory management methods and -isProxy. It also implements +initialize, which the runtime requires to exist in every class. The header is really basic and the implementation nearly as simple. The only tricky stuff at work is the inline reference count using atomic functions for thread safety.

Future Basics
To make implementing futures easier, I created a base class called MABaseFuture which provides common facilities. A basic future needs to be able to store a value, to store whether the future has been resolved yet or not, and a condition variable to make it all thread safe:

```objc
@interface MABaseFuture : MAProxy
{
    id _value;
    NSCondition *_lock;
    BOOL _resolved;
}
```

For code, the class obviously needs creation/destruction methods:

```objc
- (id)init
{
    _lock = [[NSCondition alloc] init];
    return self;
}

- (void)dealloc
{
    [_value release];
    [_lock release];

    [super dealloc];
}
```

Then, accessors for the future's value. There are both locked and unlocked setters because a subclass may want to set the future's value after already acquiring the lock:

```objc
- (void)setFutureValue: (id)value
{
    [_lock lock];
    [self setFutureValueUnlocked: value];
    [_lock unlock];
}

- (id)futureValue
{
    // skip the usual retain/autorelease dance here
    // because the setter is never called more than
    // once, thus value lifetime is same as future
    // lifetime
    [_lock lock];
    id value = _value;
    [_lock unlock];
    return value;
}

- (void)setFutureValueUnlocked: (id)value
{
    [value retain];
    [_value release];
    _value = value;
    _resolved = YES;
    [_lock broadcast];
}
```

A quick getter to see if the future has been resolved (which relies on the subclass to manually acquire the lock first):

```objc
- (BOOL)futureHasResolved
{
    return _resolved;
}
```

Then the one part that's a bit interesting, a method to wait for the future to resolve, handy for implementing background futures:

```
- (id)waitForFutureResolution
{
    [_lock lock];
    while(!_resolved)
        [_lock wait];
    [_lock unlock];
    return _value;
}
```

This class also has a `-resolveFuture` method which is abstract. Subclasses must override it and do whatever they need to do:

```
- (id)resolveFuture
{
    NSLog(@"-[MABaseFuture resolveFuture] called, this should never happen! Did you forget to implement -[%@ resolveFuture]?", NSStringFromClass(isa));
    NSParameterAssert(0);
    return nil;
}
```

Actually there are two interesting parts to this class, and the second one is here. It's an implementation of `-class`. Normally this implementation wouldn't be necessary, as the proxy mechanism will proxy that method just fine. The problem arises in the implementation of `-[NSCFString isEqual:]`, part of the `CFString` toll-free bridging, and with other bridged classes. That code checks the class of the other object, and if it's an `NSCFString` as well, hits a fast path that depends on internal implementation details of `NSCFString`. If `-class` returns `NSCFString` when the object is really a proxy, that code fails and the two strings will never compare as equal, even when they are.

The fix is simple, if bizarre. Get the real class, check to see if it starts with `NSCF`, and return the superclass if it does. If the real class is `NSCFString`, this will return `NSString`, the code goes through the general equality path, and all is well. This is the implementation of `-class`:

```
- (Class)class
{
    Class c = [[self resolveFuture] class];
    if([NSStringFromClass(c) hasPrefix: @"NSCF"])
        return [c superclass];
    else
        return c;
}
```

And that's all there is to MABaseFuture.

Deepening the Hierarchy

Building on MABaseFuture, I want to then create a tree of subclasses. First, _MASimpleFuture will contain some more common facilities for "simple" futures (futures which immediately resolve when accessed), then I'll create two subclasses of that for background and lazy futures.

_MASimpleFuture is very, well, simple. It implements -forwardingTargetForSelector: to resolve the future and return the object that resulted:

```
- (id)forwardingTargetForSelector: (SEL)sel
{
    LOG(@"%p forwardingTargetForSelector: %@, resolving future", self, NSStringFromSelector(sel));
    return [self resolveFuture];
}
```

Using this class, subclasses just need to provide an initializer method and override -resolveFuture, and they get forwarding for free.

Forwarding to nil

There's a bad corner case here, which happens if the future returns nil. Messaging nil is no problem, but forwardingTargetForSelector: takes a nil return as meaning that there is no forwarding target, and the runtime should start on the slow forwarding path instead.

And here there's a major problem, because the slow forwarding path requires a method signature, but it's impossible to get one from nil. I've partially solved this in an extremely brute-force fashion by writing a class called MAMethodSignatureCache, which will check every class registered with the runtime for a selector and return whatever method signature it can dig up. (I didn't write it solely for this, there's more handy stuff to do with it in another post.) I can use this class to implement the slow forwarding path of _MASimpleFuture to return zero:

```
- (NSMethodSignature *)methodSignatureForSelector: (SEL)sel
{
    return [[MAMethodSignatureCache sharedCache]
cachedMethodSignatureForSelector: sel];
}

- (void)forwardInvocation: (NSInvocation *)inv
{
    // this gets hit if the future resolves to nil
    // zero-fill the return value
    char returnValue[[[inv methodSignature]
methodReturnLength]];
    bzero(returnValue, sizeof(returnValue));
    [inv setReturnValue: returnValue];
}
```

The problem comes when there are multiple method signatures for a given selector, which can easily happen if two unrelated classes implement methods with the same name. In that case, there's no way to know which one is meant, and this whole approach falls apart. Unfortunately, with the way the runtime is currently written, there's no generalized way to "forward to nil".

If that's not enough, there's another problem with futures that return nil. This problem is quite simple: although the futured value may be nil, the future object itself is not nil. Any code which checks the object pointer for nil before using it will fail in weird ways. Imagine this code using an NSData:

```
NSData *data = ...;
if(data)
    [self doSomethingWithBytes: [data bytes]];
```

If data is a future that resolves to nil, then the if check will pass, but [data bytes] will return NULL, causing a crash.

Because of these two problems, you should avoid futuring any computation which might return nil.

Background Futures

To implement background futures, I created a class called _MABackgroundBlockFuture. Since computation is supposed to begin immediately in the background, I create an initializer which takes the block to compute, and uses Grand Central Dispatch to execute it in the background. Once the computation is finished, it simply calls -setFutureValue: to set the computed value and mark the future as resolved:

```
- (id)initWithBlock: (id (^)(void))block
{
    if((self = [self init]))
    {
        dispatch_async(dispatch_get_global_queue(0, 0), ^{
            [self setFutureValue: block()];
        });
    }
    return self;
}
```

The implementation of -resolveFuture is then extremely simple. Since the future is already being computed, it just waits for it to finish, then returns the result:

```
- (id)resolveFuture
{
    return [self waitForFutureResolution];
}
```

Lazy Futures

I created _MALazyBlockFuture to implement lazy futures. A lazy future doesn't begin computation right away, so it just needs to store a copy of the block when initialized, and release it when deallocating:

```
- (id)initWithBlock: (id (^)(void))block
{
    if((self = [self init]))
    {
        _block = [block copy];
    }
    return self;
}

- (void)dealloc
{
    [_block release];
    [super dealloc];
}
```

Resolution is straightforward as well. Acquire the lock. If the future hasn't been resolved yet, then call the block and set the future's value from its result:

```objc
- (id)resolveFuture
{
    [_lock lock];
    if(![self futureHasResolved])
    {
        [self setFutureValueUnlocked: _block()];
        [_block release];
        _block = nil;
    }
    [_lock unlock];
    return _value;
}
```

Wrappers

This code now has all the functionality that's needed, but I want a couple of wrappers to make it nicer to use:

```objc
id MABackgroundFuture(id (^block)(void))
{
    return [[[_MABackgroundBlockFuture alloc] initWithBlock: block] autorelease];
}

id MALazyFuture(id (^block)(void))
{
    return [[[_MALazyBlockFuture alloc] initWithBlock: block] autorelease];
}
```

Because these functions return id, the compiler won't be able to catch mistakes like:

```objc
NSArray *array = MALazyFuture(^{ return [self somethingThatReturnsNSString]; });
```

Gcc will also reject this because the block types don't match exactly (returning NSString * instead of id) even though they're completely compatible.

I worked around both of these problems by using two really scary-looking macros:

```objc
#define MABackgroundFuture(...) ((__typeof((__VA_ARGS__)()))MABackgroundFuture((id (^)(void))__VA_ARGS__))
#define MALazyFuture(...) ((__typeof((__VA_ARGS__)()))MALazyFuture((id (^)(void))__VA_ARGS__))
```

Let's unpack these a bit.

First, they take variable arguments, because block syntax doesn't play completely nice with the preprocessor. If you write a block which contains a comma that isn't inside parentheses (which can be written completely legally), the preprocessor won't realize that it's inside a block, and will use that as an argument separator. The preprocessor will therefore see two (or more) arguments, and a single-argument macro will fail. By making the macros take ..., that problem is avoided. Thus, the block parameter is represented in the macro by __VA_ARGS__.

__typeof is a gcc language extension which pretty much does what it says. You give it an expression, and it gives you the type of the expression.

The argument to __typeof is (__VA_ARGS__)(). Remember that __VA_ARGS__ is the block being passed to the macro. This expression calls the block. But since it's an argument being passed to __typeof, which is a compile-time construct, it doesn't *really* call the block. Put the two together, and you get the return type of the block.

Next, the whole __typeof combination is wrapped in another set of parentheses and put right before the call through to the real function, which casts the return value of the function.

Finally, the function argument is cast to id (^)(void), because gcc is too stupid to understand that a block which returns NSString * is compatible with a block type that returns id.

Potential Uses

Background futures are useful any time you have computation which can happen asynchronously. In essence, you can think of the future as a synchronization mechanism, like a lock, which ensures that the job is completed before the result is used. Because these futures automatically forward requests, you can pass the future into code that doesn't know what it is, and it will be resolved automatically.

For example, let's say you're building a composite image by loading one image from disk, shrinking another image that already exists, and then putting the result into an image view:

```
NSImage *image1 = [[NSImage alloc] initWithContentsOfFile:
...];
NSImage *image2 = [self shrinkImage: existingImage];

NSImage *composite = [[NSImage alloc] initWithSize: ...];
[composite lockFocus];
[image1 drawAtPoint: NSZeroPoint fromRect: NSZeroRect
operation: NSCompositeSourceOver fraction: 1.0];
[image2 drawAtPoint: NSZeroPoint fromRect: NSZeroRect
operation: NSCompositeSourceOver fraction: 1.0];
[composite unlockFocus];

[imageView setImage: composite];
```

By futuring all of the images, you allow the work for `image1` and `image2` to run in parallel, and there's at least the possibility that some of the work for `composite` could run in parallel with main thread work too:

```
NSImage *image1 = MABackgroundFuture(^{ return [[[NSImage
alloc] initWithContentsOfFile: ...] autorelease]; });
NSImage *image2 = MABackgroundFuture(^{ return [self
shrinkImage: existingImage]; });

NSImage *composite = MABackgroundFuture(^{
    NSImage *img = [[NSImage alloc] initWithSize: ...];
    [img lockFocus];
    [image1 drawAtPoint: NSZeroPoint fromRect: NSZeroRect
operation: NSCompositeSourceOver fraction: 1.0];
    [image2 drawAtPoint: NSZeroPoint fromRect: NSZeroRect
operation: NSCompositeSourceOver fraction: 1.0];
    [img unlockFocus];
    return [img autorelease];
});

[imageView setImage: composite];
```

Quick and easy parallel code, and `imageView` never has to know that it's getting a proxy instead of the real thing.

Lazy futures are useful any time you have objects that may never be needed, or simply may not be needed for a long time. Even if the object is used, deferring computation can spread out the load and improve responsiveness and startup times.

As an example, imagine some code which sets up a bunch of data file contents to be accessed through a dictionary:

```
gGlobalDictionary = [[NSDictionary alloc]
initWithObjectsAndKeys:
    [NSData dataWithContentsOfFile: ...], @"dataFile",
    [NSData dataWithContentsOfFile: ...],
@"anotherDataFile",
    [NSData dataWithContentsOfFile: ...], @"moreDataFile",
    [NSData dataWithContentsOfFile: ...],
@"fourthDataFile",
    nil];
```

You could load these files lazily by splitting them out, providing an accessor for each one, etc., but using lazy futures requires minimal changes and most of the same benefits:

```
gGlobalDictionary = [[NSDictionary alloc]
initWithObjectsAndKeys:
    MALazyFuture(^{ return [NSData dataWithContentsOfFile:
...] }), @"dataFile",
    MALazyFuture(^{ return [NSData dataWithContentsOfFile:
...] }), @"anotherDataFile",
    MALazyFuture(^{ return [NSData dataWithContentsOfFile:
...] }), @"moreDataFile",
    MALazyFuture(^{ return [NSData dataWithContentsOfFile:
...] }), @"fourthDataFile",
    nil];
```

Many other possibilities abound for parallel and lazy computation through the use of futures.

Conclusion

Futures are an interesting technique which can make it much easier to use lazy evaluation and parallel computation. Futures make it easy to use lazy evaluation even when you have no control over (or no desire to change) the code that will eventually use the value in question. They also make for a handy synchronization mechanism for performing heterogeneous parallel computations. The dynamic nature of Objective-C makes it possible to mostly hide the existence of the future from code that isn't involved in creating it.

Friday Q&A 2010-03-05: Compound Futures

Related Articles
- Blocks in Objective-C 14
- Practical Blocks 146
- Creating a Blocks-Based Object System 205
- Error Returns with Continuation Passing Style 303
- Trampolining Blocks with Mutable Code 311
- Futures 330
- Background Timers 419

Welcome back to another thrilling edition of Friday Q&A. This week I want to extend my discussion from last week about futures, and talk about compound futures, an extension to the basic futures system that I developed previously.

I'm going to assume that you've read last week's article and understand what a future is and how the `MAFuture` library works. If you haven't seen it, please read that post before continuing with this one.

Code
As before, the library is available from my subversion repository:

```
svn co http://mikeash.com/svn/MAFuture/
```

Compound Futures
The futures I discussed last week are implicit futures, which behave as a proxy to the result of the calculation being futured. They look and act like the real object. Once the proxy is messaged, then the future is resolved and the message is passed on to the real object.

A *compound* future is more complex. Whenever possible, messaging a compound future doesn't resolve the future. Instead, it *returns another future*. This is also a compound future, which will in turn return more compound futures, until you have a whole chain of futures set up. Only when you send a message that can't be futured (essentially, a message that returns a primitive rather than an object) is the future resolved, with resolution proceeding up the chain.

As an example, consider this code:

```
NSString *string = ...;
NSArray *components = [string componentsSeparatedByString:
@" "];
NSString *first = [components objectAtIndex: 0];
NSString *second = [components objectAtIndex: 1];
second = [second uppercaseString];

printf("%s: %s\n", [first UTF8String], [second
UTF8String]);
```

Nothing unusual there. Now let's toss in a compound future:

```
NSString *string = MACompoundLazyFuture(^{ return ...; });
NSArray *components = [string componentsSeparatedByString:
@" "];
NSString *first = [components objectAtIndex: 0];
NSString *second = [components objectAtIndex: 1];
second = [second uppercaseString];

printf("%s: %s\n", [first UTF8String], [second
UTF8String]);
```

Now the futures start to chain. The call to componentsSeparatedByString: returns a future that depends on the future stored in string. The calls to objectAtIndex: return futures that depend on the array future. The call to uppercaseString returns yet another future. Finally, the calls to UTF8String can't be futured because they return a primitive, and so they cause the entire chain to be resolved.

The sequence of futures ends up looking like this:

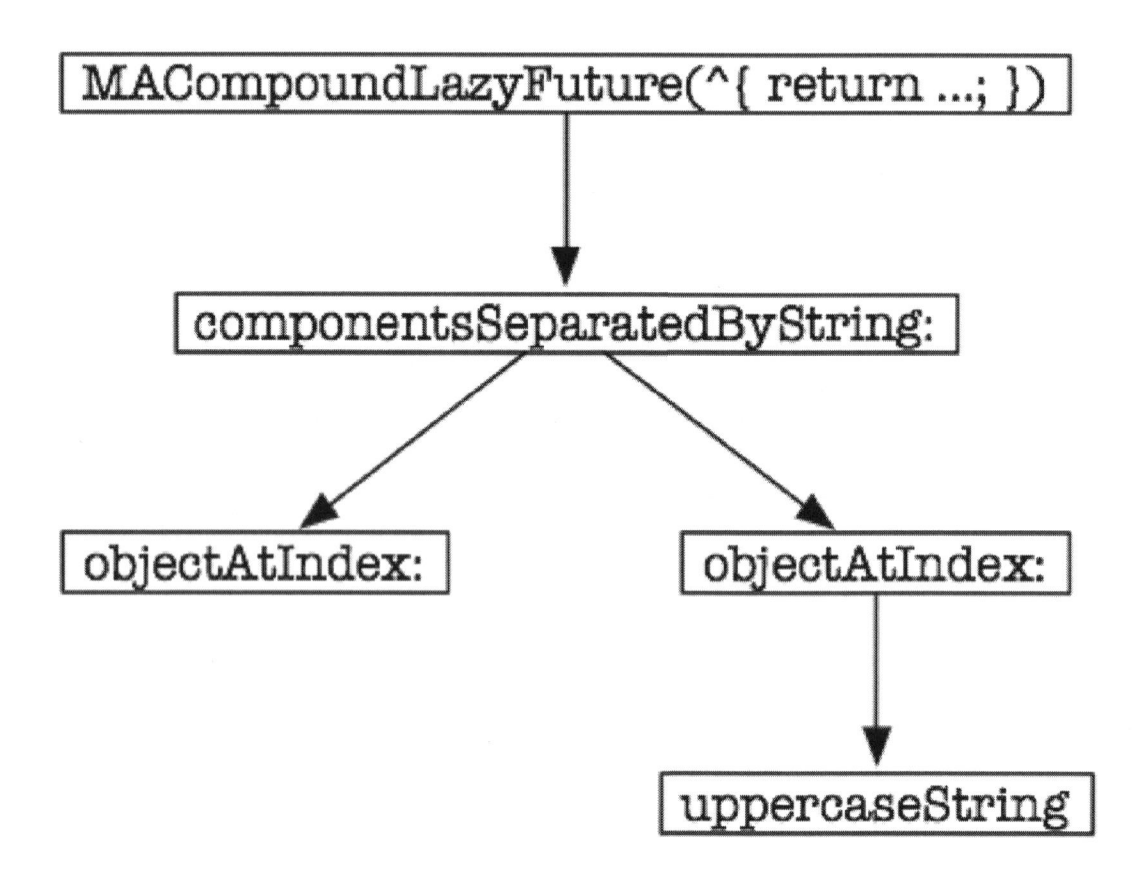

```
    MACompoundLazyFuture(^{ return ...; })
                    |
                    v
       componentsSeparatedByString:
           /                    \
          v                      v
    objectAtIndex:          objectAtIndex:
                                  |
                                  v
                           uppercaseString
```

Just like with simple futures, compound futures come in two varieties: lazy and background. A lazy compound future doesn't perform any computation until it's resolved. A background compound future begins the *initial computation* as soon as it's created, and futures additional calls until that computation completes. Note that background futures are only one layer deep: the sub-futures that they create are lazy futures. To pull from the above example, `componentsSeparatedByString:` will never execute until a future in the tree gets resolved, even if the original future was a background future.

It would be possible to develop a background compound future that performed each calculation in the tree in the background instead of just the first one, but I didn't take things that far. It would be an interesting mechanism for managing a large number of implicit, interdependent parallel computations.

Design

Compound futures are implemented in the `_MACompoundFuture` class, which is a subclass of `_MALazyBlockFuture`. This lets them inherit the behavior of wrapping a block and resolving the future represented by that block. Compound lazy futures directly wrap the block that's passed in to create the future. Compound background futures wrap the block in a `MABackgroundFuture` first, then use a small block that returns the value of the background future. This technique leverages the existing futures code to avoid duplication of effort.

Compound futures then override the forwarding machinery defined in
_MASimpleFuture to implement the compound future mechanism.

For any given call, the future needs to decide whether that call requires resolution, or whether it can return a new future. This involves checking the method signature of the call. If it returns a primitive, or any of the parameters are pointers to primitives (which could be used to return a value by reference), then the future needs to be resolved. Otherwise, a future can be returned.

I decided to get fancy, and also return futures for any pointer-to-pointer-to-object parameters. This means that things like NSError return-by-references can be futured.

If a given call requires resolution, then forwardingTargetForSelector: detects that, resolves the future, and forwards the call to the target. If the call can be futured, then forwardInvocation: takes care of returning a future for the return value, and for any return-by-reference parameters.

Method Signatures

To know whether a call can be futured, and to use forwardInvocation:, the code needs a method signature for each selector which is sent.

This is problematic, because with a compound future, you want to be able to obtain this method signature without resolving the future. This means that you can't ask the target object for a method signature, because it doesn't exist yet.

I (mostly) solved this problem with a class called MAMethodSignatureCache. This class will take a selector and search all classes registered with the runtime for that selector. If it finds a method, and if all methods have the same method signature, then it returns it. Since this is slow, the result of each search is cached, thus the class name.

What happens if two classes implement the same method but have a different method signature? This is why I said "(mostly)" above. In this case it's impossible to know which one is correct. I solved this by simply giving up on the problem; if the method signature is unknown, then the future is resolved immediately, and the message forwarded directly to the object that can handle it.

Will it Future?

As you've seen, a key question that the code needs to answer is whether a particular selector can be futured or whether it requires resolution. _MACompoundFuture answers this question using a private _canFutureSelector: method.

This method fetches the method signature for the selector from MAMethodSignatureCache. If the signature doesn't exist, or if it doesn't return an object, then the answer is immediately NO:

```objc
- (BOOL)_canFutureSelector: (SEL)sel
{
    NSMethodSignature *sig = [[MAMethodSignatureCache sharedCache] cachedMethodSignatureForSelector: sel];

    if(!sig) return NO;
    else if([sig methodReturnType][0] != @encode(id)[0]) return NO;
```

If the signature passes those two tests, it then checks the parameter types to see if there are any non-object pointer arguments. If there are, then they prevent futuring as well. If that test passes too, then the selector can be futured:

```objc
    // it exists, returns an object, but does it return any non-objects by reference?
    unsigned num = [sig numberOfArguments];
    for(unsigned i = 2; i < num; i++)
    {
        const char *type = [sig getArgumentTypeAtIndex: i];

        // if it's a pointer to a non-object, bail out
        if(type[0] == @encode(void *)[0] && type[1] != @encode(id)[0])
            return NO;
    }
    // we survived this far, all is well
    return YES;
}
```

Forwarding Target

The implementation of `forwardingTargetForSelector:` makes two checks. First, it checks to see if the future has been resolved. If it has, then it forwards the message to the result. If it hasn't, it then checks to see if the selector can be futured. If it can, then it returns `nil` to get on the `-forwardInvocation:` path. Finally, if the selector can't be futured, then it resolves the future and forwards the message to it:

```
- (id)forwardingTargetForSelector: (SEL)sel
{
    LOG(@"forwardingTargetForSelector: %p %@", self,
NSStringFromSelector(sel));
    
    id value = [self futureValue];
    if(value)
        return value;
    else if([self _canFutureSelector: sel])
        return nil;
    else
        return [self resolveFuture];
}
```

Method Signature

The -methodSignatureForSelector: method is much the same: grab a signature from the futured value if it's available, from the method signature cache if possible, and if all else fails, resolve the future and ask the real value:

```
- (NSMethodSignature *)methodSignatureForSelector: (SEL)sel
{
    LOG(@"methodSignatureForSelector: %p %@", self,
NSStringFromSelector(sel));
    
    NSMethodSignature *sig = [[self futureValue]
methodSignatureForSelector: sel];
    
    if(!sig)
        sig = [[MAMethodSignatureCache sharedCache]
cachedMethodSignatureForSelector: sel];
    
    if(!sig)
        sig = [[self resolveFuture]
methodSignatureForSelector: sel];
    
    return sig;
}
```

Invocation Manipulation

The real magic of this class happens in its gigantic -forwardInvocation: implementation.

The beginning is straightforward. Grab the future value and whether it's been resolved. If it's been resolved, forward the invocation to the value. Normally, if the future has been resolved, this would be caught in -forwardingTargetForSelector:. However, it's possible that another thread could have caused it to be resolved in between the two calls, and this makes that case behave nicely. It also allows for handling `nil` in cases where the correct method signature can be determined, as a `nil` future value will always trigger `forwardInvocation:` due to the semantics of `forwardingTargetForSelector:`.

```
- (void)forwardInvocation: (NSInvocation *)invocation
{
    LOG(@"forwardInvocation: %p %@", self, NSStringFromSelector([invocation selector]));

    [_lock lock];
    id value = _value;
    BOOL resolved = _resolved;
    [_lock unlock];

    if(resolved)
    {
        LOG(@"forwardInvocation: %p forwarding to %p", invocation, value);
        [invocation invokeWithTarget: value];
    }
    else
```

If the future hasn't been resolved, then the method needs to run through the invocation and replace any return-by-reference objects with futures. This gets pretty hairy.

If there are any return-by-reference objects, then this code is going to create multiple compound futures (one for the actual return value, and one for each return-by-reference parameter) which all depend on the same invocation. It would be incorrect to invoke the invocation each time one of the futures resolves, because the method it's calling may have side effects and shouldn't be called twice. We need a way to have the invocation be called exactly once, on demand. Fortunately I already have code to do exactly that: it's called a lazy future!

Futuring the invocation is only necessary if there are return-by-reference parameters, which I don't know yet, so I start out without one. These parameter futures all use storage which needs to be tracked, so I declare an array variable here as well, which is also created on demand:

```
    {
        // look for return-by-reference objects
        _MALazyBlockFuture *invocationFuture = nil;
        NSMutableArray *parameterDatas = nil;
```

Now loop through all the arguments to the method:

```
NSMethodSignature *sig = [invocation methodSignature];
unsigned num = [sig numberOfArguments];
for(unsigned i = 2; i < num; i++)
{
```

Examine each argument's type. If the type is a pointer to object (starts with ^@) then we need to future it:

```
const char *type = [sig getArgumentTypeAtIndex: i];
if(type[0] == @encode(void *)[0] && type[1] != @encode(id)[0])
{
```

The first thing the code has to do is fetch the parameter that the caller passed in, so we know where to store the newly-created future:

```
// get the existing pointer-to-object
id *parameterValue;
[invocation getArgument: &parameterValue atIndex: i];
```

Do a quick NULL check, since there's no need to create a future if the caller didn't ask for a value:

```
// if it's NULL, then we don't need to do anything
if(parameterValue)
{
    LOG(@"forwardInvocation: %p found return-by-reference object at argument index %u", self, i);
```

Now we know where to store the future, but we still have to pass a parameter in to the called function. We can't leave the original parameter, because that's pointing to a local variable which could be gone by the time the code actually executes, and in any case will contain a future and shouldn't be altered arbitrarily. Instead, we need to pass a pointer to some new storage where the called method can safely store the return-by-reference value.

Allocating this space is tricky, because that space eventually needs to be freed. It would make sense to free it after the future we create for that parameter has resolved, but we can't guarantee that it ever *will* resolve. It's possible that the value would be ignored, and if the space was freed on resolution, it would leak.

The solution is to allocate the space using NSMutableData, and to capture that data in the block used to create the future. This ties the NSMutableData's lifetime to that of the block. If the future is resolved, the block is destroyed, and the space is destroyed. If the future is never resolved, it's eventually destroyed, destroying the block and the allocated space.

```
                    // allocate space to receive the final computed value
         NSMutableData *newParameterSpace = [NSMutableData dataWithLength: sizeof(id)];
```

Now that we have that space allocated, we can set it as the new value for that parameter:

```
         id *newParameterValue = [newParameterSpace mutableBytes];
```

```
                    // set the parameter to point to the new space
         [invocation setArgument: &newParameterValue atIndex: i];
```

Near the top of the method, I declared invocationFuture to hold a future that would resolve the invocation. Now I have to check it, and set it if this is the first parameter to need it. This future also keeps all of the NSMutableData instances alive by capturing the parameterDatas array. The individual parameter futures may be destroyed before the invocation is invoked, so the fact that they keep their individual instances alive is not enough. Note that the future's side effect is what's important, not its value, so it just returns nil:

```objc
                        // create a future to refer to the invocation, so that it
                        // only gets invoked once no matter how many
                        // compound futures reference it
                        if(!invocationFuture)
                        {
                            parameterDatas = [NSMutableArray array];
                            invocationFuture = [[_MALazyBlockFuture alloc] initWithBlock: ^{
                                [invocation invokeWithTarget: [self resolveFuture]];
                                // keep all parameter datas alive until the invocation is resolved
                                // by capturing the variable
                                [parameterDatas self];
                                return (id)nil;
                            }];
                            [invocationFuture autorelease];
                        }
                        [parameterDatas addObject: newParameterSpace];
```

All the preliminaries are taken care of, so now we can actually create the compound future that will be returned by reference to the caller, and "return" it by saving the pointer into their parameter:

```
                        // create the compound future that we'll "return" in this argument
                        _MACompoundFuture *parameterFuture = [[_MACompoundFuture alloc] initWithBlock: ^{
                                [invocationFuture resolveFuture];
                                // capture the NSMutableData to ensure that it stays live
                                // interior pointer problem
                                [newParameterSpace self];
                                return *newParameterValue;
                        }];

                        // and now "return" it
                        *parameterValue = parameterFuture;

                        // memory management
                        [parameterFuture autorelease];
                }
            }
        }
```

Arguments are all taken care of, now it's time to create the return value. First I instruct the invocation to retain its arguments, because it needs to live in the long term, which I could do anywhere in this method but chose to do here:

```
        [invocation retainArguments];
```

Next, I create a new compound future for the return value. This future uses the value of invocationFuture if it's been created. If not, then it manually invokes the invocation. Either way, it then fetches the invocation's return value and returns it as its own value:

```
        _MACompoundFuture *returnFuture = [[_MACompoundFuture alloc] initWithBlock:^{
            id value = nil;
            if(invocationFuture)
                [invocationFuture resolveFuture];
            else
                [invocation invokeWithTarget: [self resolveFuture]];
            [invocation getReturnValue: &value];
            return value;
        }];
```

Finally, set this future as the invocation's return value, and we're done!

```
        LOG(@"forwardInvocation: %p creating new compound
future %p", invocation, returnFuture);
        [invocation setReturnValue: &returnFuture];
        [returnFuture release];
    }
}
```

Helper Functions

Like with the simple futures, I wrap this class in a couple of helper functions. MACompoundBackgroundFuture creates a compound future wrapping a regular background future:

```
id MACompoundBackgroundFuture(id (^block)(void))
{
    id blockFuture = MABackgroundFuture(block);

    _MACompoundFuture *compoundFuture =
[[_MACompoundFuture alloc] initWithBlock: ^{
        return [blockFuture resolveFuture];
    }];

    return [compoundFuture autorelease];
}
```

And MACompoundLazyFuture just wraps its block directly:

```
id MACompoundLazyFuture(id (^block)(void))
{
    _MACompoundFuture *compoundFuture =
[[_MACompoundFuture alloc] initWithBlock: block];

    return [compoundFuture autorelease];
}
```

Like with the other helpers, I wrap these in some crazy macros to get the types right:

```
#define MACompoundBackgroundFuture(...) \
((__typeof((__VA_ARGS__)()))MACompoundBackgroundFuture((id (^)(void))(__VA_ARGS__)))
#define MACompoundLazyFuture(...) \
((__typeof((__VA_ARGS__)()))MACompoundLazyFuture((id (^)(void))(__VA_ARGS__)))
```

Amazingly, this stuff all works. You can create compound futures, chain them out a long way, and verify that they only get resolved once you hit a primitive return value.

Caveats

Simple futures are pretty robust and can generally be passed to code which has no idea what they are, with a big exception being if you ever return `nil` from one, as discussed last week.

Compound futures are not so nice. They have two big problems with unsuspecting code. First, because they chain, you end up with arbitrary messages being sent, and this can include ones which return `nil`, which falls into that dangerous case. Second, methods can have side effects, and compound futures can cause those side effects to happen out of order, which will cause hilarity to ensue.

To illustrate the first problem, imagine the following method, which just happens to use old-style enumeration instead of fast enumeration:

```objc
- (NSArray *)appendedStringsFromArray: (NSArray *)array
{
    NSMutableArray *outArray = [NSMutableArray array];
    NSEnumerator *enumerator = [array objectEnumerator];
    NSString *str;
    while((str = [enumerator nextObject]))
        [outArray addObject: [str stringByAppendingString: @" suffix"]];
    return outArray;
}
```

This code is fine. However, consider what happens if you pass a compound future in as the array parameter. Nothing in this code will cause a compound future to resolve. The `enumerator` object will be a compound future, and every call to `objectEnumerator` will also produce a compound future. This code will loop forever, and eventually crash when it runs out of memory. Oops!

To illustrate the second problem, consider this code:

```objc
NSMutableArray *array = ...;
NSString *s = [[array objectAtIndex: 0] retain];
[array removeAllObjects];
NSLog(@"%@", s);
```

This code works fine normally, but if `array` is a compound future then it falls apart. The `objectAtIndex:` call will be futured, and then `removeAllObjects` will resolve the array future and remove the elements. However, `s` still contains a future. When it's resolved by the `NSLog` call, it will call `objectAtIndex: 0` on an array which is now empty, throwing a range error. Oops!

You must be careful when writing code that uses compound futures, and ensure that they never escape to code that you don't control. Making explicit calls to `resolveFuture` and passing what it returns is a way to make sure that can't happen.

Practical Uses

I'll be straight: I haven't been able to think of any.

I'm sure that there are cases where compound futures would be useful. The chaining nature makes it possible to put off computation for longer than with a basic future. However, the fact that you have to be careful never to let them escape to code you don't control (or to code you haven't written to tolerate them) places big restrictions on your code. Unlike simple futures, which I consider to be a useful tool, I see compound futures as more of an interesting programming exercise. I would love to see some real, useful applications of them, though.

Conclusion

Compound futures are an interesting concept which might, maybe, possibly have actual practical applications somewhere. They show that `NSInvocation` and forwarding are nothing to be afraid of, but can be bent to our will. And of course they continue to illustrate just how wonderful an addition blocks make to Objective-C.

Friday Q&A 2010-03-12: Subclassing Class Clusters

Welcome to another chewy edition of Friday Q&A. This week, Gwendal Roué has suggested talking about the techniques of subclassing class clusters.

Abstract Classes

To subclass a class cluster, you need to know what it is, and to understand class clusters you must first understand the concept of *abstract classes*. It's an easy concept, though.

An *abstract class* is a class which is not fully functional on its own. It must be subclassed, and the subclass must fill out the missing functionality.

An abstract class is not necessarily an empty shell. It can still contain a lot of functionality all on its own, but it's not complete without a subclass to fill in the holes.

Class Clusters

A class cluster is a hierarchy of classes capped off by a public abstract class. The public class provides an interface and a lot of auxiliary functionality, and then core functionality is implemented by private subclasses. The public class then provides creation methods which return instances of the private subclasses, so that the public class can be used without knowledge of those subclasses.

Take `NSArray` as an example. It's an abstract class which requires its subclasses to provide implementations of the `count` and `objectAtIndex:` methods. It then provides a bunch of methods built on top of those two, such as `indexOfObject:`, `objectEnumerator`, `makeObjectsPerformSelector:`, and many more.

The core functionality is then implemented in private subclasses such as `NSCFArray`. The `NSArray` creation methods such as `+arrayWithObjects:` or `-initWithContentsOfFile:` then produce instances of those private subclasses.

From the outside, the cluster nature of `NSArray` is not readily apparent most of the time. It usually makes itself known if you start introspecting the classes of objects, and confuses programmers when they create an `NSArray` and then start getting messages about an `NSCFArray`. Other than that, `NSArray` mostly looks and acts like any other class.

There is one place where the cluster nature is hugely important, and that's if you subclass the public class yourself.

Subclassing

Subclassing a class cluster (which means subclassing an abstract class) is completely different from subclassing a normal class.

When subclassing a normal class, your superclass provides full functionality for whatever it does. A subclass with an empty implementation is completely valid in this case, and will behave just like the superclass. You can then add methods to your implementation to add new functionality or override existing functionality.

When subclassing a class cluster, your superclass does *not* provide full functionality. It provides a lot of ancillary functionality, but you must provide the core yourself. This means that an empty subclass is *not* valid. There is a minimum set of methods that you must implement.

In class cluster teminology, those methods that you must implement are called *primitive methods*. How do you find them? There are two easy ways.

The first way is to crack open the documentation for the cluster class and search it for the word "primitive". The docs will tell you which methods you have to override.

The second way is to open the header for the cluster class. Apple's primitive methods are always found in the class's main `@interface` block. Additional methods provided by the cluster are always found in categories. (This, however, is not actually documented, so be careful.)

Watch out when looking at cluster classes which are themselves subclasses of another cluster class. The result inherits all primitive methods, and you must implement both sets. For example, `NSMutableArray` has five primitive methods of its own *plus* the two from `NSArray`. If you subclass `NSMutableArray`, you must provide implementations for all seven.

Techniques

Now you know what to implement, but how? There are three main ways.

First, you can simply provide your own implementation of the primitive methods, implementing them all from scratch. For example, imagine you're writing a specialized array optimized for holding two elements:

```
@interface MyPairArray : NSArray
{
    id _objs[2];
}

- (id)initWithFirst: (id)first second: (id)second;

@end

@implementation MyPairArray

- (id)initWithFirst: (id)first second: (id)second
{
    if((self = [self init]))
    {
        _objs[0] = [first retain];
        _objs[1] = [second retain];
    }
    return self;
}

- (void)dealloc
{
    [_objs[0] release];
    [_objs[1] release];
    [super dealloc];
}

- (NSUInteger)count
{
    return 2;
}

- (id)objectAtIndex: (NSUInteger)index
{
    if(index >= 2)
        [NSException raise: NSRangeException format:
@"Index (%ld) out of bounds", (long)index];
    return _objs[index];
}

@end
```

Precisely how you implement the primitives depends, of course, on precisely what you want them to do.

Second, you can keep a working instance around, obtained from the public API, and pass your calls through to it:

```objc
@interface MySpecialArray : NSArray
{
    NSArray *_realArray;
}

- (id)initWithArray: (NSArray *)array;

@end

@implementation MySpecialArray

- (id)initWithArray: (NSArray *)array
{
    if((self = [self init]))
    {
        _realArray = [array copy];
    }
    return self;
}

- (void)dealloc
{
    [_realArray release];
    [super dealloc];
}

- (NSUInteger)count
{
    return [_realArray count];
}

- (id)objectAtIndex: (NSUInteger)index
{
    id obj = [_realArray objectAtIndex: index];
    // do some processing with obj
    return obj;
}

// maybe implement more methods here

@end
```

359

This technique allows you to reuse the existing implementations of the primitive methods, and then add more functionality.

The third technique is to simply add a category to the cluster class instead of subclassing it. People often subclass simply to add new methods, and not to modify existing functionality. In Objective-C, you can add new methods in a category:

```
@interface NSArray (FirstObjectAdditions)

- (id)my_firstObject;

@end

@implementation NSArray (FirstObjectAdditions)

- (id)my_firstObject
{
    return [self count] ? [self objectAtIndex: 0] : nil;
}

@end
```

(The method is prefixed to prevent a conflict if Apple should ever add a `firstObject` method.)

Conclusion

Class clusters are different from normal classes, but are easy to subclass once you understand the differences and what they mean. You're required to implement the class cluster's *primitive methods*, which you can do by providing a from-scratch implementation, or by passing through to another instance. Finally, if your only purpose in subclassing is to add new methods, create a category instead.

Friday Q&A 2010-04-02: OpenCL Basics

I'm back in action at last, so it's time for another Friday Q&A. This week, both someone named "charles" and Brian Olsen have suggested that I talk about OpenCL, so I'm going to go through the basics of what OpenCL is and how to do some simple computation with it.

SMUGOpenCL
I made heavy use of Chris Liscio's SMUGOpenCL library, which provides some nice Objective-C wrappers for basic OpenCL functionality.

What is OpenCL?
OpenCL is a natural outgrowth of the move toward doing general-purpose computation on graphics cards using OpenGL. The graphics card is actually the most powerful number cruncher in many PCs, and taking advantage of its power for non-graphics computations has been an emerging trend in recent years. My GPULife screensaver is an example of using OpenGL to do non-graphics computations, in this particular case computing the Game of Life.

OpenGL, while providing enough power to do general-purpose computations with the GLSL, the OpenGL shader language, is awkward for non-graphical purposes. GLSL is still heavily graphics-oriented, and lacks things which many non-graphics computations need, like the ability to do random memory access for writing. Working around these limitations is possible, but is hard to do and can greatly hurt efficiency.

Not all graphics cards are capable of GLSL, and CPU emulation can be slow. A truly adaptable program will run computations on the GPU when possible and on the CPU as a fallback, ideally with vectorized, parallelized CPU code, but OpenGL doesn't make this easy.

OpenCL does make it easy. OpenCL allows you to program your GPU using normal C, with all the pointer craziness and random memory access that implies. Of course your performance will be better with more structured accesses, but when you really need random accesses, OpenCL allows it. OpenCL can also target both GPUs and CPUs, and when you need to fall back to CPUs, OpenCL will do its best to automatically vectorize and parallelize your code. OpenCL is structured so that it can do a much better job at these tasks than your normal compiler in many cases. Since you can use essentially the same code for both CPU and GPU, this means that you can maintain less code, run on any hardware, and still take full advantage of powerful GPUs when they're available.

OpenCL Overview
OpenCL is a library that you access at runtime. You give programs to OpenCL, which transforms them into *kernels*, which are functions that you can then call using OpenCL.

Unlike normal C programming, you don't compile OpenCL kernels ahead of time. Instead, you feed the raw textual source to OpenCL, which compiles them at runtime. This is necessary because you can't know in advance just what sort of hardware you're going to target. And in the case where you're targeting CPUs, this still allows OpenCL to make specializations based on the specific CPU's vector capabilities and number of cores.

These kernels are written in plain C with some basic extensions. When compiled, they can't be directly accessed as C functions. Instead, you set arguments and make calls using OpenCL functions, which then manage the execution of the kernels.

A Frequency Counter

To illustrate the use of OpenCL, I built a byte frequency counter. This just loads a file and counts the number of times each byte value occurs, and prints out the result. This is not the most useful program in the world, but it's a decent illustration of how to use OpenCL.

Code

As usual, I'll be presenting excerpts here, but the full code is available from my public subversion repository:

```
svn co http://mikeash.com/svn/OpenCLFreqCount/
```

Plain C Implementation

I first wrote a non-OpenCL implementation of the frequency counter. This is useful to understand the problem, and also for debugging, to ensure that the OpenCL version produces the correct output. The function is simple: it takes an NSData and returns an NSData containing an array of uint32_ts representing the frequency counts. The computation is straightforward:

```
static NSData *SimpleFreqCount(NSData *inData)
{
    NSMutableData *freqCount = [NSMutableData dataWithLength: 256 * sizeof(uint32_t)];
    uint32_t *freqs = [freqCount mutableBytes];
    
    const unsigned char *ptr = [inData bytes];
    NSUInteger len = [inData length];
    for(NSUInteger i = 0; i < len; i++)
        freqs[ptr[i]]++;
    
    return freqCount;
}
```

OpenCL Strategy

An OpenCL kernel gets invoked multiple times in parallel by OpenCL with the same parameters. The kernel can differentiate between these different instances by examining its work-item ID. These work-item IDs can get complex, but in the simplest case, each call to the kernel has one ID which you can fetch by calling `get_global_id(0)`.

Because the kernels can execute in parallel, there are the standard problems with concurrent data access. To avoid clashes, I decided to write the frequency count in two stages.

The first stage will go through the input data in blocks of 256 bytes and compute a *local* frequency count of the bytes just in that block. This local count will be stored into a large array which contains one local frequency count per block. The second stage will then go through and add all of the local counts together into one global count.

OpenCL Kernel Code
Here's what the start of the `freqcount` kernel, the first stage kernel, looks like:

```
__kernel void freqcount(const unsigned char *input,
unsigned short *output)
{
```

This should be pretty familiar to any C programmer. The only strange part is the `__kernel` keyword. This is an OpenCL-specific keyword which indicates that this function is a *kernel*, which is to say that it can be accessed from the outside program. It's also possible to write functions that can only be accessed by other OpenCL functions.

Next, the kernel gets its work-item ID:

```
const uint index = get_global_id(0);
```

It uses this to compute a starting place in the array. Since we're working with 256-byte blocks, the starting index is the work-item ID multiplied by 256:

```
const uint start = index * 256;
```

Then I simply loop through `input`, getting the value of each byte, and incrementing the value in the corresponding spot in `output`:

```
    for(uint i = 0; i < 256; i++)
    {
        uint value = input[start + i];
        output[start + value]++;
    }
}
```

The `freqsum` kernel is the second stage. It uses a fixed number of work items, 256, one for each entry in the frequency count. Each work item then loops through all of the local count arrays to compute a final total. This is what the kernel looks like:

```
__kernel void freqsum(const unsigned int count, unsigned
short *freqs, unsigned int *totals)
{
    const uint index = get_global_id(0);
    for(uint i = 0; i < count; i++)
        totals[index] += freqs[index + i * 256];
}
```

Calling the Kernels

Building the kernels was easy in this case, calling them is a bit more work. The first thing I do is pad the incoming data to a multiple of 256, so that it plays nice with the kernel's chunking:

```
static NSData *CLFreqCount(NSData *inData)
{
    NSMutableData *data = [NSMutableData dataWithData:
inData];

    // pad data to multiple of 256
    NSUInteger dataLength = [data length];
    NSUInteger paddedLength = dataLength + 255 -
(dataLength + 255) % 256;
    NSUInteger pad = paddedLength - dataLength;
    [data setLength: paddedLength];
```

(This will change the final frequency count, of course, so the amount of padding is kept in the `pad` variable so that it can be subtracted off at the end.)

Next I create buffers to hold the local counts and the final count. The local counts array is twice as large as the incoming data, because it needs two bytes for each byte value for each 256-byte block. The final count array is just enough to hold 256 32-bit integers:

```
    // create large output area
    NSMutableData *largeOutput = [NSMutableData
dataWithLength: paddedLength * 2];
    // and the final totals area
    NSMutableData *freqCount = [NSMutableData
dataWithLength: 256 * sizeof(uint32_t)];
```

Now it's time to set up OpenCL. I'll be doing everything through SMUGOpenCL, so you won't see any OpenCL calls here. If you want to see how the OpenCL calls work under the hood, you can look at the SMUGOpenCL source directly.

The first thing to do is to set up a context in which the kernels can be executed:

```
SMUGOpenCLContext *context = [[SMUGOpenCLContext alloc] initCPUContext];
```

Note that you can substitute `initGPUContext` instead to execute code on the GPU. It's your choice, not the system's, and it will fail if your GPU can't handle OpenCL, so you need to handle this carefully. For this simple example, I just always use a CPU context.

Next, I load the OpenCL program into the context, and fetch the two kernels out of the program. The `CLFreqCountSourceString` function just returns an `NSString` containing the code to the two kernels:

```
SMUGOpenCLProgram *program = [[SMUGOpenCLProgram alloc] initWithContext: context sourceString: CLFreqCountSourceString()];
SMUGOpenCLKernel *freqCountKernel = [program kernelNamed: @"freqcount"];
SMUGOpenCLKernel *freqSumKernel = [program kernelNamed: @"freqsum"];
```

I need to pass the buffers I created as arguments, but I can't pass them directly. Instead, I need to turn them into `cl_mem` objects. SMUGOpenCL makes this really easy:

```
cl_mem dataCL = [data getOpenCLBufferForReadingInContext: context];
cl_mem largeOutputCL = [largeOutput getOpenCLBufferForWritingInContext: context];
cl_mem freqCountCL = [freqCount getOpenCLBufferForWritingInContext: context];
```

Next, I set the arguments for both kernels. This is a little tedious. In addition to the buffers, I also need to pass a block count into the sum kernel, which I compute by just dividing the padded data length by 256:

```
    cl_int err;
    err = [freqCountKernel setArgument: 0 withSize:
sizeof(dataCL) data: &dataCL;];
    if(err)
        ERROR("OpenCL error: %lld", (long long)err);
    err = [freqCountKernel setArgument: 1 withSize:
sizeof(largeOutputCL) data: &largeOutputCL;];
    if(err)
        ERROR("OpenCL error: %lld", (long long)err);

    cl_uint sumCount = paddedLength / 256;
    err = [freqSumKernel setArgument: 0 withSize:
sizeof(sumCount) data: &sumCount;];
    if(err)
        ERROR("OpenCL error: %lld", (long long)err);
    err = [freqSumKernel setArgument: 1 withSize:
sizeof(largeOutputCL) data: &largeOutputCL;];
    if(err)
        ERROR("OpenCL error: %lld", (long long)err);
    err = [freqSumKernel setArgument: 2 withSize:
sizeof(freqCountCL) data: &freqCountCL;];
    if(err)
        ERROR("OpenCL error: %lld", (long long)err);
```

Now it's finally time to run the kernels. In addition to the kernel to run, the context also wants a global and local work size. The global work size is just the number of work items to run, and is essentially the maximum number that `get_global_id(0)` can return. The local work size is something I honestly don't quite understand, and I just use a SMUGOpenCL method to get a good size. The sizes are passed as arrays because some fancy stuff can be done (presumably for multi-dimensional data and such) by passing multiple values, but I only need one:

```
    size_t globalSizeCount[] = { paddedLength / 256 };
    size_t localSizeCount[] = { [context
workgroupSizeForKernel: freqCountKernel] };
    [context enqueueKernel: freqCountKernel
        withWorkDimensions: 1
            globalWorkSize: globalSizeCount
             localWorkSize: localSizeCount];

    size_t globalSizeSum[] = { 256 };
    size_t localSizeSum[] = { [context
workgroupSizeForKernel: freqSumKernel] };
    [context enqueueKernel: freqSumKernel
        withWorkDimensions: 1
            globalWorkSize: globalSizeSum
             localWorkSize: localSizeSum];
```

Now the kernels are running. Enqueueing the kernels just makes them eligible to run, but doesn't guarantee that they're finished, because they can run concurrent with your normal code. This could be useful for setting up computations and then doing something else while they crunch. Since the results here are needed right away, I just force the context to block until computation is complete:

```
    [context finish];
```

Now the results are sitting in freqCount, except that they're incorrect due to padding. To fix this, I do a quick fix-up of the frequency count for zero:

```
    uint32_t *freqs = [freqCount mutableBytes];
    // compensate for the padding
    freqs[0] -= pad;
```

And finally, release allocated objects and return:

```
    [program release];
    [context release];

    return freqCount;
}
```

And that's it! You can run the included test program to compute a frequency count on a file, and it produces identical results to the simple reference function.

Conclusion

OpenCL isn't too complicated to get started with, and SMUGOpenCL makes it especially easy. Performance might be trickier. With a CPU context, OpenCL was significantly slower than the non-OpenCL code for a single pass through the data. With some loops to force it to do more work, and reduce the overhead of OpenCL setup, the OpenCL version pulled ahead a bit. My Mac Pro's video card doesn't do OpenCL, so I didn't test GPU speed, but I'm going to guess that these kernels are not well adapted to the GPU. How to wrest the maximum speed out of OpenCL is beyond the scope of today's post. OpenCL is an exciting new technology, and much easier to get started with than doing general-purpose computation with OpenGL, and I hope that I've shown you enough to start experimenting on your own.

Friday Q&A 2010-04-09: Comparison of Objective-C Enumeration Techniques

Related Articles

    Intro to the Objective-C Runtime 67

    Objective-C Messaging 73

    Objective-C Message Forwarding 77

    Objective-C Class Loading and Initialization 115

    Care and Feeding of Singletons 194

    Probing Cocoa With PyObjC 240

    Using Accessors in Init and Dealloc 246

    Method Replacement for Fun and Profit 297

    Error Returns with Continuation Passing Style 303

    Implementing Fast Enumeration 373

    Implementing Equality and Hashing 412

    Zeroing Weak References in Objective-C 428

    Implementing NSCoding 459

    Defensive Programming in Cocoa 468

Welcome back to another edition of Friday Q&A. Preston Sumner has suggested that I talk about different ways of enumerating over collections in Cocoa, and how to implement Fast Enumeration. This will be a two part series. This week I will look at the different enumeration techniques and their pros and cons. Next week I will take you through implementing Fast Enumeration on a custom object.

A Baseline

To establish a baseline for comparison, consider iterating over a C array of Objective-C objects:

```
id *array = ...;
NSUInteger length = ...;
for(NSUInteger i = 0; i < length; i++)
    // do something with array[i]
```

The syntax is decent, but not great. It's somewhat redundant and a bit error prone.

For single-threaded code, this is about as fast as you're going to get for object enumeration. You have a small amount of overhead from the loop, and it's pretty much the minimum possible. (If you really want to get radical, you can try manually unrolling the loop, but that begins to get crazy, and could actually hurt performance.)

Of course, this sort of object enumeration is not usually practical in Cocoa apps. It's rare that we encounter a C array of objects. Much more common is an object that implements a collection.

NSEnumerator

In times past, the standard way of enumerating over a collection in Cocoa was to use `NSEnumerator`:

```
NSEnumerator *enumerator = [collection objectEnumerator];
id obj;
while((obj = [enumerator nextObject]))
    // do something with obj
```

This is extremely verbose and annoying to write. It also has a fair amount of overhead compared to the baseline. First, it has to allocate a whole new object just to manage enumeration. Then, each iteration involves sending a message to the enumerator. The overhead here, while relatively small compared to most activities that would happen *inside* the loop, is much larger than the baseline.

objectAtIndex:

For those who preferred something more traditional, or who disliked creating a whole new object just for enumeration, another way to enumerate over an array was to simply call `objectAtIndex:` on it repeatedly:

```
NSUInteger length = [array count];
for(NSUInteger i = 0; i < length; i++)
{
    id obj = [array objectAtIndex: i];
    // do something with obj
}
```

This still requires a message send per iteration, but avoids creating the `NSEnumerator` object so it can be a bit of a win, depending on just how fast `objectAtIndex:` is for that particular array. (The performance characteristics of `objectAtIndex:` compared to `objectEnumerator` aren't always completely obvious, especially on very large arrays, due to how `NSArray` is implemented internally.)

A big disadvantage, besides being verbose and error-prone, is that it simply doesn't work for enumerating `NSSet` or `NSDictionary`. Conversely, a big advantage is that, with careful management of the loop index, it's safe to mutate the array inside the loop, something that's not true of any other enumeration technique (unless you do something like enumerate over a copy instead).

NSFastEnumeration

In 10.5, Apple finally solved these problems. They solved the verbosity problem by introducing the `for/in` syntax. They solved the speed problem by building `for/in` on top of a protocol called `NSFastEnumeration`.

```
for(id obj in collection)
    // do something with obj
```

`NSFastEnumeration` works by fetching objects in bulk whenever possible. The compiler generates code that calls the collection and asks the collection to return as many objects as possible. For collections that store objects contiguously, the collection is able to return an interior pointer directly to those objects. If every object in the array is contiguous, the loop turns into something very much like the baseline, and with the same overall performance. If there are multiple contiguous object stores, `NSFastEnumeration` allows the collection to return interior pointers one after another, allowing for a quick loop implementation over each store, and requiring an Objective-C message only for getting the next interior pointer. For collections without contiguous storage, `NSFastEnumeration` allows the collection to copy objects out to temporary storage in bulk, reaping many of the same benefits. For collections where none of this works, `NSFastEnumeration` still allows a collection to efficiently return objects one by one.

Nice syntax and good performance, it's a great combination.

Blocks-Based Enumeration
With 10.6, Apple introduced blocks into Objective-C, and also introduced blocks-based enumeration. Blocks are a natural fit for creating new control constructs like enumeration, and Apple added blocks-based enumeration methods to their collections as well:

```
[array enumerateObjectsUsingBlock: ^(id obj, NSUInteger index, BOOL *stop) {
    // do something with obj
}];
```

For simple enumeration, the block syntax doesn't really offer any advantage over fast enumeration and the `for/in` syntax. The syntax is a bit clumsier, and iteration is a bit slower. The code has to call your block for every object. This overhead is less than that of a message send, as in the `NSEnumerator` case, but is more than the simple C `for` loop of `NSFastEnumeration`. There are two places where the block syntax is useful.

First is when you need something more than simple enumeration. Apple gives two enumeration options: to enumerate concurrently and to enumerate in reverse. Neither is directly supported by `for/in` syntax. Concurrent enumeration is very difficult to do any other way, so if your enumeration can take advantage of multithreading, this is extremely useful. Reverse enumeration can be done by sending `reverseObjectEnumerator` to an array and then using that as the target of a `for/in`, but this still has the overhead of

371

creating an `NSEnumerator` and enumerating through it indirectly, so the blocks-based method is probably a win.

Second is when you're enumerating over a dictionary and need both keys and objects. The `for/in` syntax can only give you one object at a time. This means that you have to enumerate over keys, and then ask the dictionary for objects as a separate step:

```
for(id key in dictionary)
{
    id obj = [dictionary objectForKey: key];
    // do something with key and obj
}
```

Not only is this much more verbose than a normal `for/in`, it's also much slower. The extra message send and dictionary lookup will kill the nice performance characteristics of `NSFastEnumeration`.

`NSDictionary` provides a blocks-based enumeration method that passes both key and object directly to the block:

```
[dictionary enumerateKeysAndObjectsUsingBlock: ^(id key, id obj, BOOL *stop) {
    // do something with key and obj
}];
```

This is somewhat nicer to write, and can be much faster. The dictionary is able to directly iterate over key/object pairs in its internal data structure, skipping the extra message send and key lookup required by the `for/in` loop.

Conclusion
With any code, you should always prefer the technique which is easiest to maintain and read unless you know for sure that there's a speed problem which would benefit from a more difficult approach. This is especially true with collection enumeration, where the work that you do inside the loop is virtually certain to dwarf the work that's done by the loop itself.

Fortunately, Apple has made it so that we don't have to make any tradeoffs in most cases. The `for/in` syntax is simultaneously the nicest and fastest code for enumerating over a collection in the majority of cases. For the rare cases where it's not the best, 10.6 provides blocks-based enumeration constructs which fill in the holes. You should pretty much never write an `NSEnumerator` loop unless you have to support 10.4. Manually fetching objects using `objectAtIndex:` can be handy if you need to mutate the array while enumerating, but besides that has no advantage over `for/in`.

Friday Q&A 2010-04-16: Implementing Fast Enumeration

Related Articles

    Intro to the Objective-C Runtime 67

    Objective-C Messaging..73

    Objective-C Message Forwarding 77

    Objective-C Class Loading and Initialization..115

    Care and Feeding of Singletons 194

    Probing Cocoa With PyObjC..240

    Using Accessors in Init and Dealloc..246

    Method Replacement for Fun and Profit 297

    Error Returns with Continuation Passing Style 303

    Comparison of Objective-C Enumeration Techniques 369

    Implementing Equality and Hashing 412

    Zeroing Weak References in Objective-C 428

    Implementing NSCoding 459

    Defensive Programming in Cocoa 468

Last week I discussed the various options available in Objective-C for enumerating over a collection. This week I'm going to finish up the discussion of enumeration with a guide on how to implement Fast Enumeration in your own program.

Basics
There are two benefits to implementing Fast Enumeration. One is that you can then use your object as the target in a `for/in` loop. The other is that, with a good implementation, such enumeration will be fast.

Implementing Fast Enumeration is accomplished by implementing the `NSFastEnumeration` protocol. This protocol contains only a single method:

```
- (NSUInteger)countByEnumeratingWithState:(NSFastEnumerationState *)state objects:(id *)stackbuf count:(NSUInteger)len;
```

Easy enough, right? But what's that `NSFastEnumerationState` thing?

```
typedef struct {
    unsigned long state;
    id *itemsPtr;
    unsigned long *mutationsPtr;
    unsigned long extra[5];
} NSFastEnumerationState;
```

This starts to get a little bit complex....

Deciphering Fields and Parameters
To understand how to implement this method, you need to understand what all of the fields and parameters mean, as well as the return value. I'll take these out of order.

The objective of this method is to return a series of arrays of objects. Each call returns one array, which allows objects to be returned in bulk. For speed, this uses a C array, which means that it needs a pointer and a length.

The length is provided by the return value of the method. That's what the `count` refers to in the name of the method. The array is actually the `itemsPtr` field of the `NSFastEnumerationState` struct. These two values together define the array returned by the method.

`NSFastEnumeration` is designed to allow returning a pointer to internal storage. However, not all data structures fit well with that, so it's also designed to allow copying objects into an array provided by the caller. That caller-provided array is `stackbuf`, and its size is given by `len`.

`NSFastEnumeration` is also designed to detect when a collection is mutated while being enumerated, and throw an exception if this occurs. `mutationsPtr` is indended to be pointed to a value which changes if the collection is mutated.

That's just about everything. The only fields I haven't covered yet are the `state` and `extra` fields of `NSFastEnumerationState`. These are just freeform fields which the callee can use to store whatever values it finds useful.

Generated Loop Code
Now we know what all these things are for, but to really understand how this stuff works, it's best to understand what kind of code the compiler generates. You write this:

```
for(id obj in collection)
{
    // body
}
```

What really goes on behind the scenes?

The compiler creates an NSFastEnumerationState on the stack, as well as a stack buffer. It creates two nested loops, one which repeatedly calls countByEnumeratingWithState:... and one which loops over the array it returns. It ends up being something like this:

```
// declare all the local state needed
NSFastEnumerationState state = { 0 };
id stackbuf[16];
BOOL firstLoop = YES;
long mutationsPtrValue;

// outer loop
NSUInteger count;
while((count = [collection countByEnumeratingWithState:
&state objects: stackbuf count: 16]))
{
    // check for mutation, but
    // only after the first loop
    // (note that I'm not sure
    // whether the real compiler
    // puts this in the inner
    // loop or outer loop, and
    // it could conceivably
    // change from one compiler
    // version to the next)
    if(!firstLoop && mutationsPtrValue !=
*state.mutationsPtr)
        @throw ..mutation exception...
    firstLoop = NO;
    mutationsPtrValue = *state.mutationsPtr;

    // inner loop over the array
    // returned by the NSFastEnumeration call
    id obj;
    for(NSUInteger index = 0; index < count; index++)
    {
        obj = state.itemsPtr[index];
        // body
    }
}
```

Notice how this code never touches or examines the state and extra fields. As I mentioned before, these are provided purely for the use of the collection, and to facilitate that, their value is preserved between calls while within the same loop.

375

Returning One Object At a Time

A major point of `NSFastEnumeration` is to achieve speed through bulk enumeration. Returning one object at a time defeats that point. However, it's easy to implement, and still gets you the benefit of being able to use `for/in` syntax. In the spirit of avoiding premature optimization, if returning one object at a time is easy, then go for it.

As an example, imagine you have a linked list class:

```
@implementation LinkedList : NSObject
{
    struct Node *listHead;
}
```

Now let's implement `NSFastEnumeration` for this class, in the simplest possible way, by returning one object at a time:

```objc
-(NSUInteger)countByEnumeratingWithState:(NSFastEnumerationState
*)state objects:(id *)stackbuf count:(NSUInteger)len
{
    // plan of action: extra[0]
    // will contain pointer to node
    // that contains next
    // object to iterate
    // because extra[0] is a long,
    // this involves ugly casting
    if(state->state == 0)
    {
        // state 0 means it's the first
        // call, so get things set up
        // we won't try to detect
        // mutations, so make mutationsPtr
        // point somewhere that's
        // guaranteed not to change
        state->mutationsPtr = (unsigned long *)self;

        // set up extra[0] to point
        // to the head to start in
        // the right place
        state->extra[0] = (long)listHead;

        // and update state to
        // indicate that enumeration has started
        state->state = 1;
    }

    // pull the node out of extra[0]
    struct Node *currentNode = (struct Node
*)state->extra[0];

    // if it's NULL then we're done
    // enumerating, return 0 to end
    if(!currentNode)
        return NULL

    // otherwise, point itemsPtr
    // at the node's value
    state->itemsPtr = &currentNode->value

    // update extra[0]
    if(currentNode)
```

```
        state->extra[0] = (long)currentNode->next;

    // we're returning exactly one item
    return 1;
}
```

This is really not bad at all. It gets a little ugly with the pointer/integer casting, but that's C for you....

Returning Copied Objects in Bulk

Let's say that it turns out the above method really is too slow and you want to make it faster. You can do this by returning objects in bulk. Because the objects in the linked list aren't stored contiguously, you have to do this by copying objects into the `stackbuf`. While no guarantee is given as to the size of `stackbuf`, we can assume that it's made large enough to justify this sort of thing. Here's how the code would look:

```objc
-(NSUInteger)countByEnumeratingWithState:(NSFastEnumerationState
*)state objects:(id *)stackbuf count:(NSUInteger)len
{
    // plan of action: pretty
    // much the same as before,
    // with extra[0] pointing
    // to the next node to use
    // we just iterate over
    // multiple nodes at once
    if(state->state == 0)
    {
        state->mutationsPtr = (unsigned long *)self;
        state->extra[0] = (long)listHead;
        state->state = 1;
    }

    // pull the node out of extra[0]
    struct Node *currentNode = (struct Node
*)state->extra[0];

    // keep track of how many
    // objects we iterated
    // over so we can return
    // that value
    NSUInteger objCount = 0;

    // we'll be putting objects
    // in stackbuf, so point
    // itemsPtr to it
    state->itemsPtr = stackbuf;

    // loop through until either
    // we fill up stackbuf or
    // run out of nodes
    while(currentNode && objCount < len)
    {
        // fill current stackbuf
        // location and move to the next
        *stackbuf++ = currentNode->value

        // move to next node
        currentNode = currentNode->next;

        // and keep our count
```

```
        objCount++;
    }
    
    // update extra[0]
    if(currentNode)
        state->extra[0] = (long)currentNode->next;
    
    return objCount;
}
```

This is not too much harder, and will significantly reduce the number of message sends that occur in the `for/in` loop.

Returning a Bulk Interior Pointer
For best efficiency, you can return a pointer to contiguously stored objects. For example, say you have a simple array class like this:

```
@interface Array : NSObject
{
    id *pointer;
    NSUInteger count;
}
```

Implementing `NSFastEnumeration` for this class is really easy. It can return a single interior pointer to all of the objects, and that's it

```
- (NSUInteger)countByEnumeratingWithState:(NSFastEnumerationState *)state objects:(id *)stackbuf count:(NSUInteger)len
{
    if(state->state == 0)
    {
        state->mutationsPtr = (unsigned long *)self;
        state->itemsPtr = pointer;
        state->state = 1;
        return count;
    }
    else
        return 0;
}
```

That was easy! It'll also be really fast, because the enumeration loop will basically devolve into a straight C `for` loop.

This technique can also be used, with some care, for more complex data structures. If you have a series of contiguous object pointers, you can return pointers to each one in turn, which will result in efficient enumeration over all of the objects in sequence. You can make good use of the `extra` values to keep track of where you are in your internal data structure.

A Note on Temporary Objects

You may find it useful to store Objective-C objects in the `extra` values:

```
state->extra[1] = (long)[NSArray arrayWith...];
```

But beware! This will break with this completely legal enumeration code:

```
NSAutoreleasePool *pool = [NSAutoreleasePool new];
for(id obj in collection)
{
    // do stuff with obj
    [pool release];
    pool = [NSAutoreleasePool new];
}
[pool release];
```

When the autorelease pool goes away, it'll take your array with it, and the next time you try to access it, you'll explode. And you can't retain the array, either, because there's no guarantee the caller will loop all the way to the end to let you release it; they might `break` out of the loop early, and then you've leaked the object.

There's really no general way to solve this. (I've concocted a completely insane scheme which involves tracking the position of the stack pointer to know when it's safe to destroy temporary objects, but it's, well, completely insane.) If you can, try to avoid storing temporary Objective-C objects in `extra` like this. And if you must do it, just keep in mind that you have to be careful with autorelease pools in the `for/in` loops that you use with this object. Since you're likely to be the only client of your `NSFastEnumeration` implementation, this is a reasonable constraint to make, but it's something that you have to be aware of.

Conclusion

Implementing `NSFastEnumeration` allows you to use nice, simple syntax for enumerating over your custom objects which are conceptually collections of other objects. As a bonus, it will usually speed up that enumeration as well. And while `NSFastEnumeration` can look daunting at first glance, it's actually pretty easy to write an implementation of it, depending on just how hard-core you want to get and how complex your internal data structures are.

Friday Q&A 2010-04-23: Implementing a Custom Slider

Related Articles

    Thread Safety in OS X System Frameworks 24

    The Good and Bad of Distributed Objects..56

    Care and Feeding of Singletons 194

    Dangerous Cocoa Calls...236

    Probing Cocoa With PyObjC 240

    Using Accessors in Init and Dealloc 246

    NSRunLoop Internals 273

    NSNotificationQueue..284

    Dealing with Retain Cycles 392

    What Every Apple Programmer Should Know 401

    Leopard Collection Classes..405

    Implementing Equality and Hashing 412

    Implementing NSCoding 459

    Defensive Programming in Cocoa 468

Welcome to another chilling edition of Friday Q&A. While I hope to be soaring over the scenic Shenandoah Valley on this fine Friday, I have taken the precaution of preparing my post in advance, so that you may see it even while I am incommunicado. Such is the magic of the modern world. This week, Michael Crawford has suggested that I give in example of implementing a custom control in Cocoa.

Specifically, he requested a diagonal slider. This slider works much like a regular Cocoa slider, except that it's oriented diagonally. To make the example more useful, I implemented it completely from scratch rather than trying to base it off of NSSlider (which would probably not be very easy for this anyway).

Getting the Code

As usual, the code that I wrote for this post is available in my Subversion repository:

```
svn co http://mikeash.com/svn/DiagonalSlider/
```

Planning

When building a custom control, it's helpful to break your tasks down as much as possible. The concept of building a custom control can be daunting, but when broken into small pieces, each small piece can become easy.

There are three main pieces to any custom control:

1. **Drawing:** The code with which the control draws itself. As controls are just views, this usually means implementing `drawRect:` to draw whatever you want your control to look like. In the case of the diagonal slider, it needs to draw the slider track and the knob.
2. **Event Tracking:** This involves getting and responding to events. In this case, looking at mouse down/dragged/up events and moving the slider knob around appropriately.
3. **Geometry:** This is code which figures out where the various components of the control are located. The geometry information is then used by the drawing and event tracking code to figure out where to draw things and where events are in the control. In this case, the geometry code consists of figuring out where the slider track is, where the knob is, and converting from a point to a slider value.

Interface

Before getting into the implementation, let's define the interface of the class. It will subclass `NSControl`. It will implement `setDoubleValue:` and `doubleValue` to return its position. For instance variables, it needs to store its value. Also, because `NSControl` tends to assume that you have an `NSCell`, and I don't want to build a cell, I also need instance variables to hold the control's target and action:

```
@interface DiagonalSlider : NSControl
{
    double _value;
    id _target;
    SEL _action;
}

- (void)setDoubleValue:(double)value;
- (double)doubleValue;

@end
```

Geometry

Since magic numbers are evil, the first thing I do for the geometry code is define some constants that determine the geometry of the control. The slider will extend from the bottom left corner to the top right corner of the control, but the ends need to be inset a bit to allow room to draw the slider and knob. These insets are defined here. The slider width and knob size are also defined as constants:

```
const CGFloat kInsetX = 12;
const CGFloat kInsetY = 12;
const CGFloat kSliderWidth = 6;
const CGFloat kKnobRadius = 10;
```

Now for some actual code. A major theme you'll see here is building up small methods, where each method computes a single value, relying on other methods for intermediate results. This helps enormously with simplifying the task of programming the control.

First, two methods for getting the slider endpoints:

```
- (NSPoint)_point1
{
    return NSMakePoint(kInsetX, kInsetY);
}

- (NSPoint)_point2
{
    NSRect bounds = [self bounds];
    return NSMakePoint(NSMaxX(bounds) - kInsetX, NSMaxY(bounds) - kInsetY);
}
```

Next, finding the center of the knob. To do that, I just take a weighted average of the two endpoints, using _value as the weight:

```
- (NSPoint)_knobCenter
{
    NSPoint p1 = [self _point1];
    NSPoint p2 = [self _point2];

    return NSMakePoint(p1.x * (1.0 - _value) + p2.x * _value, p1.y * (1.0 - _value) + p2.y * _value);
}
```

Next, I create a method that returns an NSBezierPath that describes the knob. You might think that this belongs in drawing, not geometry. However, I plan to use this path not only for drawing the knob, but also for determining whether the mouse is within the knob or not. Conceptually, this bezier path is part of the common geometry code:

```
- (NSBezierPath *)_knobPath
{
    NSRect knobR = { [self _knobCenter], NSZeroSize };
    return [NSBezierPath bezierPathWithOvalInRect:
        NSInsetRect(knobR, kKnobRadius, kKnobRadius)];
}
```

Next, I'll write code to determine the slider value that corresponds to a point, and whether the slider track contains a point. In order to write those, I need some utility functions. Specifically, I need vector subtraction, vector dot product, and vector length. To keep things simple, I use `NSPoint` as my "vector" type. These three utility functions are then easy to write:

```
static NSPoint sub(NSPoint p1, NSPoint p2)
{
    return NSMakePoint(p1.x - p2.x, p1.y - p2.y);
}

static CGFloat dot(NSPoint p1, NSPoint p2)
{
    return p1.x * p2.x + p1.y * p2.y;
}

static CGFloat len(NSPoint p)
{
    return sqrt(p.x * p.x + p.y * p.y);
}
```

Now, code for determining the value for a point. The math here is not complex, but may not be obvious. I start by doing a vector projection of the vector from the slider start to the point in question onto the vector of the slider itself. This projection gives me the distance of the point in question from the slider start in the direction of the slider, ignoring any side component. I then divide this length by the length of the slider, and that gives me a proportion. I want the value to be between 0 and 1, so that number is exactly what I want. Here's the code:

```
- (double)_valueForPoint: (NSPoint)p
{
    // vector from slider start to point
    NSPoint delta = sub(p, [self _point1]);

    // vector of slider
    NSPoint slider = sub([self _point2], [self _point1]);

    // project delta onto slider
    CGFloat projection = dot(delta, slider) / len(slider);

    // value is projection length divided by slider length
    return projection / len(slider);
}
```

Finally, I need code for determining whether a point is within the slider track. (This is used to determine whether a mouse click was on the slider track, and should be responded to, or whether it was outside.)

The concept for this code is similar. First, I use `_valueForPoint:` to see if the point is off the ends of the slider. If it is, instant rejection. Otherwise, I see how far to the side the point is from the slider. If this distance is within the slider width, then the point is contained by the slider.

Finding that distance is similar to the above code. Instead of projecting onto the slider's vector, I project onto a vector perpendicular to the slider. The length of that projection is the distance from the middle of the slider track:

```
- (BOOL)_sliderContainsPoint: (NSPoint)p
{
    // if beyond the ends, then it's not contained
    double value = [self _valueForPoint: p];
    if(value < 0 || value > 1)
        return NO;
    
    // vector from slider start to point
    NSPoint delta = sub(p, [self _point1]);
    
    // vector of slider
    NSPoint slider = sub([self _point2], [self _point1]);
    
    // vector of perpendicular to slider
    NSPoint sliderPerp = { -slider.y, slider.x };
    
    // project delta onto perpendicular
    CGFloat projection = dot(delta, sliderPerp) / len(sliderPerp);
    
    // distance to slider is absolute value of projection
    // see if that's within the slider width
    return fabs(projection) <= kSliderWidth;
}
```

Drawing

With all of these geometry methods, drawing is a snap. First, I draw a line between `_point1` and `_point2`. Then I get the `_knobPath` and fill it. And that's it!

Note that I'm going for technical information, not graphical prettiness, so my slider is ugly. The track is just a blue line, and the knob is just a red circle. Making it beautiful is up to you!

Here's what the drawing code looks like:

386

```objc
- (void)drawRect: (NSRect)r
{
    NSBezierPath *slider = [NSBezierPath bezierPath];
    [slider moveToPoint: [self _point1]];
    [slider lineToPoint: [self _point2]];
    [slider setLineWidth: kSliderWidth];

    [[NSColor blueColor] setStroke];
    [slider stroke];

    [[NSColor redColor] setFill];
    [[self _knobPath] fill];
}
```

Event Tracking

For tracking a mouse down/dragged/up sequence, there are two ways to do things.

One way is to implement `mouseDown:`, `mouseDragged:`, and `mouseUp:`, to do what you need in each situation. The other way is to only implement `mouseDown:`, then run your own event loop inside that to look for dragged/up events.

This second way is how most (possibly all) Apple controls work, and in my opinion generally works better. You often have state which is generated by the mouse down event, and then needs to be referenced by the dragged/up handlers, and this is easier to manage when everything is in the same place instead of scattered through several different methods. The dragged and up code is also often similar, and a single event loop allows consolidating the two cases. Because I think this way is superior, that's how `DiagonalSlider` will handle event tracking.

To do this, implement `mouseDown:`. First, figure out whether to handle the event or not. In the case of the slider, we want to handle the event if the click was in the knob or slider track, but not if it fell outside them. Handle any necessary setup, then start the inner event loop.

The slider has two cases which act slightly differently. One case is clicking in the knob itself, which does nothing to begin with, then moves the knob relative to the mouse's movements. The other case is clicking directly in the slider track, which jumps the knob to that position, then tracks further movement.

These two cases handle the same tracking at the end, but have slightly different setup. To facilitate this, I split most of the tracking into a separate method, `_trackMouseWithStartPoint`, which can then be called by these two cases.

The `mouseDown:` method first gets the location of the event, then sees if it's within the knob. If it is, then it just goes straight to tracking:

```
- (void)mouseDown: (NSEvent *)event
{
    NSPoint p = [self convertPoint: [event locationInWindow] fromView: nil];

    if([[self _knobPath] containsPoint: p])
    {
        [self _trackMouseWithStartPoint: p];
    }
```

Otherwise, it checks to see if the event is within the slider track. If it is, then it jumps the value to the current mouse position. It also sends the slider's action, to notify the target that the slider moved immediately. It then starts tracking:

```
    else if([self _sliderContainsPoint: p])
    {
        [self setDoubleValue: [self _valueForPoint: p]];
        [self sendAction: [self action] to: [self target]];
        [self _trackMouseWithStartPoint: p];
    }
}
```

If the event is not within the knob or slider, then it's just ignored.

Now for the actual event tracking. The first thing to do is compute a value offset. This is the difference between the slider's current value, and the value which corresponds to the location of the initial mouse down event. The purpose of this is to preserve the distance between the slider knob's center and the mouse cursor. If you click on the edge of the knob and drag, your cursor should stay on the edge, not have the knob suddenly jump to be centered. Note that this is only necessary when clicking the knob, not the track. However, when clicking the track, this value will be 0 and thus do nothing, so it's not necessary to conditionalize the code:

```
- (void)_trackMouseWithStartPoint: (NSPoint)p
{
    // compute the value offset: this makes the pointer stay on the
    // same piece of the knob when dragging
    double valueOffset = [self _valueForPoint: p] - _value;
```

Next, start the event loop. This consists of calling -[NSWindow nextEventMatchingMask:] in a loop, until a NSLeftMouseUp event is received. I also toss in an NSAutoreleasePool to ensure that memory doesn't build up if the loop continues for a long time:

```
    // create a pool to flush each time through the cycle
    NSAutoreleasePool *pool = [[NSAutoreleasePool alloc] init];
    // track!
    NSEvent *event = nil;
    while([event type] != NSLeftMouseUp)
    {
        [pool release];
        pool = [[NSAutoreleasePool alloc] init];

        event = [[self window] nextEventMatchingMask: NSLeftMouseDraggedMask | NSLeftMouseUpMask];
```

Once the event comes in, figure out where it is, set the slider's value appropriately, and send the action:

```
        NSPoint p = [self convertPoint: [event locationInWindow] fromView: nil];
        double value = [self _valueForPoint: p];
        [self setDoubleValue: value - valueOffset];
        [self sendAction: [self action] to: [self target]];
    }
```

And that's it for this method, just dump the last autorelease pool and exit:

```
    [pool release];
}
```

Miscellaneous

The slider needs a bit more support code. The only one that does anything of consequence is `setDoubleValue:`. It performs several tasks. First, it clamps the incoming value to be between 0 and 1. Then it assigns the value, and finally marks the control as needing a redisplay, so that the GUI updates accordingly. Note that simply redisplaying the entire view is somewhat inefficient, and it would be better to compute a minimal changed rect. However, in the spirit of avoiding premature optimization, I didn't do this.

```
- (void)setDoubleValue: (double)value
{
    // clamp to [0, 1]
    value = MAX(value, 0);
    value = MIN(value, 1);

    _value = value;
    [self setNeedsDisplay: YES];
}
```

I also have a few one-liners to return the value, and handle target/action:

```
- (double)doubleValue
{
    return _value;
}

- (void)setTarget: (id)anObject
{
    _target = anObject;
}

- (id)target
{
    return _target;
}

- (void)setAction: (SEL)aSelector
{
    _action = aSelector;
}

- (SEL)action
{
    return _action;
}
```

And that's it!

Using the Slider
Using this custom slider is much like using any other control, just with somewhat worse Interface Builder support. To create the slider in IB, you have to drag out a plain NSView, then set the class of that view to DiagonalSlider. IB doesn't know what a DiagonalSlider looks like, so it'll still show up as a plain box, but it will work correctly at runtime. IB is smart enough to notice that DiagonalSlider is an

`NSControl` subclass, and thus allows you to set the target/action of the slider right in the nib. Convenient!

Implement the action as you would for any other control. Then you can fetch the slider's current value using `doubleValue`. Update its value using `setDoubleValue:`. And that's it!

Conclusion

Building a custom control in Cocoa can be a daunting task, but if you break it down into components and build the control up from small pieces, it's really not that hard. By separating the code into geometry, drawing, and tracking sections, and building up each section from parts, building a custom control can become relatively straightforward.

Friday Q&A 2010-04-30: Dealing with Retain Cycles

Related Articles

    Thread Safety in OS X System Frameworks 24

    The Good and Bad of Distributed Objects..56

    Mac OS X Process Memory Statistics 123

    Care and Feeding of Singletons 194

    Dangerous Cocoa Calls..236

    Probing Cocoa With PyObjC..240

    Using Accessors in Init and Dealloc..246

    NSRunLoop Internals 273

    NSNotificationQueue...284

    Stack and Heap Objects in Objective-C...289

    Implementing a Custom Slider 382

    What Every Apple Programmer Should Know 401

    Leopard Collection Classes..405

    Implementing Equality and Hashing 412

    Implementing NSCoding 459

    Defensive Programming in Cocoa...468

Happy iPad 3G day to everyone. Whether you're waiting in line, waiting for the delivery guy, or just pining at home like I am, you can fill your idle moments with another edition of Friday Q&A. This week, Filip van der Meeren has suggested that I discuss retain cycles and how to deal with them.

Retain Cycles

First we need to discuss exactly what a retain cycle is. I'll assume you're familiar with standard Cocoa memory management. The simplest retain cycle is when two objects retain each other:

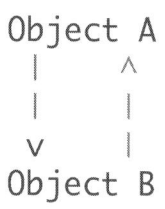

```
Object A
 |    ^
 |    |
 v    |
Object B
```

And in the general case, it can be any collection of objects which results in a circular series of links like this. It's rare, but possible, to have a chain of three, four, five, or more objects which point to each other in a cycle.

Retain cycles are a problem because the standard for Cocoa memory management is to release such retained references in an object's `dealloc` method. However, if an object is being retained, it won't `dealloc`. Objects which are part of a retain cycle will never be deallocated, and will leak if separated from the rest of the application.

Note that retain cycles can involve your own classes, but can also involve Cocoa classes. Two of the most common culprits in retain cycles in Cocoa classes are `NSTimer` and `NSThread`.

Also note that retain cycles only affect code that uses manual memory management. Cocoa's garbage collector is able to detect and destroy objects which have strong references to each other but which aren't referenced from the outside. However, retain cycles are a big threat if you're using retain/release memory management (like if you're on the iPhone), and can even show up in a garbage collected application if you use `CFRetain` and `CFRelease` to bypass the collector.

Avoiding Retain Cycles

Apple's memory management guidelines state that when two objects have a parent-child relationship, the parent should retain the child. If the child needs a reference back to the parent, that reference should be an unretained, weak reference. This allows the parent to be deallocated, which can then release its reference to the child, avoiding a cycle.

However, sometimes you have two objects which are peers. Neither one is a parent of the other, but they need to reference each other. If these references are retained, then you have a cycle.

One way to deal with this is to redefine the relationship into parent-child. You can arbitrarily choose one to be the parent object, which will have a retained reference to the other. The other can then have a weak reference to the first. The cycle diagram then looks like this:

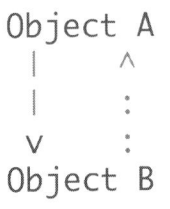

```
Object A
 |    ^
 |    :
 v    :
Object B
```

To be safe, Object A should always zero out B's weak reference when it's destroyed, to ensure that B doesn't then try to message it afterwards:

```
- (void)dealloc
{
    [_b setAReference: nil];
    [_b release];
    [super dealloc];
}
```

(This is also a good practice to follow with any weak reference, including things like `NSTableView` data sources.)

An alternative approach is to have another object act as the parent for both sub-objects. This can work with either retained or weak references between the sub-objects. With retained references:

```
         Object C
         |      |
         |      |
         V      V
Object A<=====>Object B
```

In this scenario, you still have a retain cycle, but C can break the cycle when it releases its references:

```
- (void)dealloc
{
    // break the cycle by zeroing the reference
    [_a setBReference: nil];

    // this breaks the cycle in both directions; this is optional
    [_b setAReference: nil];

    [_a release];
    [_b release];

    [super dealloc];
}
```

You can also have a weak reference between the sub-objects:

```
         Object C
         |      |
         |      |
         V      V
Object A<:::::>Object B
```

In this case, C should clear the weak references as well to be safe, but could get away without doing so.

Which way is better? They're both basically equivalent. I think that using retained references is a bit safer, both in terms of continuing to work correctly if you change the object graph later, and in being more resistant to mistakes in the code.

`NSThread` and `NSTimer`

`NSThread` and `NSTimer` are common causes of retain cycles. It's not unusual to write code like this:

```objc
- (id)init
{
    ...
    _timer = [[NSTimer scheduledTimerWithTimeInterval: 0.1
        target: self selector: @selector(whatever) userInfo: nil
        repeats: YES] retain];
    ...
}

- (void)dealloc
{
    [_timer invalidate];
    [_timer release];
    [super dealloc];
}
```

There's a retain cycle here! This object retains the timer, and the timer retains its target. And note that you can't fix this by not retaining `_timer`. The run loop will also retain the timer, and won't release it untill the call to `invalidate`. This acts as a second retained reference to the timer, causing what is essentially a cycle even without the explicit retained reference.

This exact same problem also happens with an `NSThread`, when specifying `self` as the target, and then shutting down the thread in `dealloc`. The `dealloc` method will never run, so the thread will never be shut down.

There are two ways to deal with this problem. One is to force explicit invalidation, and one is to split your code into two classes.

An `NSTimer` won't necessarily be destroyed when you release your final reference to it. As long as the timer is active, the runloop keeps a reference to it. To destroy a repeating timer, you can't just release all of your references to it, you have to explicitly invalidate it.

You can borrow this concept for your own class. Just expose your own `invalidate` method, and use that to destroy the timer:

```
- (void)invalidate
{
    [_timer invalidate];
    [_timer release];
    _timer = nil;
}
```

Of course, this leaks implementation details up into your interface, but forcing clients to explicitly declare when they're done with your object isn't always bad.

The other way is to split your code into two classes. You have a shell class which is exposed to the outside world, and which manages the thread or timer. Then you have an implementation class which is the target of the thread or timer, and which does most of the actual work:

```
@implementation MyClassImpl

- (id)init
{
    ...
    _timer = [[NSTimer scheduledTimerWithTimeInterval: 0.1 target: self selector: @selector(_timerAction) userInfo: nil repeats: YES] retain];
    ...
}

- (void)invalidate
{
    [_timer invalidate];
    [_timer release];
    _timer = nil;
}

- (void)doThingy
{
    // do stuff here
}

- (void)_timerAction
{
    // periodic code here
}

@end
```

```
@implementation MyClass

- (id)init
{
    ...
    _impl = [[MyClassImpl alloc] init];
    ...
}

- (void)dealloc
{
    [_impl invalidate];
    [_impl release];

    [super dealloc];
}

- (void)doThingy
{
    // just pass it on to the "real" code
    [_impl doThingy];
}

@end
```

By splitting the implementation from the interface, you avoid the retain cycle. In effect, `MyClass` becomes the common parent object, with `MyClassImpl` and `NSTimer` as the sub-objects. The parent then manually breaks the retain cycle between the sub-objects when it's destroyed. Externally, the parent preserves the normal retain/release semantics, with no need for explicit invalidation.

Blocks

Because blocks retain the objects they reference, they're another excellent candidate for a retain cycle. Consider this code:

```
- (id)init
{
    ...
    _observerObj = [[NSNotificationCenter defaultCenter]
addObserverForName: ... queue: [NSOperationQueue
mainQueue] usingBlock: ^(NSNotification *note) {
        [self doSomethingWith: note];
    }];
    [_observerObj retain];
    ...
}

- (void)dealloc
{
    [[NSNotificationCenter defaultCenter] removeObserver:
_observerObj];
    [_observerObj release];
    [super dealloc];
}
```

Because the notification block references `self`, the block will retain `self`. The result is a subtle retain cycle. This can happen even if you don't directly reference `self`; simply referencing an instance variable will indirectly reference `self`, which will cause the block to retain it.

The solutions used for `NSTimer` and `NSThread` will work here as well: either add explicit invalidation to the class's API, or break the class into two pieces.

There's a blocks-specific solution that you can use as well, which is to refer to `self` through a variable declared `__block`, which will not be retained:

```
    __block MyClass *blockSelf = self;
    _observerObj = [[NSNotificationCenter defaultCenter]
addObserverForName: ... queue: [NSOperationQueue
mainQueue] usingBlock: ^(NSNotification *note) {
        [blockSelf doSomethingWith: note];
    }];
```

This avoids the cycle, because `blockSelf` is not retained. Be careful if you do this to avoid referring to instance variables directly, as those will still reference the original `self`. If you need to access an instance variable, explicitly indirect through `blockSelf` by doing `blockSelf->_someIvar`.

Finding Cycles
For the most part, standard leak finding techniques will work fine for finding retain

cycles that cause a leak. Instruments is a good way to find them, both the ObjectAlloc instrument and the Leaks instrument. If you have a cycle that's hard to figure out, its ability to track `retain` and `release` calls to each object can help a lot.

If you prefer the command line, or just need text that's easier to search through, the `leaks` command-line tool is also handy.

When hunting for cycles, note that leaks tools won't always find a cycle if there's an external reference into the cycle. For example, consider a cycle involving an `NSTimer`. There's a reference from the runloop to the timer, and from the timer to your object, so they're both reachable. Both the Leaks instrument and the `leaks` tool will not consider this to be a leak. However, if they're doing nothing and build up without end, then it still is a leak, even if they're technically reachable. The ObjectAlloc tool will show this buildup even though the other tools won't identify the leak.

Conclusion

Retain cycles are an unfortunate wart on Cocoa's memory management system. However, with some care, they can be avoided or fixed with a minimum of pain, with small changes to your object hierarchy. Pay extra attention to `NSTimer` and `NSThread` (but don't ignore other code!), then either eliminate the cycle or add code that explicitly breaks it.

Friday Q&A 2010-05-14: What Every Apple Programmer Should Know

Related Articles
- Thread Safety in OS X System Frameworks 24
- The Good and Bad of Distributed Objects..56
- Care and Feeding of Singletons 194
- Dangerous Cocoa Calls 236
- Probing Cocoa With PyObjC 240
- Using Accessors in Init and Dealloc 246
- NSRunLoop Internals 273
- NSNotificationQueue..284
- Implementing a Custom Slider 382
- Dealing with Retain Cycles 392
- Leopard Collection Classes...405
- Implementing Equality and Hashing 412
- Implementing NSCoding 459
- Defensive Programming in Cocoa 468

Welcome back to another Friday Q&A. This week, Quentin Carnicelli (who is heavily involved in generating my paychecks) has suggested that I talk about things that every Apple programmer should know. In other words, common Cocoa design and implementation decisions that I'd prefer Apple not to make.

But First, a Brief Word from Our Sponsor
Before I get into the meat of the post, I have a bit of meta-business. While I greatly enjoy writing Friday Q&A and am humbled by the great feedback I get about it, it also represents a significant drain on my time that's becoming hard to sustain. Therefore, starting with this post, I will be scaling Friday Q&A back to a biweekly schedule. I'll be writing the same stuff in the same place, just not quite as often. I hope that what I'm taking away in quantity, I'll be able to make up for in quality.

And Now, Back to Our Show
While the theme of this article is common problems in Cocoa, I think this will also have a great deal of relevance to any Cocoa programmer. Ultimately, this will be a collection of common problems in API design and implementation, and large chunks of any real application count as APIs. While I really want Apple to follow these ideas, if you follow them as well, they should make your life much easier.

Without further ado, the list.

Always use `[self class]` when invoking your own class methods

A bunch of these boil down to making your code easier to subclass, and this is the first. If you hardcode your class when invoking a class method, it makes it impossible for a subclass to override that behavior. If that class method is public, then you've created a frustrating situation: the method exists, is published, can be overridden, but won't be called if you do, so you can't change the behavior.

Don't access instance variables directly if there's an accessor

This is much like the previous one. If there's an accessor, there's an expectation that you can override it in a subclass to alter the value which is used. If you access the instance variable directly, you bypass that override, making it impossible for subclasses to alter behavior. Even worse, if you use the accessor only *sometimes*, then you get bizarre inconsistent behavior that's easy to go wrong. Apple really loves to do this one, so as a user of Cocoa, be careful when subclassing and overriding accessors, and be prepared for them not to be called.

If components of functionality are exposed as public methods, the implementation should always call them when it needs that functionality

Yet another ease-of-subclassing item. Sometimes Apple provides a public method, but doesn't use it internally to accomplish the task it's built for. An example of this is `NSSliderCell`, which provides a `drawBarInside:flipped:` method, but which does its own bar drawing separately. If you want custom bar drawing, you either have to override a higher level drawing method, or you have to override the private `_usesCustomTrackImage` method to convince it to call your custom code. Another example is `NSMutableURLRequest`'s `setHTTPBodyStream:` method. If you create a custom `NSInputStream` class and pass an instance of that custom class as the parameter, it won't work. You have to override the private `_scheduleInCFRunLoop:forMode:` method for the two components to work together. Subclasses should be able to override a public method to alter functionality, or work with existing APIs, without jumping through these hoops.

Don't write empty stub methods and then make them public

`NSView` has this nifty method:

```
- (BOOL)lockFocusIfCanDrawInContext:(NSGraphicsContext *)context;
```

It's nifty until you read the documentation on it, which says, "This method was declared in Mac OS X v10.4, but is not used in that release. It currently does nothing and returns NO. However, it might be implemented in a future release."

It baffles me as to why this method is public. It's useless, so why have it at all? If they plan to implement it in the future, they could make it public once it's implemented. I can only assume that it was implemented as a stub with the intent to complete it, but then it slipped through the cracks.

Apple doesn't do this much, but suffice it to say that it shouldn't happen at all.

User data fields should be `id`
It's a common pattern to have "user data" as part of an API, which is just some arbitrary data which can be passed through a callback or attached to an object. Sometimes this is an object, but sometimes Cocoa presents user data as a `void *`. This greatly complicates memory management (especially when using garbage collection) to little benefit. The common case is to pass an object as user data, and the API should simplify that. For the rare cases where you want a different type of pointer, the programmer can always wrap it in an `NSValue`.

Make up your mind on what "thread safe" means
As I discussed in an earlier post, Apple is pretty inconsistent about what "thread safe" actually means. Sometimes it means any instance can be safely used from multiple threads simultaneously. Sometimes it means any instance can be used from one thread at a time, but that you must synchronize access. Sometimes that's described as "not thread safe" instead. It's tremendously confusing! The world is becoming heavily multithreaded, and we need more explicit descriptions of what these APIs require.

Make fewer APIs dependent on the main thread
The main thread is a huge bottleneck in a modern Cocoa app, because many APIs only work on the main thread. Most GUI manipulation can't be safely done off the main thread, even if you take care to cleanly keep each window on a single thread. Entire APIs, like WebKit, can only be used from the main thread. Fortunately, the situation is gradually improving.

Make every runloop API take a modes parameter
Do a google search for webview modal to see what the problem is here. `WebView` depends on a running runloop to do its processing, but it only runs in the default mode. If you want your `WebView` to remain functional while a modal window is running, you're out of luck. You should be able to easily schedule the `WebView` in the modal runloop mode, but the API isn't there, so you can't. While it's perfectly reasonable to schedule into one particular runloop mode *by default*, a runloop-dependent API should always provide the ability to schedule on other modes too.

Make it easy to convert between different classes with similar capabilities
An example of this is `NSImage` and `CGImage`. Before Snow Leopard, there was no easy way to convert between the two, even though they were fairly similar. (Yes, `NSImage` can contain multiple representations, isn't necessarily pixel-based, etc. They're still conceptually close.) If you had one, and needed the other, it was a bunch of work to go from one to the other.

In 10.6, Apple added APIs to `NSImage` to make it easy to convert between them, and suddenly life became a lot easier.

Toll free bridging in CoreFoundation is the pinnacle of how to do this right. The objects are interoperable, and just require a cast to convince the compiler that you're not insane. While this isn't always possible, easy methods to do explicit conversion help enormously.

There are still areas where this is lacking. `NSColor` and `CGColor` are difficult to convert between. `CFBundle` and `NSBundle` are extremely similar but not interchangeable or convertible.

Don't pollute namespaces
One of the unfortunate things missing from Objective-C is namespaces. It's all too easy for components in a framework to conflict with components in an application. If you're building a framework, then you need to minimize the possibility of this happening as much as possible.

Always prefix class names with something that should be reasonably unique. This goes *even for private classes*. They can conflict and cause problems even though they're never exposed as part of your public API.

You also need to prefix *category* methods that aren't made public. If they aren't prefixed, there's a risk of conflict with other category methods. The same also goes for private methods.

Conclusion
Overall, Cocoa is a great API, but there are a few common problems which make things a little bit less smooth than they otherwise could be. The intent is not to bash Apple, but just show how things could be made a little bit better, and give some ways that the rest of us can make our own APIs better as well.

Friday Q&A 2010-05-28: Leopard Collection Classes

Related Articles
- Thread Safety in OS X System Frameworks 24
- The Good and Bad of Distributed Objects 56
- Care and Feeding of Singletons 194
- Dangerous Cocoa Calls 236
- Probing Cocoa With PyObjC 240
- Using Accessors in Init and Dealloc 246
- NSRunLoop Internals 273
- NSNotificationQueue 284
- Implementing a Custom Slider 382
- Dealing with Retain Cycles 392
- What Every Apple Programmer Should Know 401
- Implementing Equality and Hashing 412
- Implementing NSCoding 459
- Defensive Programming in Cocoa 468

Welcome back to another edition of Friday Q&A. For this week's post, I'm going to talk about three somewhat obscure collections classes that were introduced to Cocoa in 10.5: `NSPointerArray`, `NSHashTable`, and `NSMapTable`, a topic suggested by Phil Holland.

Introduction
These classes were introduced in 10.5 and it appears that their main purpose was to add some useful capabilities for the newly-introduced Cocoa garbage collection support. However, they add a lot of other useful capabilities beyond that as well.

Each of these classes is the counterpart of a more traditional Foundation collection class. `NSPointerArray` is the counterpart of `NSArray`, `NSHashTable` is the counterpart of `NSSet`, and `NSMapTable` is the counterpart of `NSDictionary`. They are not identical, but share a lot of behaviors, and are the same basic kind of container.

One nice feature of Cocoa garbage collection (and many other collectors) is zeroing weak references. These are references to an object which don't keep that object alive. Instead, they point to the object while it's alive, but if and when it gets garbage collected, the collector zeroes out the reference. This can be really useful for object caches, parent-child object relationships, automatic deregistration of observers and others.

Individual weak references are easy to use: simply prepend `__weak` to an object pointer variable's type and that variable becomes a weak reference. (Note: this does not work for local variables.) The standard collections all hold strong references to their contents. One of the reasons for these new collection classes was that they can be configured to hold weak references to their contents, greatly expanding the uses for weak references.

These classes are also much more flexible in general. They can hold `NULL` values, they can be configured to hold opaque non-object pointers, plain integers, or even pointers to memory with custom comparison/destruction operations.

NSPointerArray

This class is a lot like an `NSMutableArray`, but with the `id` objects replaced with `void *`, and many fewer convenience functions.

The major difference from `NSMutableArray` is in how you create a new `NSPointerArray`. The class has two initializers:

```
- initWithOptions:(NSPointerFunctionsOptions)options;
- initWithPointerFunctions:(NSPointerFunctions *)functions;
```

This is where the flexibility comes in. The parameters for these initialiers allow you to fully specify how the `NSPointerArray` treats its contents. You can use an `NSPointerArray` any time you want an `NSArray` that points to special kinds of objects or otherwise needs special treatment.

NSPointerFunctions

`NSPointerFunctions` is a class whose main purpose is to hold a bunch of function pointers. There are function pointers for hashing, equality, memory management, and more. There are also two flags you can set to have it use different garbage collection read/write barriers. By stuffing function pointers into this class, you can specify how everything works.

Let's build an example. We'll create an `NSPointerFunctions` object that deals with pointers to integers. Not too useful, but a good exercise.

The first thing to do is to define all of the various functions that will be needed. Hashing is easy, just return the integer that the pointer points to:

```
static NSUInteger Hash(const void *item, NSUInteger (*size)(const void *item))
{
    return *(const int *)item;
}
```

Equality is just as easy, dereference both pointers and compare:

```
static BOOL IsEqual(const void *item1, const void *item2,
NSUInteger (*size)(const void *item))
{
    return *(const int *)item1 == *(const int *)item2;
}
```

Note the final `size` parameter to both functions. If necessary, this will get the size of the pointed-to object. We already know the size, so there's no need to use it. Since it's unnecessary, I won't provide a size function to the `NSPointerFunctions` object either.

For the description, we just return a simple string using the integer obtained from dereferencing the pointer:

```
static NSString *Description(const void *item)
{
    return [NSString stringWithFormat: @"%d", *(const int *)item];
}
```

Relinquish and acquire are a bit trickier. They assume reference counting memory management, but I want to use plain `malloc` and `free`. I decided to just have relinquish always free the item, and acquire return a copy. The relinquish function is simple:

```
static void Relinquish(const void *item, NSUInteger (*size)(const void *item))
{
    free((void *)item);
}
```

The acquire function isn't much more complicated. It `malloc`s some new memory, copies the value, and returns the new pointer:

```
static void *Acquire(const void *src, NSUInteger (*size)(const void *item), BOOL shouldCopy)
{
    int *newPtr = malloc(sizeof(int));
    *newPtr = *(const int *)src;
    return newPtr;
}
```

And now with all of this in place, we can create a new `NSPointerFunctions`, and a new `NSPointerArray` from it:

```
NSPointerFunctions *functions = [[NSPointerFunctions
alloc] init];
[functions setHashFunction: Hash];
[functions setIsEqualFunction: IsEqual];
[functions setDescriptionFunction: Description];
[functions setRelinquishFunction: Relinquish];
[functions setAcquireFunction: Acquire];

NSPointerArray *array = [NSPointerArray
pointerArrayWithPointerFunctions: functions];

int one = 1, two = 2, three = 3;
[array addPointer: &one;];
[array addPointer: &two;];
[array addPointer: &three;];
```

And it all works.

NSPointerOptions

It may work, but that was a gigantic hassle. Fortunately, Apple has provided a bunch of pre-baked `NSPointerFunctions` to work with. These can be accessed by using `NSPointerFunctionsOptions` constants.

`NSPointerFunctionsOptions` is composed of three parts. There are memory options, personalities, and flags.

Memory options determine memory management. Using `NSPointerFunctionsStrongMemory` will get you the behavior of the more standard Foundation collection classes: a strong reference for garbage collection, and a retained reference for manual memory management. `NSPointerFunctionsZeroingWeakMemory` will get you zeroing weak references under garbage collection and, I believe, a non-retained reference under manual memory management. There are also options for `malloc/free` management, for Mach virtual memory, and for completely ignoring memory management.

Personalities determine hashing and equality. `NSPointerFunctionsObjectPersonality` provides the standard Foundation behavior of using `hash` and `isEqual:`. You can also use `NSPointerFunctionsObjectPointerPersonality`, which treats the contents as objects, but uses direct pointer value comparison; this is useful if you need a collection to work with object identity rather than value. `NSPointerFunctionsIntegerPersonality` allows storing pointer-sized integers directly in the container. Note that unlike the toy example above, this doesn't deal with *pointers* to integers, but rather integers directly, like storing `(void *)42`.

This is useful if you need a collection that stores integers and don't want the code and runtime overhead of packing the integers into objects.

Apple has only given us one flag at the moment: `NSPointerFunctionsCopyIn`. When set, this flag will cause newly inserted pointers to be copied rather than simply retained. What exactly this means will depend on the personality set, but in the case of object personalities, it will use `NSCopying`.

Some examples:

- Strong references with copied objects using object value comparison: `NSPointerFunctionsStrongMemory | NSPointerFunctionsObjectPersonality | NSPointerFunctionsCopyIn`.
- Zeroing weak references and object identity: `NSPointerFunctionsZeroingWeakMemory | NSPointerFunctionsObjectPointerPersonality`.
- C strings stored in `malloc` memory, copied when inserted: `NSPointerFunctionsMallocMemory | NSPointerFunctionsCStringPersonality | NSPointerFunctionsCopyIn`.

As you can see, there's a lot of flexibility to be had here without ever having to define your own functions.

Now that you know how all of those work, let's look at the remaining two classes.

NSHashTable

`NSHashTable` is the rough equivalent of `NSMutableSet`. It's an unordered collection of objects, using hashing to allow for fast access. Again, the basic functionality is the same, but without some of the more advanced methods. And again, it has two initializers which take pointer functions and options.

There is one extra factory method on `NSHashTable`:

`+ (id)hashTableWithWeakObjects;`

Apparently Apple thought that this was a common enough use to justify making it more convenient to create a new object of this type.

Like `NSPointerArray`, you can use `NSHashTable` any time you want an `NSSet` but with some different capabilities in terms of how it treats its contents.

NSMapTable

`NSMapTable` is the final class of the three, and is the rough equivalent of `NSDictionary`. It's an unordered collection of key/object pairs, with fast access to the objects by looking them up through their keys. Like the others, it has the standard two initializers to tell it how to act.

NSMapTable also has four extra factory methods:

+ (id)mapTableWithStrongToStrongObjects;
+ (id)mapTableWithWeakToStrongObjects;
+ (id)mapTableWithStrongToWeakObjects;
+ (id)mapTableWithWeakToWeakObjects;

This gives you all four possible combinations of weak and strong.

As with the others, you can use NSMapTable in any case where you'd normally want an NSDictionary but need a little extra flexibility.

In particular, [NSMapTable mapTableWithStrongToStrongObjects] will give you an object which behaves much like an NSDictionary but which doesn't copy its keys. This is useful in all kinds of situaitons, and can save a lot of headache.

Comparison with CoreFoundation
Those of you who are intimately familiar with CoreFoundation collections probably nodded a lot at the NSPointerFunctions stuff. CoreFoundation collections such as CFArray require nearly identical functions to determine how they treat their contents. Given this, what are the advantages of each?

The new Cocoa classes are largely useful because they're vastly more convenient to set up. CoreFoundation has no equivalent for a lot of the built-in NSPointerOptions functionality, which would require you to build them all yourself. There is not, as far as I know, any way to do zeroing weak references with CoreFoundation collections. Toll-free bridging is also inconsistent when it comes to custom behavior: you can build a CFDictionary with callbacks that don't copy their keys, but using [customDictionary setObject: obj forKey: key] will still copy the key even though you expressly told it not to! (For any Apple employees reading this, I've filed this as bug #4350677, and it was returned as "behaves correctly".)

Custom CoreFoundation collections can be better due to toll-free bridging, which allows you to treat them as standard NSArrays and so forth. However, you must be careful when passing these to code you don't own, as they may make assumptions about the behavior of the collection which your custom callbacks don't respect. And as noted above, the behavior of custom callbacks with toll-free bridging is inconsistent, so watch out!

All in all, each one has its place. In pure Cocoa code, the new Cocoa classes are generally more convenient and can be more powerful.

Conclusion

The new collection classes added to Cocoa in 10.5 are a powerful, flexible addition to Foundation. They easily allow useful behaviors like storing weak references and raw integers, or just creating an object map that doesn't copy its keys.

Friday Q&A 2010-06-18: Implementing Equality and Hashing

Related Articles

    Thread Safety in OS X System Frameworks 24

    The Good and Bad of Distributed Objects..56

    Intro to the Objective-C Runtime 67

    Objective-C Messaging..73

    Objective-C Message Forwarding 77

    Objective-C Class Loading and Initialization..115

    Care and Feeding of Singletons 194

    Dangerous Cocoa Calls 236

    Probing Cocoa With PyObjC 240

    Using Accessors in Init and Dealloc 246

    NSRunLoop Internals 273

    NSNotificationQueue..284

    Method Replacement for Fun and Profit 297

    Error Returns with Continuation Passing Style 303

    Comparison of Objective-C Enumeration Techniques 369

    Implementing Fast Enumeration..373

    Implementing a Custom Slider 382

    Dealing with Retain Cycles 392

    What Every Apple Programmer Should Know 401

    Leopard Collection Classes..405

    Zeroing Weak References in Objective-C 428

    Implementing NSCoding 459

    Defensive Programming in Cocoa..468

Welcome back to a late edition of Friday Q&A. WWDC pushed the schedule back one week, but it's finally time for another one. This week, I'm going to discuss the implementation of equality and hashing in Cocoa, a topic suggested by Steven Degutis.

Equality

Object equality is a fundamental concept that gets used all over the place. In Cocoa, it's implemented with the `isEqual:` method. Something as simple as `[array indexOfObject:]` will use it, so it's important that your objects support it.

It's so important that Cocoa actually gives us a default implementation of it on `NSObject`. The default implementation just compares pointers. In other words, an object is only equal to itself, and is never equal to another object. The implementation is functionally identical to:

```
- (BOOL)isEqual: (id)other
{
    return self == other;
}
```

While oversimplified in many cases, this is actually good enough for a lot of objects. For example, an `NSView` is never considered equal to another `NSView`, only to itself. For `NSView`, and many other classes which behave that way, the default implementation is enough. That's good news, because it means that if your class has that same equality semantic, you don't have to do anything, and get the correct behavior for free.

Implementing Custom Equality

Sometimes you need a deeper implementation of equality. It's common for objects, typically what you might refer to as a "value object", to be distinct from another object but be logically equal to it. For example:

```
// use mutable strings because that guarantees distinct
objects
NSMutableString *s1 = [NSMutableString stringWithString:
@"Hello, world"];
NSMutableString *s2 = [NSMutableString stringWithFormat:
@"%@, %@", @"Hello", @"world"];
BOOL equal = [s1 isEqual: s2]; // gives you YES!
```

Of course `NSMutableString` implements this for you in this case. But what if you have a custom object that you want to be able to do the same thing?

```
MyClass *c1 = ...;
MyClass *c2 = ...;
BOOL equal = [c1 isEqual: c2];
```

In this case you need to implement your own version of `isEqual:`.

Testing for equality is fairly straightforward most of the time. Gather up the relevant properties of your class, and test them all for equality. If any of them are not equal, then return `NO`. Otherwise, return `YES`.

One subtle point with this is that the class of your object is an important property to test as well. It's perfectly valid to test a `MyClass` for equality with an `NSString`, but that comparison should never return `YES` (unless `MyClass` is a subclass of `NSString`, of course).

413

A somewhat less subtle point is to ensure that you only test properties that are actually important to equality. Things like caches that do not influence your object's externally-visible value should not be tested.

Let's say your class looks like this:

```
@interface MyClass : NSObject
{
    int _length;
    char *_data;
    NSString *_name;
    NSMutableDictionary *_cache;
}
```

Your equality implementation would then look like this:

```
- (BOOL)isEqual: (id)other
{
    return ([other isKindOfClass: [MyClass class]] &&
            [other length] == _length &&
            memcmp([other data], _data, _length) == 0 &&
            [[other name] isEqual: _name])
            // note: no comparison of _cache
}
```

Hashing

Hash tables are a commonly used data structure which are used to implement, among other things, NSDictionary and NSSet. They allow fast lookups of objects no matter how many objects you put in the container.

If you're familiar with how hash tables work, you may want to skip the next paragraph or two.

A hash table is basically a big array with special indexing. Objects are placed into an array with an index that corresponds to their hash. The hash is essentially a pseudorandom number generated from the object's properties. The idea is to make the index random enough to make it unlikely for two objects to have the same hash, but have it be fully reproducible. When an object is inserted, the hash is used to determine where it goes. When an object is looked up, its hash is used to determine where to look.

In more formal terms, the hash of an object is defined such that two objects have an identical hash if they are equal. Note that the reverse is not true, and can't be: two objects can have an identical hash and not be equal. You want to try to avoid this as much as possible, because when two unequal objects have the same hash (called a *collision*) then the hash table has to take special measures to handle this, which is slow. However, it's provably impossible to avoid it completely.

In Cocoa, hashing is implemented with the `hash` method, which has this signature:

```
- (NSUInteger)hash;
```

As with equality, `NSObject` gives you a default implementation that just uses your object's identity. Roughly speaking, it does this:

```
- (NSUInteger)hash
{
    return (NSUInteger)self;
}
```

The actual value may differ, but the essential point is that it's based on the actual pointer value of `self`. And just as with equality, if object identity equality is all you need, then the default implementation will do fine for you.

Implementing Custom Hashing

Because of the semantics of `hash`, if you override `isEqual:` then you *must* override `hash`. If you don't, then you risk having two objects which are equal but which don't have the same hash. If you use these objects in a dictionary, set, or something else which uses a hash table, then hilarity will ensue.

Because the definition of the object's hash follows equality so closely, the implementation of `hash` likewise closely follows the implementation of `isEqual:`.

An exception to this is that there's no need to include your object's class in the definition of `hash`. That's basically a safeguard in `isEqual:` to ensure the rest of the check makes sense when used with a different object. Your hash is likely to be very different from the hash of a different class simply by virtue of hashing different properties and using different math to combine them.

Generating Property Hashes

Testing properties for equality is usually straightforward, but hashing them isn't always. How you hash a property depends on what kind of object it is.

For a numeric property, the hash can simply be the numeric value.

For an object property, you can send the object the `hash` method, and use what it returns.

For data-like properties, you'll want to use some sort of hash algorithm to generate the hash. You can use CRC32, or even something totally overkill like MD5. Another approach, somewhat less speedy but easy to use, is to wrap the data in an `NSData` and ask it for its hash, essentially offloading the work onto Cocoa. In the above example, you could compute the hash of _data like so:

```
[[NSData dataWithBytes: _data length: _length] hash]
```

Combining Property Hashes

So you know how to generate a hash for each property, but how do you put them together?

The easiest way is to simply add them together, or use the bitwise xor property. However, this can hurt your hash's uniqueness, because these operations are symmetric, meaning that the separation between different properties gets lost. As an example, consider an object which contains a first and last name, with the following hash implementation:

```
- (NSUInteger)hash
{
    return [_firstName hash] ^ [_lastName hash];
}
```

Now imagine you have two objects, one for "George Frederick" and one for "Frederick George". They will hash to the same value even though they're clearly not equal. And, although hash collisions can't be avoided completely, we should try to make them harder to obtain than this!

How to best combine hashes is a complicated subject without any single answer. However, any asymmetric way of combining the values is a good start. I like to use a bitwise rotation in addition to the xor to combine them:

```
#define NSUINT_BIT (CHAR_BIT * sizeof(NSUInteger))
#define NSUINTROTATE(val, howmuch) ((((NSUInteger)val) << howmuch) | (((NSUInteger)val) >> (NSUINT_BIT - howmuch)))

- (NSUInteger)hash
{
    return NSUINTROTATE([_firstName hash], NSUINT_BIT / 2) ^ [_lastName hash];
}
```

Custom Hash Example

Now we can take all of the above and use it to produce a hash method for the example class. It follows the basic form of the equality method, and uses the above techniques to obtain and combine the hashes of the individual properties:

```
- (NSUInteger)hash
{
    NSUInteger dataHash = [[NSData dataWithBytes: _data length: _length] hash];
    return NSUINTROTATE(dataHash, NSUINT_BIT / 2) ^ [_name hash];
}
```

If you have more properties, you can add more rotation and more xor operators, and it'll work out just the same. You'll want to adjust the amount of rotation for each property to make each one different.

A Note on Subclassing

You have to be careful when subclassing a class which implements custom equality and hashing. In particular, your subclass should not expose any new properties which equality is dependent upon. If it does, then it must not compare equal with any instances of the superclass.

To see why, consider a subclass of the first/last name class which includes a birthday, and includes that as part of its equality computation. However, it can't include it when comparing equality with an instance of the superclass, so its equality method would look like this:

```
- (BOOL)isEqual: (id)other
{
    // if the superclass doesn't like it then we're not equal
    if(![super isEqual: other])
        return NO;

    // if it's not an instance of the subclass, then trust the superclass
    // it's equal there, so we consider it equal here
    if(![other isKindOfClass: [MySubClass class]])
        return YEs;

    // it's an instance of the subclass, the superclass properties are equal
    // so check the added subclass property
    return [[other birthday] isEqual: _birthday];
}
```

Now you have an instance of the superclass for "John Smith", which I'll call A, and an instance of the subclass for "John Smith" with a birthday of 5/31/1982, which I'll call B.

Because of the definition of equality above, A equals B, and B also equals itself, which is expected.

Now consider an instance of the subclass for "John Smith" with a birthday of 6/7/1994, which I'll call C. C is not equal to B, which is what we expect. C is equal to A, also expected. But now there's a problem. A equals both B and C, but B and C do not equal each other! This breaks the standard transitivity of the equality operator, and leads to extremely unexpected results.

In general this should not be a big problem. If your subclass adds properties which influence object equality, that's probably an indication of a design problem in your hierarchy anyway. Rather than working around it with weird implementations of `isEqual:`, consider redesigning your class hierarchy.

A Note on Dictionaries

If you want to use your object as a key in an `NSDictionary`, you need to implement hashing and equality, but you also need to implement `-copyWithZone:`. Techniques for doing that are beyond the scope of today's post, but you should be aware that you need to go a little bit further in that case.

Conclusion

Cocoa provides default implementations of equality and hashing which work for many objects, but if you want your objects to be considered equal even when they're distinct objects in memory, you have to do a bit of extra work. Fortunately, it's not difficult to do, and once you implement them, your class will work seamlessly with many Cocoa collection classes.

Friday Q&A 2010-07-02: Background Timers

Related Articles

    Blocks in Objective-C 14
    Practical Blocks 146
    Intro to Grand Central Dispatch, Part I: Basics and Dispatch Queues 162
    Intro to Grand Central Dispatch, Part II: Multi-Core Performance 169
    Intro to Grand Central Dispatch, Part III: Dispatch Sources 174
    Intro to Grand Central Dispatch, Part IV: Odds and Ends 179
    GCD Practicum 183
    Creating a Blocks-Based Object System 205
    A GCD Case Study: Building an HTTP Server 256
    Error Returns with Continuation Passing Style 303
    Trampolining Blocks with Mutable Code 311
    Futures 330
    Compound Futures 342

Welcome back to another Friday Q&A. This week I'm departing from my usual user-driven format to present a class I've written for what I'm calling "background timers", and discuss potential uses for it.

Periodic Cleanup
To understand the usefulness of background timers, it's important to understand what kind of problem they're trying to solve.

It's common to have a class which needs to perform some sort of periodic cleanup or dumping. For example, buffered file IO (as done by e.g. `printf`) requires occasionally flushing the buffer to the file. A cache may want to occasionally evict old entries.

As one concrete example, consider an implementation of `NSMutableArray`. The array needs to manage storage for its contents, which it allocates with `malloc`. When an object is added that exceeds the current storage size, it uses `realloc` to grow the array. When it shrinks enough to justify it, it uses `realloc` to shrink the array.

The key is "enough to justify it". When is it enough?

One strategy would be to shrink it every time the current allocation was less than half full. However, imagine that you remove a lot of elements, but leave the array at one element over half full, then let it sit for a long time. You're wasting a lot of space! You could reduce the potential for wasted space by, say, shrinking any time the array is less than 90% full. But that can be inefficient if you remove a lot of elements right away, or add and remove a lot of objects at a size that causes the array to constantly shrink and then re-grow.

Another strategy would be to shrink it every so many calls, say, every 100 calls. This could be combined with the above so that it would only shrink when there was enough wasted space to justify it. But this, too, could cause a lot of unnecessary shrinking and re-growing with an unfriendly access pattern, or a lot of wasted space if you suddenly leave the array idle on call #99.

Yet another strategy would be to base the decision not on fullness or calls, but on time. Check the array, say, once every half-second while it's in active use. If needed, resize the array. If the array isn't being used, nothing happens.

The natural way to implement this strategy would be with `NSTimer`. Whenever an object is removed from the array, check to see if a timer exists, and if it doesn't, create one with a half-second delay. When the timer fires, resize the array if it's necessary.

Trouble is, `NSTimer` requires an active runloop. If the array is manipulated a lot without returning to the runloop, it won't resize during that period. Worse, if the array is manipulated on a thread that doesn't have an active runloop, it will never resize.

To fix this, you'd want the timer to run on some sort of dedicated background thread. And you'd want to make sure that your normal array code was synchronized with that background thread so that all of your data access was safe.

Of course, Mac OS X already has an API that lets you do work on background threads and synchronize accesses with them: Grand Central Dispatch. GCD even includes timers, although they're not 100% what's wanted here.

Thus, I created a class, `MABGTimer`. It wraps GCD timers to provide the functionality needed to perform these periodic maintenance tasks based on time and in the background.

Code
As usual, you can get the code that goes along with this post from my public subversion repository:

```
svn co http://mikeash.com/svn/BackgroundTimer/
```

Or just click on the link above to browse it.

API
The key public methods of `MABGTimer` are:

```
- (void)afterDelay: (NSTimeInterval)delay do: (void (^)(id self))block;
- (void)performWhileLocked: (void (^)(void))block;
- (void)cancel;
```

After creating the timer, you set up a task by calling `afterDelay:do:`. You give it a delay, and a block to perform after that delay passes. If you call this method multiple times before the delay expires, the timer is either extended or coalesced, depending on settings.

Notice that the block passed to `afterDelay:do:` takes a parameter called `self`. The idea is that `MABGTimer` is initialized with a pointer to the object it's supposed to operate on, and it then passes a pointer to that object as a parameter to the block.

You might wonder, what's the point? After all, the block could simply capture `self` from the enclosing scope. That's what blocks are all about, after all.

The reason for the `self` parameter is that capturing `self` from the enclosing scope sets up a retain cycle. The object will be kept alive by the block until the timer fires. `MABGTimer` keeps a *weak* reference to the object, so that it can be destroyed at any time. When it is, the object can cancel the timer using the `cancel` method. This allows an object to set up long-term maintenance tasks and then cancel them early if the object is destroyed and no longer needs to perform them. `MABGTimer` then passes that weak reference into the block so it can use the original object without forcing a strong reference.

(Note: it is possible to give the block a weak reference to something in the enclosing scope by declaring a local variable with the `__block` qualifier and capturing that. However, that's more work than simply having a parameter passed in that you can use, so `MABGTimer` does a little extra work to make the client's job easier.)

As I mentioned above, since the timer executes in the background, synchronization is important. The `performWhileLocked:` method takes care of synchronization. Any time you do something with data that is also accessed in the timer block, wrap that code in a call to `performWhileLocked:`, and the timer will ensure that access is synchronized.

To clarify, here's an example of how these methods might be used:

```objc
    // do some work with non-shared data
    _someIvar++;
    [_someOtherIvar addObject: parameter];
    
    // do some work with timer-accessed data
    __block id resultObject;
    [_timer performWhileLocked: ^{
        // retain here to ensure the object stays live, since
        // this is multithreaded!
        resultObject = [[_cache objectForKey: parameter] retain];
    }];
    // balance the retain
    [resultObject autorelease];
    
    // clean the cache periodically
    [_timer afterDelay: 1.0 do: ^(id self) {
        // DON'T directly access ivars here
        // that will implicitly capture self, and cause a retain cycle
        [self _flushCache];
    }];
    
    return resultObject;
```

Behaviors

Each call to `afterDelay:do:` does not necessarily result in an invocation of the block passed in. If it's called multiple times before the timer fires, the block is only called once. This means that you should pass the same block each time; if they do different things, some of those things won't get done!

What exactly happens when you call it multiple times depends on how the timer was configured. This is done using *behaviors*, and I currently implement two.

When set with the **coalesce** behavior, the timer fires at the earliest time specified by the calls. In other words, calling with 2 seconds and then with 1 second will fire after 1 second. Calling with 10 seconds, then waiting 1 second, then calling with 5 seconds, will fire at the 6-second mark.

Coalesce is good for periodic maintenance tasks. You can call the timer many times, and it will fire periodically as needed. By passing different delays into the timer, you can handle events with varying urgency. For example, if you write some very low-priority data to a file handle, you might specify a 60-second delay. If you write high-priority data, you might specify a 0.1-second delay. `MABGTimer` will intelligently combine those so that high-priority data following low-priority data will flush the entire cache.

When set with the **delay** behavior, the timer's firing time is reset with each call. This essentially implements an idle timer. As long as your class is active, the timer will continue to reset, but after it's quiet for a while, it will fire. This could be used to implement a GUI control which refreshes an expensive view only when the mouse has stopped moving.

Behaviors are specified when creating the timer object using this method:

```
- (id)initWithObject: (id)obj behavior:
(MABGTimerBehavior)behavior;
```

There is also a convenience initializer:

```
- (id)initWithObject: (id)obj;
```

This defaults to **coalesce** behavior, because I think it's the more common one.

Target Queue

There's also one method for advanced GCD users:

```
- (void)setTargetQueue: (dispatch_queue_t)target;
```

This allows you to specify a dispatch queue where the `MABGTimer` will execute its code. This includes the timer block as well as the block passed to `performWhileLocked:`.

By default, `MABGTimer` runs everything on a private queue targeted to the default-priority global queue. This method could be used to retarget it to a global queue of different priority, to another private queue (to manage suspension behavior) or even to the main queue so you can do GUI work in the timer.

Implementation

`MABGTimer` has the following instance variables, which should be self-explanatory:

```
id _obj;
dispatch_queue_t _queue;
dispatch_source_t _timer;
MABGTimerBehavior _behavior;
NSTimeInterval _nextFireTime;
```

The initializers and `dealloc` are also pretty simple:

```objc
- (id)initWithObject: (id)obj
{
    return [self initWithObject: obj behavior: MABGTimerCoalesce];
}

- (id)initWithObject: (id)obj behavior: (MABGTimerBehavior)behavior
{
    if((self = [super init]))
    {
        _obj = obj;
        _behavior = behavior;
        _queue = dispatch_queue_create("com.mikeash.MABGTimer", NULL);
    }
    return self;
}

- (void)dealloc
{
    if(_timer)
    {
        dispatch_source_cancel(_timer);
        dispatch_release(_timer);
    }
    dispatch_release(_queue);
    [super dealloc];
}
```

And `setTargetQueue:` and `performWhileLocked:` just call through to the appropriate dispatch function:

```objc
- (void)setTargetQueue: (dispatch_queue_t)target
{
    dispatch_set_target_queue(_queue, target);
}

- (void)performWhileLocked: (dispatch_block_t)block
{
    dispatch_sync(_queue, block);
}
```

The `cancel` method calls through to an internal `_cancel` method that's run on the queue. This ensures that cancellation is synchronized with timer activity:

```
- (void)cancel
{
    [self performWhileLocked: ^{
        [self _cancel];
    }];
}
```

And the `_cancel` method is also simple: if the timer is active, cancel it and destroy it:

```
- (void)_cancel
{
    if(_timer)
    {
        dispatch_source_cancel(_timer);
        dispatch_release(_timer);
        _timer = NULL;
    }
}
```

The meat of the functionality is in `afterDelay:do:`. The first thing it does is run everything synchronized to avoid race conditions and the like:

```
- (void)afterDelay: (NSTimeInterval)delay do: (void (^)(id self))block
{
    [self performWhileLocked: ^{
```

It then checks to see whether it needs to reset the timer or not. It needs to reset the timer if the GCD timer doesn't exist (no pending fire has been set up), if the timer is in delay mode, or if the timer is in coalesce mode and the new fire time is before the previous fire time:

```
        BOOL hasTimer = _timer != nil;

        BOOL shouldProceed = NO;
        if(!hasTimer)
            shouldProceed = YES;
        else if(_behavior == MABGTimerDelay)
            shouldProceed = YES;
        else if(_behavior == MABGTimerCoalesce && [self _now] + delay < _nextFireTime)
            shouldProceed = YES;
```

Next, if the timer needs to be reset and the GCD timer doesn't exist, create it:

425

```
            if(shouldProceed)
            {
                if(!hasTimer)
                    _timer =
dispatch_source_create(DISPATCH_SOURCE_TYPE_TIMER, 0, 0,
_queue);
```

Then it first sets the GCD timer and the _nextFireTime instance variable:

```
                dispatch_source_set_timer(_timer,
dispatch_time(DISPATCH_TIME_NOW, delay * NSEC_PER_SEC), 0,
0);
                _nextFireTime = [self _now] + delay;
```

Then it sets the event handler on the timer. The event handler first calls the block that's passed in. Since GCD timers are always repeating, it then calls _cancel to make sure it only fires once, and also to signal to any future calls that the timer is no longer active:

```
                dispatch_source_set_event_handler(_timer, ^{
                    block(_obj);
                    [self _cancel];
                });
```

Finally, if the timer was newly created, resume it so it can become active:

```
                if(!hasTimer)
                    dispatch_resume(_timer);
            }
        }];
}
```

One last thing, we need an implementation of the _now method. This is simple: call mach_absolute_time, convert it to seconds:

```
- (NSTimeInterval)_now
{
    uint64_t t = mach_absolute_time();
    Nanoseconds nano =
AbsoluteToNanoseconds(*(AbsoluteTime *)&t;);
    NSTimeInterval seconds = (double)*(uint64_t *)&nano /
(double)NSEC_PER_SEC;
    return seconds;
}
```

Conclusion
Background timers are a useful technique for decoupling the timing of calls to an API from the tasks it performs. The repository contains `BackgroundResizingArray`, an implementation of `NSMutableArray` which uses a background timer to implement resizing. Background timers can be useful for networking as well, especially on iOS devices where you want to batch up transmissions to reduce power usage on the cellular radio, or any case where you have a lot of non-urgent messages to send.

Friday Q&A 2010-07-16: Zeroing Weak References in Objective-C

Related Articles

Code Injection	40
Intro to the Objective-C Runtime	67
Objective-C Messaging	73
Objective-C Message Forwarding	77
Objective-C Class Loading and Initialization	115
Care and Feeding of Singletons	194
Probing Cocoa With PyObjC	240
Using Accessors in Init and Dealloc	246
Method Replacement for Fun and Profit	297
Error Returns with Continuation Passing Style	303
Comparison of Objective-C Enumeration Techniques	369
Implementing Fast Enumeration	373
Implementing Equality and Hashing	412
Zeroing Weak References to CoreFoundation Objects	447
Implementing NSCoding	459
Defensive Programming in Cocoa	468

It's that time of the biweek again. For this week's Friday Q&A, Mike Shields has suggested that I talk about weak references in Objective-C, and specifically zeroing weak references. I've gone a bit further and actually implemented a class that provides zeroing weak references in Objective-C using manual memory management.

Weak References

First, what is a weak reference? Simply put, a weak reference is a reference (pointer, in Objective-C land) to an object which does not participate in keeping that object alive. For example, using memory management, this setter creates a weak reference to the new object:

```
- (void)setFoo: (id)newFoo
{
    _foo = newFoo;
}
```

Because the setter does not use `retain`, the reference does not keep the new object alive. It will stay alive as long as it's retained by other references, of course. But once those go away, the object will be deallocated even if `_foo` still points to it.

Weak references are common in Cocoa in order to deal with retain cycles. Delegates in Cocoa are almost always weak references for exactly this reason.

Zeroing Weak References

Weak references are useful for things like avoiding retain cycles, but their utility is limited due to their inherent danger. With a plain weak reference in Objective-C, when the target object is destroyed, you're left with a dangling pointer. If your code tries to use that pointer, it will crash or worse.

Zeroing weak references eliminate this danger. They work just like a regular weak reference, except that when the target object is destroyed, they automatically become `nil`. At any time you access an object through a zeroing weak reference, you're guaranteed to either access a valid, live object, or get `nil`. As long as your code can handle `nil`, then you're perfectly safe.

Because of this safety, a zeroing weak reference can be useful for much more than the unsafe kind. One example is an object cache. An object cache using weak references can refer to objects as long as they're alive, and then let them deallocate when no longer needed. If a client requests an object that's still alive, it can obtain it without having to create a new object. If the object has already been destroyed, the cache can safely create a new object.

They can be used for much more mundane purposes as well, for any case where you want to keep a reference to an object but don't want to keep that object in memory beyond its normal lifetime. For example, you might track a window but not want to keep it in memory after it's closed. You could deal with this by setting up a notification observer and seeing when the window goes away, but a zeroing weak reference is a much simpler way to do it. As another example, a zeroing weak reference to `self` used in a block can prevent a retain cycle while ensuring that your program doesn't crash if the block is called after `self` is deallocated. Even a standard delegate pointer is made better with a zeroing weak reference, as it eliminates rare but annoying bugs which can appear if the delegate is deallocated before the object that points to it.

If you're using garbage collection in Objective-C, then good news! The Objective-C garbage collector already supports zeroing weak references using the type modifier `__weak`. You can just declare any instance variable like so:

```
__weak id _foo;
```

And it's automatically a zeroing weak reference. The compiler takes care of emitting the appropriate read/write barriers so that access is always safe.

What if you aren't using garbage collection, though? While it would be great if we all could, many of us can't for various reasons, one of the most common being that garbage collection simply isn't supported on iOS. Well, until now you've been out of luck when it comes to zeroing weak references with manual memory management in Objective-C.

Introducing MAZeroingWeakRef

Those of us who use manual memory management can now benefit from zeroing weak references! MAZeroingWeakRef implements the following interface:

```
@interface MAZeroingWeakRef : NSObject
{
    id _target;
}

+ (id)refWithTarget: (id)target;

- (id)initWithTarget: (id)target;

- (void)setCleanupBlock: (void (^)(id target))block;

- (id)target;

@end
```

Usage is extremely simple. Initialize it with a target object. Retrieve the target object when you need to use it. The -target method will either return the target object (retained/autoreleased to guarantee that it will stay alive until you're done with it) or, if the target has already been destroyed, it will return nil.

The -setCleanupBlock: method exists for more advanced uses. Normally a zeroing weak reference is a passive object. You can query its target at any time, and it either gives you an object or nil. But sometimes you want to take some additional action when the reference is zeroed out, such as unregistering a notification observer. The block passed to -setCleanupBlock: runs when the reference is zeroed out, allowing you to set up additional actions like that.

As an example, here's how to write the standard delegate pattern using MAZeroingWeakRef:

```
// instance variable
MAZeroingWeakRef *_delegateRef;

// setter
- (void)setDelegate: (id)newDelegate
{
    [_delegateRef release];
    _delegateRef = [[MAZeroingWeakRef alloc]
initWithTarget: newDelegate];
}

- (void)doSomethingAndCallDelegate
{
    [self _doSomething];

    id delegate = [_delegateRef target];
    if([delegate respondsToSelector:
@selector(someDelegateMethod)])
        [delegate someDelegateMethod];
}
```

This is only slightly harder than using normal, dangerous weak references, and provides complete safety. (If you use this pattern, remember that you must now release `_delegateRef` in `-dealloc`!)

`MAZeroingWeakRef` is completely thread safe, both in terms of accessing it from multiple threads, and in terms of having the target object be destroyed in one thread while the weak reference is accessed from another thread.

How Does it Work?
The concept of how a zeroing weak reference works is pretty straightforward. Track all such references to a target. When an object is destroyed, zero out all of those references before calling `dealloc`. Wrap everything in a lock so that it's thread safe.

The details of how to accomplish each step can get tricky, though.

Tracking all zeroing weak references to a target isn't too tough. A global `CFMutableDictionary` maps targets to `CFMutableSet` objects which hold the zeroing weak references to each target. I use the CF classes so that I can customize the memory management; I don't want the targets or weak references to be retained.

Zeroing all of the weak references before calling `dealloc` gets a little trickier....

The answer to that is to use dynamic subclassing, as done in the implementation of Key-Value Observing. When an object is targeted by a zeroing weak reference, a new subclass of that object's class is created. The `-dealloc` method of the new subclass takes care of zeroing out all of the weak references and then calls through to `super` so that the normal chain of deallocations can occur. The new subclass also overrides `-release` to take a lock so that everything is thread safe. (Without that override, it would be possible for one thread to `release` an object with a retain count of 1 at the same time that another thread retrieved the object from a `MAZeroingWeakRef`. The retrieval would then try to resurrect the object after it had already been marked for destruction, which is illegal.)

Of course you don't want to make a new subclass for every single targeted object, but only one subclass is necessary per target class. A small table of overridden classes ensures that no more than one new subclass is created for each normal class.

As the final step, the class of the target object is set to be the new subclass, ensuring that the new methods take effect.

CoreFoundation Trickiness
The above strategy runs into a snag with toll-free bridged classes like `NSCFString`. Because of the way they're implemented, changing the class of such an object causes infinite recursion and a crash the moment that something tries to use them. The CoreFoundation code sees the changed class, assumes it's a pure Objective-C class, and calls through to the equivalent Objective-C method. The `NSCF` method then calls back to CoreFoundation. A crash rapidly ensues.

While I did figure out a solution to this problem, it is so hairy and complicated that I will save it for a separate article to be posted in two weeks.

Code
As usual, you can get the code for `MAZeroingWeakRef` from my public Subversion repository:

```
svn co http://mikeash.com/svn/ZeroingWeakRef/
```

I will be walking through a somewhat abbreviated version of `MAZeroingWeakRef`. Due to the crazy nature of the CoreFoundation workaround I mentioned above, I will skip over those parts and only discuss the sane Objective-C bits this week. There is a macro called `COREFOUNDATION_HACK_LEVEL` which allows control over how much CoreFoundation hackery is enabled. At level `2` you get full-on hackery with full support for weak references to CoreFoundation objects. With level `1`, some less important private symbols are referenced and used to reliably decide whether an object is bridged or not, and the code simply asserts if trying to create a weak reference to a bridged object. At level `0`, the code asserts when trying to create a weak reference to a bridged object, and checks for bridging simply by looking for a prefix of `NSCF` in the class name. For this week, I will be discussing the code as if it were compiled with level `0`.

Globals

`MAZeroingWeakRef` makes use of some global variables for various housekeeping uses. First off is a mutex:

`static pthread_mutex_t gMutex;`

This is used to protect the other global data structures, as well as the table of zeroing weak references that's attached to each target object.

Next up, a `CFMutableDictionary` is needed to map the target objects to the weak references which target them:

`static CFMutableDictionaryRef gObjectWeakRefsMap;` // *maps (non-retained) objects to CFMutableSetRefs containing weak refs*

Next, an `NSMutableSet` is used to track the dynamic subclasses that are created, and an `NSMutableDictionary` is used to map from normal classes to their dynamic subclasses:

`static NSMutableSet *gCustomSubclasses;`
`static NSMutableDictionary *gCustomSubclassMap;` // *maps regular classes to their custom subclasses*

Finally, implement `+initialize` to set up all of these variables. The only tricky business here is that it uses a recursive mutex rather than a regular one. There are cases where the critical section can be re-entered, such as creating a `MAZeroingWeakRef` pointing to another `MAZeroingWeakRef`, and using a recursive mutex allows that to function.

```
+ (void)initialize
{
    if(self == [MAZeroingWeakRef class])
    {
        CFStringCreateMutable(NULL, 0);
        pthread_mutexattr_t mutexattr;
        pthread_mutexattr_init(&mutexattr;);
        pthread_mutexattr_settype(&mutexattr, PTHREAD_MUTEX_RECURSIVE);
        pthread_mutex_init(&gMutex, &mutexattr;);
        pthread_mutexattr_destroy(&mutexattr;);

        gCustomSubclasses = [[NSMutableSet alloc] init];
        gCustomSubclassMap = [[NSMutableDictionary alloc] init];
    }
}
```

I also write a quick helper to execute a block of code while holding the lock:

```
static void WhileLocked(void (^block)(void))
{
    pthread_mutex_lock(&gMutex;);
    block();
    pthread_mutex_unlock(&gMutex;);
}
```

And three more helpers to deal with adding a weak reference to an object's CFMutableSet, removing a weak reference from an object, and clearing out all weak references to an object:

```
static void AddWeakRefToObject(id obj, MAZeroingWeakRef
*ref)
{
    CFMutableSetRef set = (void
*)CFDictionaryGetValue(gObjectWeakRefsMap, obj);
    if(!set)
    {
        set = CFSetCreateMutable(NULL, 0, NULL);
        CFDictionarySetValue(gObjectWeakRefsMap, obj, set);
        CFRelease(set);
    }
    CFSetAddValue(set, ref);
}

static void RemoveWeakRefFromObject(id obj,
MAZeroingWeakRef *ref)
{
    CFMutableSetRef set = (void
*)CFDictionaryGetValue(gObjectWeakRefsMap, obj);
    CFSetRemoveValue(set, ref);
}

static void ClearWeakRefsForObject(id obj)
{
    CFMutableSetRef set = (void
*)CFDictionaryGetValue(gObjectWeakRefsMap, obj);
    [(NSSet *)set makeObjectsPerformSelector:
@selector(_zeroTarget)];
    CFDictionaryRemoveValue(gObjectWeakRefsMap, obj);
}
```

Implementation of MAZeroingWeakRef

With those basics in place, I'll now take a top-down approach to the rest of the implementation.

First, the convenience constructor and initializer. Mostly straightforward:

```objc
+ (id)refWithTarget: (id)target
{
    return [[[self alloc] initWithTarget: target] autorelease];
}

- (id)initWithTarget: (id)target
{
    if((self = [self init]))
    {
        _target = target;
        RegisterRef(self, target);
    }
    return self;
}
```

The only tricky bit is that call to `RegisterRef`. That's an internal utility function which takes care of connecting the weak reference object to the target object, subclassing the target's class if necessary, and changing the target's class to be the custom subclass.

The `dealloc` implementation similarly calls a utility function to remove the weak reference object:

```objc
- (void)dealloc
{
    UnregisterRef(self);
    [_cleanupBlock release];
    [super dealloc];
}
```

Toss in a simple `description` method so we can see what's going on internally:

```objc
- (NSString *)description
{
    return [NSString stringWithFormat: @"<%@: %p -> %@>",
        [self class], self, [self target]];
}
```

And a standard setter for setting the cleanup block:

```
- (void)setCleanupBlock: (void (^)(id target))block
{
    block = [block copy];
    [_cleanupBlock release];
    _cleanupBlock = block;
}
```

The `target` method gets a little more complicated. Because the target can be destroyed at any time, it needs to fetch its value while holding the global weak reference lock. It also needs to retain the target while holding that lock, to ensure that, if the target is alive, it *stays* alive until the receiver is done using it. This is of course balanced with an autorelease afterwards:

```
- (id)target
{
    __block id ret;
    WhileLocked(^{
        ret = [_target retain];
    });
    return [ret autorelease];
}
```

Finally there's a private method used to zero out the target, which is called by the internal machinery when the target object is deallocated. Since the global lock is already held by that machinery, there's no need to explicitly lock it here too. This method simply calls and releases the cleanup block if there is one, and clears out the target:

```
- (void)_zeroTarget
{
    if(_cleanupBlock)
    {
        _cleanupBlock(_target);
        [_cleanupBlock release];
        _cleanupBlock = nil;
    }
    _target = nil;
}
```

And that's it! Easy, right? Of course, all the interesting bits are in those utility functions, the utility functions *they* call, and on and on....

Implementation of Utility Functions

The implementation of `UnregisterRef` is simple. Get the target out of the `MAZeroingWeakRef`, get the table of references to the target, and remove the given reference. Wrap it all in a lock to ensure that the target can't be deallocated in the middle of this operation:

```
static void UnregisterRef(MAZeroingWeakRef *ref)
{
    WhileLocked(^{
        id target = ref->_target;
        
        if(target)
            RemoveWeakRefFromObject(target, ref);
    });
}
```

`RegisterRef` is similar. In addition to adding the reference to the table of references, it also calls `EnsureCustomSubclass`. That function will, if necessary, create a new custom subclass and set the class of the target object to that subclass.

```
static void RegisterRef(MAZeroingWeakRef *ref, id target)
{
    WhileLocked(^{
        EnsureCustomSubclass(target);
        AddWeakRefToObject(target, ref);
    });
}
```

The implementation of `EnsureCustomSubclass` is broken into many pieces. First it checks to see if the object is *already* an instance of a custom subclass. If it is, then nothing has to be done. If it's not, it then looks up the custom subclass that corresponds to the object's current class, and sets the class of the target object accordingly. If no custom subclass has yet been created, it creates it.

```
static void EnsureCustomSubclass(id obj)
{
    if(!GetCustomSubclass(obj))
    {
        Class class = object_getClass(obj);
        Class subclass = [gCustomSubclassMap objectForKey: class];
        if(!subclass)
        {
            subclass = CreateCustomSubclass(class, obj);
            [gCustomSubclassMap setObject: subclass forKey: class];
            [gCustomSubclasses addObject: subclass];
        }
        object_setClass(obj, subclass);
    }
}
```

The implementation of `GetCustomSubclass` is easy. Get the object's class, and check to see if it's in the `gCustomSubclasses` set. If not, get the superclass, and follow it up the chain until one is found. If none are found, then there is no custom subclass for this object. (The reason for following the chain is so that this code will still behave correctly even if some other code, such as Key-Value Observing, sets its own custom subclass after `MAZeroingWeakRef` set one.)

```
static Class GetCustomSubclass(id obj)
{
    Class class = object_getClass(obj);
    while(class && ![gCustomSubclasses containsObject: class])
        class = class_getSuperclass(class);
    return class;
}
```

Again, not too hard. The real fun begins in `CreateCustomSubclass`. The first thing it does is check to see if the object is a CoreFoundation toll-free bridged object. As I discussed above, the subclassing approach breaks for those objects, so they need to be rejected:

```
static Class CreateCustomSubclass(Class class, id obj)
{
    if(IsTollFreeBridged(class, obj))
    {
        NSCAssert(0, @"Cannot create zeroing weak reference to object of type %@ with COREFOUNDATION_HACK_LEVEL set to %d", class, COREFOUNDATION_HACK_LEVEL);
        return class;
    }
    else
    {
```

(COREFOUNDATION_HACK_LEVEL is the `#define` which determines how much CoreFoundation hackery to enable. As I mentioned above, I'm going through the code as through it's not enabled.)

The implementation of `IsTollFreeBridged` simply checks to see if the class name starts with NSCF:

```
static BOOL IsTollFreeBridged(Class class, id obj)
{
    return [NSStringFromClass(class) hasPrefix: @"NSCF"];
}
```

For the `else` branch, the first order of business is to create a name for the new class. Since Objective-C class names have to be unique, it constructs a new name based on the original name and a unique suffix:

```
NSString *newName = [NSString stringWithFormat: @"%s_MAZeroingWeakRefSubclass", class_getName(class)];
const char *newNameC = [newName UTF8String];
```

Next, call `objc_allocateClassPair` to create a new class pair. (In Objective-C, each class has a corresponding metaclass, which is related to how the runtime works. The `objc_allocateClassPair` function creates both in one shot.)

```
Class subclass = objc_allocateClassPair(class, newNameC, 0);
```

The new class implements two methods, `release` and `dealloc`. The next step is then to add those two methods to the class, pointing them to the functions which implement them:

```
        Method release = class_getInstanceMethod(class,
@selector(release));
        Method dealloc = class_getInstanceMethod(class,
@selector(dealloc));
        class_addMethod(subclass, @selector(release),
(IMP)CustomSubclassRelease,
method_getTypeEncoding(release));
        class_addMethod(subclass, @selector(dealloc),
(IMP)CustomSubclassDealloc,
method_getTypeEncoding(dealloc));
```

Finally, call `objc_registerClassPair` to register the new class with the runtime, and return the newly created class:

```
        objc_registerClassPair(subclass);
        
        return subclass;
    }
}
```

Next, `CustomSubclassRelease`. Conceptually, the implementation of this class is simple. Acquire the global weak reference lock, and call `[super release]` while it's acquired. The purpose of this is to ensure that the final release for an object and its deallocation happens atomically, and an object can't be resurrected in between the two by a weak reference that hasn't yet been zeroed out.

The trouble is that simply writing `[super release]` won't work, because the compiler only allows that in a true, compile-time method implementation. In order to perform the equivalent action, it's necessary to figure out the superclass of the custom weak reference subclass. This is done using a simple helper function which calls `GetCustomSubclass` and returns the superclass of that class:

```
static Class GetRealSuperclass(id obj)
{
    Class class = GetCustomSubclass(obj);
    NSCAssert(class, @"Coudn't find ZeroingWeakRef subclass in hierarchy starting from %@, should never happen", object_getClass(obj));
    return class_getSuperclass(class);
}
```

With that helper in place, the implementation of `CustomSubclassRelease` can use it to look up the superclass, use that to look up the superclass's implementation of `release`, and then call that with the lock held:

```
static void CustomSubclassRelease(id self, SEL _cmd)
{
    Class superclass = GetRealSuperclass(self);
    IMP superRelease = class_getMethodImplementation(superclass, @selector(release));
    WhileLocked(^{
        ((void (*)(id, SEL))superRelease)(self, _cmd);
    });
}
```

Almost done! The one remaining function is CustomSubclassDealloc. It gets the table of weak references to the object and tells all of them to _zeroTarget. It then invokes the superclass implementation of dealloc using the same technique as CustomSubclassRelease uses.

```
static void CustomSubclassDealloc(id self, SEL _cmd)
{
    ClearWeakRefsForObject(self);
    Class superclass = GetRealSuperclass(self);
    IMP superDealloc = class_getMethodImplementation(superclass, @selector(dealloc));
    ((void (*)(id, SEL))superDealloc)(self, _cmd);
}
```

That's it! You now have zeroing weak references to Objective-C objects (except to bridged CoreFoundation objects, which I'll get to next week).

Examples:

Basic usage of MAZeroingWeakRef is simple:

```
NSAutoreleasePool *pool = [[NSAutoreleasePool alloc] init];
NSObject *obj = [[NSObject alloc] init];
MAZeroingWeakRef *ref = [[MAZeroingWeakRef alloc] initWithTarget: obj];

NSLog(@"%@", [ref target]);
[obj release];
[pool release];

NSLog(@"%@", [ref target]);
```

The first NSLog will print the object, and the second will print (null). The autorelease pool is used to ensure that the object is truly destroyed, because the use of target will put the object into the pool and otherwise it will stay alive longer.

Using a cleanup block is similarly simple:

```
NSObject *obj = [[NSObject alloc] init];
MAZeroingWeakRef *ref = [[MAZeroingWeakRef alloc]
initWithTarget: obj];
[ref setCleanupBlock: ^(id target) { NSLog(@"Cleaned
object %p!", target); }];
[obj release];
```

The log will print when [obj release] is called. Of course you can take more actions than simply printing. However, because the cleanup block is called while the global weak reference lock is held, you should try to keep your activities in there to a minimum. If you need to do a lot of work, set up a deferred call, using performSelectorOnMainThread:, GCD, NSOperationQueue, etc. and do the extra work there.

A simple way to turn a regular instance variable into a zeroing weak reference is to use MAZeroingWeakRef in your getter and setter, and then make sure to always use your getter in other code:

```
// ivar
MAZeroingWeakRef *_somethingWeakRef;

// accessors
- (void)setSomething: (Something *)newSomething
{
    [_somethingWeakRef release];
    _somethingWeakRef = [[MAZeroingWeakRef alloc]
initWithTarget: newSomething];
}

- (Something *)something
{
    return [_somethingWeakRef target];
}

// use
- (void)doThing
{
    [[self something] doThingWithObject: self];
}
```

And of course if you do that, you have to be sure to release your reference in -dealloc, just like any other object you allocate. Just don't release the target.

For a more advanced use, here's an addition to NSNotificationCenter that eliminates the need to manually remove an observer in dealloc:

```objc
@implementation NSNotificationCenter (MAZeroingWeakRefAdditions)

- (void)addWeakObserver: (id)observer selector: (SEL)selector name: (NSString *)name object: (NSString *)object
{
    [self addObserver: observer selector: selector name: name object: object];
    
    MAZeroingWeakRef *ref = [[MAZeroingWeakRef alloc] initWithTarget: observer];
    [ref setCleanupBlock: ^(id target) {
        [self removeObserver: target name: name object: object];
        [ref autorelease];
    }];
}

@end
```

Note the use of a cleanup block to remove the notification observer when the object is destroyed. All you have to do is call addWeakObserver: instead of addObserver: in notification observers, and you'll never again forget to remove an observer in dealloc.

Similarly, if you're tired of mysterious crashes caused by NSTableView data sources being deallocated before the views themselves, you can easily fix it:

```objc
@implementation NSTableView (MAZeroingWeakRefAdditions)

- (void)setWeakDataSource: (id
<NSTableViewDataSource>)source
{
    [self setDataSource: source];

    MAZeroingWeakRef *ref = [[MAZeroingWeakRef alloc]
initWithTarget: observer];
    [ref setCleanupBlock: ^(id target) {
        if([self dataSource] == target) // double check for safety
            [self setDataSource: nil];
        [ref autorelease];
    }];
}

@end
```

If you anticipate a scenario where you change the data source of a table view frequently, you'll want to write some more sophisticated code to clear out the old weak reference when adding a new one. However that is not a common scenario.

Essentially, any time you have a weak reference (an object reference that you don't retain or copy), you should use a `MAZeroingWeakRef` instead of a raw unretained pointer. It will save you trouble and pain and is extremely easy to use.

ZeroingCollections

The repository includes `MAWeakArray` and `MAWeakDictionary`, subclasses of `NSMutableArray` and `NSMutableDictionary` which use zeroing weak references to their contents. `MAWeakDictionary` uses strong keys to weak objects, which would be useful for many caching scenarios. I won't go through their code here, but they're simple, and you can look at the code in the repository if you're curious.

Although I didn't write them, it would be possible to create a weak version of `NSMutableSet` and `NSMutableDictionary` which uses weak keys instead of, or in addition to, weak objects. These would be trickier due to hashing/equality issues with the weak references, but could certainly be done.

Conclusion

Zeroing weak references are an extremely useful construct present in many languages. Even Objective-C has them when running under garbage collection, but without GC, Objective-C code has been stuck using non-zeroing weak references, which are tricky and dangerous.

`MAZeroingWeakRef` brings zeroing weak references to manual memory managed Objective-C. Although it uses some trickery on the inside, the API is extremely simple to use. By automatically zeroing weak references, you avoid many potential crashers and data corruption. Zeroing weak references can also be used for things like object caches where non-zeroing weak references aren't very practical at all.

The code is made available under a BSD license.

Friday Q&A 2010-07-30: Zeroing Weak References to CoreFoundation Objects

Related Articles

    Code Injection..40

    Creating a Blocks-Based Object System 205

    Probing Cocoa With PyObjC...240

    Toll Free Bridging Internals...293

    Method Replacement for Fun and Profit 297

    Trampolining Blocks with Mutable Code...311

    Zeroing Weak References in Objective-C 428

It's time for another friendly edition of Friday Q&A. For my last Friday Q&A, I talked about `MAZeroingWeakRef` and how it's implemented for pure Objective-C objects. For this one, I'm going to discuss the crazy hacks I implemented to make it work with toll-free bridged CoreFoundation objects as well.

Code

Just as before, you can get the code for `MAZeroingWeakRef` from my public Subversion repository:

```
svn co http://mikeash.com/svn/ZeroingWeakRef/
```

Prior Reading

This post assumes fairly good knowledge of CoreFoundation and how CF-ObjC bridging works. If you haven't already, you may wish to read or at least refer to Friday Q&A 2010-01-22: Toll Free Bridging Internals.

Recap

A zeroing weak reference is a reference to an object which does not participate in keeping that object alive. When the target object is destroyed, the zeroing weak reference automatically becomes `NULL`. When a zeroing weak reference's target is requested, the caller is guaranteed to either get a valid reference, or `NULL`. This is useful for all kinds of things as covered in the previous article.

In order to accomplish this in Cocoa, `MAZeroingWeakRef` overrides the `dealloc` method of the target object by dynamically creating a subclass of the target's class, and changing the class of the target. This overridden `dealloc` method zeroes out `MAZeroingWeakRef` objects that point to the target.

There is a problem with thread safety and resurrection (trying to retain an object scheduled for destruction) if you stop there. Imagine one thread calls `release` on the last strong reference to an object, causing it to then call `dealloc`. Imagine that between these two, another thread accesses the object through a zeroing weak reference. Since `dealloc` has not yet been called, it returns a reference to the object. However, because the `dealloc` call is already set to go, the `retain/autorelease` dance done by `MAZeroingWeakRef` can't save the object from being destroyed. Disaster!

This problem is solved by also overriding `release`. By having `release` acquire a lock that's also used when retrieving a zeroing weak reference target, it's assured that this resurrection scenario can't occur.

Toll-Free Bridged Objects
This scheme works great for normal Objective-C objects, but fails hard for bridged CoreFoundation objects. Changing out the class of a bridged object causes infinite recursion. The first thing a CoreFoundation function does is check the class of the object it's being called on. If that class doesn't match the official `NSCF` class, it assumes it's a pure Objective-C class and calls through to the Objective-C equivalent method. The Objective-C equivalent method on an `NSCF` class just calls the CoreFoundation function. Rinse, lather, repeat, and crash.

The dynamic subclass wouldn't be strictly necessary in this case. I could instead swizzle out the `dealloc` and `release` methods on the `NSCF` class directly, and have them do my dirty work. This is a bit less efficient (since I'm affecting every object of that class, not just weak-referenced ones) but that shouldn't matter.

The trouble is that this doesn't work. If you call `CFRelease` on such an object, it goes directly to the refcounting and deallocation of that object without ever calling the Objective-C methods. So this solution can only catch one side of things, which is basically useless.

After working through all of this, I hunted around for a solution. Short of patching `CFRelease` (which I really didn't want to do, not the least of which because this approach won't work on the iPhone, where modifying executable code is forbidden) I couldn't come up with a way.

I nearly gave up on the problem, resigned to simply forbidding weak references to CoreFoundation objects, when I finally happened upon....

The Solution
I had started looking through the CoreFoundation source code (available from opensource.apple.com) trying to find a way to hook into release events when I happened up on this little gem in the code for `CFRelease`:

```
void (*func)(CFTypeRef) =
__CFRuntimeClassTable[typeID]->finalize;
if (NULL != func) {
    func(cf);
}
// We recheck lowBits to see if the object has been
retained again during
// the finalization process.  This allows for the
finalizer to resurrect,
// but the main point is to allow finalizers to be able to
manage the
// removal of objects from uniquing caches, which may race
with other threads
// which are allocating (looking up and finding) objects
from those caches,
// which (that thread) would be the thing doing the extra
retain in that case.
if (isAllocator || OSAtomicCompareAndSwap32Barrier(1, 0,
(int32_t *)&(((CFRuntimeBase *)cf)->_rc)) {
    goto really_free;
}
```

The comment about resurrection is key. While I can't intercept the CFRelease to eliminate the race condition, I can detect it and allow the object to resurrect so that I can recover from the situation. I was on my way!

Implementing this solution requires overriding the CoreFoundation finalize function. CoreFoundation has no supported mechanism for this, so I had to get down and dirty with the CF source code and hack my way in. This means that everything I'm doing is not entirely supported and could break, although I believe that this stuff is actually pretty stable.

CoreFoundation Classes

A CoreFoundation class is just a struct that looks like this:

```
typedef struct __CFRuntimeClass {           // Version 0 struct
    CFIndex version;
    const char *className;
    void (*init)(CFTypeRef cf);
    CFTypeRef (*copy)(CFAllocatorRef allocator, CFTypeRef cf);
    void (*finalize)(CFTypeRef cf);
    Boolean (*equal)(CFTypeRef cf1, CFTypeRef cf2);
    CFHashCode (*hash)(CFTypeRef cf);
    CFStringRef (*copyFormattingDesc)(CFTypeRef cf, CFDictionaryRef formatOptions);    // str with retain
    CFStringRef (*copyDebugDesc)(CFTypeRef cf);      // str with retain
    void (*reclaim)(CFTypeRef cf);
} CFRuntimeClass;
```

It's basically just a table with a few function pointers in it for common operations that all CF objects support. All class-specific functionality is implemented as functions and has no dynamic lookup at all (except for the stuff present in toll-free bridging support).

Overriding the finalize function then becomes easy. First, look up the `CFRuntimeClass` for the given CF type ID with this function:

```
extern CFRuntimeClass *
_CFRuntimeGetClassWithTypeID(CFTypeID typeID);
```

I can then replace the `finalize` function pointer with my own function. I still need to call through to the original, so I make my own table for the original function pointers, indexed by CF type ID:

```
typedef void (*CFFinalizeFptr)(CFTypeRef);
static CFFinalizeFptr *gCFOriginalFinalizes;
static size_t gCFOriginalFinalizesSize;
```

If you'll remember from last time, my utility function `CreateCustomSubclass` is responsible for creating a dynamic Objective-C subclass for a given object. The original implementation checked to see if the object was a bridged CoreFoundation object and simply asserted if it was. The new implementation handles swizzling out the `finalize` function pointer to my custom function:

```
static Class CreateCustomSubclass(Class class, id obj)
{
    if(IsTollFreeBridged(class, obj))
    {
        CFTypeID typeID = CFGetTypeID(obj);
        CFRuntimeClass *cfclass =
_CFRuntimeGetClassWithTypeID(typeID);

        if(typeID >= gCFOriginalFinalizesSize)
        {
            gCFOriginalFinalizesSize = typeID + 1;
            gCFOriginalFinalizes =
realloc(gCFOriginalFinalizes, gCFOriginalFinalizesSize *
sizeof(*gCFOriginalFinalizes));
        }

        do {
            gCFOriginalFinalizes[typeID] =
cfclass->finalize;
        }
while(!OSAtomicCompareAndSwapPtrBarrier(gCFOriginalFinalizes[typeID],
    CustomCFFinalize, (void *)&cfclass->finalize));
        return class;
    }
    else
        // original ObjC dynamic subclassing code is here
```

There's nothing too complicated here. The first part just gets the requisite information. The `if` statement in the middle handles resizing the table if it's too small. (CF type IDs are small integers, so a flat array indexed by them works nicely.) The last part swizzles out the original function pointer, using an atomic call to ensure that it's thread safe just in case anybody else happens to be trying the same thing at the exact same time.

With this change, it's now critical that `IsTollFreeBridged` be 100% reliable. The old implementation simply looked for a class name that started with `NSCF`, and that's not good enough. I came up with a completely reliable test using a private CoreFoundation table of Objective-C classes:

`extern Class *__CFRuntimeObjCClassTable;`

This table maps a CF type ID to the `NSCF` Objective-C class. Checking for bridgedness is then just a matter of getting the type ID of the object in question, getting the bridged class of the type ID, and seeing if the object's class matches it or not:

```
static BOOL IsTollFreeBridged(Class class, id obj)
{
    CFTypeID typeID = CFGetTypeID(obj);
    Class tfbClass = __CFRuntimeObjCClassTable[typeID];
    return class == tfbClass;
}
```

The `finalize` swizzling re-points to `CustomCFFinalize`. This function simply checks for resurrection by looking at `CFGetRetainCount`, and then if resurrection has not taken place, it clears out all weak references to the object and calls the original `finalize` function:

```
static void CustomCFFinalize(CFTypeRef cf)
{
    WhileLocked({
        if(CFGetRetainCount(cf) == 1)
        {
            ClearWeakRefsForObject((id)cf);
            void (*fptr)(CFTypeRef) =
gCFOriginalFinalizes[CFGetTypeID(cf)];
            if(fptr)
                fptr(cf);
        }
    });
}
```

Easy! Right? Right...?

Resurrection Comes Back From the Dead

Unfortunately, there's a race condition here. Imagine the following sequence:

1. **Thread 1**
    1. `CFRelease(obj)`
    2. `CFRelease` calls `CustomCFFinalize`
    3. Before `CustomCFFinalize` begins executing, the thread is preempted
2. **Thread 2**
    1. `[ref target]` obtains reference to `obj`
    2. `obj` is retained and autoreleased by `MAZeroingWeakRef`
    3. The enclosing autorelease pool is drained, resulting in `CFRelease(obj)`
    4. `CFRelease` calls `CustomCFFinalize`
    5. `CustomCFFinalize` clears weak references and calls the original `finalize`

6. `CustomCFFinalize` returns
3. **Thread 1**
    1. Resumes execution at the beginning of `CustomCFFinalize`
    2. `CustomCFFinalize` checks the retain count, which is still 1
    3. `CustomCFFinalize` calls the original `finalize` a second time on the same object
    4. A horrible flaming crash occurs

What's worse, `CFRelease` isn't even safe in the presence of resurrecting finalizers. It checks the object's reference count a second time after the finalizer returns. However, the object could have been resurrected and destroyed in the intervening time, causing a bad memory access. In order to make this safe, we *can't* allow any possibility that the object is destroyed until `CFRetain` itself returns.

Thus there is an extremely narrow, difficult-to-hit, but entirely real race condition that could cause this code to crash.

Hack Level Three

In order to solve this problem, I divide CoreFoundation objects into two categories. Some objects are the target of a weak reference, and the rest are not. This serves two purposes. First, it allows me to take a fast path when destroying an object that was never the target of a weak reference. Second, I can track whether a referenced object can still potentially be resurrected or not.

This is implemented by simply keeping a `CFMutableSet` where referenced objects are stored. Checking the status of an object is simply a matter of testing set membership. Objects are inserted into the set when calling `RegisterRef`. Objects are removed when the finalize executes with a retain count of 1, which ensures that it can no longer be resurrected.

The new `CustomCFFinalize` is then split in two. If the object has weak references, it first checks for a retain count of 1 to see whether it's been resurrected:

```
static void CustomCFFinalize(CFTypeRef cf)
{
    WhileLocked({
        if(CFSetContainsValue(gCFWeakTargets, cf))
        {
            if(CFGetRetainCount(cf) == 1)
            {
```

If the retain count is still 1 then the object has not been resurrected. It's still not safe to destroy, however, as multiple threads may be sitting in this spot. Instead, the code clears out all weak references, *retains* the object to deliberately resurrect it, and then arranges for it to be released later:

```
            ClearWeakRefsForObject((id)cf);
            CFSetRemoveValue(gCFWeakTargets, cf);
            CFRetain(cf);
            CallCFReleaseLater(cf);
        }
    }
```

If the object has no weak references, then simply call through to the original finalize function without any fuss:

```
    else
    {
        void (*fptr)(CFTypeRef) = gCFOriginalFinalizes[CFGetTypeID(cf)];
        if(fptr)
            fptr(cf);
    }
});
}
```

Easy enough, right? But how exactly does that `CallCFReleaseLater` function work?

Using `autorelease` would do the trick, except that this is pure CF code and there's no guarantee that the caller actually has an autorelease pool in place. A nice idea, but it just doesn't work out.

Some way to hook `CFRelease` to see when it exits would be ideal. But as discussed before, there's simply no available hook, so that goes out as well.

Ultimately I obtained some serious inspiration from Ed "Master of All Things Arcane" Wynne that it could really be done by using a completely insane technique similar to the cache-cleanup scheme in the Objective-C runtime.

The Crazy Scheme

To restate the problem: I need to call `CFRelease` on the object sometime after the original call to `CFRelease` has completed. Since there's no way to arrange this on the thread that made the original call to `CFRelease`, I make use of a background thread.

How can the background thread know when the original call to `CFRelease` has completed?

It's possible for one thread to access the PC (program counter, the location of the currently executing instruction) of another thread. Normally this is not very useful, but the Objective-C runtime uses it to see whether it's safe to destroy stale cache data by looking to see if any other threads are in a function that accesses it.

Likewise, this code can check the PC of the original calling thread and see if it's still within `CFRelease` or not. If it's not, then the call must have finished, so it's now safe to release the object again.

The only way (that I know of) to get the PC of another thread on OS X is to use mach calls, so the first step is to get a reference to the current mach thread. This reference is also "retained" (mach ports are reference counted, just like Objective-C objects) so that it doesn't go invalid in case the thread is destroyed in the mean time:

```
static void CallCFReleaseLater(CFTypeRef cf)
{
    mach_port_t thread = pthread_mach_thread_np(pthread_self());
    mach_port_mod_refs(mach_task_self(), thread, MACH_PORT_RIGHT_SEND, 1 ); // "retain"
```

Next up, send this thread reference and the CF object pointer to a background thread. I use `NSOperationQueue` to handle the backgrounding. I create an `NSInvocationOperation` to handle the release (pointing it towards a class method on `MAZeroingWeakRef`, since it can't deal with pure functions) and add it to the queue. Everything is wrapped in an autorelease pool in case this code is being called from a context which doesn't already have one:

```
    NSAutoreleasePool *pool = [[NSAutoreleasePool alloc] init];
    SEL sel = @selector(releaseLater:fromThread:);
    NSInvocation *inv = [NSInvocation invocationWithMethodSignature: [MAZeroingWeakRef methodSignatureForSelector: sel]];
    [inv setTarget: [MAZeroingWeakRef class]];
    [inv setSelector: sel];
    [inv setArgument: &cf atIndex: 2];
    [inv setArgument: &thread atIndex: 3];

    NSInvocationOperation *op = [[NSInvocationOperation alloc] initWithInvocation: inv];
    [gCFDelayedDestructionQueue addOperation: op];
    [op release];
    [pool release];
}
```

The code for `releaseLater:fromThread:` is based around a loop. It continuously checks the PC of the target thread until that PC has moved out of the target range. Once it's out, it releases the object as well as the thread that was passed in to it. To start with, the loop:

```
+ (void)releaseLater: (CFTypeRef)cf fromThread:
(mach_port_t)thread
{
    BOOL retry = YES;

    while(retry)
    {
```

Next, fetch the PC of the target thread. (`GetPC` is a helper function I'll get to in a moment.)

```
        BLOCK_QUALIFIER void *pc;
        // ensure that the PC is outside our inner code when fetching it,
        // so we don't have to check for all the nested calls
        WhileLocked({
            pc = GetPC(thread);
        });
```

Now start checking the PC for validity. First see if it contains anything at all. If not, assume a transient error occurred and try again (this may not be the best strategy...):

```
        if(pc)
        {
```

Next, see if the PC is within `CustomCFFinalize`. Since that's called from `CFRelease`, it's possible that the target is still in there, and we need to wait for it to exit. To do this, check the PC to see if it's between the start of that function and the start of the one following it. (The compiler lays out functions in order in memory, so the beginning of `IsTollFreeBridged` is right after the end of `CustomCFFinalize`):

```
            if(pc < (void *)CustomCFFinalize || pc > (void *)IsTollFreeBridged)
            {
```

If that test passes, see if the PC is within `CFRelease`. I don't know the order of functions in CoreFoundation so I can't use that same trick. Instead, I use the `dladdr` call. This returns the last symbol that comes before the specified address, among other info. I can just check that against `_CFRelease` (the private function that actually handles the guts of a `CFRelease` call). If it matches, try again later:

```
                    Dl_info info;
                    int success = dladdr(pc, &info;);
                    if(success)
                    {
                        if(info.dli_saddr != _CFRelease)
                        {
```

If all the tests pass, then it's good to go. Clear `retry` to indicate that the test succeeded, call `CFRelease`, and dispose of the thread reference:

```
                            retry = NO; // success!
                            CFRelease(cf);

mach_port_mod_refs(mach_task_self(), thread,
MACH_PORT_RIGHT_SEND, -1 ); // "release"
                        }
                    }
                }
            }
        }
    }
}
```

One last thing, the `GetPC` function. The implementation is highly architecture-specific. The generalized part looks like this:

```
static void *GetPC(mach_port_t thread)
{
    // arch-specific code goes here

    kern_return_t ret = thread_get_state(thread, flavor,
(thread_state_t)&state, &count;);
    if(ret == KERN_SUCCESS)
        return (void *)state.PC_REGISTER;
    else
        return NULL;
}
```

The real code in the repository has conditionals that define `state`, `flavor`, and the rest for Intel 32/64, PPC 32/64, and ARM.

And that's it!

Odds and Ends

In the previous post, I mentioned the `COREFOUNDATION_HACK_LEVEL` macro that controls how much hack `MAZeroingWeakRef` contains. When set to 0, it makes use of no private API. It refuses to reference CoreFoundation objects, and detects them by checking the class name for an `NSCF` prefix. When set to 1, it only uses private API to make a reliable CoreFoundation object check. Level 1 is now the default.

When I wrote the previous post, I didn't actually know about this subtle resurrection race condition. As such, I've added an extra hack level. Hack level 2 uses private CoreFoundation calls to allow referencing CF objects, but does not eliminate the resurrection race condition I described above. Finally, the newly-added hack level 3 goes into full-on CoreFoundation hackery as described above, and eliminates the race condition by doing the final `CFRelease` in a background thread.

These can be controlled using the `COREFOUNDATION_HACK_LEVEL` macro at the top of the file. I recommend level 1 for Mac development (weak references to CoreFoundation objects are not commonly needed) and level 0 for iOS development (Apple gets their underwear in a twist over private API usage). However, if you're adventurous or need weak references to CF objects, you can set it to 3 and everything *should* still work.... If you do, keep in mind that the really horrible hacks don't activate until you actually create a weak reference to a CF object, so you can enable it just in case you inadvertently reference a CF object, but not worry about it doing anything terrible in the normal case.

Conclusion
In the last post I showed how to create zeroing weak references to Objective-C objects with relative ease. In this post, I show that doing the same to CoreFoundation objects is, if not easy, at least possible. A great deal of mucking about with private APIs is required, but the solution should be fairly robust.

This kind of hackery is extremely challenging but it's also a lot of fun. The CoreFoundation source code is a valuable resource for this kind of thing, but as always you must beware of private symbols which may change in the future. Other low-level open source code like the Objective-C runtime can also be a handy read. Finally, `otx` is an extremely useful tool for when you need to see how a library works when Apple doesn't provide source.

That's it for this edition of Friday Q&A. Come back in two weeks for more wacky hijinks.

Friday Q&A 2010-08-12: Implementing NSCoding

Related Articles
- Thread Safety in OS X System Frameworks 24
- The Good and Bad of Distributed Objects 56
- Intro to the Objective-C Runtime 67
- Objective-C Messaging 73
- Objective-C Message Forwarding 77
- Objective-C Class Loading and Initialization 115
- Care and Feeding of Singletons 194
- Dangerous Cocoa Calls 236
- Probing Cocoa With PyObjC 240
- Using Accessors in Init and Dealloc 246
- NSRunLoop Internals 273
- NSNotificationQueue 284
- Method Replacement for Fun and Profit 297
- Error Returns with Continuation Passing Style 303
- Comparison of Objective-C Enumeration Techniques 369
- Implementing Fast Enumeration 373
- Implementing a Custom Slider 382
- Dealing with Retain Cycles 392
- What Every Apple Programmer Should Know 401
- Leopard Collection Classes 405
- Implementing Equality and Hashing 412
- Zeroing Weak References in Objective-C 428
- Defensive Programming in Cocoa 468

Welcome back to another frightening edition of Friday Q&A. This time around, friend and local OS X coder Jose Vazquez has suggested that I discuss how to implement `NSCoding` in Objective-C classes.

Serialization
Objects in memory can't be directly saved or moved to other programs. They contain data, such as pointers, which are only valid in the context of your process's memory space. Move the contents of an object into another program and all of those pointers suddenly make no sense. Serialization is the process of converting the non-portable, in-memory representation of an object into a portable stream of bytes that can be stored and moved between processes.

Cocoa offers two built-in serialization methods. The most commonly-used method is property list serialization, implemented in the `NSPropertyListSerialization` class. Property list serialization is fast and produces output that's easy to understand, but is fairly limited in what it can do. It can only store a limited number of classes which support property list serialization, such as `NSDictionary` and `NSString`, and it's not possible to extend the classes it supports.

The other method offered by Cocoa is archiving. Archiving can serialize arbitrary objects connected in arbitrary ways, and reconstitute the entire thing on demand. It's extremely powerful, however it's not completely automatic, and requires the programmer to write some code in order to allow their classes to be archived.

Archiving is split into two pieces. One piece is the actual archiver and unarchiver classes. These are `NSKeyedArchiver` and `NSKeyedUnarchiver` (and their non-keyed equivalents). They handle the nuts and bolts of translating a bunch of objects into a bunch of bytes.

The other piece is the `NSCoding` protocol. This is code that *you* implement in order to tell the archiver how to encode and decode instances of your class.

NSCoding

The `NSCoding` protocol is short and simple, containing only two methods:

```
@protocol NSCoding

- (void)encodeWithCoder:(NSCoder *)aCoder;
- (id)initWithCoder:(NSCoder *)aDecoder;

@end
```

You implement `encodeWithCoder:` to tell the archiver how to serialize your object into bytes, and `initWithCoder:` to tell the archiver how to transform the serialized representation into a new object. It is necessary to implement both methods.

Note that the parameter to `encodeWithCoder:`, although typed as `NSCoder`, is actually the particular archiver instance (for example, an `NSKeyedArchiver`) that you're working with. Likewise, the parameter to `initWithCoder:` is actually the particular unarchiver instance (e.g. `NSKeyedUnarchiver`) that you're using.

Basic Implementation of `NSCoding`

To implement `encodeWithCoder:`, you should go through all of the essential properties of your object and use the various methods on `NSCoder` to encode them. For object properties, just use `encodeObject:forKey:`. The key can just be a short string that describes the property being encoded:

```objc
- (void)encodeWithCoder: (NSCoder *)coder
{
    [coder encodeObject: [self name] forKey: @"name"];
    [coder encodeObject: [self title] forKey: @"title"];
}
```

The `initWithCoder:` implementation is then more or less symmetrical. However, there are a few different ways to implement it, depending on your particular taste.

One way is to implement it as a normal initializer, directly setting your instance variables:

```objc
- (id)initWithCoder: (NSCoder *)coder
{
    if((self = [self init]))
    {
        _name = [[coder decodeObjectForKey: @"name"] retain];
        _title = [[coder decodeObjectForKey: @"title"] retain];
    }
    return self;
}
```

Important note: if you use this style and are not using garbage collection, *you must retain the objects that come out of decodeObjectForKey:*. It's easy to forget to do this, but this method follows the standard Cocoa memory management rules and returns an object that you do not own. If you don't retain it, it will disappear and you will crash.

Another way is to use setter methods rather than setting the instance variables directly:

```objc
- (id)initWithCoder: (NSCoder *)coder
{
    if((self = [self init]))
    {
        [self setName: [coder decodeObjectForKey: @"name"]];
        [self setTitle: [coder decodeObjectForKey: @"title"]];
    }
    return self;
}
```

Whether it's better to use a setter or set the instance variable directly is, of course, a matter of some debate.

Finally, you can implement it in terms of your normal initializer. Decode the objects first, then call through to your normal initializer:

```
- (id)initWithCoder: (NSCoder *)coder
{
    NSString *name = [coder decodeObjectForKey: @"name"];
    NSString *title = [coder decodeObjectForKey: @"title"];

    return [self initWithName: name title: title];
}
```

Of all the possibilities, this last one probably makes things simplest overall. Among other things, it gives your class a single override point for subclasses that need to implement initializers.

Keyed Versus Unkeyed Archiving

If you look at `NSCoder`, you'll notice that most methods have one variant that takes a key, and one variant that doesn't. For example:

```
- (void)encodeObject:(id)object;
- (void)encodeObject:(id)objv forKey:(NSString *)key;
```

So why are there two?

Back in the dark days before Mac OS X 10.2 shipped, the non-keyed variants were all that existed. They require that the exact same sequence of calls be made to encode and decode. Any variation causes an error, because the archiver has no way of knowing what you intended. This caused enormous problems when making changes to a code base over time. If you add a third property that needs to be encoded and you want your code to still be able to read old archives (using a default value for the new property) then you had to jump through many painful hoops.

The keyed variants are enormously more flexible. You can encode and decode in any order. You can encode data and neglect to decode it. When decoding, you can check for the presence of a key and supply a default value or take a different action if it's missing.

Today, there is essentially no reason to support non-keyed archiving. (It can still be useful if you're using `NSPortCoder` with Distributed Objects, but that is an extremely rare situation.) Therefore, in general, you should write your `NSCoding` implementation to assume keyed coding, and use `NSKeyedArchiver` and `NSKeyedUnarchiver`.

If for some reason you do need to support both, you can simply check `[coder allowsKeyedCoding]` to see what kind you're dealing with, and take the appropriate actions.

Conditional Encoding

The great thing about NSCoding is that it makes it easy to encode large, complex object graphs. The coder automatically ensures that cyclical references don't cause an infinite loop, and that multiple references to the same object don't result in multiple copies of that object being encoded.

However, sometimes you don't want to encode the entire object graph. Imagine an implementation of a board game, with classes for the board and for the pieces:

```
@interface GameBoard : NSObject <NSCoding>
{
    NSMutableArray *_gamePieces;
}
@end

@interface GamePiece : NSObject <NSCoding>
{
    GameBoard *_gameBoard; // weak reference to avoid retain cycles
}
@end
```

You want to be able to serialize an entire board and have all of the pieces automatically included. This is easy, of course: just have GameBoard encode its _gamePieces array. You also want to ensure that the GamePiece back reference to the board is preserved. This can be done by simply encoding it and decoding it. Since it's a weak reference, you would decode it and not retain it.

This approach works fine as long as you're serializing an entire board. But perhaps you also want to serialize a single piece by itself. What happens then?

With the simple approach to implementing NSCoding, you'll end up serializing not only the piece, but the board that it's a part of, every other piece on the board, and any other data that's part of the game board. Worse, because the _gameBoard reference is weak, the board will be destroyed after decoding, causing a dangling pointer. Your archives are large and your code sometimes mysteriously crashes when loading them. Not what you want!

In order to solve this problem, NSCoder provides *conditional objects*. This allows you to encode an object *only if something else unconditionally encodes it*. If nothing *needs* the object, then it doesn't get encoded. In that situation, when you decode, you get nil.

Conditional objects are perfect for encoding just one piece of a larger object graph. The GamePiece can use a conditional object when encoding _gameBoard. If you explicitly encode the entire board, then the conditional object will point to it. However, if

463

you encode an individual game piece, then the board will *not* be encoded, because nothing ever encoded it unconditionally.

Thus, to solve this problem, you simply change `-[GamePiece encodeWithCoder:]` to look like this:

```
- (void)encodeWithCoder: (NSCoder *)coder
{
    [coder encodeConditionalObject: _gameBoard forKey: @"gameBoard"];
}
```

In general, anything that's a weak reference in memory should be a conditional object in your `NSCoding` implementation.

Encoding Non-Object Data

So far I've talked a lot about encoding objects, but what about all of that non-object data floating around?

For primitives, `NSCoder` provides a variety of methods to encode various integer and floating-point types. You can simply call `encodeInteger:forKey:` or `encodeDouble:forKey:` to save your individual values. For types that aren't supported, for example `short`, you can simply encode as a bigger compatible type that is supported, like `int`.

Structs can get more difficult. Non-keyed archiving actually supported encoding and decoding of arbitrary structs, but for some reason this capability was removed in the keyed archivers. Perhaps because it made things too fragile; you couldn't alter the struct without breaking all of your archives.

In general, the best way to handle a struct is to simply encode and decode each field of the struct separately. If that is too unwieldy, then you should consider rewriting the struct as an Objective-C class that supports `NSCoding` itself, so that you can just directly encode instances of it.

For built-in Cocoa structs like `NSRect`, use the built-in functions to transform them to `NSString`. For example, call `NSStringFromRect` and encode the resulting string, and call `NSRectFromString` on the decoded object. This is somewhat less efficient, but much easier to code and debug.

The worst part is arrays. There is no built-in support for archiving C arrays. There are a few workarounds you can use, depending on how big your arrays are and how much code you want to write:

1. Transform your C array into an `NSArray` containing instances of `NSValue`, and encode that. You can either construct a temporary `NSArray` from your C array in your `-initWithCoder:` implementation, or you can do a complete conversion use the `NSArray` throughout.

2. Construct keys dynamically and encode each entry in the array separately. You can write a loop like this:

   ```
   for(int i = 0; i < arrayLength; i++)
       [coder encodeInt: intArray[i] forKey:
   [NSString stringWithFormat: @"intArray%d", i]];
   ```

   Then write a similar loop for decoding.

3. Encode raw bytes using `encodeBytes:length:forKey:`. This requires paying special attention to things like endianness and data type issues. (If you have an array of `NSInteger` or `CGFloat`, they will *not* be the same size between machines. If you have an array of any multi-byte values, they may not be in the same format between machines.) How to handle these issues is somewhat beyond the scope of this article, but research on endianness and serializing raw C data should cover it.

For C strings, which are a special case of arrays, the simplest way to handle it is probably to simply convert it to an `NSString` and encode that. It would also be safe to run a C string through `encodeBytes:length:forKey:`.

Reading Old Archives

If your code lives long enough, eventually you'll change what you encode and decode. Normally, you still want your code to be able to read old archives despite the changes.

For simple changes, like adding a new property to a class, you often don't need to do anything. Your call to `decodeObject:forKey:` will return `nil`. Calls to methods like `decodeIntForKey:` will return `0`. Write your new code to tolerate this, and your job is done.

Sometimes you need to do more. If your changes are complicated enough, you may want to create two separate code paths, one for the old data structure and one for the new. In that case, it's easy to differentiate between the two by adding a `version` key to your `NSCoding` implementation. Check the value of the key when decoding, and you'll know which path to take.

Note that adding a `version` key isn't something that needs to be done ahead of time. You can add it in your new code. The lack of a `version` key in the old archives will identify them as such. If you encode a simple integer, set the new version as `1`, and then trying to get the version of an old archive will conveniently give you 0, and you'll have room to expand further if you need more changes.

If you refactor your code, you might change class names. If these classes are archived, then you have an incompatibility. The old class name exists in the old archive, and when the unarchiver tries to find it at decoding time, it will fail.

This can be worked around by using the `-setClass:forClassName:` before unarchiving:

```
[unarchiver setClass: [NewClass class] forClassName: @"OldClass"];
```

Reading New Archives With Old Code
You often want to go in reverse as well. Just because you added some new information to your archive format doesn't mean you want to make new archives incompatible with old versions of your software. It's not always possible to maintain backwards compatibility, but if your changes are simple then it can be easy.

If you add a new property to a class, ensure that the existing properties remain consistent amongst each other, and complete in terms of what the old version of your software needs. Then old versions will continue to work with little effort. For example, imagine if you add a `title` property to a `Person` class. The old version will only see the old `name` property, and will lose `title`, but will otherwise continue to work.

If you completely revamp a class, you might consider archiving both the new properties *and* a set of compatibility properties intended for old code. New code can read the new properties, and old code can read the old properties and continue to work, at least in some fashion.

Finally, if you rename a class, that will break old versions of the software unless you compensate for it, just as renaming a class will break old archives. To fix this, you can tell the archiver to save your class under its old name using the `setClassName:forClass:` method:

```
[archiver setClassName: @"OldClass" forClass: [NewClass class]];
```

Backwards compatibility can be difficult, particularly if you add a lot of new data or capabilities. It's also generally much less important than forward compatibility. Consider all of the tradeoffs involved and don't be afraid to break backwards compatibility. Just ensure that, if you do, trying to load a new archive into an old version of your software fails gracefully.

Conclusion

`NSCoding` is a powerful way to serialize objects so that you can pass them between processes or save it to a file. Implement the `NSCoding` protocol on your custom objects that you want to serialize, then use `NSKeyedArchiver` to serialize them and `NSKeyedUnarchiver` to deserialize them.

Friday Q&A 2010-08-27: Defensive Programming in Cocoa

Related Articles

    Thread Safety in OS X System Frameworks 24

    The Good and Bad of Distributed Objects..56

    Intro to the Objective-C Runtime 67

    Objective-C Messaging..73

    Objective-C Message Forwarding 77

    Objective-C Class Loading and Initialization..115

    Care and Feeding of Singletons 194

    Defensive Programming 200

    Dangerous Cocoa Calls...236

    Probing Cocoa With PyObjC 240

    Using Accessors in Init and Dealloc 246

    NSRunLoop Internals 273

    NSNotificationQueue..284

    Method Replacement for Fun and Profit 297

    Error Returns with Continuation Passing Style 303

    Comparison of Objective-C Enumeration Techniques 369

    Implementing Fast Enumeration..373

    Implementing a Custom Slider 382

    Dealing with Retain Cycles 392

    What Every Apple Programmer Should Know 401

    Leopard Collection Classes..405

    Implementing Equality and Hashing 412

    Zeroing Weak References in Objective-C 428

    Implementing NSCoding 459

Welcome back to another word-laden edition of Friday Q&A. About a year ago, I wrote a post on defensive programming. That post covered defensive programming in a general sense, and Scott Gould has requested that I write one specific to various standard Cocoa practices, which is what I will be talking about today.

Recap

Defensive coding essentially boils down to constantly asking yourself, "what if it fails?" and coding appropriately. Your code's response to failure can be ranked:

1. Corrupt/delete user data

2. Crash/freeze
3. Fail silently
4. Display an error
5. Work around the failure

The goal is to get as far down the list as is possible and reasonable.

When it comes to defensive Cocoa programming, a lot of failures are really just unanticipated changes. What happens if something makes a subclass of your class? What happens if your superclass's `dealloc` implementation changes? What happens if the behavior of an object changes but remains within the API contract?

Initializers

What better place to start than at the beginning of an object's lifecycle?

I wrote a full post on implementing Cocoa initializers, so I won't go into too much detail here. The main things you need to do to write a defensive initializer are to always ensure that your superclass's initializer gets called (even if it doesn't do anything, it could start doing something later), always assign `self` to the result, and always check the result for `nil`. Thus:

```
- (id)init
{
    self = [super init];
    if(self)
    {
        // ... initialize instance variables here
    }
    return self;
}
```

Deallocation

When your object is destroyed, it must clean up after itself. Naturally, you need to be careful when doing this.

First, always write your `dealloc` implementation to tolerate an uninitialized or partially initialized object. It's possible that your initializer, or a superclass initializer, will encounter an error and decide to destroy your object before it's fully formed, and your code should tolerate this. You can take advantage of the fact that Objective-C objects start out zero-filled. For example:

```
- (void)dealloc
{
    // if statement guards against uninitialized object
    if(someStructPointer)
        [someStructPointer->object release];
    
    [super dealloc];
}
```

Note that most of the time, you can simply take advantage of the fact that messages to `nil` do nothing, and not have to write any extra code to handle the case of an uninitialized object.

Setters
The same thing goes for setters, especially those which are overridden from a superclass. The superclass may call the setter with `nil` to destroy an object rather than directly using `release`. Always write your code to tolerate this. For example:

```
- (void)setFoo: (id)newFoo
{
    // make sure we don't do something bad if newFoo is nil!
    if(newFoo)
        [[NSNotificationCenter defaultCenter]
          addObserver: self
          selector: @selector(_fooChanged)
          name: FooDidChangeNotification
          object: newFoo];
    [super setFoo: newFoo];
}
```

You should always do this even if you're sure it will never get called with `nil`. It's just good practice, and doesn't hurt.

+initialize

Just as you have to code defensively when initializing your objects, so do you have to for initializing your classes.

The `+initialize` method is extremely useful for doing basic setup of class-wide data. It's invoked automatically by the runtime the first time any message (such as `alloc`) is sent to your class.

For example, say you need a global dictionary to hold certain items:

```
static NSMutableDictionary *gDictionary;

+ (void)initialize
{
    gDictionary = [[NSMutableDictionary alloc] init];
}
```

However, this is dangerous and wrong! The trouble occurs if there's a subclass which doesn't implement +initialize. The runtime still *sends* the message, and so it ends up invoking your version instead. Suddenly you've leaked the old dictionary and lost all of the data in it. Whoops.

The fix is simple: just check the identify of self before you do your initialization.

```
static NSMutableDictionary *gDictionary;

+ (void)initialize
{
    if(self == [MyClass class])
        gDictionary = [[NSMutableDictionary alloc] init];
}
```

As a general rule, the first line of any +initialize implementation should always be a check of self to ensure that it's the correct class.

You might be thinking that you didn't write any subclasses and don't plan to, so you don't need to do this. There are two problems with that approach.

First is the obvious one that you might simply be wrong about your future plans. If in a year you change your mind and decide that you do need a subclass, you don't want this code to suddenly break in mysterious and hard-to-debug ways.

Less obvious is the fact that subclasses of your class can be created dynamically at runtime. This is done by Cocoa's key-value observing system, a key component of Cocoa bindings. These dynamic subclasses still cause +initialize to execute, so be prepared for it.

Memory Management

If you have an object pointer instance variable, never assign to that variable except in init, dealloc, and a setter method. In other words, don't write code that does this directly:

```
[myObjIvar release];
myObjIvar = [[self makeNewObj] retain];
```

471

If you write that code directly, it's easy to forget a retain or release and cause havoc. It makes your code less dangerous and easier to understand to call through to a setter:

```
[self setMyObjIvar: [self makeNewObj]];
```

That way all of the memory management code is contained in just one place, instead of being scattered all about.

On the subject of setters, if you're writing your own setter, remember that you must either do an `if` check to make sure that the object you have is genuinely new, or you must do a `retain` (or `copy`) *before* you do a `release`, to make your code robust against calling the setter with the same object as is already held in the variable. In other words, don't do this:

```
- (void)setMyObjIvar: (id)obj
{
    [myObjIvar release]; // could destroy obj!
    myObjIvar = [obj retain];
}
```

Instead, either do this:

```
- (void)setMyObjIvar: (id)obj
{
    if(obj != myObjIvar)
    {
        [myObjIvar release];
        myObjIvar = [obj retain];
    }
}
```

Or this:

```
- (void)setMyObjIvar: (id)obj
{
    [obj retain]; // or obj = [obj copy];
    [myObjIvar release];
    myObjIvar = obj;
}
```

Which one is better is essentially a matter of taste.

Copying

Object copying is a source of horrors when it comes to subclassing Cocoa objects, due to the two different ways that exist to create a copy of an object in the top-level implementation of `copyWithZone:`.

The *sane* way to implement `copyWithZone:` is to either return `[self retain]` (only if the object is immutable) or to create a new instance of the object's class and populate it to hold the same values using accessors or direct instance variable access:

```
- (id)copyWithZone: (NSZone *)zone
{
    // note use of [self class] rather than MyClass
    // this is defensive programming against subclassing!
    MyClass *newObj = [[[self class] alloc] init];
    [newObj setFoo: _foo];
    [newObj setBar: _bar];
    return newObj;
}
```

The completely *insane* way to implement `copyWithZone:` is to use the `NSCopyObject` function. This function allocates a new object of the same class and returns it. The problem is that it also *performs a bitwise copy of all instance variables*. These instance variables include things like pointers to objects. It does not retain them, merely copies their value.

Never, ever, ever use `NSCopyObject`. Easy, right? The problem is that *Cocoa* uses it, and if you ever subclass Cocoa objects, you have to be aware.

Even worse: you often can't count on the Cocoa implementation using one technique or another. It could use either one, and which one it uses could switch at any time. So if you ever subclass a Cocoa object that implements `NSCopying`, and you add instance variables, you need to write a `copyWithZone:` override that handles both cases correctly. Fortunately this is easier than it sounds.

First, let's examine the problem in more detail. Here's an example NSCell subclass:

```
@interface MyCell : NSCell
{
    NSString *_someString;
}

- (void)setSomeString: (NSString *)newString;

@end
```

```
@implementation MyCell

- (void)setSomeString: (NSString *)newString
{
    [newString retain];
    [_someString release];
    _someString = newString;
}

- (void)dealloc
{
    [_someString release];
    [super dealloc];
}

@end
```

Now you write a bit of code that uses it:

```
MyCell *cell = [[MyCell alloc] init];
[cell setSomeString: string];
MyCels *cell2 = [cell copy];
[cell release];
[cell2 release];
```

You run this and it crashes! Why?

The implementation of -[NSCell copyWithZone:] uses NSCopyObject. This means that it copies the _someString pointer, but does no memory management on it. You end up with two pointers to the string but only one of which is retained. They both get released in dealloc. Crash.

The solution is simple: override copyWithZone: and retain or copy the instance variable:

```
- (id)copyWithZone: (NSZone *)zone
{
    MyCell *newObj = [super copyWithZone: zone];
    [newObj->_someString retain];
    return newObj;
}
```

This works, but is brittle. If the NSCell implementation changed to no longer call NSCopyObject, this implementation will fail, because newObj->_someString will be nil. It won't crash, but the copy won't be a proper copy either. And you can't just switch to using `[newObj setSomeString: _someString]` because that crashes the `NSCopyObject` case. We need code that works equally well for both.

The answer is to directly assign to the instance variable of the other object and do memory management at the same time, like so:

```
- (id)copyWithZone: (NSZone *)zone
{
    MyCell *newObj = [super copyWithZone: zone];
    newObj->_someString = [_someString retain];
    return newObj;
}
```

You'll note that it works for both cases. For the sane case, it retains the string and puts the value into the new object's instance variable. For the `NSCopyObject` case, it overwrites the existing pointer with a new one, but without releasing the old one.

Note that `NSCell` is by far the most commonly subclassed class that conforms to `NSCopying`. If you ever subclass `NSCell` or one of its subclasses, you *must* implement `copyWithZone:`, and you *must* do it correctly using the above technique. Otherwise you leave yourself open to extremely mysterious crashes and corruption problems. I've been there, it's no fun.

Error Returns

A lot of Cocoa methods take `NSError **` parameters to tell you why something went wrong. Always check the retun value from these methods! And always at least log the error if there is one.

Don't do this:

```
NSString *string = [NSString stringWithContentsOfFile:
path encoding: NSUTF8StringEncoding error: NULL];
[self corruptImportantDataIfNil: string];
```

Instead, check `string` and use the error if it's `nil`. At the very least, use an assert to nicely stop the current operation rather than continuing with bad data:

```
NSError *error;
NSString *string = [NSString stringWithContentsOfFile:
path encoding: NSUTF8StringEncoding error: &error];
NSAssert(string, @"Could not load string, error: %@",
error);
[self corruptImportantDataIfNil: string];
```

If possible and reasonable, try to either fail gracefully (maybe try a different, backup source of data) or at least report the error to the user in the GUI and allow the program to continue executing normally.

Always at least check for failure and log the error. Even if subsequent code won't corrupt data in the error case, it's still much easier to figure out why your code isn't working if you can catch the failure as early as possible.

A Note on Checking Errors

This has been repeated in many other places, but bears another mention. Always check *the return value* of such a method, and not the `NSError` variable directly. For example, this is wrong:

```
NSError *error = nil;
NSString *string = [NSString stringWithContentsOfFile:
path encoding: NSUTF8StringEncoding error: &error];
NSAssert(!error, @"Could not load string, error: %@",
error);
```

Apple reserves the right to fill your `error` variable with junk upon success. This is a stupid policy, but it's the policy which is there, so you must take it into account.

Weak References

The standard way to set up an `NSTableView` using a data source is to create an object to be the data source, implement the required methods, and then hook up the `dataSource` outlet of the table view. However, if you don't do anything else, this is actually a dangerous setup.

The problem is that the order of object destruction isn't defined. If your data source gets destroyed before the table view, the table view could potentially message the data source after it's been destroyed, causing your program to crash.

To ensure that this never happens, you must zero out the data source in your `dealloc`. However, simply adding that isn't safe either! It's possible for the table view to be destroyed first, and then your message to it will crash. What to do?

The answer to this conundrum is to *retain* the table view outlet. Don't rely on direct instance variable twiddling, but rather write a setter for it that retains it. Then you can write your `dealloc` like this:

```
- (void)dealloc
{
    [tableView setDataSource: nil];
    [tableView release];
    [super dealloc];
}
```

This is safe because it ensures that the table view is never destroyed before you zero out the weak reference.

Most weak references are subject to this problem, including most delegate references from Cocoa objects. Most of the time you can get away with ignoring it, but it's much safer to do it right.

For a more comprehensive solution to the problem of weak references, check out MAZeroingWeakRef. By using the `MAZeroingWeakProxy` class and the Objective-C associated object API, it becomes trivial to create delegate and data source connections which are completely safe.

Categories

Categories are a great feature of Objective-C. It's really handy to be able to add new methods to Cocoa classes that you can then use anywhere in your program. However, it can also be dangerous.

The danger comes when your method name clashes with one that Apple has put in the class. Your method will override the existing one. If they do different things, trouble will ensue. Even worse, your category method could be just fine today, but conflict with a method added by Apple in the next release of the OS.

For example, say you add a `map:` method to NSArray:

```
@interface NSArray (MyAdditions)

- (NSArray *)map: (id (^)(id obj))block;

@end
```

This is fine now, but if Apple adds their own `map:` method in 10.7, and it doesn't have identical semantics, you'll be in big trouble.

The only way to avoid this is to ensure that your category methods on Apple classes will never have a name conflict. The most obvious way to ensure this is to add a prefix to the method name:

```
- (NSArray *)ma_map: (id (^)(id obj))block;
```

This is ugly, but effective. As a bonus, it's often easier to find your category methods with Xcode's code completion, since you can just type in your prefix and let Xcode show all of them.

Another way to ensure that you never have a conflict is to give your method an extremely specific name that you can be confident will never be used by Apple. For example:

```
- (NSArray *)arrayByMappingMyFooElements: (id (^)(MyFoo *foo))block;
```

But this can be a dangerous game to play. When in doubt, prefix.

Conclusion

Cocoa is a complex system that can have some hidden gotchas. However, for the most part, all you need to do is be aware of the fact that your application is really just one component in a larger system. Write your application to be a good citizen and cooperate nicely with the other components that get loaded into your process. Be particularly careful when subclassing and when making modifications to framework classes. The cases presented above are just a sampling of useful defensive programming techniques in Cocoa. Keep defensive programming on your mind no matter what you write, and your code will be better for it.

That's it for this round of Friday Q&A. I will probably be taking a few weeks off for (good) personal reasons, so don't panic if two weeks go by and I haven't posted another one. I will resume before too long, but won't make any promises as to when just yet.

Index

Accessors
    Using Accessors in Init and Dealloc 246

Advice
    What Every Apple Programmer Should Know 401

Apple
    What Every Apple Programmer Should Know 401

Assembly
    Trampolining Blocks with Mutable Code 311

Blocks
    Blocks in Objective-C 14
    Practical Blocks 146
    Creating a Blocks-Based Object System 205
    Error Returns with Continuation Passing Style 303
    Trampolining Blocks with Mutable Code 311
    Futures 330
    Compound Futures 342
    Background Timers 419

Bridging
    Toll Free Bridging Internals 293

C
    Type Qualifiers in C, Part 1 127
    Type Qualifiers in C, Part 2 131
    Type Qualifiers in C, Part 3 135
    Format Strings Tips and Tricks 141
    Writing Vararg Macros and Functions 158

ChemicalBurn
    Multithreaded Optimization in ChemicalBurn 82

Clang
    Using the Clang Static Analyzer 63

Cocoa
    Thread Safety in OS X System Frameworks 24
    The Good and Bad of Distributed Objects 56
    Care and Feeding of Singletons 194

　　　　Dangerous Cocoa Calls 236
　　　　Probing Cocoa With PyObjC 240
　　　　Using Accessors in Init and Dealloc 246
　　　　NSRunLoop Internals 273
　　　　NSNotificationQueue 284
　　　　Implementing a Custom Slider 382
　　　　Dealing with Retain Cycles 392
　　　　What Every Apple Programmer Should Know 401
　　　　Leopard Collection Classes 405
　　　　Implementing Equality and Hashing 412
　　　　Implementing NSCoding 459
　　　　Defensive Programming in Cocoa 468

Code Injection
　　　　Code Injection 40

Collections
　　　　Leopard Collection Classes 405

Continuations
　　　　Error Returns with Continuation Passing Style 303

Controls
　　　　Implementing a Custom Slider 382

CoreFoundation
　　　　Toll Free Bridging Internals 293
　　　　Zeroing Weak References to CoreFoundation Objects 447

Dangerous
　　　　Dangerous Cocoa Calls 236

Defensive
　　　　Defensive Programming 200
　　　　Defensive Programming in Cocoa 468

Encoding
　　　　Character Encodings 324

Enumeration
　　　　Implementing Fast Enumeration 373

Error Handling
　　　　Error Returns with Continuation Passing Style 303

Evil
    Code Injection..40
    Creating a Blocks-Based Object System 205
    Method Replacement for Fun and Profit 297
    Trampolining Blocks with Mutable Code..311
    Zeroing Weak References to CoreFoundation Objects.................................447

Frameworks
    Linking and Install Names..233

Futures
    Futures..330
    Compound Futures...342

Garbage Collection
    Zeroing Weak References in Objective-C 428

GCD
    Intro to Grand Central Dispatch, Part I: Basics and Dispatch Queues 162
    Intro to Grand Central Dispatch, Part II: Multi-Core Performance 169
    Intro to Grand Central Dispatch, Part III: Dispatch Sources 174
    Intro to Grand Central Dispatch, Part IV: Odds and Ends..............................179
    GCD Practicum..183
    A GCD Case Study: Building an HTTP Server...256
    Background Timers..419

Generators
    A Preview of Coming Attractions..215
    Generators in Objective-C 216
    A GCD Case Study: Building an HTTP Server...256

Hack
    Code Injection..40
    Probing Cocoa With PyObjC...240
    Zeroing Weak References in Objective-C 428
    Zeroing Weak References to CoreFoundation Objects.................................447

Hash
    Implementing Equality and Hashing 412

Heap
    Stack and Heap Objects in Objective-C...289

HTML
    Building Standalone iPhone Web Apps...250

HTTP
    A GCD Case Study: Building an HTTP Server 256

IPC
    Interprocess Communication 29
    The Good and Bad of Distributed Objects 56

iPhone
    Building Standalone iPhone Web Apps 250

isEqual:
    Implementing Equality and Hashing 412

Javascript
    Building Standalone iPhone Web Apps 250

KVO
    How Key-Value Observing Works 33

Libraries
    Linking and Install Names 233

Linking
    Linking and Install Names 233

LLVM
    Code Generation with LLVM, Part 1: Basics 88
    Code Generation with LLVM, Part 2: Fast Objective-C Forwarding 96

Macro
    Writing Vararg Macros and Functions 158

Memory
    Mac OS X Process Memory Statistics 123
    Stack and Heap Objects in Objective-C 289
    Dealing with Retain Cycles 392

Networking
    A GCD Case Study: Building an HTTP Server 256

Notifications
    NSNotificationQueue 284

Nscoding
    Implementing NSCoding 459

NSFastEnumeration
    Comparison of Objective-C Enumeration Techniques 369

NSOperationQueue
    Operations-Based Parallelization 53

Objective-C
    Intro to the Objective-C Runtime 67
    Objective-C Messaging 73
    Objective-C Message Forwarding 77
    Objective-C Class Loading and Initialization 115
    Care and Feeding of Singletons 194
    Probing Cocoa With PyObjC 240
    Using Accessors in Init and Dealloc 246
    Method Replacement for Fun and Profit 297
    Error Returns with Continuation Passing Style 303
    Comparison of Objective-C Enumeration Techniques 369
    Implementing Fast Enumeration 373
    Implementing Equality and Hashing 412
    Zeroing Weak References in Objective-C 428
    Implementing NSCoding 459
    Defensive Programming in Cocoa 468

OpenCL
    OpenCL Basics 361

Override
    Method Replacement for Fun and Profit 297

Parallelism
    Multithreaded Programming and Parallelism Overview 11

Performance
    Multithreaded Programming and Parallelism Overview 11
    Profiling With Shark 45
    Operations-Based Parallelization 53
    The Good and Bad of Distributed Objects 56
    Holistic Optimization 60
    Multithreaded Optimization in ChemicalBurn 82
    Mac OS X Process Memory Statistics 123
    Intro to Grand Central Dispatch, Part I: Basics and Dispatch Queues 162
    Intro to Grand Central Dispatch, Part II: Multi-Core Performance 169
    Intro to Grand Central Dispatch, Part III: Dispatch Sources 174
    Intro to Grand Central Dispatch, Part IV: Odds and Ends 179
    GCD Practicum 183

Pointless
    Highlights From a Year of Friday Q&A 272

Private API
    Pros and Cons of Private APIs 21

PyObjC
    Probing Cocoa With PyObjC 240

Python
    Probing Cocoa With PyObjC 240

Rant
    Holistic Optimization 60

Release
    Dealing with Retain Cycles 392

Retain
    Dealing with Retain Cycles 392

Runloop
    NSRunLoop Internals 273

Serialization
    Implementing NSCoding 459

Shark
    Profiling With Shark 45

Singleton
    Care and Feeding of Singletons 194

Source Code
    GCD Practicum 183

Stack
    Stack and Heap Objects in Objective-C 289

Static Analysis
    Using the Clang Static Analyzer 63
    Introduction to Valgrind 118

Swizzling
    Method Replacement for Fun and Profit 297

Text
    Character Encodings 324

Threading
    Multithreaded Programming and Parallelism Overview 11
    Thread Safety in OS X System Frameworks 24
    Multithreaded Optimization in ChemicalBurn 82
    Dangerous Cocoa Calls 236

Trampoline
    Trampolining Blocks with Mutable Code 311

Unicode
    Character Encodings 324

Valgrind
    Introduction to Valgrind 118

Vararg
    Writing Vararg Macros and Functions 158

Web
    Building Standalone iPhone Web Apps 250

Printed in Great Britain
by Amazon.co.uk, Ltd.,
Marston Gate.